D0995455

Cathedral Shrines
of
Medieval England

UNIVERSITY LIBRARY
DATE DUE FOR RETURN

21 JAN 2008

The shrine of St Alban in St Alban's Abbey. The substructure has been restored very recently, and of all surviving examples gives the best impression of how a greater shrine once looked. The gabled object on top of the base is neither original nor based on any evidence, but does have some of the appearance of a moveable cover or canopy when lowered over the feretrum.

Cathedral Shrines
of
Medieval England

BEN NILSON

UNIVERSITY LIBRARY
NOTTINGHAM

THE BOYDELL PRESS

© Ben Nilson 1998

All Rights Reserved. Except as permitted under current legislation
no part of this work may be photocopied, stored in a retrieval system,
published, performed in public, adapted, broadcast,
transmitted, recorded or reproduced in any form or by any means,
without the prior permission of the copyright owner

First published 1998
The Boydell Press, Woodbridge
Reprinted in paperback 2001

ISBN 0 85115 540 5 (hardback)
ISBN 0 85115 808 0 (paperback)

The Boydell Press is an imprint of Boydell & Brewer Ltd
PO Box 9, Woodbridge, Suffolk IP12 3DF, UK
and of Boydell & Brewer Inc.
PO Box 41026, Rochester, NY 14604–4126, USA
website: http://www.boydell.co.uk

A catalogue record for this book is available
from the British Library

Library of Congress Cataloging-in-Publication
Card Number: 97–52221

This publication is printed on acid-free paper

Printed in Great Britain by
Athenæum Press Ltd, Gateshead, Tyne & Wear

Contents

To my Mother

Sorry the candles didn't work

Acknowledgements

I would like to thank first of all my supervisor, Prof. R.B. Dobson of Christ's College, Cambridge, for guidance and counsel far above the norm. His wisdom and genuine concern are largely responsible for any merit this book may contain. Additional help and advice were generously provided by Prof. C.N.L. Brooke of Gonville and Caius College. Dr C. Wilson of University College London, who read and commented on chapters two and three, was also very helpful. Assistance also was provided by Ms R.H. Frost. Abundant help with the paperback edition was provided by Dr M. Treschow of Okanagan University College.

Many thanks must also go out to numerous archivists and librarians across England. These include the staffs of the British Library manuscript room, the manuscript room of the Cambridge University Library, the archivists at Canterbury, Worcester, Lichfield, Hereford, York, Salisbury and Durham cathedrals, the muniment room of Westminster Abbey, and the County Record Offices at Lincoln, Lichfield and Norwich. Special thanks must go out to A. Piper at Durham and S. Eward at Salisbury, who were especially helpful in pointing out documents and facts. Special thanks should also go to the Centennial Museum of Kelowna, British Columbia, for processing photographs.

Financial support for the doctoral thesis on which this book is based was provided primarily by a Doctoral Fellowship from the Social Sciences and Humanities Research Council of Canada. Further funding was provided by an Overseas Research Studentship from the University of Cambridge. Research grants were generously supplied by the History Faculty of the University of Cambridge and Corpus Christi College, Cambridge.

Abbreviations

An. Boll.	*Analecta Bollandiana*
Ant. J.	*The Antiquaries Journal*
Arch. J.	*Archaeological Journal*
Arch. Cant.	*Archaeologia Cantiana*
Ass.	Association
BAACT	*British Archaeological Association Conference Transactions*
BL	British Library
CCA	Canterbury Cathedral Archive
CUL	Cambridge University Library
Concilia	*Concilia Magnae Britanniae et Hiberniae*, ed. D. Wilkins (London, 1737)
EHR	*English Historical Review*
DDCA	Durham Dean and Chapter Archives
HCA	Hereford Cathedral Archive
J.	Journal
JBAA	*Journal of the British Archaeological Society*
Liberate Rolls	*Calendar of the Liberate Rolls*
LCA	Lincoln County Archive
LJRO	Lichfield Joint Record Office
NCA	Norwich County Archive
ns	new series
Patent Rolls	*Calendar of the Patent Rolls*
PL	*Patrologia Latina*
RS	Rolls Series
SCA	Salisbury Cathedral Archive
ser.	series
Soc.	Society
SS	Surtees Society
Trans.	Transactions
trans.	translator
VCH	*Victoria History of the Counties of England*
vol.	volume
WAM	Westminster Abbey Muniments
WCA	Worcester Cathedral Archive
YMLA	York Minster Library Archive

Introduction

In the holiest sanctuaries deep within many English cathedrals there once could be found some of the most precious objects in the world: the shrines of saints. They were imbued with value not only through the accumulation of gold and silver, but also through the miraculous holy radiance that was believed to emanate from the saint's body. Given the almost axiomatic importance of saints and relics in medieval Christian religion, the exact role played by shrines must be crucial to an understanding of religious practice in that period. These golden monuments had a financial, architectural, religious and historical impact on the churches they graced. Yet shrines have long since disappeared from England and now seem strange and ancient, their most basic nature little understood. A descriptive analysis of shrines as both objects and institutions is thus necessary in order to explain their role in the wider religious world of the middle ages.

For a long time, however, denominational bias and modern contempt towards saint worship and miracle stories brought about a general avoidance of medieval relic worship as a topic for serious research. The cathedral clergy were often treated as unscrupulous forgers and fraud artists perpetrating relic cults on a gullible and naive populace.[1] Pilgrims and shrines did not become a popular subject in England until the turn of this century, when many books written to appeal to a general audience began to appear. Although dealing with diverse aspects of the topic, these early works suffer from the lack of a scholarly apparatus.[2] With the recent emergence of increased interest in social history and traditional religion, saints and their relics are being treated with greater respect and are now a popular and common field of study. Scholars like D. Rollason and M. Biddle have explored much of the English archaeological and historical material for the period before the Conquest.[3] R.C. Finucane, J. Sumption, and B.

---

[1] See for example J.T. Fowler's exhumation of St Cuthbert for the purpose of disproving his incorruption: J.T. Fowler, 'On an Examination of the Grave of St. Cuthbert in Durham Cathedral in March 1899', *Archaeologia*, 2nd ser. vol. 57 (1900), pp. 1–28; Fowler's motives are discussed in R.N. Bailey, 'St Cuthbert's Relics: Some Neglected Evidence', in *St Cuthbert, His Cult and his Community to AD 1200*, eds G. Bonner, D. Rollason and C. Stancliffe (Woodbridge, 1989), pp. 231–46.

[2] See especially S. Heath, *In the Steps of the Pilgrims* (2nd ed., London, no date); J.C. Wall, *Shrines of British Saints* (London, 1905); B.C. Boulter, *Pilgrim Shrines of England* (London, 1928); C. Hole, *English Shrines and Sanctuaries* (London, 1954); D.J. Hall, *English Medieval Pilgrimage* (Bath, 1965).

[3] These authors' best general works on shrines are M. Biddle's 'Archaeology, Architecture, and the Cult of Saints in Anglo-Saxon England', in *The Anglo-Saxon Church*, eds L.A.S. Butler and R.K. Morris (London, 1986), pp. 1–31, and D.W. Rollason's *Saints and Relics in Anglo-Saxon England* (Oxford, 1989).

Ward have all pioneered the use of *miracula* (collections of miracle stories) to examine the history of pilgrimage from a wider perspective.[4] However, these studies have been more concerned with pilgrimage than with shrines, and have been so wide-ranging that there is much work left to be done. At the other end of the spectrum, there has been a significant amount of careful research on individual shrines, often using archaeological and architectural evidence. Some of the better examples range in date from R. Willis's many monographs on English cathedrals written in the middle of the nineteenth century to J. Crook's recent work on Winchester.[5]

This combination of general and specific works has progressed to the point where it is now possible to produce a broadly based study of the entire body of evidence relating to medieval English shrines. Information on any one shrine is limited, but by choosing a large enough sample and comparing one shrine with another it should be possible to discover the underlying patterns in worship, offerings, organisation and shrine structure. A cross-sectional study of all shrines, not just the largest or most unusual, should therefore allow us to distinguish the 'normal' or conventional practices and beliefs from exceptional local variations. This has not yet been done. The goal of this book is to use such a survey to illustrate the nature and importance of shrines in the greater churches of medieval England, and in particular of the major shrines in English cathedrals.

It is crucial to confine the scope of any survey to comparable times, objects and places. The period under examination in this study is a long one, marked at beginning and end by dramatic events. The arrival of the Normans provides a convenient starting point: they rebuilt every cathedral, moved several old sees to new sites, created others, reorganised the chapters and set a new standard throughout English ecclesiastical life. Thereafter, shrines and the traditions surrounding them did not undergo any absolutely radical changes for the next four and a half centuries, at the end of which period they were destroyed by order of Henry VIII. This stability not only allows but actually requires the historian to study shrines over a long period. The relative lack of change meant that shrines and the activities surrounding them were rarely described, since they were considered to be an eternal part of life and there for anyone to see. Not until the very end could the

---

4   See R.C. Finucane's 'The Use and Abuse of Medieval Miracles', *History*, vol. 1, no. 198 (1975), pp. 1–10, for an interesting historiographic survey. His *Miracles and Pilgrims: Popular Beliefs in Medieval England* (London, 1977) is a standard reference work for this subject, as is J. Sumption's *Pilgrimage: An Image of Medieval Religion* (London, 1975). Ward's *Miracles and the Medieval Mind: Theory, Record and Event 1000–1215* (2nd ed., Aldershot, 1987) is a valuable work on miracles and their perception.
5   Especially useful has been R. Willis's *The Architectural History of Canterbury* (London, 1845). For J. Crook's works see especially 'St Swithun of Winchester', in *Winchester Cathedral: Nine Hundred Years, 1093–1993* (Chichester, 1993), pp. 57–68, 'The Romanesque East Arm and Crypt of Winchester Cathedral', *JBAA*, vol. 142 (1989), pp. 1–36, and 'King Edgar's Reliquary of St Swithun', *Anglo-Saxon England*, vol. 21 (1992), pp. 177–202.

monks and clerics guarding shrines conceive that they would ever be destroyed. When that end came, however, the political situation was such that devotion to shrines could be dangerous. In only one case, *The Rites of Durham*, has a determined effort to record what was lost come down to us.[6] As a result, whole centuries of scattered references must be collected and examined for relevant information.

In order to understand the nature of a saint's shrine it is also necessary to make certain definitions concerning relics, the shrine's *raison d'être*. Relics have been divided by the Roman Catholic Church into primary and secondary classes.[7] Primary relics are the actual bodily remains of a saint while secondary relics are those objects, such as clothing or personal possessions, that were sanctified by close contact with a saint's body. This basic theoretical distinction was in existence from the beginnings of the cult of relics, and was made stronger by late Roman laws forbidding the disinterment, dismemberment and sale of bodies. These rules seem to have been obeyed by the early church, with the result that only secondary relics could be brought away from the tomb of a saint.[8] When England was first converted, the lack of indigenous saints meant that secondary relics were much more common. By the Conquest, however, churches had acquired the remains of numerous saints, both foreign and indigenous, while the disinterment and division of saints' remains had not only become legal but was universally accepted. Bones and other body parts soon greatly outnumbered secondary relics in the collections of greater churches.

Although not formally acknowledged, there was in fact another distinction made between different sorts of primary relics, which I call 'major' (or 'greater') and 'lesser'. Although contemporaries did not make this distinction clear, the difference is implicit in medieval attitudes and practices. Almost all primary relics were at first preserved as whole, entire bodies. As the old prohibitions vanished and the odd bone was separated from the remains, so a distinction arose between these separated and isolated relics and what remained. Even if the relics still

---

6 *Rites of Durham, Being a Description or Brief Declaration of All the Ancient Monuments, Rites and Customs Belonging or Being within the Monastical Church of Durham before the Suppression*, ed. J.T. Fowler (SS, vol. 107, 1903).

7 J. O'Connell, *Church Building and Furnishing: the Church's Way* (London, 1955), p. 194; J.A. Hardin, *Modern Catholic Dictionary* (London, 1981), p. 461. This distinction is apparently traditional and not part of canon law.

8 Rollason, *Saints and Relics*, pp. 27–8. These prohibitions led to the manufacture of 'representative' relics: objects, usually pieces of cloth, placed on or near real relics in order to absorb their sanctity. For a lucid discussion of representative relics, see N. Herrmann-Mascard, *Les Reliques des Saints: Formation Coutumière d'un Droit* (Paris, 1975), pp. 45ff. By the high middle ages representative relics had all but disappeared. 'But the absolute pre-eminence acquired by corporeal relics is not the result of a conscious evolution guided by the ecclesiastical authorities. It is fully the fruit of circumstances and the anarchic development of the devotion to relics' (Mais la prééminence absolue acquise par les reliques corporelles n'est pas résultat d'une évolution consciente et guidée par les autorités ecclésiastiques. C'est plutôt le fruit des circonstances et du dévelopement anarchique de la dévotion aux reliques): Herrmann-Mascard, *Reliques des Saints*, p. 70.

resting in their tomb or shrine were only disarticulated fragments of the original corpse, they were still collectively considered to be the 'body' of the saint, a classification that imbued them with special importance. Although acknowledged to be both in heaven and virtually omnipresent, a saint was at the same time thought to dwell specially in his or her body, and would arise at the Resurrection wherever it rested. For example, Hugh Candidus made a lengthy list of saints' resting places 'that whosoever desireth to visit some saint may know where he may seek him'.[9] An account of the translation of St Thomas calls his tomb 'the place where the glorious martyr abode'.[10] This association of the tomb with the saint's home is vividly demonstrated by the frequent reports of visions of saints exiting their tomb or shrine. One such was experienced by Elias, a monk of Canterbury, in which he saw St Dunstan trying to leave his tomb but prevented from doing so by its heavy lid.[11] A famous piece of thirteenth-century stained glass in the same cathedral depicts a similar vision by showing St Thomas projecting half-way out of his shrine.[12] In another vision St William of Norwich declared that he had to turn uncomfortably in his tomb in order to gaze at the cross, and desired another to be placed by his feet so that he could look at it without turning.[13] It was no doubt this belief in tombs and shrines as the homes of saints that, above all, made greater relics the centres of pilgrimage.

Lesser relics, on the other hand, usually consisted of a small fragment of bone or a secondary relic enclosed in a small reliquary. Like all relics, they facilitated contact with the saint in heaven but, unlike greater relics, did not mark the grave or home of the saint and therefore did not in themselves create a holy place. They were also not unique, since one body could supply a great many bones or hairs. The greater saints, like Peter or Mary Magdalene, had relics in hundreds and possibly thousands of churches across Europe. Only the institution that boasted the actual tomb could claim to be that saint's resting place and home. A greater shrine thus vastly increased a church's reputation as a holy place and gave it a special celestial patron.[14]

---

[9] Hugh Candidus, *The Peterborough Chronicle of Hugh Candidus*, eds C. Mellows and W.T. Mellows (Peterborough, 1941), p. 32.

[10] 'Ou le martyr glorious fust demore': from the Canterbury chronicle called the *Polistorie*, written after 1313. The passage relating to the translation is printed in A.J. Mason, *What Became of the Bones of St Thomas?* (Cambridge, 1920), pp. 72–3.

[11] Elias and Archbishop Anselm managed to open the tomb, upon which Dunstan sat upright and predicted Anselm's death: Eadmer of Canterbury, *The Life of Anselm, Archbishop of Canterbury*, ed. R.W. Southern (Oxford, 1972), pp. 154–5.

[12] M.H. Caviness, *The Early Stained Glass of Canterbury* (Princeton, 1977), fig. 164.

[13] Thomas of Monmouth, *The Life and Miracles of St. William of Norwich*, eds A. Jessopp and M.R. James (Cambridge, 1896), p. 214.

[14] I thus disagree with Duchesne: 'Any relic whatever . . . was sufficient to represent him [the saint] at a distance from his resting place. To possess an object of this nature was to possess the body of the saint itself. To translate it and depose it in a church was equivalent to interring the body there': L. Duchesne, *Christian Worship: Its Origin and Evolution*, trans. M.L. McClure (5th edn, London, 1919), p. 402. An obvious exception to the uniqueness of a greater shrine occurred when there were conflicting claims as to which church possessed a

Major relics were physically distinguishable from other cult objects. They were honoured with full-scale shrines complete with a large reliquary resting on a sculpted stone base which was usually situated in a special chapel, as opposed to lesser relics which were kept in small, easily portable reliquaries. Inevitably there were borderline cases, but these were quite rare. Some objects, such as the hand of St James at Reading Abbey and the arm of St Oswald at Peterborough, acted as greater shrines without containing the full body of a saint. In general, however, such relics were not as successful as tomb-shrines unless they were the bodily members of truly great saints with one or more exceptional attributes. Obviously, James was a great apostle and his hand was already legendary when it arrived at Reading, while Oswald was a very popular Anglo-Saxon saint who had the rare fate of having been dismembered and his parts dispersed on the battlefield, with the result that no one church could easily claim his grave and monopolise his cult.

It is also the case that some relic collections attracted worship as a whole. Thus, each of a list of twenty-five miracles in the annals of Tewkesbury under 1232 is annotated as 'received at the memorial of the holy relics'.[15] Certain special relics, usually mementoes of either Christ or St Mary, could create great pilgrimage centres without containing a fraction of a saint's body. However, even a relic of such potent figures as these could not sustain a cult without being of especially miraculous origin or nature. The shrine at Walsingham, for example, was not only believed to have been constructed on directions from angels but also to have held a miraculous statue. Similar relics languished in numerous other collections without attracting pilgrim cults, largely because they did not set themselves apart from innumerable others of the same ilk. Crosses and Marian shrines, such as the statues of the Virgin in Worcester and Carlisle cathedrals, were commonly worshipped in English medieval cathedrals but are outside the scope of this study.[16] Although sometimes called 'shrines' by modern scholars, they were never referred to as 'scrinia' or 'feretra' (the technical terms for saints' shrines) by contemporaries.

The object of this book, therefore, will be those shrines which had as their physical centre the bodies of saints. However, the total number of English saints' shrines is still too large to study in full, and so the scope must be reduced further. The cathedrals of medieval England form a finite, complete group of comparable host churches. With the sole exception of Carlisle (which in any case did not possess a major saint's shrine), English cathedrals were administered in one of only two ways: either by secular canons or Benedictine monks. Architecturally,

---

certain saint. English examples of disputed relics include the two tombs of St Alban (at St Alban's and Ely), St Dunstan (at Canterbury and Glastonbury) and St Wilfrid (at Canterbury and Ripon).

[15] 'Recepit ad memoriam sanctarum reliquiarum': *Annales de Theokesberia*, in *Annales Monastici*, ed. H.R. Luard (RS, vol. 36, 1864), vol. 1, p. 86.

[16] For a comparable but not strictly parallel development of events in Germany see L. Rothkrug, 'Popular Religion and Holy Shrines: Their Influence on the Origins of the German Reformation and their Role in German Cultural Development', in *Religion and the People, 800–1700*, ed. J. Obelkevich (Chapel Hill, 1979), pp. 20–86.

cathedrals have comparable histories of construction and were built for similar purposes. While local variation was significant, it is not enough to render comparisons and general conclusions invalid *per se*. There were nineteen cathedral churches at the Reformation, by which time fourteen are known to have acquired a major saint. The exceptions were Carlisle, Exeter, Wells, Bath and Coventry (see table 1). Of the fourteen shrine churches, eight were fortunate enough to possess an Anglo-Saxon saint while six acquired the relics of post-Conquest saints. Two of the former cathedrals (Canterbury and Rochester) had their Anglo-Saxon shrines superseded by more fashionable newcomers in the post-Conquest period. The various English cathedrals possessed at least twenty-six major saints' shrines and many lesser ones. These will form the primary object of this study. Where information from within this group is scarce or when another shrine is too important to ignore, then occasional reference will be made to some of the greater abbeys and collegiate churches, particularly those at St Albans, Bury St Edmunds, Westminster, Beverley, Tynemouth and St Augustine's Canterbury. However, the number of churches with saints' shrines which could be examined in this study is so large that all cannot be examined with the exactitude they merit.

An important reason for studying cathedral shrines is the high survival rate and informative nature of their documents. Most cathedral libraries and archives have survived (at least in part), and the administrative documents pertaining to a local shrine are often extant. Most informative are the accounts and inventories of the officials responsible for shrine income and expenditure, which usually cover the period from c.1275 to 1540. These sources have been under utilised until now, and will form a major part of the information for this book. Other useful administrative documents include bishops' registers, chapter acts and statute books. While the fourteenth and fifteenth centuries are well represented by administrative documents, the main sources for earlier periods are quite different in character. The two main types of hagiographical literature which deal with posthumous saints' cults are *vitæ* and *miracula*, the latter of which deal specifically with events occurring after the saint's death. Sometimes the translation of a saint is either the subject of its own chapter in a *miracula* or merits a separate work of short length (a *translatio*). The historical sources are mostly confined to brief references in chronicles, although these are sometimes of great importance and so have been used extensively in this study.

The limits of this survey are therefore defined as saints' shrines existing in the greater churches of England, specifically cathedrals, from 1066 to about 1540. Their examination is divided by subject matter into seven chapters. Chapter 1 provides an account of how cathedrals first came into possession of shrines, dealing especially with the processes of canonisation and translation. It will show that the steps leading up to the establishment of a proper saint's shrine were expensive and elaborate. The importance of canonisation is well known, but translation perhaps less so. The latter's established rituals and procedures influenced much of what later went on at shrines and in many ways symbolised and encapsulated their place in medieval religion.

The next two chapters venture into the field of art history, dealing with the structure of the shrine monument itself and its relationship with the cathedral around it. The disparate and difficult nature of the evidence has resulted in the physical design of English shrines as a whole being under studied. Chapter 2 attempts to provide an accurate description of the elements that were necessary to make up shrines at various stages of their development. It will emphasise the prevalence of standardisation and consistent traditions over radical or unusual structures. The third chapter, besides describing the architectural setting of shrines, is mostly concerned with disproving certain asserted relationships between shrines and their surroundings. It suggests that the shrine was not as important to the design of a cathedral as has often been assumed. In particular, post-Conquest English shrines bore little relationship to crypts, ambulatory plans or retrochoirs. Also, the extent to which they were intended to be seen from points west is debated. Despite general opinions to the contrary, shrines were not visible from the nave, and possibly not from the choir.

Chapters 4 and 5 delineate activities at the shrine, first from the perspective of the pilgrim and second from that of the clergy and cathedral. Pilgrims have been the source of much interest, yet their behaviour when actually at a major shrine has not been treated fully before. Not only is the nature of pilgrims' devotions and offerings examined, but also their numbers and the behaviour of exceptional devotees. Chapter 5 discusses how the shrine was important to a cathedral both symbolically and financially. It describes the administration of the shrine, along with other matters of importance to the clergy such as security. The final two chapters examine in detail the nature of offerings. Chapter 6 is devoted to a detailed analysis of financial accounts from shrines. They have not been so examined before, and require careful consideration, both as to their general nature and trustworthiness. Each cathedral's records are then discussed in turn. Chapter 7 is involved with analysing the results of this survey. In particular, it puts forward a model of the rise and fall of shrine income over the centuries, along with certain theories to explain the fluctuations revealed. The last chapter also examines the importance of the offerings to the finances of a cathedral, weighing the profit and loss, and concludes that (despite some previous views to the contrary) shrines were very profitable for almost all of their history.

1

The Origins of Shrines:
Canonisation and Translation

At the Conquest only eight English cathedrals are known to have contained major shrines. Most of those were the tombs of early bishops, namely Sts Dunstan and Alphege at Canterbury, Indract and Paulinus at Rochester, Erkenwald at London, Chad at Lichfield, Swithun at Winchester, Oswald at Worcester and Cuthbert at Durham. Ely, not yet but soon to be a cathedral, was the one exception, possessing the famously uncorrupted body of St Etheldreda, royal virgin and abbess. Of course, many of the greater abbeys also held ancient shrines, notably those at St Albans and Bury St Edmunds.

Despite some speculation by historians about Norman contempt towards Anglo-Saxon saints, all the major cathedral shrines were not just maintained by the new administration but were actively supported by it. For example, Lanfranc at first denigrated St Alphege but later promoted his cult after it was defended by Anselm, and although St Dunstan was left out of a new calendar he and Lanfranc were portrayed as allies in a *Vita* written during Lanfranc's own lifetime.[1] The Normans promoted the older saints that came under their protection through new hagiography and sumptuous translations of their shrines into new and more glorious positions. When the Norman re-organisation of dioceses and cathedrals was complete, however, eleven cathedrals were still without a major shrine. This number includes Hereford, whose relics of St Ethelbert had been stolen and probably burnt by a Welsh army in 1055.[2]

In time the Normans and their successors added new shrines, and there came to be no practical difference between those shrines containing Anglo-Saxon or post-Conquest saints once their cults had become established. There were several reasons why the newly canonised saints were predominantly bishops. Firstly, bishops were among very few people buried within cathedrals, and thus the mother church automatically had possession of their relics in the event of saint-

---

1 The work in question is Osbern's *Vita Dunstani*: see S.J. Ridyard, '*Condigna Veneratio*: Post-Conquest Attitudes to the Saints of the Anglo-Saxons', in *Anglo-Norman Studies*, vol. 9, ed. R.A. Brown (Woodbridge, 1987), pp. 201–3; N. Ramsay and M. Sparks, 'The Cult of St Dunstan at Christ Church, Canterbury', in *St Dunstan: His Life, Times and Cult*, eds N. Ramsay, M. Sparks and T. Tatton-Brown (Woodbridge, 1992), pp. 314–16.
2 *The Anglo-Saxon Chronicle, a Revised Translation*, ed. D. Whitelock (Westport, 1961), pp. 130–1.

hood. Secondly, bishops dominated the religious scene, a prominence which made any saintly qualities more likely to be noticed. Finally, as canonisation became more expensive the wealth and influence of living bishops, who were likely to expend funds on enhancing the prestige of an episcopal predecessor, became very useful. Cathedral chapters were also powerful advocates of potential saints, and were especially proud of the bishops buried within the walls of their church.

Six post-Conquest bishop-saints became particularly important. The first and most famous was Archbishop Thomas Becket, whose tomb supplanted Dunstan's as the premier shrine of Canterbury and became England's only truly international saint's shrine. Wulfstan, the eleventh-century bishop of Worcester, joined St Oswald in Worcester cathedral after his canonisation in 1203. Bishop Hugh of Avalon's death in 1200 and canonisation in 1220 gave Lincoln the saint it had long looked for. Less well-known today are William Fitzherbert, the archbishop of York canonised in 1226, Richard de Wych of Chichester, canonised in 1262, and Thomas Cantilupe of Hereford, whose death in 1287 finally provided that cathedral with relics to replace those of St Ethelbert. The last of all cathedrals to possess a saint was Salisbury, which did not obtain the canonisation of Bishop Osmund until 1456.

Saints who were not bishops were much rarer. Before the Conquest saintly kings were relatively common but, partly because cathedrals did not often receive royal bodies for burial and partly because the Papacy was reluctant to canonise royalty, Edward the Confessor was the last English king to be canonised. It has been argued that in the later middle ages anti-monarchical cults aroused greater interest at a popular level than official ones.[3] One type of saint that appears to have originated at Norwich was the so-called 'boy martyr'. The Norwich townsmen may have invented what is now known as the 'blood libel', the claim that a world-wide Jewish conspiracy organised ritual slayings of young boys at yearly intervals in mockery of Christ. It was held that Norwich had been chosen by lot as the place where the ritual had to take place in 1144, and that local Jews, following orders from their religious leaders, were responsible for the murder of a boy named William.[4] Another boy martyr, 'Little St Hugh', was hailed at Lincoln. His case evolved in a way similar to the events at Norwich, except that there may also have been some royal involvement in the cult in the person of Edward I.[5] Neither Little Hugh or William were actually canonised, yet both were treated as official saints to an uncommon degree.

It is possible to explain the blood libel myth in part as a desire for martyrs, who

---

[3] E.M. Hallam, 'Royal Burial and the Cult of Kingship in France and England, 1060–1330', *J. of Medieval History*, vol. 8, no. 4 (1982), p. 362–3. For a discussion of royal saints in general see J. Nelson, 'Royal Saints and Early Medieval Kingship', *Studies in Church History*, vol. 10, ed. D. Baker (Oxford, 1973), pp. 31–44. For Edward the Confessor in particular see B.W. Scholz, 'The Canonization of Edward the Confessor', *Speculum*, vol. 36 (1961), pp. 51–60.

[4] Thomas of Monmouth, *Life of St William*, esp. pp. 14–23.

[5] This connection is emphasized by D. Stocker in 'The Shrine of Little St Hugh', in *Medieval Art and Architecture at Lincoln Cathedral* (*BAACT*, vol. 8, 1986), pp. 115–16.

can be defined as those killed by heathens for their faith. With more aggressive heathens having been eliminated from England, 'the Norwich Jews were a group of non-Christians readily available'.[6] However, it was not necessary to be killed by heathens in order to be granted the reputation of martyrdom. Other murder victims were also enshrined as martyrs, mostly unofficially. The pilgrim William of Perth, murdered near Rochester in 1201, was soon buried in the cathedral and canonised, but the cults of the variously slain Simon de Montfort, Edward II, Richard Scrope, Henry VI and Thomas of Lancaster were all unofficial despite being very popular. It is very likely that they all owed their posthumous reputations to their violent deaths.

The origins of a saint cult

For our purposes, a relic cult began with the burial of a holy figure within a church. In medieval England intramural burial was not uncommon for high ecclesiastics and upper nobility, but even those buried outside the church could be moved inside if sanctity was suspected. Thus, William of Norwich, discovered half-buried in a wood, was translated to four progressively more honourable sites until his tomb-shrine found its final place in the cathedral's choir aisle.[7] Recognition of sanctity, at first unofficial, led to veneration of a saint's tomb and, eventually, steps towards canonisation. The latter was not absolutely essential for a successful cult, but did enhance its chances of survival by ensuring that the church would work to preserve the saint's memory. 'By this papal proclamation a liturgical cult of the new saint was approved and extended to the universal church, his feast day was established, his veneration endorsed and the invocation of his intercession by the faithful encouraged.'[8]

At first sanctity was authorised by local bishops or councils, but by the mid-eleventh century it was widely held that the Pope should be consulted when there was some doubt about the candidate. In 1099 Urban II created a new precedent when he appointed an archbishop to look into the sanctity of Nicholas of Trani.[9] Papal control was extended under Alexander III (1159–81) and Innocent III (1198–1216), who secured the sole right of the Papacy to judge such matters. Witnesses to miracles now had to come forward, some even being required to appear at Rome.[10] In England the first papal canonisations took place in the

6 V.D. Lipman, *The Jews of Medieval Norwich* (London, 1967), p. 56.
7 Thomas of Monmouth, *Life of St William*, pp. 33, 54, 123, 186, 221.
8 P.H. Daly, 'The Process of Canonization in the Thirteenth and Early Fourteenth Centuries', in *St Thomas Cantilupe, Bishop of Hereford: Essays in his Honour*, ed. M. Jancey (Hereford, 1982), p. 125.
9 M.R. Toynbee, *S. Louis of Toulouse and the Process of Canonisation in the Fourteenth Century* (Manchester, 1929), p. 137.
10 D.H. Farmer, 'The Cult and Canonization of St Hugh', in *St Hugh of Lincoln: Lectures Delivered at Oxford and Lincoln to Celebrate the Eighth Centenary of St Hugh's Consecration as Bishop of Lincoln*, ed. H. Mayr-Harting (Oxford, 1987), p. 82; Toynbee, *S. Louis of*

twelfth century with those of Edward the Confessor (1161) and Thomas of Canterbury (1173).

Public acclamation of sainthood often ignored official proclamations. William of Perth, for example, was immediately hailed as St William on his death in 1201, even though formal recognition did not come until 1256.[11] While popular devotion arose swiftly, 'by the end of the thirteenth century the process whereby a saint won official papal recognition was a protracted exercise in litigation'.[12] The process began with 'letters of postulation' to the papal court requesting consideration. The backers of the canonisation (usually a group of clergy) sometimes sent form letters to eminent people, especially bishops, to be copied, collected and dispatched in one consignment. Several batches of letters, sent to cardinals as well as the Pope, were usually needed before matters could progress further. Letters of postulation for Thomas of Hereford, for example, were first sent to Rome in April 1290, with more consignments following in 1294, 1299 and 1305.[13] By 1305 Cantilupe's file at Rome included letters from Edward I, the archbishop of York, fifteen bishops, seven abbots, eleven earls and many nobles.[14] In the case of Robert Grosseteste a large petition was sent to Rome in 1288 and 1289, endorsed by the dean and chapter of Lincoln, the bishops of Worcester, Lincoln, Hereford, St David's, Durham and Ely, the archbishop of York and many others. In 1307 the dean and chapter sent a canon to Rome to plead the case with more letters, this time including some from the bishop of Lincoln, the archbishop of York, the dean and chapter of St Paul's, the University of Oxford and Edward I.[15]

By the mid-thirteenth century the normal practice was for the Pope to pass the testimonials, postulatory letters and *vitae* to a committee of cardinals. If their report was positive the Pope appointed a commission of three or four eminent members to investigate further. An inquiry of 1202 into the merits of Wulfstan of Worcester, for example, was conducted by the archbishop of Canterbury, the bishop of Ely and the abbots of Bury and Woburn.[16] The commission for St Hugh of Lincoln, the first surviving document for which dates from 1219, was made up of Archbishop Stephen Langton, Bishop William of Coventry and Abbot John II of Fountains.[17]

Toulouse, p. 138; E.W. Kemp, *Canonization and Authority in the Western Church* (Oxford, 1948), pp. 97–106.

11 J.S. Richardson, 'Saint William of Perth, and his Memorials in England', *Trans. of the Scottish Ecclesiological Soc.*, vol. 2, pt 1 (1906–7), p. 123.

12 Daly, 'Process of Canonization', p. 125.

13 Daly, 'Process of Canonization', pp. 126–8. See an example in *Registrum Ade de Orleton, Episcopi Herefordensis, A.D. mcccxvii–mcccxxvii*, ed. A.T. Bannister (Canterbury and York Soc., vol. 5, 1908), pp. 76–7.

14 E.M. Jancey, *St. Thomas of Hereford* (Newport, 1978), p. 14.

15 R.E.G. Cole, 'Proceedings Relative to the Canonization of Robert Grosseteste, Bishop of Lincoln', *Ass. Architectural Soc. Reports and Papers*, vol. 33 (1915), pp. 7–8, 30–2. Despite this massive support the petitions were ultimately unsuccessful.

16 *Annales Monasterii de Wigornia*, in *Annales Monastici*, vol. 4, ed. H.R. Luard (RS, vol. 36, 1869), p. 391.

17 Farmer, 'Cult and Canonization of St Hugh', p. 101; 'The Canonization of St. Hugh of

The commissioners interviewed those familiar with the saint or his reputation and examined testimonials of miracles but did not pass judgement. The judges-delegate into Thomas Cantilupe's case, for example, established that Thomas died in communion with the church and heard evidence on his life and miracles at London and Hereford before sending their findings to the papal court.[18] A commission's report passed through several layers of papal bureaucracy before it was decided upon by the college of cardinals and then, if their decision was positive, by all the prelates then at the curia. The final ceremony was elaborate and usually included the proclamation of a new indulgence. The bull of canonisation announced the feast day, listed the more conclusive miracles, and ordinarily commanded that the saint be translated to a shrine. To take one example, the bull on the canonisation of St Hugh issued by Honorius III in 1220 declared that his body 'should be translated from the place it now is and more honourably situated'.[19]

The recognition of a saint required two things: sanctity of life and posthumous miracles.[20] The latter eventually became the more important of the two, since a virtuous life did not guarantee that the prospective saint had not fallen from grace soon before his death, while miracles proved that the candidate was with God. Investigations into miracles accordingly became the standard method of testing sanctity. An early example occurred when Abbot Lawrence told two papal legates about some miracles of Edward the Confessor, and also showed them a piece of his shroud which they agreed was miraculously undecayed, thus helping to secure Edward's 1161 canonisation.[21] Hagiography was a key element of the canonisation process. *Vitae* and *miracula* were used as evidence, as in the *Registrum in Causa Canonizacionis Beati Viri Osmundi olim Saresbiriensis Episcopi in Anglia*, a collection, primarily of miracles, presented at Rome in 1424.[22] Famous writers were sometimes enlisted for this purpose. In order to aid their petition for the canonisation of Remigius of Lincoln, the dean and chapter of that place contracted Giraldus Cambrensis to write the *Vita Remigii*, which he did in c.1198.[23]

Three less explicit but just as important requirements for canonisation were

Lincoln: The text of Cotton Roll xiii, 27', ed. H. Farmer, *Lincolnshire Architectural and Archaeological Soc. Reports and Papers*, vol. 6, pt 2 (1986), p. 90.

18 *Acta Sanctorum, October*, vol. 1, ed. J. Ghesquiero (Antwerp, 1765), pp. 584–96.

19 'A loco in quo est transferendum sit et dignius collocandum': *Registrum Antiquissimum of the Cathedral Church of Lincoln*, vol. 1, ed. C.W. Foster (Lincoln Record Soc., vol. 27, 1931), p. 237.

20 'Virtue of morals and virtue of signs': Kemp, *Canonization and Authority*, p. 104.

21 The two legates were Hyacinthus and Othos, who sent a letter to Pope Alexander marvelling that the shroud could so have retained its colour and form. They felt that it had to have been a miracle for it to have lain next to a human body without decomposing, and so they begged the Pope to advance the cause: *Spicilegium Liberianum*, ed. F. Liverani (Florence, 1863), pp. 733–4; Scholz, 'Canonization of Edward', pp. 52–3.

22 This text makes up the body of *The Canonization of Saint Osmund*, ed. A.R. Malden (Salisbury, 1901), pp. 1–90.

23 Giraldus Cambrensis, *Vita S. Remigii et Vita S. Hugonis*, in *Opera*, vol. 7, ed. J.F. Dimock (RS, vol. 21, 1877), p. xi.

power, money and patience. The canonisation of William of York, for example, was secured through the money and influence of Bishop Antony Bek and Archbishop Walter de Grey.[24] The cost and effort proved prohibitive for many churches. Four English bishops (Robert Grosseteste of Lincoln, Walter of Worcester, Walter Suffield of Norwich and Thomas Cantilupe of Hereford) were candidates for canonisation at the same time, but only the last named was successful despite the fact that all had thriving cults with miracles.[25] Higden, in his *Polychronicon*, attributed the failure of Grosseteste's canonisation to his *Epistola* on papal abuses.[26] John Schalby was less certain: 'And although the Dean and Chapter of Lincoln wrote repeatedly to the apostolic see on behalf of his canonisation, . . . in no way . . . have they been able to make progress, for what reason God knows.'[27] In 1324 the canons of Lincoln tried again, this time attempting to secure the canonisation of Bishop John D'Alderby based on reports of miracles at his tomb. A 1331 letter of postulation from the bishop of Lichfield describes D'Alderby as a new light in England, with miracles as much at his tomb as elsewhere. A feast day and antiphons recording his miracles were even prepared, but all to no avail.[28] The first attempt to secure recognition for Edward the Confessor, begun in 1138, was officially rejected by the Pope because there was not enough testimony, but in fact was probably denied due to bad timing and political considerations, whereas the final success was due to the Pope's need of English support in 1161.[29]

Even with success the time taken to attain canonisation varied considerably. The quickest canonisation in medieval England was that of Thomas Becket on 21 February 1173, less than twenty-six months after his murder and the sixth fastest in the history of the medieval church.[30] The canonisation of St Osmund, who died in 1099, was the longest and hardest fought. The first campaign was undertaken in 1228 by Bishop Richard Poore, who sent messengers to Rome asking for a canonisation process, and another unsuccessful effort was made in about 1370.[31]

24   W.H. Dixon, *Fasti Eboracenses* (London, 1863), pp. 227–8; Grey's involvement is outlined in P. Draper, 'Bishop Northwold and the Cult of Saint Etheldreda', in *Medieval Art and Architecture at Ely Cathedral (BAACT*, vol. 2, 1979), p. 19.
25   The miracles of Grosseteste are mentioned in *Annales de Theokesberia*, where he is erroneously described as having been canonised: *Annales de Theokesberia*, p. 159. See also *Annales de Burton*, in *Annales Monastici*, vol. 1, ed. H.R. Luard (RS, vol. 36, 1864), p. 336. For a full discussion of the canonisation attempt, see Cole, 'Proceedings Relative to the Canonization of Robert Grosseteste', pp. 1–34.
26   John de Shalby, *The Book of John de Shalby, Canon of Lincoln (1299–1333) Concerning the Bishops of Lincoln and their Acts*, trans. with notes by J.H. Srawley, Lincoln Minster Pamphlets, no. 2 (Lincoln, 1949), p. 28.
27   John de Shalby, *The Book of John de Shalby*, p. 12.
28   'The Register of Bishop Norburgh', LJRO, B/A/1/3, f. 15v; D. Owen, *History of Lincolnshire, vol. v: Church and Society in Medieval Lincolnshire* (Lincoln, 1971), p. 126.
29   Scholz, 'Canonization of Edward', pp. 47–8, 50–1.
30   A.J. Duggan, 'The Cult of St Thomas Becket in the Thirteenth Century', in *St Thomas Cantilupe, Bishop of Hereford: Essays in his Honour*, ed. M. Jancey (Hereford, 1982), p. 22.
31   W.J. Torrance, *The Story of Saint Osmund, Bishop of Salisbury* (Salisbury, 1978), p. 37; *Canonization of St Osmund*, p. iv.

In the early fifteenth century Bishops Hallam and Chandler came close to obtaining a canonisation but were foiled by confusion at Rome and the swift death of three popes in succession.[32] In 1416 Dean Chandler summoned a chapter to discuss the matter, wherein canons agreed to pay one tenth of their prebendal income for seven years and to use the entrance fees of new canons towards the expenses of canonisation. Many letters from the chapter's proctor at Rome in the fifteenth century show a continual lack of funds, papal respect and attention.[33] The costs to Salisbury cathedral, 'discounting the expenses of the commission, the cause and the process, since no accurate estimate of those may be given', but including red and white carpet, banquets for the Pope and cardinals, ornaments at the celebration, cantors, bell ringers, and a host of solicitors and servants, totalled 847 ducats, but Malden gives the full cost at £731 13s.[34] Osmund was finally canonised in 1456, no less than 228 years after the first attempt.

Translations: theory and causes

The translation which inevitably followed canonisation came to be the most important event in the local cult of a saint.[35] Simply put, a translation was the ritual movement of a saint's bodily remains from one place to another, usually accompanied by extreme degrees of ceremony and pageantry. It was in fact among the greatest of medieval ecclesiastical celebrations. The sources for translations consist of written descriptions varying in length from the single sentences found in chronicles to the lengthier chapters contained within saints' lives and *miracula*. The earliest significant account which I have used is the *Translatio Sancti Augustini*, describing the translation of St Augustine at his abbey in Canterbury in 1091, and the latest is the account of the last translation of St Swithun at Winchester in 1476.[36] Because my research focuses on cathedrals, the information in this chapter is no doubt biased towards the bigger translation ceremonies.

The practice of translation was limited to saints' shrines. Lesser relics were not

---

[32] Torrance, *Story of St Osmund*, pp. 37–8.

[33] *Canonization of St Osmund, passim*.

[34] *The Register of John Morton, Archbishop of Canterbury 1486–1500*, ed. C. Harper-Bill (Canterbury and York Soc., vol. 75, 1987), vol. 1, pp. 51–2; *Canonization of St Osmund*, p. xxxij. For the increased difficulty of obtaining a canonisation, see Finucane, *Miracles and Pilgrims*, p. 197.

[35] For a good examination of the gradual extension of exceptions to the Roman rule of funerary inviolability, a process which led to translations, see Herrmann-Mascard, *Reliques des Saints*, pp. 35–41. For Gaul as England's source for the practice of translation, see Rollason, *Saints and Relics*, p. 49; A. Thacker, 'Lindisfarne and the Origins of the Cult of St Cuthbert', in *St Cuthbert, History, Cult and Community to AD 1200*, eds G. Bonner, D. Rollason, C. Stancliffe (Woodbridge, 1989), pp. 105–6.

[36] Goscelin, 'Historia Translationis S. Augustini Episcopi', ed. J.-P. Migne (*PL*, vol. 155, 1854), cols 13–46; *Concilia Magnae Britanniae et Hiberniae*, ed. D. Wilkins (London, 1737), vol. 3, pp. 610–11. A version of the Winchester translation rendered into English is in *Register of John Morton*, no. 184, pp. 52–3.

specially connected to a location; whole collections could be relocated with little or no ceremony. Greater relics, on the other hand, had associations with specific sites. Even though feretra (the chests within which the saintly bodies lay) were sometimes portable they were only removed from their bases temporarily, always to be returned (see Chapter 2). Permanently moving the relics was tantamount to moving the saint's home and therefore required a special ritual, an event that became the translation ceremony.

But why exhume and move a saint's corpse in the first place? The translation was the culmination of several earlier stages in the cult of a saint. In medieval England the initial burial of saints did not differ ceremonially or in technical details from that of non-saints, for the simple reason that no one could be officially recognised as a saint until some time after death. Even obvious martyrs like Thomas Becket were not immediately enshrined. Despite their own lax use of the term saint, in ceremonial matters the medieval clergy of major churches were fastidious: without canonisation, there could be no shrine. As a result, a burial might be conducted with great honour, but was still a burial in a tomb or grave and not an enshrinement. Even the tombs of the two boy martyrs (William of Norwich and Little St Hugh of Lincoln), who were widely called saints despite never being canonised, were not, strictly speaking, shrines. In other words, their bones are not known to have ever been lifted into reliquary chests.

Before the eleventh century canonisation was subsumed within translation. When a cult had grown up around a tomb and the occupant was commonly considered to be a saint, then the local bishop or abbot ordered his body to be moved into a shrine. This symbolic act was sufficient for canonisation.[37] Cuthbert and Etheldreda are notable examples of saints canonised in this way. However, when the Pope obtained a monopoly of canonisation in the early twelfth century the relationship between it and translation changed. Canonisation became concerned with the universal observance of the cult of the saint, while translation dealt with the official recognition of the local cult and the formal commencement of the shrine as an institution of the local church. The first English example of this division was the canonisation of Edward the Confessor in 1161 followed by his translation in 1163.

Two examples demonstrate the strength of papal control over canonisation and the link between it and translation. The divine punishment believed to be incurred by proceeding with translation before receiving due authority can be seen at Worcester, where several people had experienced visions of St Wulfstan commanding that his body be translated. Accordingly, one night in 1198, five years before Wulfstan's canonisation, the tomb was opened by Bishop John in the

---

[37] 'The elevation of the body during the entire high middle ages was the sole source of sanctity; it was the exhumation of a body extracted from its ancient tomb for placement in a sepulchre more worthy of the reverence that it is due' (L'elevation du corps qui pendant tout le Haut Moyen Age va être la seule source de sainteté: c'est l'exhumation d'un corps saint extrait de son tombeau primitif pour être placé dans un sépulcre plus digne de la révérence qui lui est due): Herrmann-Mascard, *Reliques des Saints*, p. 82.

presence of the monks. The vestments and ornaments were taken out and deposited in one shrine and the bones in another. Just over three weeks later, John died. St Oswald appeared in a vision to declare that this was not a coincidence, but a punishment for actions conducted without the approval of the Pope and without due reverence. St Wulfstan's bones were replaced before being properly translated in 1218.[38] Another telling example is that of Osmund of Salisbury. In 1452 the bishop of Salisbury's proctor in Rome warned the advocate of the papal consistory court that the local people were angry at the lack of attention given to their saint and were threatening to translate him without papal canonisation. This would greatly weaken papal authority and therefore it was better to hasten the official process. He was advised that the inclusion of this fact in letters of postulation would increase the likelihood of the pope considering the case.[39] Osmund was finally raised to the altars in 1456. Having waited so long, the locals wasted no time in translating him later that same year. These two cases clearly demonstrate how canonisation was thought to be a prerequisite for enshrinement and translation, and how breaking that tradition was a serious breach of both custom and the divine order. A command to translate became part of bulls of canonisation. Often the bull's language was obscure, but that for Thomas Becket was explicit: 'we command you by this our apostolic rescript to hold a solemn procession on some high feast-day when the clergy and the people are met together, to inter his body devoutly and reverently behind the altar, or to place it in a chest, elevated above the altar, whichever be more convenient'.[40]

The question remains as to why canonisation implied that a saint should be exhumed and moved. In other words, why were saints enshrined and what was the difference between a tomb and a shrine? There existed a general feeling that saintly relics should not remain below ground like those of the ordinary dead. Some monks at Westminster thought it shameful that a saint like Edward the Confessor, whose canonisation was delayed, was still 'concealed in a tabernacle of mortality'. 'How much longer', they grumbled, 'is our precious treasure to lie hidden buried in the earth?'[41] Of St Erkenwald it was said that 'Someone who shines forth so gloriously in the heavens surely should not have been buried in such a foul garment as the earth.'[42] Even a crypt was not good enough: Stephen

---

[38] The bones were 'raised irreverently and by night (noctu et irreverenter levata)': *Annales de Wigornia*, pp. 392, 409–10; E. Mason, *St Wulfstan of Worcester, c. 1008–1095* (Oxford, 1990), p. 278.

[39] A letter of 10 Aug., 1452: *Canonization of St Osmund*, p. 109.

[40] See *English Historical Documents, 1042–1189*, eds D.C. Douglas and G.W. Greenaway (London, 1953), p. 775; *Materials for the History of Thomas Becket*, eds J.C. Robertson and J.B. Sheppard (RS, vol. 67, 1885), vol. 7, p. 545.

[41] 'Usquequo celabitur in terra defossus thesaurus noster pretiosus?': Richard of Cirencester, *Speculum Historiale de Gestis Regum Angliæ*, ed. J.E.B. Mayor (RS, vol. 30, 1863, 1869); translated in F. Barlow, *Edward the Confessor* (London, 1970), p. 278.

[42] 'Qui tanta in celestibus emicat gloria non debuit tam uili scemate sepeliri in terra': *The Saint of London: The Life and Miracles of St. Erkenwald*, ed. E.G. Whatley (Birmingham, N.Y., 1989), pp. 119–20, hereafter referred to as the *Miracula Erkenwaldi*.

Langton performed the translation of St Thomas, having seen 'that he lay igno-
bly, almost in the foundation of the church and in stone'.[43] By medieval English
definitions, a saint needed to be moved from a place of little dignity (buried
underground) to a more exalted position (a shrine in the quire). Accounts of
translations often describe the new shrine position as a better or more suitable
place; for example, the movement of St Osmund was to be to 'a more proper
place'.[44] The need for translations was thus, in the first instance, a matter of
religious sentiment.

This improvement in location occurred in one or both of two directions.
Firstly, the body was lifted vertically out of the tomb above the pavement of the
church and placed in a casket on an elevated base. Secondly, it was moved horizontally, usually to the east, towards a holier and more convenient part of the
building. Shrines differed from tombs primarily in the elevation of the coffin,
and indeed translations could be described as movements to 'higher' positions,
such as St William of York's translation *'ad altiorem locum'*.[45] Although tombs
in general gradually became higher and more elaborate during the middle ages,
until they rivalled and in some cases exceeded shrines in magnificence of structure, the body remained, in almost all cases, buried beneath the level of the floor.
The bulk of a tomb monument was therefore a superstructure, while a shrine
monument was a base for a reliquary chest.

The process of elevation (the raising of a body into a shrine without changing
its horizontal location) may originally have been separate from translation
proper. After the Conquest, however, only Thomas of Hereford, who was enshrined directly above his grave in 1320, is known to have been elevated without
being moved horizontally. His old tomb was converted into a base for the reliquary chest (or 'feretrum'), and can still be seen. However, this event was called
a translation (*translatio*) and seems to have been functionally identical to other
translations despite the purely vertical direction of the move. In any case, it was
only a temporary measure until Thomas was properly translated into his final
shrine in the far east end of Hereford cathedral in 1349 (see Chapter 3).

As time went on, new shrines could be built for saints on the same site as their
old monuments without a full translation ceremony. The shrine of Edward the
Confessor, for example, was moved two feet to the west to accommodate Henry
V's tomb, but with no known ceremony.[46] Such later shrine reconstructions were
relatively casual in nature because the structural improvements did not involve a
change in the sacred location and, furthermore, all the saints in question had

---

43 'quod ignobiliter jacuit, quasi in fundamento ecclesie et in lapide': Matthew Paris, *Historia
    Anglorum*, ed. F. Madden (RS, vol. 44, 1866), vol. 2, p. 241. In his sermon on that occasion
    Langton described the tomb as 'locis humilibus': Stephen Langton, 'Tractatus de
    Translatione Beati Thomae', ed. J.P. Migne (*PL*, vol. 190, 1854), col. 419.
44 'Digniori loco', from the Papal Bull of Canonisation: *Canonization of Saint Osmund*, p. 234.
45 William Rishanger, *Willelmi Rishanger, Quondam Monachi S. Albani, et Quorundam
    Anonymorum, Chronica et Annales, Regnantibus Henrico Tertio et Edwardo Primo*, in
    Chronica Monasterii S. Albani, ed. H.T. Riley (RS, vol. 28, 1865), p. 106.
46 W.R. Lethaby, *Westminster Abbey Re-Examined* (London, 1925), p. 266.

already been translated at least once before. Although this suggests that the first move was the most important, most translations of the post-Conquest era were from already existing shrines to new and improved ones. A saint could be moved several times, each calling for a new translation ceremony. St Swithun, for example, was translated at least four times.[47]

The main reason for moving existing shrines was the disruption caused by the reconstruction of churches. The Norman building campaign resulted in the demolition of all the old cathedrals, and in the process of rebuilding most shrines had to be relocated. During the thirteenth and fourteenth centuries many of the great churches of England were again re-built and their east ends extended. The high altar was usually moved eastward, and naturally the shrine had to be moved as well if the two objects were to maintain their spatial relationship. Few English translations involved migration over a significant distance, almost all being from one part of a church to another, newer section, or even from one part of the quire to another. St Frideswide, for example, was translated at Oxford 'near the site where she had formerly been placed' in 1289.[48] If construction was likely to be lengthy, then the shrine might need a temporary home while the cathedral was re-built. For this reason St Cuthbert was removed to what would become the cloisters at Durham during the construction of the first Norman Church, while Erkenwald was moved into the first part of St Paul's to be rebuilt, the crypt, after it burned down in 1087.[49]

The primary reasons for translations were thus two: religious sentiment and architectural necessity. Whatever the causes, the ceremonial relocation of saints' bodies was as impressive as the new architecture. Far from being seen as a burden, the translation was a great opportunity to refurbish the shrine and celebrate the prestige of the church. There were two other incidental but important purposes of the translation ceremony: continuity and consecration. When a disruption in the history of a church occurred its shrine became a symbol of the past. The translation ceremony highlighted the fact that although other things had changed, the community and its sanctity remained. A major disjunction was, of course, the Norman Conquest. The new ecclesiastical hierarchy linked itself to the holiness and prestige of its Anglo-Saxon predecessors by ostentatiously translating the old saints into newly re-built churches. They thereby acquired the saint as patron and linked themselves with the entire history of the see and its possessions, negating the discontinuity of tradition and reaffirming the ancient heritage of the church.

Similarly, when a community of clergy entered a new or re-built church, their official occupation was symbolised by the placement of their saintly patron in his or her new home. A notable example occurred at Winchester in 1093, when

---

47 The translations were in 971, 1093, 1150 and 1476, with a possible translation in 974. For an overview of Swithun's history see Crook, 'Swithun of Winchester', pp. 57–68. See also table 1.

48 'Prope situm quo prius fuerat collocatum': *Chronicon Vulgo Dictum Chronicon Thomae Wykes*, in *Annales Monastici*, vol. 4, ed. H.R. Luard (RS, vol. 36, 1869), p. 318.

49 The temporary site of Cuthbert's body was later venerated and marked with a monument: *Rites of Durham*, pp. 64, 74; *Miracula Erkenwaldi*, p. 128.

the clergy marked their formal move to the new cathedral, which was being built alongside the old, by a solemn procession with the body of their patron, St Swithun, to his new shrine behind the high altar of the Norman church.[50] A more obscure instance is the translation of St Milburga. The Anglo-Saxon community at Much Wenlock had died away, but the Cluniacs imported in 1079 went to great lengths to find the relics of Milburga and rejuvenate her cult with a translation.[51]

Translations had an impact on the consecration of churches and high altars. Relics were required by canon law for every altar but, since they were sealed into the structure during the consecration ceremony, the relics used were usually small and, from that point on, hidden from view. The close proximity of major relics in a shrine could be more emphatic. Although there was no explicit link between altar or church consecration and the translation of a major shrine, the two cere- monies technically being distinct and separate, they were often performed in such close conjunction that a relationship was directly implied. The translation of St Wulfstan at Worcester in 1218, for example, occurred immediately after the new church had been consecrated.[52] Even St William of Norwich had his altar dedicated on the same day as the re-built church.[53] The shrine and the high altar might be connected symbolically by changing the dedication of the church to include the main shrine's saint. The dedication of the cathedral at Ely, for example, was changed to include St Etheldreda when she was translated into the new choir in 1252.[54] The translation ceremony of a great shrine could thus function as a kind of super-consecration for the church. It announced the completeness of the church and showed that despite other changes the holy site had been preserved.

Translations: preparation

When it had been decided to translate a saint, and all canonical requirements had been met, practical considerations still had to be overcome. Lack of ideal condi- tions often produced a considerable delay between canonisation and translation, the longest in England being sixty years in the case of St Hugh of Lincoln. A delay of ten to twenty years was common, and was usually the result of long-term problems like church reconstruction or extended political turmoil. Some periods were unfavourable to big ecclesiastical celebrations, such as that from about 1200 until 1218, during part of which England was suffering from interdict and civil war. Political conditions including the Baronial Wars and Bishop Berstead's exile

---

50 *Annales de Wigornia*, p. 37.
51 See Odo of Ostia, 'An Early Twelfth-Century Account of the Translation of St. Milburga of Much Wenlock', trans. A.J.M. Edwards (*Trans. of the Shropshire Archaeological Soc.*, vol. 57, 1961–4), pp. 143–51.
52 The high altar was consecrated in honour of St Mary and St Oswald and the middle (*medium*) altar in honour of St Peter and St Wulfstan: *Annales de Wigornia*, pp. 409–10.
53 Bartholomew de Cotton, *Historia Anglicana*, ed. H.R. Luard (RS, vol. 16, 1859), p. 157.
54 'Chronicon Ecclesiae Eliensis', BL, Harl. MS 3721.

in Rome delayed the translation of Richard of Chichester.[55] Some delay was necessary in order to allow for the construction of the shrine itself, which could take a considerable length of time. Marble for the shrine of St Thomas was in Canterbury as early as 1181, and work began at least five years in advance of the 1220 translation.[56] The construction of the shrine of Edward the Confessor, which is the best documented, took over thirty years.[57]

Time was also needed to raise the huge sums of money required for extravagant festivals. Stephen Langton's expenses on the translation of Thomas Becket contributed to a debt that was still being paid off by Archbishop Boniface, the fourth after Langton.[58] At Chichester in 1276 Bishop Stephen spent more than £1,000 on the translation of St Richard.[59] We can only guess at the total cost of the more extraordinary celebrations at Lincoln and Canterbury, but one to two thousand pounds seems to have been the usual expense for a major translation, part of which may have gone towards the structure of the new shrine.

In most instances we know that the local bishop paid the bill. At least some of the elaborate festivities at Lincoln in 1280, however, were paid for by Thomas Bek, consecrated bishop of St David's the same day, just as the translation of St William of York had been paid for by Bek's brother Antony when he was consecrated bishop of Durham.[60] Sometimes bishops were less willing or able to fund a translation, particularly in later centuries. In 1320 Bishop Reynolds of Hereford appealed to the clergy of the diocese for contributions to the new shrine of Thomas Cantilupe, and in the same year seven men were appointed by the bishop of Hereford to collect money for the shrine and church. Sufficient funds were still missing in 1348, when Bishop John Trillek pleaded that he could not afford St Thomas's translation on his own.[61] It is interesting that bishops were so often the sponsors, and not cathedral corporations. After all, the community

55 D.J. Jones, 'The Cult of St Richard of Chichester in the middle ages', *Sussex Archaeological Collections*, vol. 121 (1983), p. 80.
56 T. Tatton-Brown, 'The Trinity Chapel and Corona Floors', *Canterbury Cathedral Chronicle*, no. 75 (1981), p. 54.
57 The earliest notice of work on the shrine in the Liberate Rolls appears in 1239, and the last in 1272 (when two marks of gold dust were purchased for it): *Calendar of the Liberate Rolls*, ed. H.C.M. Lyte (London, 1916), vol. 1, p. 404, vol. 6, p. 225.
58 Thomas Burton, *Chronica Monasterii de Melsa*, ed. E.A. Bond (RS, vol. 43, 1868), vol. 1, p. 406; Ralph Higden, *Polychronicon Ranulphi Higden Monachi Cestrensis*, eds C. Babington and J.R. Lumby (RS, vol. 41, 1865), vol. 8, p. 200. Much of this debt, however, was the result of building the palace hall: F. Woodman, *The Architectural History of Canterbury Cathedral* (London, 1981), p. 133. Langton's expenses on free victuals in the city are outlined in the *Polistorie*, see Mason, *Bones of St Thomas*, pp. 70–1.
59 M.E.C. Walcott, 'The Bishops of Chichester from Stigand to Sherbourne', *Sussex Archaeological Collections*, vol. 28 (1878), p. 35.
60 'Translatio Corporis Sancti Hugonis Lincolniensis Episcopi', *Catalogus Codicum Hagiographicorum Bibliothecae Regiae Bruxellensis, pars I, Codices Latini Membranei, vol. I.*, eds Hagiographi Bollandiani (Brussels, 1886), p. 193; *Chronicon Abbatie de Parco Lude*, ed. E. Venables (Horncastle, 1891), p. 19.
61 P.E. Morgan, 'The Effect of the Pilgrim Cult of St. Thomas Cantilupe on Hereford Cathedral', in *St Thomas Cantilupe, Bishop of Hereford: Essays in his Honour*, ed. M.

directly benefited from the shrine and received pilgrims' offerings, which in almost all cases the bishop saw nothing of.[62] Bishops therefore seem to have been involved in a sort of pious largesse calculated for its enormous prestige value.

There were rare exceptions to episcopal sponsorship. Some eleventh and early twelfth-century translations seem to have been organised, and therefore presumably paid for, by other local clergy. In an obscure and apparently unique case, the 1148 translation of St Erkenwald appears to have been supported by collections (collectiones) set up about the city by the poor, to which the wealthy reportedly contributed little or nothing.[63] Kings were infrequently involved, as in the funding of the shrine of St Cuthbert by Edgar, later king of Scotland, and the second translation of Edward the Confessor by King Henry III, whose devotion to Edward is well known.[64] Sometimes permission from the authorities was sought. In 1185 the Canterbury monks solicited the authorisation and support of the king before preparing the translation of St Thomas.[65]

While most greater shrines were funded by a bishop or king, some cathedrals were less fortunate. The trials and tribulations of the dean and chapter of Salisbury while trying to gather resources for a new shrine in the late fifteenth century make tragic reading in light of its destruction so soon after, but also give us rare details of the efforts such fund-raising could involve. When St Osmund was translated in 1456 he was installed in a temporary shrine. Fifteen years later Edward Bowden, Goldsmith of London, appeared with a proposal drawn on paper for a new shrine which the bishop of Salisbury, who was present, took away. The next day all concerned went to the treasury to view the jewels, precious metals and other valuables collected and offered to St Oswald since his translation.[66]

Unfortunately, the bishop did not bear the brunt of the cost, despite his interest in the plans. Some of the money came from gifts. In 1472 the outgoing shrine-keeper, W. Crowton, gave 100s. in gold money to the new work, and several other donations were reported in 1473. Although unpriced, the latter included twelve old nobles for gilding and six silver dishes left by the widow Alice Browning. Some of the funds were obtained by sequestering cathedral revenues. In 1472/3 seven canons' subsidies were diverted to the new shrine.[67] This was not enough,

Jancey (Hereford, 1982), p. 150; Calendar of Patent Rolls, Edward II, 1317–1321, ed. H.C.M. Lyte (London, 1903), p. 526; Registrum Johannis de Trillek, Episcopi Herefordensis, A.D. mcccxliv–mccclxi, ed. J.H. Parry (Canterbury and York Soc., vol. 8, 1912), pp. 147–8.

62 The exception is Worcester. See Chapters 5 and 6.
63 From a miracle concerning a woman who wanted to contribute but was prohibited by her husband: Miracula Erkenwaldi, pp. 132–4.
64 See for example Walter of Coventry, The Historical Collections of Walter of Coventry, ed. W. Stubbs (RS, vol. 58, 1872–3), vol. 1, p. 123; Annales Prioratus de Dunstaplia, in Annales Monastici, vol. 4, ed. H.R. Luard (RS, vol. 36, 1866), p. 252; The accounts of the Keepers of the Works at Westminster survive for 1264–72 (Exchequer pipe rolls, 110, 112, 113–16), printed in Building Accounts of King Henry III, ed. H.M. Colvin (Oxford, 1971), p. 416.
65 Materials for a History of Becket, vol. 7, pp. 581–2.
66 SCA, 'Machon Register', f. 39.
67 SCA, 'Machon Register', ff. 48, 59, 61, 57.

and in 1485 the income of the prebend of Horton was also devoted to the cause.[68] A letter sent to the thirty-eight non-residentiary canons asked them to donate to the shrine, since the work on the shrine had only just begun whereas they had hoped to see it half completed. This was due to the common treasury being empty and the residentiaries having given all they could, what with the lingering debts from the translation and declining offerings.[69] Other resources came from bequests. In 1501 John Doget left £10 'towards the completion of the shrine of St Osmund'.[70]

The canons were not ungrateful for patronage. Prayers written on the inside of the cover of a processional were 'in especial' for ye soules of theym whiche have gyven or gyve any parte of theyr godes to the performyng of the shryne of seynt Osmunde'.[71] There are several records of the purchase of materials for the same shrine. Silver plate, for example, was bought, 'fabricando sumtuose', for £66 13s. 4d.[72] An account of the Warden of the Shrine of St Osmund, 1493/4, shows Arnold Goldsmith paid for coming from London, making a furnace, and working on the shrine for twenty-one weeks and two days. William Aurifabro was also paid for seventeen weeks, and a carpenter and smith for smaller periods of time. Gilding the shrine cost a total of £34 11d., mostly to the above-mentioned Arnold.[73] When completed the shrine only had about forty years left to exist.

Once funds had been assured plans for a translation could proceed. Setting the date was of some importance since it became a feast in the church calendar. The date of a saint's death, and thus the date of his or her first feast-day, was essentially random and did not necessarily suit the convenience of the church he would be buried in. A translation, however, could be planned. For example, Becket's murderers slew him on 29 December, which was a difficult time of the year for pilgrims to travel. This was remedied by holding the 1220 translation on 7 July, which set a major feast of St Thomas in the best summer weather.[74] Those few saints translated in the winter, such as William of York and Frideswide of Oxford, had other feasts at more clement times of the year. In at least one case the preferred day seems to have been Easter: according to Gervase, the relics of Dunstan and Alphege at Canterbury were originally to have been moved on Easter day, but this

---

68 *Ceremonies and Processions of the Cathedral Church of Salisbury*, ed. C. Wordsworth (Cambridge, 1901), p. 281.n.
69 SCA, 'Machon Register', f. 128.
70 *Sede Vacante Wills: A Calendar of Wills proved before the Commissary of the Prior and Chapter of Christ Church Canterbury, During Vacancies in the Primacy*, ed. C.E. Woodruff (Kent Archaeological Soc., Records Branch, vol. 3, 1914), p. 16.
71 *Ceremonies and Processions of Salisbury*, p. 32.
72 SCA, 'Machon Register', f. 47.
73 SCA, 'Account of the Warden of the Shrine of St Osmund', 1493/4.
74 The 7th of July was also the tenth day (by Langton's calculations) of the seventh month after seven times seven years after the martyrdom. Langton, who was one of the day's greatest theologians, thus calculated the jubilee according to details in Leviticus xxv, 8–9. The day was also a Tuesday (significant in Thomas's history) and a leap year, a sign of good fortune: Duggan, 'The Cult of St Thomas', p. 39; R. Foreville, *Le Jubilé de Saint Thomas Becket* (Paris, 1958), p. 7.

proved impossible, so they were re-enshrined beforehand.[75] The convenient date of the translation feast often resulted in it overtaking the deposition or death date in importance. Indeed, shrine accounts show that more money was offered on the translation feasts than at any other time (see Chapter Seven). In the unique case of Canterbury, the fifty year anniversaries of the first translation were turned into jubilees, extraordinary festivals in which some of the excitement of the original celebration was revived.

Once set the date was announced. St Cuthbert's translation was proclaimed 'far and wide' while preparations were still under way.[76] Langton gave two years' notice of St Thomas's translation in a proclamation circulated throughout Europe.[77] Even those not invited to attend could be asked to participate spiritually. In 1284 Archbishop Wickwane sent a letter from York to Beverley asking the canons to pray during the translation of St William.[78] Beverley held the tomb of St John of Beverley, and one wonders how such letters were received by churches with rival shrines. Invitations to attend, however, seem to have been greeted with eagerness. It has been said of the translation at York that 'on no other occasion has the cathedral received within its walls a more illustrious assemblage'.[79] Chroniclers were certainly impressed by the presence of senior ecclesiastics. Perhaps the largest episcopal attendance was the twenty-four bishops and archbishops who came to the translation of Thomas Becket.[80] St Swithun's 1093 translation, however, was claimed to have been 'in the presence of almost all the bishops and abbots of England'; a large turnout.[81]

Among royalty, Henry III and his son Edward were specially devoted to translations, each attending at least three in different cathedrals while king. Their reigns included most of the biggest celebrations, so opportunity rather than personal piety may have accounted for their good record. Among earlier kings, the first known attendance is that of Henry II at Westminster in 1163. Surprisingly, there is no record of a king attending the translations of the eleventh and early twelfth centuries. The most likely reason is that the early translations were not as spectacular as those in the thirteenth century. Although celebrated with some pomp, they seem to have been primarily local events, reflected in the fact that the

75 Gervase of Canterbury, *The Chronicle of the Reigns of Stephen, Henry II, and Richard I, by Gervase, the Monk of Canterbury*, in *The Historical Works of Gervase of Canterbury*, vol. 1, ed. W. Stubbs (RS, vol. 73, 1879), p. 22.
76 'Meanwhile the day of the translation was preached long and wide' (Interea promulgato longe lateque venturae translationis die): Symeon of Durham, *Historia Ecclesiæ Dunhelmensis*, in *Symeonis Monachi Opera Omnia*, vol. 1, ed. T. Arnold (RS, vol. 75, 1882), p. 255.
77 Heath, *Steps of the Pilgrim*, p. 156; Henry of Avranches, *The Shorter Latin Poems of Master Henry of Avranches Relating to England*, eds J.C. Russell and J.P. Hieronymous (Cambridge, Mass., 1935), p. 73.
78 *Historians of the Church of York*, ed. J. Raine (RS, vol. 71, 1879–94), vol. 3, p. 211.
79 Dixon, *Fasti Eboracenses*, p. 228.
80 Walter of Coventry, *Collections*, vol. 2, p. 245.
81 'In praesentia omnium fere episcoporum atque abbatum Angliae': *Annales Monasterii de Wintonia*, in *Annales Monastici*, vol. 2, ed. H.R. Luard (RS, vol. 36, 1865), p. 37.

clergy was often led by 'only' one or two bishops and some local abbots. After Edward I royal attendance dropped off once more, largely because big translations became rarer. The last royal participation in a translation was by Edward III at that of St Thomas of Hereford in 1349.[82]

Except for the very greatest members of the nobility the aristocracy's presence is recorded only in collective terms. At Worcester in 1218, for example, there were two earls, eight barons, 'and other nobles in an infinite multitude'.[83] At Lincoln we are given the impressive attendance figure of 230 knights.[84] Those even lower on the social scale were described simply as crowds or masses. The Canterbury crowd in 1220 was 'innumerable', while that at Westminster in 1269 was 'not a small crowd'.[85] Those attending could sometimes approach near the actual handling of the relics and were of both sexes: at Oswald's translation it was said that 'around the tomb was a large crowd of men and women'.[86] At Durham in 1104, however, it seems that the people had to wait outside the doors of the church for the body of Cuthbert to be carried out to them.[87]

It is not surprising that lay people were attracted to translations. The greater ceremonies were turned into massive festivals, sometimes lasting a whole week. As in so many other instances, the Thomas Becket example is the most extreme. During the whole celebration, which lasted two weeks, hay and provender were provided along the entire route from London to Canterbury. A banquet was given four days before, reportedly for 33,000 persons.[88] Tuns of wine were placed at strategic locations about the city, distributed free to all. On the actual day of Becket's translation wine is said to have run in the gutters.[89] Wine is also supposed to have run in the gutters of the bishop's palace at St Hugh of Lincoln's translation in 1280.[90] While perhaps not the most salubrious means of serving drinks, this practice must have been an impressive display. Pilgrims were also encouraged to attend by indulgences granted on the day. For example, the bishop of Hereford

82 G. Marshall, 'The Shrine of St. Thomas de Cantilupe in Hereford Cathedral', *Trans. of the Woolhope Naturalists' Field Club*, vol. 27 (1930–2), p. 42.
83 'Et aliorum nobilium multitudine infinita': *Annales de Wigornia*, p. 409.
84 Candidus, *Peterborough Chronicle*, p. 40.
85 Walter of Coventry, *Collections*, vol. 2, p. 245; 'turba non modica': *Chronicon Thomæ Wykes*, p. 226.
86 'Circa tumulum praesens erat multa turba virorum ac feminarum': Eadmer, *Vita Sancti Oswaldi*, p. 47.
87 Symeon of Durham, *Historiæ Ecclesiae Dunhelmensis*, p. 260.
88 Henry of Avranches, *Shorter Latin Poems*, pp. 68–9, 73.
89 'The archbishop caused the barrels of wine to be laid on their sides in bowers in the middle of the street, and his servants to be set there to give liberally to the people during the heat without any payment of money'; '. . . en my la rue les toneaus de vin en foylis fist cocher lerseueske, et ces mynistres mettre pur largement au puple doner en la chalyne sauns paer accune moneye': *Polistorie*, in Mason, *Bones of St Thomas*, pp. 71–2; A.P. Stanley, 'The Shrine of St. Thomas of Canterbury', in *Historical Memorials of Canterbury* (12th ed., London, 1891), p. 200; 'Fecit etiam per totam diem translationis vinum jugiter in canalibus per varia, urbis loca distillare': Higden, *Polychronicon*, vol. 8, p. 200; Thomas Burton, *Chronica Monasterii de Melsa*, vol. 1, p. 406.
90 Giraldus Cambrensis, *Vita Hugonis*, app. F, p. 220.

obtained seven years and seven quadragesimas of remission for the day of the 1349 translation of St Thomas itself, and 100 days for the octaves, from Pope Clement VI.[91] For the poorest there were alms: at the 1284 translation at York, Edward I and his queen paid 12s. 6d. for one hundred poor to be fed.[92]

The translation ceremony had many of the elements of good spectacle: crowds were provided by the people themselves, costumes by the clergy wearing their best vestments, and celebrity by the presence of nobles and high ecclesiastics. Music was present in the hymns and services of the choir, the playing of organ music and the performance of hired minstrels. Even the sense of smell was tantalised by incense (if not by the un-washed mob itself). A spectacle that is rare in modern times, but which is almost universally reported in our accounts of translations, was the miraculous cure. At the Chichester translation of 1276 'it is said that God worked very many miracles'.[93] When St Augustine was enshrined the alleged miracles included the reconciliation of enemies.[94] In earlier accounts of translations miracles often serve to convert a sceptical figure. At Worcester, for example, a doubting abbot was convinced of St Oswald's sanctity by the cure of a leper during his translation.[95] Miracles were important in confirming the sanctity of the shrine and saint, and showing that God celebrated the translation as much as his people did. This is explicitly stated of the translation of two shrines containing relics of Amphibalus and his companions sent by Abbot William (1214–1235) of St Albans to Redbourn church: 'Because of the manifest miracles which God celebrated openly there in honour of the said saints we believe that this honourable translation very much pleased him.'[96]

Translations: the exhumation and translation ceremony

The translation itself began with the exhumation of a corpse. Judging by the space devoted to exhumations in descriptive accounts, this was the most interesting phase for contemporaries. It was usually carried out in the dead of the night, not only to guard against theft but also through fear of what might or might not be found in the tomb. In the case of St Erkenwald, the crowds at the exhumation of 1140 tore doors off hinges in their eagerness to see the event, causing the priests

91   *Calendar of Entries in the Papal Registers Relating to Great Britain and Ireland, Petitions,* vol. 1, ed. W.H. Bliss (London, 1896), p. 163.
92   A.J. Taylor, 'Royal Alms and Oblations in the Later 13th Century', in *Tribute to an Antiquary: Essays Presented to Marc Fitch by Some of his Friends,* eds F. Emmison and R. Stephens (London, 1976), p. 100.
93   'Plurima operatus est Dominus miracula, ut dictum est': *Annales Monasterii de Wintonia,* p. 122.
94   'There were then great miracles from Augustine in aid of bodily healings, but there were more cases of healed hearts' (Magna erant tunc de Augustini præsidio miracula corporalium sanitatum, sed majora sunt cordium sanatorum): Goscelin, 'Historia Translationis S. Augustini', p. 19.
95   Eadmer, *Vita Sancti Oswaldi,* pp. 48–9.
96   Matthew Paris, *Chronicles of Matthew Paris,* ed. R. Vaughan (Gloucester, 1984), p. 49.

to flee with the lead coffin to its new home. Perhaps the memory of this incident was why the 1326 exhumation occurred 'in the middle of the night, in order to evade a disturbance of people'.[97] A clandestine confirmation of the relics was prudent, but could cause problems. The nocturnal transfer of St Cuthbert from his grave to a waiting position in the choir in the presence of only nine Durham monks was judged to be suspicious by some of the prelates attending the translation in 1104, who demanded to see and examine the corpse.[98] When Dunstan and Alphege were translated nocturnally and in secret the monks who were left out were offended 'for they had supposed (as was proper) to translate these fathers with great and devout solemnity'.[99]

The exhumation was a ceremony in itself. At the 1140 translation of St Erkenwald the canons arrived at his tomb in procession singing litanies and bearing candles and crucifixes.[100] Fasting and ritual purity were required before coming into contact with the sanctity of a holy tomb, and those who had not recently confessed were not allowed to help. At Canterbury the monks selected to open the grave and remove the bones were supposedly chosen for their holy living.[101] The solemn nature of the work was accentuated by accompanying prayers and hymns. Accounts of translations often display a vivid terror of the undertaking. When they came to unearth Cuthbert in 1104 the Durham monks, trembling and tearful, prostrated themselves before his tomb. Symeon of Durham devoted two whole pages (in the Rolls Series printed volume) to the hesitations and dread they experienced, and included a short speech by a bold monk urging the others on.[102] The monks exhuming St Augustine in 1091 lost their nerve and tried to replace the stones covering the tomb before being ordered to remove them again by the abbot.[103] This attitude is very understandable, given the punishments which saints were believed to inflict when their bodies were disturbed without their blessing. When the monks at Bury translated St Edmund in 1095 they must have been thinking of the fate of Abbot Leofstan, who had inspected the body in the mid-tenth century. Edmund had been decapitated, but Leofstan found the corpse not only uncorrupted but with the head re-attached to the body. In an attempt to test how well the two were bonded together, the abbot had a monk pull on the saint's feet while he pulled on the head. For this irreverence he was struck blind and dumb and his hands were withered. Contrition healed the first two ills, but the hands remained damaged as a reminder of his impertinence. This grim

[97] *Miracula Erkenwaldi*, p. 152; 'in media nocte, propter tumultum populi evitandum': *Chronicles of the Reigns of Edward I and Edward II*, ed. W. Stubbs (RS, vol. 76, 1882–3), vol. 1, p. 311.

[98] Symeon, *Historia Ecclesiæ Dunhelmensis*, p. 256.

[99] Gervase of Canterbury, *Chronicle*, vol. 1, p. 23; *Of the Burning and Repair of the Church of Canterbury in the Year 1174*, trans. C. Cotton (2nd edn, Cambridge, 1930), p. 13.

[100] *Miracula Erkenwaldi*, p. 152.

[101] The *Polistorie*, in Mason, *Bones of St Thomas*, p. 71.

[102] Symeon, *Historia Ecclesiæ Dunhelmensis*, pp. 249–51.

[103] Goscelin, 'Historia Translationis S. Augustini', cols 17–18.

story must have been well known at Bury when the next translation was performed forty years later.[104]

The removal of the covering of a tomb revealed the relics. Essentially, saintly remains came in two forms: corrupt and incorrupt, decomposed or miraculously preserved. Incorruption was, of course, the preferred condition, and the state of preservation was sometimes exaggerated. Hugh of Lincoln was described as 'almost whole'; he was not as decomposed as expected, and when his head fell off his severed neck was believed to be too red for a corpse which had lain in the ground for eighty years.[105] Incorruption is a very interesting and relatively common phenomenon, having been claimed for Sts Cuthbert, Etheldreda, Edmund, Hugh and Edward the Confessor, among others. This is not as unusual as we might think, for two main reasons. Firstly, there are many possible causes for the lengthy preservation of bodies, the most obvious of which is mummification (which was the most likely cause of St Hugh's resistance to decay, for example). Secondly, it did not take much to amaze medieval observers, who had a strong belief in the inevitable corruption of matter and the flesh, and were therefore surprised by the least amount of preservation. Gervase recorded an exhumation at Canterbury which illustrates this attitude:

> When the tomb of Archbishop Theobald, which was constructed of marble, was opened, and the stone coffin discovered, the Monks who were present, thinking that he was reduced to dust, ordered wine and water to be brought, to wash his bones; but the upper stone of the coffin being removed, he appeared perfect and stiff, adhering together by the bones and nerves, and a small degree of skin and flesh. The spectators were surprised, and, placing him on the bier, thus carried him into the vestry as they had done Lanfranc, that the convent might determine what was proper to be done with them both. Meanwhile the story was divulged abroad, and many, on account of his unusual preservation, styled him St Theobald.[106]

Modern excavators would not be surprised by the state of the corpse as described above, but it obviously made a great impression on the medieval spectators.

An exhumation could produce other miraculous side effects. In some cases, such as those of St William of York and St Hugh of Lincoln, a clear oil was discovered among the relics, the latter *'quantitas non modica'*.[107] No matter what the state of the body, a sweet smell was, more often than not, described as coming from holy graves. This was the 'odour of sanctity', and was thought to be the scent of paradise leaking through the grave which was, after all, a place where heaven and earth met. It is possible that the natural chemical by-products of long term

104 Samson, *Samsonis Abbatis Opus de Miraculis Sancti Ædmundi*, in *Memorials of St Edmund's Abbey*, ed. T. Arnold (RS, vol. 96, 1890), vol. 1, pp. 133–4.

105 *'Translatio Sancti Hugonis'*, p. 192.

106 Gervase of Canterbury, *Chronicle*, vol. 1, pp. 25–6; *Burning and Repair*, p. 16.

107 William's oil, which flowed in 1223, was 'Oleum lucidissimum': Johannes de Oxenedes, *Chronica Johannis de Oxenedes*, ed. H. Ellis (RS, vol. 13, 1859), p. 148; *Chronicon Petroburgense*, ed. T. Stapleton (Camden Soc., no. 47, 1849), p. 40.

decomposition can have a sweet and not unpleasant smell, and so the report of an odour of sanctity does not in itself prove that sophisticated embalming techniques were used at the burials of English bishops, which some have advanced to explain the reported cases of incorruption. Indeed, extremely slow decay is more common than is generally assumed, especially in the dry and aseptic conditions existing under a cathedral floor, and exaggeration and hagiographic convention can account for the rest of the stories.[108] It is therefore also unnecessary to postulate widespread, intentional monastic fraud.

Once the body was uncovered it needed to be lifted out of the grave. If bones and dust alone were involved, this was a simple process, some clerks being selected to enter the tomb and lift them out. At Canterbury the chosen monks handed the bones of St Thomas out to the archbishop who lovingly placed them in a chest.[109] Less corrupt bodies presented more of a problem. St Hugh was hoisted up whole using bands passed under his body.[110] At Durham two monks lifted Cuthbert by the head and feet, but he was in such a perfectly flexible condition that he bent in the middle, forcing a third to hold him about the waist.[111] The relics, in whatever condition, were taken either to a secure spot such as the sacristy or set up in the choir where they would be ready for the morrow's services. In one case at least, the translation at Winchester in 1476, the chest containing the relics was temporarily placed on the high altar itself.[112]

The overnight delay between exhumation and translation was no doubt entirely necessary. One could not judge how long an excavation might take and, since important guests could not be kept waiting, it was better to prepare everything the night before. This also provided time to give the relics special treatment, such as carefully washing them with water and wine. For example, the bones of St Milburga, discovered to be 'beautiful and luminous' in 1101, were washed twice before they were put in a shrine and placed on the altar where they remained until translated.[113] This water was usually carefully preserved as a secondary relic and curative potion.[114] Ironically, washing was probably damaging to relics, since moisture sped up the decay that had been held in check by the dry conditions of the tomb. The relics were also given new clothes if the body was whole, or the bones wrapped in silk if not. The old articles of Dunstan and Alphege, for example, were removed and replaced with more decent palls bound with linen girdles.[115] The old vestments were usually retained as relics, as was the chasuble

---

[108] See an interesting discussion in P. Barber, *Vampires, Burial and Death* (New Haven, 1988).

[109] *Materials for a History of Becket*, vol. 4, p. 427.

[110] *'Translatio Sancti Hugonis'*, p. 192.

[111] Symeon of Durham, *Historia Ecclesiæ Dunhelmensis*, p. 253.

[112] *Concilia*, vol. 3, pp. 610–11.

[113] Odo of Ostia, 'The Translation of St. Milburga', pp. 145–6.

[114] See for example Reginald of Durham, *Reginaldi Monachi Dunelmensis Libellus de Admirandis Beati Cuthberti Virtutibus quae Novellis Patratae sunt Temporibus*, ed. J. Raine (SS, vol. 1, 1835), pp. 90–1.

[115] Gervase of Canterbury, *Chronicle*, vol. 1, p. 22.

of St Oswald discovered in 1002 and still being used in the time of Eadmer.[116] The period between exhumation and translation was occupied by a vigil. This had a precedent in the ceremony used in the consecration of an altar, when a vigil was kept with the relics used in the rite. Although dedicated to prayer, the vigil was also intended as a guard against the very real threat of theft. The possible degree of suspicion can be seen at Durham in 1104: when Cuthbert was examined by the doubting abbots only one was allowed to touch him, and a crowd of monks stood by watching in case one of the abbots tried to pilfer so much as a hair.[117]

After the exhumation but before the shrine was sealed there was a brief opportunity for access to the relics. This was the time when relics were divided and given away to special recipients. Archbishop Langton himself placed the bones of Thomas Becket in a feretrum, 'except a few little bones, which were kept outside the chest, for distributing to great men and churches in honour of the martyr'.[118] Incorrupt saints were saved this fate. St Edward the Confessor's hair was even miraculously strong, and could not be removed from his beard by Bishop Gundulf when his grave was opened in 1102. A verse life of Edward had Gundulf declare that he would have considered the hair more precious than gold, 'But since it is his pleasure/ to be entire without losing anything/ Let all his body be entire/ Until the day of Judgement.'[119] Others were not so respectful. Bishop Sylvester of Worcester was suspected of using an axe to divide the bones of St Wulfstan at the latter's 1218 translation.[120]

Saints so unfortunate as to decompose were open to depredation by the visiting clergy. The rules or customs as to the distribution of relics are unclear and were perhaps completely informal. It seems that many visiting bishops carried away a token and that the local bishop had special liberties, particularly if he was sponsoring the event. Archbishops appear to have commanded a major relic as a fee for attending. At the translation of Edward the Confessor, Thomas Becket declined to ask for a portion of the body and instead requested the gravestone into which St Wulfstan had plunged his staff.[121] Becket could not have taken away a piece of Edward's incorrupt body, but a right to do so is implied. Shortly after Becket's own translation some of his bones were in turn taken by Archbishop Langton to Rome and presented to the Pope and cardinals.[122] We know that

116 Eadmer, *Vita Sancti Oswaldi*, p. 50.
117 Symeon of Durham, *Historia Ecclesiæ Dunhelmensis*, pp. 256, 259.
118 'Exceptis paucis ossiculis, quae extra capsam retinuit, magnis viris et ecclesiis ad ipsius martyris honorem distribuenda': *Materials for a History of Becket*, vol. 4, p. 427.
119 'Mais ke li vent a plaisir k'enter seit sanz ren partir, Eit tut sun cors entierment, De ke le jur de judgement': *Lives of Edward the Confessor*, ed. H.R. Luard (RS, vol. 3, 1858), p. 156, translated p. 310. Edward did not remain inviolable, as a tooth of the Confessor was delivered into Edward III's chapel: *Patent Rolls, 1327–1330*, p. 440.
120 *Annales Monasterii de Waverleia*, in *Annales Monastici*, vol. 2, ed. H.R. Luard (RS, vol. 36, 1865), p. 289.
121 Gervase of Canterbury, *The Gesta Regum, with its Continuation the Actus Pontificum, and the Mappa Mundi*, in *The Historical Works of Gervase of Canterbury*, vol. 2, ed. W. Stubbs (RS, vol. 73, 1880), p. 285.
122 Walter of Coventry, *Collections*, vol. 2, p. 246.

Langton also took away the arm of Wulfstan and Archbishop Kilwardly the arm of Richard of Chichester at their respective translations, so perhaps an arm was the standard charge which an archbishop imposed for attendance at a translation.[123] With the other bones taken away a translation could literally cost an arm and a leg. Guests other than bishops do not seem to have had an absolute right to a relic. The abbot of St Albans, William de Trumpington, was said to have obtained a rib of St Wulfstan 'by industry' at his translation.[124] Presumably he had to work and connive to secure it. In other instances, monks of Canterbury obtained an arm bone at the translation of St Osmund on behalf of the prior and convent, and a girdle once belonging to St Thomas was apparently given to Chester by a bishop of Norwich who had been at Becket's translation.[125]

Apparently it did not matter greatly if large numbers of bones were removed; the shrine was still the grave of the saint and the centre of his power. The dispersed Swithun, missing at least his head and an arm, existed as much at Winchester as the incorruptible and therefore undivided Cuthbert did at Durham. This was proved by the attention paid to Swithun's translation as late as 1476 even though the relics were by then so few that they could fit into a relatively small ivory chest.[126] Sometimes bones and other pieces of the body were removed to be kept in smaller reliquaries in the possession of the same house, as at Lichfield where the head, an arm and unspecified bones of St Chad were kept in individual reliquaries separate from the main shrine.[127]

The division of relics led to a strange custom which appears to have been a general and almost required treatment of those saints whose bodies were not incorrupt. This was the separation of the head from the rest of the relics and its placement in another shrine. In the case of St Hugh the separation of head and body was portrayed as a miraculous accident. When exhumed in 1280, Hugh was found in what must have been a semi-mummified state. While lifting him out of the grave it happened, not surprisingly, that his head fell off (as mentioned above). This proved to be fortunate, for when the body was placed in the new shrine it was found to just fit inside without the head. If the head had not fallen off the feretrum would have been too small, and therefore the separation was proclaimed to be a miracle and the head was placed in a temporary shrine.[128] It was later given its own reliquary chest and base, the latter still in existence at Lincoln. Separations of head and body at other cathedrals may have occurred at times other than

123 Gervase of Canterbury, *Chronicle*, vol. 1, p. 285.
124 'Per industriam': Thomas Walsingham, *Gesta Abbatum Monasterii Sancti Albani a Thome Walsingham*, ed. H.T. Riley (RS, vol. 28, 1867), vol. 1, p. 283.
125 John Stone, *The Chronicle of John Stone*, ed. W.G. Searle (Cambridge Antiquarian Soc., vol. 34, 1902), p. 71; F. Bennett, *Chester Cathedral* (Chester, 1925), p. 87.
126 Swithun's head was at Canterbury, one arm in Peterborough and another in Stavenger. The depredations of Swithun's relics are summarised in P. Draper, 'The Retrochoir of Winchester Cathedral', *Architectural History*, vol. 21 (1978), p. 10.
127 'Sacrist's Roll of Lichfield Cathedral Church, A.D. 1345', ed. J.C. Cox (Collections for a History of Staffordshire, vol. 6, pt 2, appendix I, 1886), p. 199.
128 'Translatio Sancti Hugonis', p. 192.

translations. The crown of St Thomas at Canterbury, for example, was in existence some time before his translation. However, plans for a head shrine usually
could not begin until the translation, which provided the best opportunity for
dividing the bones. St Dunstan's head, for example, remained with his body until
it was inspected in 1508, when it was removed and set in silver.[129] Translations
thus resulted in a multiplication of shrines. Besides the new main shrine and
head shrine, there was also an empty tomb, which was still venerated in many
cases. After a translation a cathedral could thus convert the tomb of one saint
into three separate pilgrimage sites.

After the exhumation the translation ceremony itself was almost anti-
climactic, described very briefly and without much detail by medieval chroniclers.
The *Translatio Sancti Wulfstani*, after pages of description of the exhumation,
and the visions and miracles attendant to it, covers the translation itself in a
single sentence.[130] It can be determined, however, that there were three stages to
the translation ceremony, each a common element of medieval ritual: procession,
consecration and mass.

The procession, the first and most important stage of the translation, usually
occurred at the hour of tierce, or about nine in the morning.[131] The relics were
taken from wherever they were kept during the vigil to the site of the new shrine,
borne on a bier by those of the highest rank present. In 1220 at Canterbury young
King Henry III, the papal legate Pandulf, Archbishop Langton, the archbishop of
Rheims and Hubert de Burgh led the way, bells ringing, 'with a solemnity
previously unheard of'.[132] At Lincoln in 1280 the head was carried on a silver
platter by the archbishop of Canterbury in front of six bishops bearing the
body.[133] The translation of Little St Hugh in the same cathedral was described in
very sanguine tones: 'They raised it [the relics] aloft, and with candles, crosses
and thuribles leading, and with everyone in vestments and placed and arranged
in due order, they bore it to the greater monastery of the Blessed Virgin, singing
and weeping, and praising God together with string instruments, organ, and
sweetly toned voices.'[134]

The procession ended in the saint's chapel. If the relics had been carried in the
final feretrum this was lifted onto the shrine base. At Winchester in 1476 the new

---

129 That very year Dunstan's head received 2s. 4d. in offerings: CCA, Reg. R, ff. 183–8; CCA,
     MS MA11, ff. 71, 102.
130 William of Malmesbury, *The Vita Wulfstani of William of Malmesbury*, ed. R.R. Darlington
     (Camden Soc., 3rd ser., vol. 40, 1928), pp. 180–85.
131 For example, the translations of Sts Edmund and Thomas Becket: Heremannus the Arch-
     deacon, *Miraculis S Edmundi*, in *Memorials of St. Edmund's Abbey*, vol. 1, ed. T. Arnold
     (RS, vol. 96, 1890), p. 88; *Thómas Saga Erkibyskups*, ed. E. Magnússon (2 vols, RS, vol.
     65, 1875–83), vol. 2, p. 205, translated in Mason, *Bones of St Thomas*, p. 78.
132 Stanley, 'Shrine of St Thomas', p. 209; 'cum solemnitate prius inaudita': *Chronicon
     Thomæ Wykes*, p. 62.
133 'Translatio Sancti Hugonis', p. 193.
134 'Illud etiam elevantes, præcedentibus cereis, crucibus, et thuribulis, revestitis etiam
     quibusque, loco debito dispositis et ordinatis, ad majus monasterium beatae Virginis
     psallentes et flentes, et in cordis organo voce dulcisona Deum collaudantes, portaverunt':
     Annales de Burton, p. 344.

feretrum of silver and gold was built onto the shrine beforehand, so that the bishop and prior had to ascend a wooden ladder in order to slide the relics of Swithun into an opening in the reliquary.[135] In 1180 Dunstan and Alphege were translated to new shrines where, unusually, their coffins were enclosed in tomb structures sealed with lead rather than placed on top in feretra.[136] Once the relics were in place the shrine altar was consecrated and dedicated to the saint in the fashion normal for all altars, and a mass was celebrated. Sermons were also delivered; that delivered at Canterbury by Stephen Langton survives.[137]

There could be elaborations to this basic procedure. At Winchester in 1476 the procession first went out of the church and around the town before returning to the choir, then mass was celebrated by the bishop of Winchester and a sermon in English given to the people by the bishop of Chichester. Only then were the relics carried on a second, shorter procession to the site of the new shrine.[138] At Bury St Edmunds and Durham the procession went out of doors as well. At the latter, God showed his mercy when a timely shower of rain cut short an over-long sermon by the bishop.[139]

It is hard to compare the numerous translations of the twelfth and thirteenth centuries with the very few translations before and afterwards. Many of the major translations of the 'golden age' were the first and biggest translations of important saints; second and third translations did not have the same power. Descriptions of the events were also generally longer in the period of the greatest translations. For these reasons it is difficult to describe a chronological development of translation. The importance of the ceremony to the local cult of a saint and his or her relics, however, is indisputable. It pronounced the official confirmation of the cult and miracles locally, and was the chief celebration of that saint. It spread the cult by informing distant people, especially clergymen, of the new shrine and even brought them to the cathedral as witnesses. A translation festival sealed a great saint's relics as the primary treasure of his or her church, not only by the new physical placement of the shrine with all its grandeur, but also by the sheer scale of the celebration. The ceremony incorporated the main elements of the liturgy and medieval ecclesiastical pageantry. Furthermore, it symbolised, perhaps better than anything else, the medieval attitude towards the saintly dead and their relics.

---

[135] *Concilia*, vol. 3, pp. 610–11.
[136] Gervase of Canterbury, *Chronicle*, vol. 1, p. 22.
[137] Langton, 'Tractatus de Translatione Beati Thomae', cols 407–424.
[138] *Concilia*, vol. 3, pp. 610–11.
[139] Symeon, *Historia Ecclesiæ Dunhelmensis*, p. 260.

2

The Shrine as Object:
Feretra and Shrine Bases

It is not surprising that the physical form of English shrines has attracted great interest, covered as they were with precious metal, jewels and artwork of many kinds. Nevertheless, their structure and shape have never been systematically analysed on a large scale. While a proper presentation of the subject would require a more comprehensive art-historical study than can be attempted here, the basic form of shrines and the changes they underwent can be shown. There was a basic conformity of design across England, despite some recent attempts to propose unusual positions or structures for certain major shrines. Most of this chapter will describe this norm.

The origin and development of early shrines are related to tomb structure. Before the Conquest burial inside churches was reserved for patrons, royalty and high ecclesiastics, all of whom were likely candidates for sainthood. At first even an exposed coffin lid was a great honour, but eventually saints, prospective or actual, received monuments standing on the floor of the church. These tended to be in the shape of rectilinear chests surmounted by gabled roofs. For example, Bede described Chad's first burial place as 'covered with a wooden coffin in the form of a little house'.[1] Stone chests of this shape that survive from Jedburgh, St Andrews and St Ninian's Isle are made up of interlocking pieces: 'The decoration of these structures, their house shaped form and their suitability to stand on the floor of a church all suggest that they were intended to receive the remains of saints.'[2] Occasionally, especially in the eleventh and twelfth centuries, the monument of a saint is referred to as a 'pyramid'. Both St Dunstan's first tomb and that of St John of Beverley, for example, were so described.[3] 'Pyramid' was used in a general if not geometrically precise sense to refer to tomb chests with gabled

[1] Bede, *Bede's Ecclesiastical History of the English Nation*, trans. J. Stevens (London, 1910), p. 3. See C. Thomas, *The Early Christian Archaeology of North Britain* (London, 1971), pp. 147–8.

[2] Rollason, *Saints and Relics*, p. 47.

[3] Eadmer of Canterbury, 'Edmeri Cantvariensis Nova Opvscvla de Sanctorum Veneratione et Obsecratione', ed. A. Wilmart, *Revue de Sciences Religieuses*, vol. 15 (1935), p. 367; *Miracula Sancti Johannis Eboracensis Episcopi*, in *The Historians of the Church of York and Its Archbishops*, ed. J. Raine (RS, vol. 71, 1879), vol. 1, p. 332.

roofs.[4] Despite the presence of the monuments described above, the bodies of early saints almost always remained underground. Eventually, however, the increasingly common practice of elevation resulted in a distinction between tomb and shrine. The latter now had two distinct parts: a jewelled reliquary and a stone base.

The feretrum

The Latin word *feretrum* could refer to various related objects but most commonly pertained to reliquaries. That of St Alban, for example, was the 'exterior chest, which we call a "feretrum" (*thecam exteriorem, quam nos "feretrum" appellamus*)'.[5] For the sake of clarity, I will confine my use of 'feretrum' to describe house shaped chests containing relics. This includes some relatively small examples used to keep individual relics, although lesser relics could be kept in vessels of many other shapes. Greater relics, on the other hand, were universally preserved in feretra. There was some variation in size: those saints whose remains consisted only of dry, disarticulated bones and dust could be interred within a feretrum that was under two feet in length. For major shrines, however, it was the ideal, and for those with incorrupt saints a necessity, that the feretrum be large enough to contain a full-sized body. Thus, before its completion in the mid-twelfth century St Erkenwald's feretrum could be lain in (blasphemously) by Eustace the silversmith, even though Erkenwald was not incorrupt.[6] Similarly, the shrine of St Thomas was 'long and broad, so that a middle-sized person could lie in it'.[7] For this reason most major saints' feretra were at least five feet long.

Feretra were embellishments on the idea of a coffin. Except in a few ancient cases where stone sarcophagi were employed (particularly the first shrine of St Etheldreda),[8] the inner structure of a feretrum was made of wood. The wooden portion of the shrine of St Edward cost Henry III ten marks in 1241; little compared to the total value of the shrine but still considerable for what was essentially a box that would later be concealed under silver plates.[9] Technically, the lid of a feretrum was as removable as a coffin's, but in practice was usually kept shut. For example, Erasmus reported that St Thomas of Canterbury's bones were not permitted to be seen.[10] It can be assumed that most shrine lids remained firmly secured, perhaps even nailed shut, to avoid the casual theft of their precious

---

4   See Ramsay and Sparks, 'The Cult of St Dunstan at Christ Church', p. 312, for a similar interpretation.
5   Walsingham, *Gesta Abbatum*, vol. 1, p. 189.
6   *Miracula Erkenwaldi*, p. 142.
7   From Tetzel's account of Ambassador Leo of Rozmital's visit in 1446: printed in Mason, *Bones of St Thomas*, p. 85.
8   *Liber Eliensis*, ed. E.O. Blake (Camden Soc., 3rd. Ser., vol. 92, 1962), pp. 43–4.
9   *Liberate Rolls*, vol. 2, pp. 83–4.
10 Desiderius Erasmus, *Pilgrimages to Saint Mary of Walsingham and Saint Thomas of Canterbury*, trans. J.G. Nichols (2nd edn, London, 1875), p. 49.

contents. Many were integral to the chest itself. In 1476, for example, the bishop and prior of Winchester inserted the relics of St Swithun into his new shrine not through an opened lid but through a small door in the east end of the feretrum.[11]

Although no English post-Conquest feretra survive, the existing evidence shows that in basic shape and detail they were much like surviving Continental shrines: long rectangular chests with gabled and ridged roofs.[12] The form was so standardised that feretra could even be interchangeable between saints. At Evesham St Egwin was put in a shrine originally built for St Odulf, while St Oswald of Worcester was placed in the shrine he built for relics of St Wilfrid.[13] This form remained constant until the Reformation, differing only in artistic style from century to century.

The plain wooden feretrum was usually decorated according to the wealth of the shrine and its patrons. The most modest shrines were of carved and painted wood, while more favoured reliquaries were gilded. For example, a feretrum of gilt wood was built by Prior Goldston (1494–1517) for St Ouen at Canterbury.[14] In 1325 the Norwich Sacrist spent 36s. 1d. on 140 gold leaves, 350 silver leaves, 12 pounds of white lead, vermilion and orpiment (white, red and yellow pigments), oil for painting and the painter's wages, all for decorating the shrine of St William in the cathedral.[15] The shrine of St Mellitus at St Paul's merited a covering of silver plate on the front.[16] The most opulent feretra, including most major cathedral shrines, were completely covered in such plates. This gave the chests the appearance of being made entirely of silver, since the underlying wood was concealed, and they were often described as such. For example, the feretrum of St Richard of Chichester was called a 'silver and gilt chest' in 1276.[17]

The silver plates were usually gilded and embellished with precious stones, a process which could continue over a considerable length of time. Bishop Geoffrey Ridel (1174–89) repaired the two sides of the shrine of Etheldreda with silver, but it was not gilded until the time of Bishop Geoffrey de Burgo (1225–28).[18] St

---

11 *Concilia*, vol. 3, p. 611. See p. 45, n. 135.

12 Many examples of smaller house-shaped reliquaries survive on the Continent, two of which are probably of Anglo-Saxon origin: Rollason, *Saints and Relics*, pp. 29–33. A good collection of plates of Romanesque shrines from the Continent can be found in P. Lasko, *Ars Sacra, 800–1200* (Harmondsworth, 1972), for example pls 184, 295.

13 *Chronicon Abbatiæ de Evesham, ad Annum 1418*, ed. W.D. Macray (RS, vol. 29, 1863), pp. 37–44; Eadmer, *Vita Sancti Oswaldi*, pp. 31–2.

14 W. St John Hope and J.W. Legg, *Inventories of Christchurch Canterbury* (Westminster, 1902), p. 123.

15 H.W. Saunders, *An Introduction to the Obedientiary and Manor Rolls of Norwich Cathedral Priory* (Norwich, 1930), p. 111.

16 'The shrine, which is said to be that of St Mellitus, is made entirely of wood, with only the front covered with silver plates and images' (Feretrum quod dicitur Sancti Melliti totum ligneum, fronte solum cooperto platis argenteis et ymaginibus): 'Two Inventories of the Cathedral Church of St Paul, London, dated Respectively 1245 and 1402', ed. W.S. Simpson, *Archaeologia*, vol. 50 (1887), p. 470.

17 'Capsa argentea et deaurata': Rishanger, *Chronica*, p. 89.

18 'He repaired the two sides of the feretrum of St Etheldreda and part of the tomb with very

Erkenwald's shrine also gradually developed in magnificence. The first Norman shrine appears to have been covered in silver, and an inventory from 1245 described it as wooden with silver plates and precious stones. In the early fourteenth century, however, it was adorned with gold and precious stones. Contracts with London goldsmiths survived for 1339 and 1401, the latter describing work performed on the feretrum in some detail. Forty-three gems were set in the shrine, eight new images purchased, four carved and another ten gilded, while silver angels were placed at either end of the shrine.[19]

Most great shrines were entirely gilded, so that some, like that of Edward the Confessor, appeared to be not just silver but solid gold.[20] In at least one case this appearance may have been reality. There was a Canterbury legend that when the common people heard that the archbishop had resolved to convert the offerings to St Thomas into a feretrum 'they would hear of his shrine being made of no other metal but gold alone'.[21] Stow described the shrine at the dissolution as 'covered with plates of gold, damasked with gold wire'.[22] Simon Fitzsimons, a pilgrim passing through Canterbury in 1322, believed the shrine was 'a case made of most pure gold and adorned with innumerable precious stones, with shining pearls like unto the gate of Jerusalem, and sparkling gems, and even crowned with a regal diadem'.[23] Although the inner structure of St Thomas's shrine was made of wood, it may have been plated in solid gold rather than gilt silver, an extravagance which perhaps only this of all English shrines could have afforded.

The golden exteriors of wealthier shrines were encrusted with gems, either as part of images or set in their own right. The surface of the shrine of St Etheldreda was of silver plate with figures in high relief, some gilded and some not, and set with beryls, onyxes, alemandines, pearls, amethysts, carnelians, sardines, emeralds and one topaz. By far the most common stone on her shrine was 'crystal' (presumably quartz).[24] These gems could dominate the appearance of a greater feretrum, such as that of St Alban which 'shone marvellously with gold and gems'

beautiful silver' (Duo latera feretri sancte Etheldrede et partem tumuli de argento perpulcre reparauit); 'He also had a large part of the tomb around the feretrum of St Etheldreda gilded' (Eciam fecit magnum partem tumuli de feretro sce Etheldrede deaurari. Ad crestam autem faciend' dedit magnum et magni precij discum argenteum): 'Chronicon Ecclesiae Eliensis', BL, Harl. MS 3721, ff. 34, 36.

19 'The shrine of the Blessed Erkenwald is wood inside covered with silver plates with images and stones. The sum of the stones is, it is said, 130' (Feretrum beati Erkenwaldi est interius ligneum extra coopertum platis argenteis cum ymaginibus et lapidibus. Est autum summa lapidum, ut dicitur, C. et XXX): 'Two Inventories of St Paul's', p. 469; W. Dugdale, *The History of St Paul's Cathedral in London from its Foundation* (2nd ed., London, 1716), pp. 22–3.

20 Edward's shrine was made by Henry III 'out of purest gold and most precious gems (ex auro purissimo et gemmis preciosis)': Matthew Paris, *Matthaei Parisiensis, Monachi Sancti Albani, Chronica Majora*, ed. H.R. Luard (RS, vol. 57, 1877), vol. 4, pp. 156–7.

21 This legend was heard by the writer of the *Thómas Saga Erkibyskups*, p. 213.

22 John Stow, *The Annales of England* (London, 1592), p. 972.

23 In E. Hoade, *Western Pilgrims* (Jerusalem, 1970), pp. 3–4.

24 *Liber Eliensis*, p. 289.

in 1129.[25] Erasmus, perhaps consciously exaggerating, had a fictional character claim of the shrine of St Thomas that 'The least valuable portion was gold; every part glistened, shone and sparkled with rare and very large jewels, some of them exceeding the size of a goose's egg.'[26] A Bohemian in England recounted his 1446 visit to the shrine in very similar terms: 'The shrine that St Thomas lies in, the poorest thing about it is gold; . . . it is adorned with pearls and precious stones in so costly a fashion that they say there is no costlier shrine in Christendom.'[27] Stow described the shrine as 'covered with iewels of golde, as rings 10 or 12 cramped together with gold wier into the saide grounde of golde, many of those rings having stones in them, brooches, images, and angels, and other pretious stones, and great pearls, &c'.[28] Gems could claim marvellous powers: the shrine of St Egwin at Evesham was made of silver, gold and precious stones, 'in which were three stones illuminating a large part of the church by night'.[29] Precious stones were often used for healing purposes since they were believed to possess magical properties.[30] Although it seems odd to modern sensibilities, shrine-keepers were in the habit of attaching newly acquired jewellery and coins directly to the surface of the feretrum. In 1251 Henry III sent gold coins to be fixed to Becket's shrine, and in 1327 Archbishop Walter Reynolds bequeathed some of his rings, including his pontifical ring, to be attached to the same.[31] A long list of goods 'attached to the shrine of St William' at York includes a gilt silver heart, breast, hand, four pieces of coral and some belts, as well as seven gilt silver ships belonging to the tomb of Richard Scrope.[32]

The lids of feretra were crowned with elaborate crests. The new crest of gold made for St Thomas's feretrum in 1314, for example, cost £7 10s.[33] Crests were sometimes greatly embellished. Henry VII bequeathed a figure of himself made of gold plates on a silver gilt base, 'holding betwixt his hands the croune which it pleased God to give us, with the Victorie of our Enemye at our furst felde', which was to be placed 'in the mydds of the Creste of the Shryne of Saint Edward King in such a place as by us in our life, or by our executors after our decease shall be thought most convenient and honourable'.[34] The most amazing crest was probably that added to St Alban's shrine in the early fourteenth century, which was

---

25 'Feretrum mirabiliter auro et gemmis choruscum': Henry of Huntingdon, 'Historia Anglorum', CUL, MS Ii.2.3, f. 385; *Miracula Erkenwaldi*, p. 203 n.25.
26 Erasmus, *Pilgrimages to Saint Mary and Saint Thomas*, p. 49.
27 From Tetzel's account of Ambassador Leo of Rozmital's trip, translated in Mason, *Bones of St Thomas*, p. 85.
28 Stow, *Annales*, p. 972.
29 'In quo erant tres lapides magnam partem ecclesiæ de nocte illuminantes': *Chronicon Abbatiæ de Evesham*, p. 86.
30 The innate power of gems may have added to the attraction of feretra studded with them: *Miracula Erkenwaldi*, p. 220 n.27.
31 *Liberate Rolls*, vol. 3, p. 1251; *Sede Vacante Wills*, p. 68.
32 *Historians of the Church of York*, vol. 3, pp. 389–90. For more on objects fixed to shrines, see chapter 4, p. 146.
33 'List of Works of Henry of Eastry', CCA, MS Reg. K, f. 220.
34 *Testamenta Vetusta: Being Illustrations from Wills*, ed. N.H. Nicolas (London, 1826), pp.

long in the making and featured a golden eagle with outstretched wings and two suns with jewel-tipped rays.[35]

The surface of a feretrum was subdivided into a number of niches and panels filled with images, either in relief or as free-standing sculptures. When the shrine of St Richard of Chichester was taken down his feretrum was used as a chest to carry away fifty-seven gilt silver images, as well as fifty-five more images and untold jewels, rings, relics and pieces of broken silver in eight more coffers and boxes.[36] A list of ornaments provided (and then pawned) by Henry III for the shrine of St Edward included images of Sts Edmund and Peter, six kings, a set of five golden angels, a Virgin and Child, and a Majesty, for a total value of £1,210.[37] Henry III also commissioned three golden images for the shrine of St Thomas Becket in 1243, for which he paid 250 marks.[38]

Descriptions of the artwork on English feretra are not as common as might be hoped. The shrine of St Aldhelm, erected at Malmesbury in 837, was embossed with scenes of miracles of the saint and figures in solid silver on the front.[39] Majesties (images of Christ enthroned) seem to have been a common motif for shrines, appearing for example on the shrines of St Oswald at Worcester and St Edmund at Bury.[40] A relatively detailed description survives of the feretrum of St Etheldreda. On the east end were two crystal lions and other images, and the two sides supported sixteen figures each. On the western face were two images, including a majesty and a cross that was probably fixed to the apex of the lid.[41] The shrine of St Alban had images from his life in relief on both sides, a crucifixion scene on the east end and on the west a Virgin and Child enthroned.[42] From these few descriptions it seems that the most common scheme was to have images from the life of the saint on the sides, but that the ends were reserved for more universally Christian icons such as Majesties and Madonnas.

Shrines shone with many colours besides those provided by gold and gems.

31–2; J. Perkins, *Westminster Abbey; Its Worship and Its Ornaments* (3 vols, London, 1938), vol. 2, p. 58.

[35] Walsingham, *Gesta Abbatum*, vol. 3, p. 384; An inventory includes 'Item, one crest of the shrine of Blessed Alban, over which stands a silver and gilt eagle, made of marvelous work, of the gift of Lord Thomas, Abbot': *ibid.*, vol. 2, pp. 334–5.

[36] *Sussex Chantry Records*, ed. J.E. Ray (Sussex Record Soc., vol. 36, 1931), pp. 134–5.

[37] Several of the items were worth £200 in themselves, including the above-mentioned Majesty and Virgin and Child: *Patent Rolls, 1266–1272*, pp. 139; Perkins, *Westminster Abbey*, vol. 2, p. 39.

[38] *Liberate Rolls*, vol. 2, p. 196.

[39] William of Malmesbury, *De Gestis Pontificium Anglorum*, ed. N.E.S.A. Hamilton (RS, vol. 52, 1870), pp. 330, 389–90.

[40] A Worcester inventory, presumably fifteenth-century, entitled '*Hec sunt iocalio super feretrum sci Oswaldi patroni nostri*', describes the feretrum itself, or at least the jewels on it, including a majesty on the summit. The jewels on Wulfstan's shrine included small and large crucifixes: WCA, MS A22, f. 18; Jocelin of Brakelond, *The Chronicle of Jocelin of Brakelond*, ed. H.E. Butler (London, 1949), p. 107.

[41] *Liber Eliensis*, p. 289.

[42] Walsingham, *Gesta Abbatum*, vol. 1, p. 189.

Goldsmiths at work on the shrine of St Edward over 1267–71 were using enamels of various hues as well as gold leaf.[43] The net effect of this ornamentation was that English feretra could compare with any in wealth. When political pressures forced Henry III to put all the treasures accumulated for the shrine of St Edward in pawn in 1267 they were valued at no less than £2,555 4s. 8d.[44] An Italian visiting Edward's shrine in about 1500 declared that 'neither St Martin of Tours, a church in France, which I have heard is one of the richest in existence, nor anything else that I have ever seen, could be put into any sort of comparison with it. But the magnificence of the tomb of St Thomas the Martyr, Archbishop of Canterbury, is that which surpasses all belief.'[45]

Feretra were not allowed to shine forth in full glory at all times. In many cases cloth covers shielded the shrine from both dust and sight. Linen covering cloths were purchased and painted for the shrines of St Wulfstan and St Oswald in 1375/6 and 1401/2.[46] Miracle stories indicate that the early shrine of St Cuthbert was covered by coloured sheets, the outer of silk and the inner of linen.[47] At Canterbury the wooden cover was replaced every year from the 5th to the 21st of July by an elaborate cloth canopy donated in the late fourteenth century by Joan, the countess of Kent and Archbishop Arundel's sister.[48]

By the later middle ages most major shrines were protected by wooden covers that mimicked the feretrum's shape (see the frontispiece for a modern reproduction). These canopies were lifted vertically off the shrine by means of ropes which passed either through a pulley fixed to the underside of the vault or through a hole in the vault to a winch-like mechanism above. The wooden cover of St Edmund was hanging suspended over the shrine when it was caught up in the fire of 1465, and when the ropes burnt through it dropped over top of the feretrum.[49] Many shrine accounts record repairs to the 'wheels' or 'pulleys' used to lift the covers, which is not surprising since they were the shrine's only moving parts. In 1534 Canterbury paid 3s. 4d. 'concerning the wheels of the shrine of St Thomas', which mechanism Erasmus had seen in action a few years earlier.[50] From 1424 to 1426 five ropes ('cordis'), and more in 1448/9, were purchased for

---

[43] *Building Accounts of Henry III*, p. 428.

[44] *Patent Rolls 1266–1272*, pp. 52, 64–5, 135–40.

[45] *A Relation, or Rather a True Account, of the Island of England*, ed. C.A. Sneyd (Camden Soc., vol. 37, 1847), p. 30.

[46] Wulfstan's cloth cost 16s. 8d. and was painted for 20s.: Tumbarius Accounts for 1375/6, 1401/2: WCA, MSS C.453, C.466.

[47] Reginald of Durham, *Libellus de Admirandis Beati Cuthberti*, pp. 134, 161; V. Tudor, 'The Cult of St Cuthbert in the Twelfth Century: The Evidence of Reginald of Durham', in *St Cuthbert, History, Cult and Community to AD 1200*, eds G. Bonner, D. Rollason, C. Stancliffe (Woodbridge, 1989), p. 460. The tomb of St Augustine, at least until his translation in 1091, was also protected by cloth covers: Goscelin, 'Historia Translationis S. Augustini', col. 13.

[48] 'Customary of the Shrine of St Thomas', BL, Add. MS 59616, f. 8.

[49] See M.R. James, *On the Abbey of S. Edmund at Bury* (Cambridge Antiquarian Soc., vol. 28, 1895), p. 207.

[50] 'Circa Rotas capse feretri sancti Thomas': CCA, DCc/DE 163; 'The golden shrine is

the shrine of St Edward. The 'wheels' of the same shrine were repaired by a carpenter in 1488/9 and 1493/4, made new in 1495/6, and greased in 1505/6. The fact that a smith of London was paid in 1425/6 for making a '*barell*' to lift the '*capsella*' suggests that an earlier mechanism at Westminster was a winch of some kind, with a cylinder for winding the ropes around.[51] Ironwork that presumably held the mechanism for the rope suspending the cover of St Swithun's last shrine remains above the retrochoir vault at Winchester.[52]

As befitted objects in such a position, these canopies were opulently decorated. In 1455 the new cover for the shrine of Etheldreda cost £12 7s. 6d. for carpentry, painting, gilt nails, and a lining of eleven ells of linen cloth.[53] On some shrine bases there is still physical evidence of the former existence of a canopy. The top of the upper tier of the early shrine at Hereford, for example, is sunk a few inches in order to receive a cover, and stubs of iron bars at each corner appear to be the remains of vertical guide rails. The remnants of a strap in the centre of the west end was probably for locking the same.[54] The one surviving English cover, at Westminster, is atypical. St Edward's canopy is a large, two-tiered structure, with a flat rather than gabled top, made either during the Marian Restoration or before the Reformation. If the latter is the case then it is one of the earliest classical forms in the country.[55]

All feretra were probably portable *in extremis*, as when the shrine of St Oswald was carried out of the church in the fire of 1113.[56] In practice, many were completely immobile. At the translation of St Hugh, for example, his feretrum was firmly secured to its stone support.[57] Others must have been rendered immovable by the sheer weight of their ornamentation. Many, however, were intended to be borne forth at intervals, as, for example, were the shrines of St Egwin at Evesham and St Oswin at Tynemouth.[58] Sometimes a feretrum was borne in procession on specific days of the year, such as when the shrine of St Ouen was carried about the city of Canterbury on his feast day.[59] Bede's shrine was 'accus-

covered by one of wood; and, when that is drawn up with ropes, inestimable treasures are open to view': Erasmus, *Pilgrimages to Saint Mary and Saint Thomas*, p. 49.

[51] WAM, MSS 19666, 19667, 19698, 19736, 19745, 19747, 19761.

[52] See photo in Crook, 'Swithun of Winchester', p. 66.

[53] D.J. Stewart, *On the Architectural History of Ely Cathedral* (London, 1868), p. 131.

[54] Marshall, 'The Shrine of St. Thomas', pp. 36–7.

[55] It was perhaps made in the 1530s since it matches the style of the Kings' College Chapel screen of that date, and also fits exactly the base as it would have been before its disassembly at the Reformation: J.G. O'Neilly, 'The Shrine of Edward the Confessor', *Archaeologia*, vol. 100 (1966), pp. 153–4.

[56] Eadmer, *Vita Sancti Oswaldi*, pp. 55–6; R.D.H. Gem, 'Bishop Wulfstan II and the Romanesque Cathedral Church of Worcester', in *Medieval Art and Architecture at Worcester Cathedral* (BAACT, vol. 1, 1978), p. 19.

[57] 'Translatio Sancti Hugonis', p. 193.

[58] For an instance of Oswin's shrine performing a miracle while being borne abroad, see *Vita Oswini*, in *Miscellanea Biographica*, ed. J. Raine (SS, vol. 8, 1838), p. 35.

[59] 'In the day of St Ouen there was a procession by the prior and convent in the city, that is to say Wednesday with the feretrum of the same confessor' (In die sancti Audoeni [24 Aug.]

tomed to be taken down every festival daie when there was any sollempe proces-sion, and caried with iiij mounckes . . . which being ended they dyd convey yt into ye gallely and sett yt upon ye said tumbe againe'.[60] Special processions were frequently made to avert catastrophe, as when a procession with the body of St John of Beverley was believed to have ended a drought in Yorkshire.[61] The shrine of St Oswald of Worcester seems to have been a portable shrine *par excellence*. In 1139 it was used to fend off an approaching army: 'We however, fearing for the ornaments of the sanctuary, wearing albs and with the whole group singing, bore the relics of our most gracious patron Oswald in humble procession outside [the church], and on account of the attacks of the enemy we carried it from door to door through the cemetary.' [62] On other occasions St Oswald's body was led in proces-sion about the town to avert fire and pestilence.[63] By the late fourteenth century Oswald seems to have specialised in meteorological miracles. An account of 1390/1 itemises 44lb. of wax torches bought 'for Saint Oswald when they were carried out in time of exceeding dryness'.[64] In 1437 the prior and convent of Worcester were ordered to carry his relics in procession 'as we byn enformed that hyt hath byn afore this time for cessyng of such continual reyne'.[65] A procession with torches 'for peaceful air (*pro serenitate aeris*)' is frequently mentioned in the accounts of the Worcester tumbarius.[66]

A greater shrine, with its weight of precious metal, must have been difficult to move. As a result, some shrines apparently had a second and presumably smaller feretrum for processional purposes. St Chad's principal relics were divided between two reliquaries, described in 1345 as 'the great shrine of Saint Chad' and 'a certain portable shrine'.[67] St Chad's portable feretrum was sometimes taken far afield in search of offerings, in which case bells were rung both when it left and when it returned to Lichfield cathedral.[68] It is said of St William of York that '. . . some lesser relics were placed in a reliquary which was carried around the city in solemn procession on the anniversaries of his death and of his translation'.[69]

erat processio a priore et conuentu in ciuitate, scilicet feria iiij cum feretro eiusdem confessoris): Stone, *Chronicle*, p. 87.

60 *Rites of Durham*, pp. 44–5.

61 *Miracula Sancti Johannis*, pp. 269–71.

62 'Nos autem timentes ornamentis sanctuarii, benignissimi patroni nostri Oswaldi reliquias albis induti, tota sonante classe cum humili processione foris extulimus, et ob hostium irruptionem de porta ad portam, per cœmiterium deportavimus': Florence of Worcester, *Florentii Wigorniensis Monachi Chronicon ex Chronicis*, ed. B. Thorpe (2 vols, London, 1849), vol. 2, pp. 119–20.

63 See Eadmer, *Vita Sancti Oswaldi*, pp. 55, 57.

64 'Pro sancto Oswaldo quando exportata tempore nimie siccitatis': WCA, MS C.457.

65 J. Noake, *The Monastery and Cathedral of Worcester* (London, 1866), p. 116.

66 Worcester Tumbarius Accounts, 1397/8, 1399/1400 and others of about the same time: WCA, MSS C.462, C.464.

67 'Feretrum magnum sancti Cedde', 'quodam feretro portabili': 'Sacrist's Roll of Lichfield', p. 199.

68 A Lichfield statute of 1190, in *Statutes of Lincoln Cathedral*, eds H. Bradshaw and C. Wordsworth (Cambridge, 1897), vol. 2, p. 22.

69 Wilson, *Shrines of St William*, p. 9.

The shrine base

In order for a saint's body to be elevated above the floor of the church, one of the major reasons for a translation, the feretrum needed a base. Because most shrines were rebuilt in the later middle ages little survives of bases dating from the Norman Conquest to the mid-thirteenth century. What information there is suggests that there were two basic types in the eleventh and twelfth centuries. One, known almost entirely from descriptions and illustrations, consisted of a stone slab lifted on pillars. For example, a scene from the late twelfth-century *Guthlac Roll* shows St Guthlac's 1095 shrine supported on several short columns.[70] According to Ailred of Rievaux, the relics of Acca, Alkmund and Frithebert at Hexham were placed on a three-legged table near the high altar.[71] St Cuthbert's third shrine, made c.1104, was reportedly supported on nine stone columns, while the nearby shrine of Bede rested on five.[72]

The only physical remains of this type of shrine (the 'table' or 'columnar' type) in England may be several pieces of pink marble at Canterbury.[73] These could be from the shrine completed in 1220, and which is depicted in stained glass around the Trinity Chapel as having six columns and wide, round-headed arches supporting a flat table.[74] One of the pieces is a capital with a hole bored to take an iron rod, suggesting that the shrine was supported by slender columns needing reinforcement.[75] This would match the stained glass images. There is no record of St Thomas's shrine ever being rebuilt; certainly it is unlikely to have become any taller since it was described in the sixteenth century as 'about a man's height'.[76] Perhaps Canterbury did not modify its shrine because it was more Continentally influenced than other cathedrals. Although English shrines were almost univer-

[70] *The Guthlac Roll*, ed. G. Warner (Oxford, 1928), pl. XVII.

[71] Ailred of Rievaux, *De Sanctis Ecclesiæ*, in *The Priory of Hexham; Its Chroniclers, Endowments, and Annals*, ed. J. Raine (SS, vol. 44, 1864), p. 200.

[72] J. Raine, *St. Cuthbert: With an Account of the State in Which his Remains were Found Upon the Opening of his Tomb in Durham Cathedral, in the Year MDCCCXXVII* (Durham, 1828), p. 95.

[73] They are described in W. Urry, 'Some Notes on the Two Resting Places of St Thomas Becket at Canterbury', in *Thomas Becket, Actes du Colloque International de Sédières*, ed. R. Foreville (Paris, 1975), pp. 204–6.

[74] Caviness, *Early Stained Glass of Canterbury*, pl. 164. Fifteenth-century glass at Nettleshead, Kent, shows the base as a long box with three niches on either side and twin columns at each end: N. Coldstream, 'English Decorated Shrine Bases', *JBAA*, vol. 129 (1976), p. 28.

[75] P. Tudor-Craig, 'Archbishop Hubert Walter's Tomb and its Furnishings: The Tomb', in *Medieval Art and Architecture at Canterbury before 1220 (BAACT, vol. 5, 1982)*, p. 76.

[76] Stow, *Annales*, p. 972. According to an analysis of the handwriting made by D.T. Baird, keeper of the MSS at the British Museum in 1917, the Cottonian drawing of the shrine was made by Cotton himself. It appears to have been an attempt to draw the shrine from Stow's description (not the other way around). His weights of the finials and the pointing angel do not come from Stow and perhaps had some other, and now lost, source: Mason, *Bones of St Thomas*, p. 109.

sally replaced in the late thirteenth century and later with more solid bases, the table shrine was 'used in France for major shrines throughout the middle ages'.[77]

The *foramina* tomb, consisting of a stone chest pierced with large holes, was the other post-Conquest style of monument connected with saints. The shrine of St Candida, the only English shrine with its relics *in situ*, is of this type. The relic chest is set upon a base placed laterally against a wall and having three large openings (*foramina*) on the side facing the church.[78] It dates from no later than c.1220, when its surroundings in the north transept of Whitechurch Canonicorum were rebuilt, and the primitive form of the plain stone relic chest suggests a much earlier date. All the other surviving *foramina*-type monuments, namely the tomb of St Osmund at Salisbury (long used as a shrine), St Bertram's shrine at Ilam and fragments of another at Melrose Abbey, lack relics.[79] The tomb of Osmund, which is now in the south nave arcade of Salisbury cathedral, has three oval openings on each long side, each hole measuring 46cm. by 35cm. These *foramina* are mentioned in miracles of Osmund, the earliest being from 1384.[80] The base of Bertram's shrine is similar, but with *foramina* at either end as well as three per side, and showing signs of once having borne a feretrum atop its upper surface.[81] Other examples are known from pictorial evidence. The tomb of St Thomas, illustrated more than fifty times in the stained glass at Canterbury, appears to have been much like Osmund's monument, except for having only two holes per side.[82] Illuminations in 'the Cambridge Life' of St Edward, compiled about 1250, show the Confessor's tomb as of *foramina* type, complete with pilgrims in three circular holes.[83] The shrine is of two stages, the bottom plain except for masonry and *foramina*, the top more decorated and consisting of a slab raised on elaborate columns. A feretrum rests on the slab.[84] The early shrine of St Edward may thus have been a hybrid of the table and *foramina* types, the former built on top of the latter. The nature of some monuments is known entirely from descriptions. In 1208, for example, a woman was cured after falling asleep with her head resting 'in a circular hole' in St Hugh's tomb at Lincoln.[85]

77 Wilson, *Shrines of St William*, p. 5.
78 E.K. Prideaux, 'Illustrated Notes on the Church of St. Candida and Holy Cross in Whit-church Canonicorum, Dorset', *Arch. J.*, vol. 64 (1907), pp. 138–9.
79 Wilson, *Shrines of St William*, p. 23 n.13.
80 D. Stroud, 'The Cult and Tombs of St Osmund at Salisbury', *The Wiltshire Archaeological and Natural History Magazine*, vol. 78 (1984), pp. 50–2. See plate 1; *Canonization of St Osmund*, p. 58.
81 Browne has an interesting theory about this shrine: 'The quatrefoil openings are worn, and it seems pretty clear that worshippers at the shrine crawled in at one opening and out at another, and so round the shrine, four times in and four times out': G.F. Browne, *An Account of the Three Ancient Cross Shafts, the Font and St Bertram's Shrine at Ilam* (London, 1888), p. 19.
82 For the glass at Canterbury see Caviness, *Early Stained Glass of Canterbury*, figs 120, 159, 160, 197f, 207, 210 and 211, all of which are consistent in their depiction of the tomb; Urry, 'Two Resting Places', pp. 196–7. See plate 2.
83 'La Estoire de Seint Aedward le Rei', CUL, MS Ee.3.59, ff. 29, 30, 33. See plate 3.
84 'La Estoire de Seint Aedward', f. 36.
85 'In uno circulari foramine': Giraldus Cambrensis, *Vita S. Hugonis*, p. 140.

The tombs of St Thomas and St Osmund were never shrine bases: no feretra were ever placed on top of them. These, like several other examples of the *foramina* style of monument, were built to hold prospective but not yet confirmed saints. The *foramina* design may therefore have been used when a tomb needed to fulfil the function of a shrine without offending propriety by actually enshrining and elevating the un-canonised occupants. The origin of this design is unknown. However, very early shrines were sometimes pierced with holes giving access to the relics: St Chad's first shrine had 'an aperture in its side, through which those who visit it with devotion can insert their hands and take out a little dust'.[86] It has been suggested that *foramina* monuments were the earliest form of Norman shrine, but were abandoned because pilgrims became stuck in the holes while searching for a cure: 'No doubt the recurrence of this form of miracle led to the adoption of a different form of shrine base for [St Thomas's] relics when they were translated into the Trinity Chapel in 1220.'[87] The dates of the known examples, however, do not make it clear that the *foramina* tomb-shrine predated the table type. After all, the *foramina* tomb of St Thomas was made in 1171, while the table shrine of Guthlac was built in the late eleventh century.

Anglo-Norman bases seem to have been significantly lower than those which succeeded them. The shrine of Candida, for example, is about the height of an altar, and St Thomas's columnar shrine was described as 'about a man's height'.[88] Evidence from miracle stories suggests that the Norman shrine of St Cuthbert was no taller than someone kneeling in front of it.[89] The early shrine of St Erkenwald, however, 'stood higher than the height of a man'.[90] It can be expected that over time there was a continuous upward development. Every new shrine had to be more impressive, and thus usually taller, than its predecessor, else it would not be replaced. Perhaps, however, there was a structural limit to the height of certain types of shrine. The slender columns of table shrines like that of St Thomas must have been kept low in order to preserve reasonable proportions and strength.

With the introduction of the solid base in the mid-thirteenth century a transformation in shrine shape began. Rather than bases made up of columns or pierced boxes, shrines became highly decorated but solid plinths. Without exception they were pierced with tall niches in which praying pilgrims could kneel, the supplicants' heads pressed against the stonework of the base and their elbows resting on a sort of table which often filled the niche to a height of two or three feet (see the frontispiece for an example). Sometimes niches were placed in the ends of the base as well, but the west face was usually reserved for an altar.

The development from one type of shrine to another is wholly unclear. P. Tudor-Craig has suggested that the open base supported by columns was

---

[86] Bede, *Ecclesiastical History*, IV, p. 3; See Thomas, *Early Christian Archaeology*, pp. 147–8.

[87] Tudor-Craig, 'Hubert Walter's Tomb', p. 75.

[88] Prideaux, 'Notes on the Church of St Candida', pl. xi, no. 1; Stow, *Annales*, p. 972.

[89] Tudor, 'The Cult of St Cuthbert in the Twelfth Century', p. 460. Interestingly the *Rites of Durham* proclaim that the shrine of that time was three yards high: *Rites of Durham*, p. 67.

[90] *Miracula Erkenwaldi*, pp. 120, 126–7. This may include the height of the feretrum.

abandoned because there was no private place to pray.[91] While the utility of spaces for pilgrims undoubtedly had an effect on the development of the shrine base, other factors must also have been at work. In particular, fashions in tomb structure could have provided many ideas and impulses; they certainly changed more completely over time than did shrines. Tombs in churches were not only rare in the twelfth and thirteenth centuries, but were only occasionally allowed to rise above the pavement.[92] The few occupants of monumental tombs were usually candidates for canonisation, and so saints enjoyed something of a monopoly on free-standing monuments of any height. In the thirteenth century, however, tombs began to develop upward. Two possible forms of influence between tombs and shrines suggest themselves. Firstly, the new shrine bases could have begun to imitate the solidity of tomb chests. In this theory the shrine of St Etheldreda (1254) would be a transitional form, having a somewhat solid core yet not quite relinquishing its columns.[93] The second form of influence could have been the increased height and magnificence of tombs, which must have been a stimulus in pushing shrines to a new height. Because shrines could not use architectural canopies (since they needed space on top for the cover), the base itself had to be taller, a difficult thing to achieve using the table or foramina designs.

We can be much more certain about the later middle ages, since most shrine bases that survive in whole or in part date from after 1275.[94] They were composed of three main elements: the base itself, steps around the shrine, and the shrine altar. The best preserved example, and one that can be taken as typical in form if not décor, is the shrine base of St Edward the Confessor at Westminster. Reassembled incorrectly during the reign of Queen Mary, its original appearance has been reconstructed by O'Neilly.[95] The base itself was seven feet seven inches tall and sat on four steps, each of which was five inches thick. The bottom of the feretrum would therefore have been nine feet three inches above the level of the chapel floor. The surviving canopy shows from its internal dimensions that the feretrum must have been less than four feet tall, making a maximum total height with the cover removed of about thirteen feet.

The first shrine of St Thomas Cantilupe is another interesting example. In 1282 Thomas was buried in the Lady Chapel of Hereford cathedral, but five years later he was moved to a new tomb in the north transept. Sometime later this tomb was modified into a shrine by the addition of a second tier, consisting of short arcades

91 Tudor-Craig, 'Hubert Walter's Tomb', p. 76.
92 F.H. Crossley, *English Church Monuments A.D. 1150–1550* (London, 1921), p. 42.
93 Coldstream, 'Shrine Bases', p. 17.
94 Coldstream, 'Shrine Bases', p. 21. Coldstream thought that the fragments discovered in 1921, which date from 1275, were from Swithun's shrine. They are actually the remains of a screen. For a full discussion, see P. Tudor-Craig and L. Keen, 'A Recently Discovered Purbeck Marble Sculptured Screen of the Thirteenth Century and the Shrine of St Swithun', in *Medieval Art and Architecture at Winchester Cathedral* (BAACT, vol. 6, 1983), pp. 63–72.
95 O'Neilly, 'The Shrine of Edward'; see especially the figures on pp. 17–18 for the measurements to follow.

springing from the original tomb chest. Cantilupe's brass (now missing) was allowed to remain and could be seen through the arcades.[96] The feretrum rested on the topmost surface and was protected by a movable cover. It is usually believed that these modifications were made soon or immediately after the 1287 translation.[97] However, building a feretrum before official canonisation would have been highly irregular, and there is no record of such a project in the expenses of 1287. In 1317 and early 1320, however, money was bequeathed to a new shrine should Thomas be canonised.[98] It seems that this was only a fraction of the money available, since various receipts of London artisans show that £130 was spent on electrum, marble and goldsmiths for a new shrine in 1320 and 1321.[99] This documentary evidence for work in 1320 is backed up by the physical evidence of the existing monument, which shows signs of having been altered and whose second tier is by a different sculptor than the first.[100] It therefore seems likely that a typical 'altar-tomb' existed until Cantilupe's canonisation in 1320, and that the recorded expenses indicate its modification to a shrine shortly after 1320, rather than all the work being performed in 1287.[101]

The shrine in the north transept was only a temporary home for Thomas's relics. They were translated, after delays caused by lack of funds, into his final shrine in 1349.[102] Because his relics were removed, the modified tomb was not destroyed at the Reformation and has remained little changed. As an essentially makeshift arrangement pending a proper translation to a better shrine in a more prestigious location, Cantilupe's shrine illustrates the minimum changes thought necessary to transform a tomb into a shrine. The main requirement was that the

[96] The brass was stolen about the year 1652, according to antiquary Silas Taylor (c.1660): E.G. Benson, 'The Lost Brass of the Cantilupe Shrine', *Trans. Woolhope Field Club*, vol. 33 (1949–51), pp. 68, 70.

[97] For example, Marshall, 'The Shrine of St Thomas', p. 39.

[98] Morgan, 'Effect of the Pilgrim Cult on Hereford', p. 150; Will of John de Aquablanca, 1320, in *Charters and Records of Hereford Cathedral*, ed. W.W. Capes (Hereford, 1908), p. 186.

[99] Receipt of 1321 from William Sprot of London for £80 of 'electrum' (a type of brass) sold for the feretrum is printed in *Charters and Records of Hereford*, pp. 195–6. A goldsmith received £10 for various works in late 1420, £10 in part payment of £40 was paid to Adam le Marbrer of London in March 1321, and Michael the 'Imaginer' of London gave a receipt of payment for all his work on the shrine: HCA 1440, 1437 and 1436.

[100] Marshall, 'The Shrine of St Thomas', p. 46. 'A close inspection of the tomb in the north transept will at once disclose . . . that it has been altered from the original design, and that the alterations it has undergone were made within a comparatively few years of its inception, and it may be stated that there is no evidence that it has undergone any subsequent structural change': *ibid.* p. 35.

[101] This opinion has been independently reached by R. Emmerson, who states that although both upper and lower parts have sections carved in a short-lived naturalistic style of the late thirteenth century, the west part of the arcade has some 'bubble-foliage' of the fourteenth century: 'St Thomas Cantilupe's Tomb and Brass of 1287', *Bull. of the International Soc. for the Study of Church Monuments*, vol. 2 (1980), pp. 41–5.

[102] *Registrum Johannis de Trillek*, p. 148.

relics be moved from beneath the tomb to an elevated feretrum, and that this be protected by a cover. Fixtures for a cover can still be seen on the topmost surface of this slab.[103] The monument was also made taller by raising the uppermost slab on arcades, incidentally providing open spaces for placing offerings or inserting diseased limbs. The final height was still only five feet ten inches, far too short for a proper fourteenth-century shrine, but no one expected the new shrine to take as long to build as it did. The Hereford shrine illustrates that the essential differences between a tomb and a shrine were three: a flat upper surface for the placement of an elevated feretrum, increased height of the main structure, and niches or holes to facilitate worship.

Given that Thomas Cantilupe's first shrine was makeshift, almost all known shrine bases of the 'solid with niches' type were roughly eight feet tall.[104] I suggest that this was the practical maximum, being the highest a man could reach to lift the reliquary on and off, lock the cover, or do other necessary tasks about the feretrum without the aid of a ladder. Anything higher would have been inconvenient and of artistically unappealing proportions, anything lower less impressive and too accessible to light-fingered pilgrims. The reliquary above would have added about three feet to the total height, and the steps below as much as two feet. The width of the shrine base was usually about four feet, while length was consistent at about eight feet. The remains of Etheldreda's shrine at Ely indicate an unusually wide monument at six feet two inches.[105] The shrine of St William of York, built in 1472, was truly exceptional at seven feet six inches wide, almost fourteen feet long and eleven feet high.[106] The fact that the 1476 shrine at Winchester could only be reached by a ladder suggests that it may have been equally high.[107] Perhaps English fashion had reached a new stage in its evolution in the late fifteenth century, and new shrines were becoming considerably taller. Some of the practical obstacles to increased height may have been negated by fixing the feretra permanently to the top of the base so that they never needed to be removed. However, there were too few new shrines late in the middle ages for us to be certain about general trends in shrine design.

Shrine bases were invariably described as being made of marble. The fragments of Thomas of Canterbury's shrine are of an exceptionally rare, hard rose-pink marble, probably imported from the Mediterranean area and also used for the mosaic paving around the shrine area.[108] The usual material for shrine bases, however, was some sort of indigenous 'marble', often purbeck. During 1469–70 Master Mason Robert Spillesby went looking for 'marblers', presumably to make a new shrine of St William of York, and eventually used a blue-grey

103 Marshall, 'The Shrine of St Thomas', p. 36.
104 Coldstream, 'Shrine Bases', p. 17.
105 See the plan of the shrine in E.M. Hampson and T.D. Atkinson, 'The City of Ely', in *VCH: Cambridge and the Isle of Ely*, vol. 4, ed. R.B. Pugh (1953), p. 71.
106 Wilson, *Shrines of St William*, p. 26 n.47.
107 *Concilia*, vol. 3, pp. 610–11.
108 Tatton-Brown, 'Chapel Floors', pp. 51, 53.

limestone that probably originated from Teesdale.[109] The great weight of stone in a shrine base often required special foundations. Excavation has revealed part of what was very likely a foundation for the shrine of St Chad, and a 'flint solid' was added to the retrochoir crypt at Winchester to support the shrine of St Swithun built above in 1476.[110]

Most shrines were set on a number of shallow steps forming a sort of dais, some of which can be reconstructed. The uneven pattern and wear marks on the edges of certain stones laid in the middle of the Trinity Chapel floor at Canterbury indicate that they are the shrine steps re-laid.[111] If rearranged they would form the edges of three concentric platforms measuring 28 by 17ft, 26.5 by 15ft, and 23.5 by 12.5ft plus a topmost podium measuring 14 by 9ft on which the shrine itself sat.[112] The shrine of St Edward at Westminster was originally on four steps, each five inches high, which fit into the pattern of the Cosmati flooring.[113] Fragments of steps from the shrine of St Cuthbert were also five inches high, suggesting that this was a typical height.[114] The passage of pilgrims up and around the steps at Canterbury has worn a groove into the original paving stones just west of the shrine area.[115] The steps around the last shrine of the other St Thomas at Hereford, found in a nineteenth-century restoration, also showed wear.[116]

The one major element of the shrine base that remains to be discussed is the altar attached to the western face of all greater shrines. That belonging to the shrine at Westminster was typical in that it was no more than the width of the shrine.[117] Inventories of shrine goods frequently mention candelabra, vestments, altar cloths, and other equipment common to all altars. Objects pertaining to St Edward's altar included Turkish carpets for laying over stools, four frontals for the shrine altar (one with ostrich feathers), plus twenty-two other assorted altar cloths, four corporase cases and two mass books.[118] Rods for hanging curtains at the sides of the altar (riddels) projected from the end of the shrine. Occasionally a beam was suspended before the shrine altar. One of St Erkenwald's miracles was

---

[109] *The Fabric Rolls of York Minster*, ed. J. Raine (SS, vol. 35, 1859), p. 73; Wilson, *Shrines of St William*, p. 21.

[110] R. Willis, 'On the Foundations of Early Buildings Discovered in Lichfield Cathedral', *Arch. J.*, vol. 18 (1861), p. 24; Crook, 'Swithun of Winchester', p. 66.

[111] See plate 4.

[112] Tatton-Brown, 'Chapel Floors', p. 53, reconstructed plan p. 52.

[113] O'Neilly, 'The Shrine of Edward', pp. 134–6.

[114] Fowler, 'Examination of the Grave of St. Cuthbert', p. 16.

[115] E. Eames, 'Notes on the Decorated Stone Roundels in the Corona and Trinity Chapel in Canterbury Cathedral', in *Medieval Art and Architecture at Canterbury before 1220* (*BAACT*, vol. 5, 1982), p. 67.

[116] J. Morris, 'English Relics: I – St. Thomas of Hereford', *The Month*, vol. 44 (Jan.–Apr., 1882), p. 117.

[117] There is now a modern altar of the same size. See O'Neilly, 'The Shrine of Edward', p. 131.

[118] 'Inventories of Westminster Abbey at the Dissolution', ed. M.E.C. Walcott, *Trans. of the London and Middlesex Archaeological Soc.*, vol. 4 (1875), pp. 350–2.

worked on a man who placed wax eyes on such a beam.[119] One of the jobs of the junior clerk at the shrine of St Thomas Becket was to maintain twelve large, square candles on the beam there.[120]

Feretory chapels

The shrine sat in a chapel of varying dimensions. Perhaps the typical feretory chapel was that of St Erkenwald at London, where one and a half bays of the retrochoir were screened off.[121] St Etheldreda was more magnificently set apart in an enclosure at least two, but probably three bays long.[122] If a shrine was behind the high altar then the feretory chapel could be higher than the ambulatory by virtue of being set on a platform created by extending the raised presbytery towards the east. Platforms of this type can still be seen at Durham and Winchester, while the feretory platform at Chichester remains despite being reduced in size in 1829.[123] The ground under Edward the Confessor's shrine, although not on a platform of this type, was raised by earthen infill which later legend erroneously held to have been brought in shiploads from the Holy Land.[124] The paving of such holy places sometimes received special treatment as well. The Cosmati flooring at Westminster is exceptional, while the floor of the Canterbury shrine chapel 'is certainly the most splendid and expensive pavement of which so great an area remains'.[125]

The feretory chapel was filled with many types of shrine 'furniture'. Candelabra were common, the most impressive of which were tall candlesticks, usually brass, meant to stand near the shrine. A Canterbury sacrist's roll of 1432/3, for example, mentions four candelabra around the shrines of Sts Dunstan and Alphege.[126] Lights were carefully specified by statute, and thus we sometimes know in great detail when and what sort of candles were to be used at a shrine. In 1270 Bishop Stephen Berstead of Chichester ordered that the dean and chapter of Chichester cathedral perpetually maintain ten square (*quadratos*) and two round candles at the shrine of St Richard, plus another nine round candles burning day

---

119 'He diligently placed those same two eyes upon the beam which was suspended above' (Super hastem que imminebat eosdem oculos diligenter apposuit): *Miracula Erkenwaldi*, pp. 138–9.
120 'Maioris et quadrate forme': 'Customary of the Shrine of St Thomas', f. 2.
121 G.H. Cook, *Old St Paul's Cathedral: a Lost Glory of Medieval London* (London, 1955), p. 39.
122 See Hampson and Atkinson ('The City of Ely', p. 70), who give three bays, S.I. Ladds (*The Monastery of Ely* (Ely, 1930), p. 11), who gives two, and Draper ('Northwold and Etheldreda', pp. 14–15), who believes two bays were later changed to three.
123 W.K.L. Clarke, *Chichester Cathedral in the Nineteenth Century*, Chichester Papers no. 14 (Chichester, 1959), p. 2. See plate 5.
124 Perkins, *Westminster Abbey*, vol. 2, p. 36.
125 Eames, 'Stone Roundels', p. 70. See plate 4.
126 CCA, DCc/Sacrist Roll 26; C.E. Woodruff, 'The Sacrist's Rolls of Christ Church Canterbury', *Arch. Cant.*, vol. 48 (1936), pp. 27, 58.

and night on feasts of the first, second and third dignity, all of two pounds weight.[127] Candles often stood on the shrine itself. Some of the illuminations in Lydgate's 'Life of St Edmund' show the shrine at Bury with four candles standing at the corners of either the feretrum or base.[128] The eight candles standing on the shrine of St Thomas, along with four on his altar, were alternately red and green and were decorated with golden flowers.[129] The shrine was often the best lit place in the cathedral, but all these candles came at great cost. Special grants to maintain lights were common, such as the taper kept burning at the shrine of St Etheldreda by an annual rent of one mark, or the two silver basins for lamps provided by Henry III to hang over the shrine at Westminster.[130]

Some basins which hung about shrines were not for lighting, but for holding holy water, the Corpus Christi, or offerings.[131] Hanging an object in the presence of the shrine was a good way to conserve space and attract attention. In the north transept chapel at Hereford, which once held the shrine of St Thomas, William Stukeley, travelling sometime before 1724, saw a painting of Cantilupe on the wall and remarked that 'all around are the marks of hooks where the banners, lamps, reliques, and the like presents were hung up in his honor'.[132] The space about the shrine was usually hung with rich curtains. At Westminster in 1520 there was 'a cloth hangyng abowte the shryne of the lyff of saynt Edward'.[133] There was also a valance (a type of drapery) of blue velvet with flowers of gold and images of Sts Edward and John the Evangelist (perhaps that made in 1497/8 and having four embroidered gold flowers, eight virgates of buckram and six ounces of silk fringe), and another of blue damask 'to hange the shryne and a creiste [crest] of tymbre and of bron golde'.[134] Banners were frequently hung at shrines, most notably the flag of the saint. The latter could be a powerful relic in itself, as was

---

127 Another candle was to burn at the tomb: 'The Early Statutes of the Cathedral Church of the Holy Trinity, Chichester, with Observations on its Constitution and History', ed. M.E.C. Walcott, *Archaeologia*, vol. 45 (1877), p. 173. The candles that had to be provided about the cathedral by the treasurer in the twelfth century (i.e. before St Richard) are given on pp. 165–6.

128 'Lydgate's Life of St Edmund', BL, Harl. MS 2278, ff. 4, 9, 100.

129 '[They] ought to be decorated with paintings of comely red and green, the one of red and the other of green, with roses and flowers of gold and other colours delicately inserted' (Qui decenti pictura rubei et viridis debent adornari, unus reby et alter viridis coloris cum rosis et ffloribus de auro et alijs coloribus subtiliter insertis): 'Customary of the Shrine of St Thomas', f. 9.

130 J. Bentham, *The History and Antiquities of the Conventual and Cathedral Church of Ely* (Norwich, 1812), p. 146; *Customary of the Benedictine Monasteries of Saint Augustine, Canterbury, and Saint Peter, Westminster*, ed. E.M. Thompson (Henry Bradshaw Soc., vol. 33, 1902, 1904), vol. 2, p. 45.

131 Such as the cord which was bought for 4d. in 1404/5 to hang a basin at the shrine of St Oswald, Worcester: WCA, MS C.469.

132 W. Stukeley, *Itinerarium Curiosum, or, an Account of the Antiquitys and Remarkable Curiositys in Nature or Art, observ'd in Travels thro' Great Brittan* (London, 1724), p. 67.

133 The 1520 inventory is printed in H.F. Westlake, *Westminster Abbey* (2 vols, London, 1923), vol. 2, pp. 504–5.

134 WAM, MS 19751.

the banner of St Edmund borne before the victors of the battle of Fornham in 1173.[135]

Books belonging to the shrine, such as the 'two very old books which are called the books of St Chad' kept at Lichfield,[136] were stored in secure chests or chained to a convenient spot. However, written material for the use of pilgrims was often painted on wooden boards called tables (*tabulæ*) which were displayed about the shrine chapel. The whole history of the canonisation of St William, for example, was written on a table in York Minster, along with a list of his miracles.[137] Perhaps more commonly, *tabulæ* were covered with pictorial representations. This was probably the case with the *tabulæ* placed before the altar of St Edward, a silver one in 1377/8, and a painted wood one made in 1394/5 for 153s. 4d.[138]

It was common for a feretory chapel to house the cathedral relic collection. In smaller churches relics could be kept in lockers or cupboards, often in the wall north of the main altar.[139] Greater churches usually kept their collections somewhere behind the high altar, as with the relics around the tomb of St Cuthbert in the twelfth century, and the two silver feretra with relics of diverse saints noted behind the altar at Lichfield in 1345.[140] The relics at Westminster were in the shrine chapel by 1346, when offerings were recorded as 'to the shrine and the other relics in the same place'.[141] Not surprisingly, relics were securely locked up: in 1504 two keys and three plates were bought for the locks in the chest of the relics at Canterbury.[142] A sixteenth-century reliquary chest (with some iron work from the thirteenth century) found near St Richard's shrine, and measuring no less that eight by twenty feet, contains a door for the exhibition of relics and a slit for the reception of offerings.[143] Often the relics were displayed and preserved in special cupboards called almeries. The thirteenth-century almeries at Gloucester in the north transept were twenty-seven feet long, eighteen feet high and three feet deep, and made of stone with broad, shallow recesses holding painted wooden cupboards.[144] At Winchester some relics were probably placed in the feretory chapel, since the front of the platform in the east end evidently once contained an

---

135 Roger of Hovedon, *Chronica Magestri Rogeri de Houedene*, ed. W. Stubbs (RS, vol. 51, 1868–71), vol. 2, p. 55.

136 In the inventory of 1345: 'Sacrist's Roll of Lichfield', p. 204.

137 Dixon, *Fasti Eboracenses*, pp. 227–8.

138 WAM, MSS 19637, 19654.

139 W. St John Hope, 'On the Great Almery for Relics of Late in the Abbey Church of Selby, with Notes on Some Other Receptacles for Relics', *Archaeologia*, vol. 60, pt 2 (1907), pp. 412–13. See the plate on p. 413 of that article for a remarkable cupboard with attached offering box from Wensley church, Yorks.

140 Reginald of Durham, *Libellus de Admirandis Beati Cuthberti*, p. 165; 'Sacrist's Roll of Lichfield', p. 199.

141 'Ad feretrum et alias reliquias ibidem': WAM, MS 19622. Some of the relics were moved to recesses in the walls when Henry V's chantry was built, others to an almery beside the tomb of Henry III: Hope, 'Great Almery', p. 418.

142 CCA, Lit. MS C11, f. 47.

143 M.E.C. Walcott, *Memorials of Chichester* (Chichester, 1865), pp. 40–1.

144 Hope, 'Great Almery', pp. 416–17.

almery protected by an arcade and, probably, an iron grating with a small door at either end.[145] In the sixteenth century most relics at Winchester were in the sacristy, including St Philip's foot (covered in plate gold), seven tables with infixed relics, five saints' heads, five saints' arms, and 'One and twenty shrines, some all silver and gilt, and some part silver and gilt, and part copper and gilt, and some part silver and part ivory, and some copper and gilt, and some set with garnished stones'.[146] At least some of Canterbury's best relics were displayed to the north of the high altar in a 'great almery'.[147] The Martilogium of Lichfield cathedral is an example of a relic chapel that was an institution in itself. Besides holding relics of Chad and other saints it had its own financial accounts, endowments and fabric fund.[148]

Spread about the feretory chapel were miscellaneous objects used by the shrine such as chests, rugs, images and cushions. The net effect must have been one of sumptuous clutter. It was certainly a display of great wealth, and monitoring all these priceless objects was an obvious concern of the cathedral staff. In several places an elevated structure, called a watching loft, was built so that shrine wardens could look down from it into the feretory chapel. The most famous example survives at St Albans, where a seventeen by eight and a half foot chamber sits atop a large relic almery, the entire height being seventeen feet.[149] At Oxford a chamber built over a wooden chantry chapel under the last southern arch could have doubled as a watching loft for the shrine of St Frideswide.[150]

Another way to guard a shrine was to enclose the feretory chapel with stout defences. Stuckley noted that St Thomas's shrine in the north transept at Hereford was 'well guarded and barricado'd to prevent thieves from making free with his superfluitys'.[151] At Ely the feretory area was enclosed by iron fences and tombs on three sides and by the reredos of the high altar on the fourth. An iron grill surrounding the platform for the shrine at Chichester was removed in 1829.[152] Doors in lateral screens extending the reredos into the Lichfield aisles controlled entry to the 'Lady Choir', and thus St Chad's shrine.[153] At Westminster not only did the ambulatory through which pilgrims passed have iron gates at each end and

---

[145] R. Willis, 'The Architectural History of Winchester Cathedral', *Proceedings at the Annual Meeting of the Archaeological Institute*, vol. 1 (1845), p. 50; Hope, 'Great Almery', p. 415; Crook, 'Swithun of Winchester', p. 61.

[146] *Monasticon Anglicanum*, ed. W. Dugdale (London, 1655), new edition, eds J. Caley, H. Ellis and B. Bandinel (London, 1830), vol. 1, pp. 202–3.

[147] Hope and Legg, *Inventories of Christchurch*, p. 37.

[148] See various notices in the *The Great Register of Lichfield Cathedral known as the Magnum Registrum Album*, ed. H.E. Savage (London, 1926), pp. 96, 109, 172–3, 319, 172.

[149] See Hope, 'Great Almery', p. 420.

[150] F.B. Bond, *An Introduction to English Church Architecture from the Eleventh to the Sixteenth Century* (2 vols, London, 1913), vol. 1, p. 82, plate p. 81.

[151] Stukeley, *Itinerarium Curiosum*, p. 67.

[152] Clarke, *Chichester Cathedral in the Nineteenth Century*, p. 2.

[153] Willis, 'Foundations of Early Buildings Discovered in Lichfield', p. 19; B. Willis, *A Survey of the Cathedrals of York, Durham, Carlisle, Chester, Man, Lichfield, Hereford, Worcester, Gloucester and Bristol* (London, 1727), plan p. 371.

fences on both sides, but all chapels were gated and locked, and tombs fenced, by the fourteenth century.[154] A shrine's custodians were willing to invest considerable sums in these defences. The grate about the shrine at London was only 5ft 10in. high, but complete with locks and doors it cost no less than £64 2s.[155]

Head relics and empty tombs

There were two common types of subsidiary shrine associated with major saints: head reliquaries and empty tombs. The practice of separating heads from saintly bodies may have originated at Canterbury where the crown of St Thomas, sliced off by his murderers in 1170, provided a conveniently separate relic that was later enclosed in a reliquary and called a 'head'. There are, of course, earlier examples of head relics: Canterbury already had several, including those of Sts Furseus, Austroberta and Swithun.[156] However, Thomas's crown seems to be the earliest English example of a head or part thereof removed and set up separately yet in the same church as the main shrine. It was installed in the easternmost chapel at Canterbury, which came to be called the Corona.

There is some doubt about St Thomas's head shrine. Erasmus saw 'the perforated skull of the martyr' in the crypt and there was also a major head relic of some sort in the Corona, even though no record of the rest of the head being removed from the shrine exists.[157] A deception was claimed after the Dissolution: 'They found his head hole with the bones, which had a wounde in the skull, for the monkes had closed another skull in silver richly, for people to offer to, which they sayd was St. Thomas skull, so that nowe the abuse was openly knowne that they had used many yeres afore.'[158]

Duplicate head relics were relatively common. In a letter of 28 Dec. 1538, for example, Dr London, scouring the monasteries, reported that he had two silver-gilt heads of St Ursula which he was holding until he could obtain a third, which he believed he would within thirteen days.[159] Even setting conscious fraud aside, head relics were particularly susceptible to multiplication. Portions of skulls, however small, were sometimes put in bust-shaped reliquaries and called 'heads', and in time these might be believed to be the entire skull. If this were done more than once, or if the majority of the skull existed somewhere else, the result could easily be a saint with more than one 'head'. Perhaps this is the cause of the confusion at Canterbury.

[154] F. Bond, *Westminster Abbey* (London, 1909), p. 67.

[155] Dugdale, *St Paul's*, p. 24.

[156] Eadmer of Canterbury, 'Edmeri Cantvariensis Nova Opvscvla de Sanctorum Veneratione et Obsecratione', pp. 365–6.

[157] Erasmus, *Pilgrimages to Saint Mary and Saint Thomas*, p. 42.

[158] Charles Wriothesley, *A Chronicle of England During the Reigns of the Tudors*, ed. W.D. Hamilton (Camden Soc., ns vol. 11, 1875), p. 86.

[159] *Three Chapters of Letters Relating to the Suppression of the Monasteries*, ed. T. Wright (Camden Soc., vol. 26, 1843), p. 234.

Among English cathedrals, head shrines existed along with a major shrine of the same saint at Canterbury, Lichfield, Lincoln, York, Chichester, Salisbury, Worcester and Hereford. The other cathedrals either had no major shrines or possessed an incorrupt saint (whose head could therefore not be removed). The only notable exception is Winchester, where St Swithun's head was taken to Canterbury. Some of these head shrines are not well known today. At Worcester, for example, separate heads of Sts Oswald and Wulfstan were frequently mentioned in manuscripts. They appear, for example, in a fifteenth-century inventory and were supplied with a beam in 1390/1, probably near the main shrines.[160] In 1521/2 the subtumbarius was in charge of oblations 'at the heads of Saints Oswald and Wulfstan'.[161]

These reliquaries were made to look like heads set on bases. The head reliquary of St William of York, for example, was in the form of a bust supported by angels. Surmounted by a jewelled canopy, William's head was kept in a silver chest and carried about using a silver belt to hold its weight.[162] The head of St Osmund, made by John Iewe, was gilded and garnished with stones and had both a mitre and a 'fote' or base.[163] That of St Chad could be disassembled into two parts, the lower weighing 110 ounces and the upper 146 ounces.[164] The head shrine of St Hugh, replaced by the treasurer John Welbourn after being stolen and stripped by thieves, was made of gold, silver and gems and, unusually, was house-shaped, having three niches per side and a plain 'roof'.[165] The stone base, which survives, has two niches on either side and one on each end, all of which originally held statues (see plate 6). According to a contemporary will, the figure in the western niche represented the Virgin Mary.[166]

Head shrines often had many of the same accoutrements as the main shrines. St Chad's head, for example, had its own warden.[167] There are many records of

---

[160] WCA, MS C. 456; WCA, MS A22, f. 18.

[161] *Accounts of the Priory of Worcester for the Year 13–14 H. VIII, AD. 1521–2*, eds J.H. Bloom and S.G. Hamilton (London, 1907), p. 25.

[162] The pertinences of the head are contained in an inventory, and include 'a chest of silver and a belt ornamented with silver gilt, for carrying the head of St William' (Item unus arcus argenti. Una zona, garnishyt cum argento deaurato, pro portando capite Sancti Willielmi): *Historians of the Church of York*, vol. 3, p. 389.

[163] Found in a heavily damaged memorandum of expenses from 1457: *Canonization of St Osmund*, pp. 217–18.

[164] From an eighteenth-century transcript in Shrewsbury Public Library, MS 2, ff. 92 and 94, a photocopy of which was supplied to me by Prof. R.B. Dobson.

[165] R.E.G. Cole, and J.O. Johnston, 'The Body of Saint Hugh', *Associated Architectural Soc. Reports and Papers*, vol. 36, pt 1 (1921–22), illustration opposite p. 47; 'He also after the theft and plundering of the head of St Hugh made it new with repairs of gold, silver and precious stones' (Qui etiam post furacionem et spolacionem capitis sancti Hugonis de novo fecit cum auro et argento et lapidibus preciosis ornari et reparari): Venables, 'The Shrine and Head of St. Hugh of Lincoln', *Arch. J.*, vol. 50 (1893), p. 50, from the 'Welbourn Chantry Book'.

[166] Cole and Johnston, 'The Body of St Hugh', p. 64.

[167] See Lichfield Cathedral Library, MSS XXVI–XXVIII, labelled 'Cantaria Sancti Blasii'. For a discussion of this chapel see J. Hewitt, 'The "Keeper of Saint Chad's Head" in

head shrines receiving offerings, such as the £16 19s. 'to the head and shrine' at Salisbury in 1493/4.[168] Heads, being easily portable, were more flexible for use in miracle cures. In 1302 a young monk of Worcester was cured of a 'perturbed brain' by touching the head of Wulfstan to his own head.[169] The smaller head shrine required less space than a major shrine and thus could also be situated wherever convenient. Although no one location appears to have been favoured over another, in general they were not placed in the feretory chapel. The head shrine of St Hugh, for instance, was (and the base still is) on the north side of the Angel Choir, across the ambulatory from the main shrine.[170] At Lichfield, 'There are very strong reasons for supposing that the head of the Saint was kept in the chapel over the sacristy in the south choir aisle; and there was the altar to the head of St Chad, which was distinct from the chief altar dedicated to his memory.'[171] In the will of Bishop de Lenne (d.1373) the head of Richard of Chichester was described as being in the north side of the chapel of Mary Magdalene.[172] This physical separation ensured that there were at least two major sites of the saint's cult.

A second common type of subsidiary shrine was the saint's original tomb, which often functioned as a shrine (by receiving pilgrims and offerings) before canonisation. Holy tombs could be given special marks of honour. The tomb of St Wulfstan, for example, was raised above ground level, covered by a tapestry, and provided with candles and a kneeling mat for petitioners. Thus 'Wulfstan's cult was clearly sanctioned to some degree by prior and monks, if not by his immediate episcopal successors.'[173] Veneration of the tomb did not cease after the body was translated to a proper shrine. The grave of St Swithun, where he was buried in 862 outside the west door of the church as it then was, continued to be venerated into the fifteenth century. The original site, north of the new cathedral's nave, was marked by a modest chapel and surrounded by graves of high status.[174] Tombs could also continue to be adapted and improved. After the translation of St William of York his now empty tomb received a new monument, fragments of which survive, at the expense of Archbishop Melton (1317–40).[175] By the end of

Lichfield Cathedral, and other Matters Concerning that Minster in the Fifteenth Century', *Arch. J.*, vol. 33 (1876), pp. 72–3.

168 'Ad caput et scrinium': SCA, 'Account of the Warden of the Shrine of St Osmund', 1493/4.

169 St Wulfstan came to the monk in a dream, saying 'My head was placed upon yours; behold I come to you with my head, and you have been made whole' (Caput meum super tuum positum fuit; ecce ego venio cum capite meo, et sanus factus es): *Annales de Wigornia*, pp. 552–3.

170 Cole and Johnston, 'The Body of Saint Hugh', p. 64; plate 6.

171 'Sacrist's Roll of Lichfield', p. 214 n. 6. See W. Rodwell, 'Archaeology and the Standing Fabric: Recent Studies at Lichfield', *Antiquity*, vol. 63 (1989), pp. 285–6.

172 An image from St Richard's 'historia' was 'towards the left part in which, namely, the head of the Blessed Richard rested' (ad sinestram partem in qua, scilicet, Capud B. Ricardi reponitur): 'Early Statutes of Chichester', p. 169.

173 William of Malmsbury, *De Gestis Pontificium Anglorum*, p. 289; Mason, *Wulfstan*, pp. 262–3.

174 M. Biddle, 'Archaeology, Architecture, and the Cult of Saints', p. 24.

175 'Truly he renewed the tomb of St William at the cost of twenty pounds' (Tumbam vero sancti Willielmi sumptibus xx. librarum renovabat): T. Stubbs, *Chronica Pontificium*

the middle ages more than half of shrine cathedrals continued to venerate an empty tomb as well as the main shrine, and those at Canterbury, York and Winchester were substantial shrines in their own right.

Beams and reredoses as bases

Head and empty tomb-shrines differed in shape, size and location from the standard late-medieval saint's shrine described earlier in this chapter, largely because they were different in their basic nature. Basically, there was no reason that a head had to be enshrined in the same fashion as a body. However, it was possible for saint's bodies to be enshrined somewhat differently from the norm if they were of lesser prestige. The mid thirteenth-century shrine of St William of Rievaulx, for example, rested on a slab suspended within an arch in the west wall of the Chapter House of Rievaulx Abbey.[176] Were there other types of base for greater shrines besides the monumental stone plinths described above?

There are several well-known English examples of reliquaries carried on a beam, usually that which commonly crossed the quire behind and above the high altar. As a result of a fire at Canterbury in 1174, 'The chests of relics, thrown from the lofty beam above the pavement, were broken, and the relics scattered.'[177] In 1294 Archbishop Winchelsey made a station behind the high altar of Canterbury under the shrine of St Blaise on the beam, and in 1443 Archbishop Stafford, as part of his enthronization, also knelt under that shrine.[178] Shrines on beams over lesser altars at Canterbury included the reliquaries of Sts Swithun, Wulgan and many others.[179] There is even a translation account of the shrine of St Fleogild, taken up from the high altar in 1448 and carried past the shrine of St Thomas to the beam between it and the Corona chapel.[180] These examples show that a beam was an acceptable position for a minor shrine, where it was loftier than on a regular base and could lend its glory to nearby altars. Equally important, this arrangement did not take up floor space like a stone base since it was possible to walk right under the shrine. This position was possible because, unlike major shrines, lesser shrines were small enough to be perched on a beam and did not need to accommodate pilgrims and an altar.

A similar type of placement would be a position on top of the reredos. A diagrammatic drawing made in about 1414 of the interior of the eastern arm of St Augustine's Abbey, Canterbury, shows a beam supporting three large house-

---

Ecclesiæ Eboraci, in *Historiæ Anglicanæ Scriptores X*, no editer given (London, 1652), col. 1731.

[176] C.R. Peers, 'Rievaulx Abbey: The Shrine in the Chapter House', *Arch. J.*, vol. 86 (1929), pp. 23–4.

[177] Gervase of Canterbury, *Burning and Repair*, p. 8.

[178] C. Cotton, *The Saxon Cathedral at Canterbury and the Saxon Saints buried therein* (Manchester, 1929), p. 37; Stone, *Chronicle*, p. 34.

[179] Hope and Legg, *Inventories of Christchurch*, pp. 36, 40.

[180] Stone, *Chronicle*, p. 44.

shaped reliquaries labelled *Reliquie* and *Letardus*.[181] Below the beam the solid and reasonably lofty reredos supported several more objects, including six books, two arm reliquaries and, apparently, the shrine of St Ethelbert. Even here, however, the main shrine (of St Augustine himself) was in the usual position in the axial apse, and the area behind the reredos was stuffed with no less than thirteen full-sized shrines. The obvious lack of space in the more suitable regions of the church was doubtless part of the reason for Ethelbert's unusual enshrinement. Also, it was not the object of a significant pilgrimage cult and therefore did not need to be accessible, its small size gave more latitude in its placement, and Ethelbert did not need his own altar since the high altar was partially dedicated to him.

The only supposed English instances of major shrines on the reredos are at Beverley, York and Lincoln. Sometime after 1330 a great reredos was built at Beverley with a stair at the north end giving access to an upper platform. While the prevailing view regarding the shrine at Beverley is that 'St John's main relics were in the conventional place behind the high altar',[182] J. Bilson, who cited A.F. Leach in agreement, pointed out that the shrine base is not mentioned in a contract for the shrine's construction and that the reliquary, which was to be five and one half by one and one half feet, could have easily fitted on the reredos platform.[183] Yet, it is to be expected that contracts for feretra and shrine bases would have been drawn up separately, since one called for a goldsmith and the other for a stone carver or mason. Therefore, the only apparent support for this theory is that it was physically possible. N. Coldstream has tentatively postulated that St William was on top of the wooden screen at York, based on the fact that otherwise it could not have been seen from the west.[184] As we shall see in the next chapter, this assumption of the importance of visibility is unfounded. Other evidence places William's shrine in a more normal position behind the reredos, where it certainly was after 1472.[185]

The most recent and strongly argued candidate for a reredos base is the shrine of St Hugh at Lincoln, for which the evidence is complex. Bishop Sanderson recorded in 1641 that six stubs of iron from Hugh's shrine could still be seen set in the pavement north of the central axis and east of the high altar, and in 1667–75 Bishop Fuller erected a monument to St Hugh over that site.[186] Because the irons

181 Thomas of Elmham, *MS history of St. Augustine's Canterbury*, now Trinity Hall Cambridge, MS I.f. 63, reproduced in W. St John Hope, *English Altars* (London, 1899), pl. ix.
182 C. Wilson, 'The Early Thirteenth-Century Architecture of Beverley Minster: Cathedral Splendours and Cistercian Austerities', in *Thirteenth Century England*, vol. 3, eds P.R. Coss and S.D. Lloyd (Woodbridge, 1991), p. 193. Little is known about this shrine. In the twelfth century a pilgrim gave a wax candle 'in the presence of the relics of the man of God over the altar': *Miracula Sanct Johannis*, p. 310.
183 Cited in Coldstream, 'Shrine Bases', pp. 21–2, from correspondence between Bilson and St John Hope.
184 Coldstream, 'Shrine Bases', p. 23.
185 See Wilson, *Shrines of St William*, pp. 19–20.
186 D. Stocker, 'The Mystery of the Shrines of St Hugh', *St Hugh of Lincoln: Lectures*

enclosed a mere eight by four foot area and were in an off-centre position it is unlikely that they were the remains of a grate about a major shrine. D. Stocker has proposed that the seventeenth-century reports were mistaken:

> It seems more reasonable to suggest that both Sanderson and Fuller, and probably the cathedral tradition on which they were drawing, had confused the site of the shrine of the bishop between 1280 and 1540 with the site where the contents of the feretory had been reburied after the shrine's destruction. When Sanderson said that the shrine had occupied the position marked by the irons, he was using the word 'shrine' loosely; what he should have said, perhaps, was that they marked the saint's most recent grave.[187]

Stocker further suggests that the irons were the remains of a grill erected around St Hugh's new grave in the sixteenth century in order to mark it in a non-idolatrous fashion.

Stocker dismisses the possibility that the shrine could have been destroyed without leaving a record, and suggests that the relics sat on a very different type of structure, one whose role as a shrine base could have been forgotten over time: 'The practice of elevating the feretory behind the high altar so that it could be seen from the west was not at all uncommon in England, and the placing of the feretory on top of the reredos is no more than a logical extension of this well-known pattern.'[188] He goes on to point out that the shrine of Little Saint Hugh, in the south aisle of Lincoln cathedral, has similarities with the shrine built for the Crown of Thorns in the Ste Chapelle, and suggests that the royal interest in the building of the Angel Chapel makes it likely that the new shrine adopted the 'peculiar, but very prestigious, French model'. In accordance with this theory, he gives a reconstruction of the shrine including a spire rising from a stonework canopy over the central part of the reredos.[189] This theory cannot be true.

The Lincoln reredos was removed by Essex in 1769, leaving only three pieces of evidence as to its nature. A plan published in 1730 shows a ten foot wide screen with a spiral staircase in the northern end.[190] This roughly matches a description by Sanderson of 1641: 'In the east part of the choir stood the altar. A door into the room there at each end. Upon the room stood the tabernacle. Below many closets in the wall.'[191] Thus, the only thing known about the upper part of the reredos is that a tabernacle stood there. The term 'tabernacle' was used in the middle ages

---

delivered at Oxford and Lincoln to celebrate the eighth centenary of St Hugh's Consecration as Bishop of Lincoln, ed. H. Mayr-Harting (Oxford, 1987), p. 91; F. Peck, Desiderata Curiosa (London, 1779), p. 317. The position is marked in the plan by B. Willis, A Survey of the Cathedrals of Lincoln, Ely, Oxford and Peterborough (London, 1730), between pp. 2 and 3. See plate 7.

187 Stocker, 'Mystery of the Shrines', p. 95.
188 Stocker, 'Mystery of the Shrines', pp. 96, 99.
189 Stocker, 'Mystery of the Shrines', p. 102.
190 Willis, Survey of Lincoln, etc., between pp. 2 and 3.
191 R. Sanderson, Lincoln Cathedral: an Exact Copy of All the Ancient Monumental Inscriptions there, as they stood in 1641 (London, 1851), p. 11.

to refer either to open structures with fixed, architectural canopies or, more specifically, to a special place where the sacrament was kept. The financial accounts of the shrine of St Hugh show that it had a movable cover suspended by a cord and lifted by means of a wheel above the vault.[192] The action of this cover made any stone tabernacle work over the shrine impossible. The Lincoln tabernacle was probably a smaller structure attached high on the front of the reredos and intended to hold the sacrament, an arrangement that became popular in France in the thirteenth century and was officially recommended, if less popular, in England.[193] A tabernacle for this purpose above the high altar at York was bequeathed 100s. in 1448.[194] The last piece of evidence produced by Stocker derives from the antiquary John Leland. In Lincoln some time between 1534 and 1543, Leland claimed that 'S. Hughe liethe in the body of the est parte of the chirche above the highe altare.'[195] However, the word 'above' was synonymous with 'east' in ancient parlance when in reference to church topography, and thus the shrine would have been described as above the high altar in any event (see Chapter Three). Besides the lack of English precedent or evidence in favour of a position on the reredos (with the exception of St Ethelbert mentioned above), there is no mention of the shrine in references to the reredos or vice versa. In 1482, for example, John Waltham, the keeper of the high altar, was allotted his commons for activity concerning the 'reredos of the high altar', with nothing said about the shrine.[196] Conversely, the shrine base was 'a marble structure that is fitting in construction and height', which does not seem to describe a reredos.[197]

A position for the shrine on the Lincoln reredos loft would have created insuperable problems of space. We know that the body (minus the head) fitted whole into the feretrum, which therefore must have been about five feet long internally. The lead coffin, wooden walls, jewelled relief work and room for the cover would have made the external dimensions much greater. The feretrum rested on a base of some sort, and had an altar which was presumably on one end. All this would have fitted on the ten foot wide loft only with difficulty. In 1308 the shrine received an iron trellis that, besides being highly unusual on a loft,

192 It was made or significantly repaired in 1360 for £17 1s.: LCA, D&C Bj/5/16/1, f. 45. A 1446 example of a regular expense was 'to William Muskam for supervising the wheel that is situated above the vault of the church from which hangs the shrine of St Hugh – 6d.' (domino Willielmo Muskam pro supervisione Rote existente supra Doma ecclesie oer quam pendet fferetrum Sancti Hugonis – 6d.): *ibid.*, f. 131.

193 G. Dix, *A Detection of Aumbries* (Westminster, 1942), pp. 36–42. Suspended pyxes were a more common receptacle for the sacrament in England.

194 From the will of Thomas Morton: J. Browne, *The History of the Metropolitanical Church of St Peter, York* (2 vols, London, 1847), p. 238.

195 J. Leland, *The Itinerary of John Leland in or about the Years 1535–1543*, ed. L. Toulmin-Smith (London, 1907), part XI, p. 122; Stocker, 'Mystery of the Shrines', pp. 93–4.

196 'Reredose Magni Altaris': D.M. Williamson [Owen], *Lincoln Muniments*, Lincoln Minster Pamphlets no. 8 (Lincoln, 1956), p. 25.

197 'Fabricam marmoream decentis structuræ altitudinisque': *'Translatio Sancti Hugonis'*, p. 193.

would have reduced the space.[198] Furthermore, devotees and attendants alike seeking access to the shrine would have had to pass the high altar, enter the door in the reredos, go through the room, mount the spiral staircase, then move along the loft. There access to the south side of the shrine would have been blocked.

Stocker acknowledged this difficulty and assumed that the head shrine was used as a source of direct contact. Yet, the general impression given by the shrine accounts is that pilgrims had access to the shrine. For example, offering money was collected by the shrine custodian and not the chaplain of the tomb.[199] Other facts suggest a larger shrine with more room. The mass celebrated at the shrine ('ad feretrum') on St Hugh's day 1360 involved two chaplains, a deacon and sub deacon, six or more singers, and two servants with censers.[200] It is unlikely that the fifteen or more celebrants were on the loft of the reredos, or that some remained below at the high altar. All is clear if the shrine was on the pavement behind the reredos. The order in which the cathedral was censed confirms this. The thurifers began in the choir:

> And then, when the high altar has been censed, they will kiss the middle of the altar. Next they should cense the tomb of Remigius. And this done they should say together in unison the psalm *The Magnificat*. And they should cense the vicinity of the altar where they celebrate the mass of the blessed Mary in the hour of prime. Next, they should cense the tomb of St Hugh, and then divide themselves, one censing on the south side, the other on the north side.[201]

The most logical interpretation is that first the area around the high altar was censed (including the tomb of Remigius, which is still directly north of the original site of the high altar), then the censers left the presbytery, presumably through the north door and aisle, and entered the Angel Choir (the site of the mass of St Mary). They next censed the 'tomb' of St Hugh, which in this case probably refers to the shrine rather than an empty tomb, since no separate tomb is known of for Lincoln at this time. A ground-level shrine of Hugh in the retrochoir would be easily accessible through doors in the fencing of the feretory chapel. A shrine on the reredos, however, necessitated a return to the area of the high altar, because it was only from there that the spiral staircase in the reredos could be approached.

---

[198] Venables, 'The Shrine and Head of St Hugh', p. 61, from Lincoln Chapter Acts 1308, f. 15.

[199] LCA, D&C, Bj/5/16/1, f. 1

[200] LCA, D&C, Bj/5/16/1, f. 45. This was an annual event.

[201] 'Vnde magno altari incensato medietatem osculabuntur altaris. Deinde incensent tumbam sancti remigij. Et hoc facto dicant insimul in eundo psalmum *Magnificat*. Et incensent ambo altare vbi celebratur missa beate marie hora prime. Deinde tumbam sancti hugonis et tunc diuident se vno incensante ex parte australi et altero ex parte boriali': *Liber Niger*, being *Statutes of Lincoln Cathedral*, vol. 1, eds H. Bradshaw and C. Wordsworth (Cambridge, 1892), p. 368. The dating of parts of the *Liber Niger*, which underwent continuous development, is complex. The order of censing was probably first written down in the episcopate of Richard de Gravesend (1258–79), when the Angel Choir was being planned, and transcribed into the *Liber Niger* in about 1400, long after it was built (*ibid.*, pp. 68–9). It was therefore undoubtably applicable to the post-1280 arrangement.

*

There was considerable continuity in the history of the physical aspect of greater shrines in England. Feretra remained house-shaped throughout the middle ages, changing relatively little. Shrine bases underwent a gradual evolution from the table and *foramina* shrines of the Norman period to solid bases with niches starting in the thirteenth century. The development was continually upward, with shrines becoming ever taller. More unusual bases, such as reredoses or beams, were left to lesser shrines. It was the greater shrine's popularity that made the standard arrangement, which was well suited to the reception of pilgrims, so common. In most cases the saint's head was removed and separately enshrined, and the empty tomb also venerated, creating sub-centres of the saint's cult which were in essence extensions of the main shrine. The combination of these sub-shrines with a fully furnished feretory chapel meant that a shrine could take up a significant proportion of a cathedral's ritual space. It is the relationship between shrines and their architectural settings that occupies the next chapter.

3

The Architectural Setting

Many historians have emphasised the importance of relics and the cult of saints for medieval ecclesiastical architecture. F. Bond went so far as to suggest that all parts of a greater church were subordinate to the shrine: the nave existed primarily to provide shelter and points of assembly for pilgrims while the aisles gave them access to the shrines without disturbing the *opus dei* in the choir or presbytery.[1] If this view is correct, then the study of saints' shrines is virtually a pre-requisite for medieval architectural history. However, in the only general survey of post-Conquest shrine structures made in recent years, N. Coldstream noted that 'The subject of shrines is large and complicated. The main problem, which is concerned with how the English developed the arrangements of the east ends of their churches, has never been satisfactorily worked out.'[2]

We are now well beyond the pioneering period of medieval architectural history. Scholarship on the ancient arrangements of individual cathedrals has passed the point where a general re-assessment of the place of shrines within churches is possible. In this chapter I will attempt to describe and critically examine the architectural setting of shrines, and in particular the relationship between medieval English shrines and the crypts, high altars and eastern terminations of cathedrals. I will also examine the question of the visibility of shrines from various parts of the church.

The position of the shrine

While there was no set rule for the location of a shrine, some positions were more popular than others. This was partly due to practical considerations such as accessibility, space and quiet. In the late twelfth century Thomas of Monmouth described the final location of the shrine-tomb of St William of Norwich 'as a fitting spot for the holy martyr as being large, as situated in a quiet place outside the processional path, and as being consecrated to the name of the Martyrs'.[3] According to one source, the shrine of St Oswin at Tynemouth was set up in a place convenient for the circulation of pilgrims, 'so that those approaching could

1   Bond, *English Church Architecture*, p. 83.
2   Coldstream, 'Shrine Bases', p. 15.
3   Thomas of Monmouth, *Life of St William*, p. 221.

more quietly, freely and spaciously continue their devotions around the shrine'.[4] Shrine position was also influenced by symbolism, prestige and historical significance. The shrine chapel at Canterbury, for example, was built over the site of St Thomas's tomb in the crypt and in the supposed spot where he said his first mass.[5]

Perhaps the best way to begin looking at the location of shrines is to analyse their structural relationship to the high altar. The association between relics and altars was close from very early times, with the practice of installing relics in a special cavity in or under the altar slab already an old custom when it was confirmed by canon law at the second Council of Nicaea in 787 and the councils at Carthage in 801 and 813.[6] This use of relics in the consecration of altars helped to establish their central position in medieval religion.[7]

In England several factors prevented the actual physical combination of major shrines and high altars. Almost all English churches already had a functional high altar, complete with enclosed relics, when they came into possession of a local saint's body. There would be no real need to replace the existing relics with those of the saint. Furthermore, the combination of high altar and shrine would concentrate and thus reduce the number of holy sites within the church, forcing pilgrims to congregate inconveniently around the high altar. The only known English examples of major relics in altars are from Canterbury, but except for St Wilfrid, whose relics were enclosed 'in the high altar' in 948, the post-Conquest examples are limited to lesser saints in minor altars. Even Wilfrid's relics were moved into an independent shrine after the 1067 fire.[8] The practical obstacles, and the lack of concrete examples, makes it, as Batsford and Fry concluded, 'safe to assume that few high altars were ever built around relics'.[9] However, there is a theory that the structure and location of greater shrines evolved from the practice, of which there are many illustrations and descriptions, of displaying portable reliquaries on the

4   'Ut advenientes quietius, liberius, capacius possent circa martyrem suas devociones continuare': Walsingham, *Gesta Abbatum*, vol. 2, pp. 379–80.
5   Gervase of Canterbury, *Chronicle*, vol. 1, p. 21.
6   D. Sox, *Relics and Shrines* (London, 1985) p. 11; Rollason, *Saints and Relics*, pp. 5, 25; Wilson, *Shrines of St William*, p. 5. This tradition, while no longer required by canon law, is still preserved. Canon 1237 §2 states: 'The ancient tradition of keeping the relics of martyrs and other saints under a fixed altar is to be preserved according to the norms given in the liturgical books': *Code of Canon Law, Latin-English Edition*, ed. Canon Law Soc. of America (Washington, 1983), p. 443. Indeed, the technical description of an altar in canon law remains 'a tomb containing the relics of saints': Sox, *Relics and Shrines*, p. 8.
7   See C.R. Cheney, 'Church Building in the middle ages', *Bulletin of the John Rylands Library*, vol. 34 (1951–2), pp. 25–26.
8   Eadmer, 'Opuscula', pp. 364–5; Eadmer, *Vita Wilfride*, in *Historians of the Church of York*, vol. 1, pp. 225–6; Among several examples, Bregwyn was 'In the altar of St Gregory in the south part of the choir' (in altari sancti Gregorii ex australi parte chori) and Archbishop Living 'In the altar of St Martin in the north part of the choir' (in altari Sancti Martini ex boriali parte chori): Hope and Legg, *Inventories of Christchurch*, p. 40. See also Gervase of Canterbury, *Chronicle*, vol. 1, p. 24.
9   H. Batsford and C. Fry, *The Greater English Church of the middle ages* (2nd edn, London, 1943–4), p. 105.

altar table.[10] This argument supposes that while minor shrines could be placed on the altar-top, major shrines would have completely covered the altar surface and so were placed immediately behind, with the west end of the shrine forming a sort of retable (backdrop) for the high altar. The physical connection between the two was severed when churches were extended towards the east in the twelfth and thirteenth centuries, thus creating space for a free-standing shrine.

Although more likely on the Continent, this development probably did not occur in England. Reliquaries seem to have been placed on altars only on special occasions such as the Feast of Relics, since the altar usually needed to be clear for mass. Much confusion has arisen as a result of the words *super* or *supra* being taken literally to mean 'above' or 'on', so that shrines and relics described as *supra altare* are assumed to have been sitting on the top of the altar. As R. Willis pointed out in 1845, *super* used in medieval church descriptions usually meant 'beyond or behind the altar. The Eastern parts of a church were the upper parts, and the western the lower, in the ancient nomenclature.'[11] This usage was also followed in the English language at least into the eighteenth century.[12]

The first Norman shrines were inevitably in close proximity to the high altar since Romanesque churches had very little space behind the latter, yet evidence for major post-Conquest shrines actually attached to the high altar is extremely rare. There is only one possible example: the shrine of St Alban which in the late twelfth century appears to have been placed 'above the high altar, set before the celebrant side, so that whoever is celebrating mass over the same altar should have the memorial of the martyr in face and in heart: to that purpose the martyrdom of the same, that is to say his decapitation, is sculpted in the object of vision of the celebrant'.[13] Even this is not a clear example, although if any shrine was attached to a high altar then St Alban was a likely candidate, since the high altar was dedicated primarily to him and doubled as his shrine altar. A possible further example is the shrine of St Oswin at Tynemouth, explicitly stated to have been 'connected (*connexum*)' to the high altar and not separated until freer movement around the shrine was needed in 1345.[14] However, Oswin's shrine

---

10 For an example of this theory see E. Bishop, 'On the History of the Christian Altar', *Downside Rev.*, vol. 5, no. 2 (1905), pp. 162–70. An illuminated initial 'P' in a Westminster Missal shows an altar on which are five reliquaries: a head, two hands and two which resemble chalices with covers: Perkins, *Westminster Abbey*, vol. 1, pl. opposite p. 42.

11 Willis, *Architectural History of Canterbury*, p.16 n.M.

12 For example, Dugdale referred to Erkenwald's shrine 'above the high altar', meaning beyond the reredos: Dugdale, *St Paul's*, p. 5.

13 'Supra majus altare, contra frontem celebrantis collocavit, ut in facie et in corde habeat quilibet celebrans Missam super idem altare Martyris memorium: idcirco in objectu visus celebrantis, Martyrium ejusdem, scilicet decollatio, figuratum': Walsingham, *Gesta Abbatum*, vol. 1, p. 189. It is possible that this does not refer to the shrine but to a 'front' made for the high altar at the same time, since the object described here bore an image of the martyrdom of St Alban while a Virgin and Child was on the side of the shrine facing west.

14 From an account of the translation of St Oswin in that year. 'And before all, caring for the decorum of the house of God, the shrine of the Saint, King and Martyr Oswin, connected to the high altar, he moved from its place, and replaced it where it magnificently stands' (Et

appears to have had its own altar attached to its west end before 1345.[15] This must have separated the shrine from the high altar, suggesting that the 'connection' was due to proximity alone.

The shrine of St Erkenwald at St Paul's is the only post-Conquest cathedral shrine claimed to have been connected to a high altar.[16] This is primarily the result of an engraving and plan made in 1657 showing what is supposedly Erkenwald's shrine abutting the back of the reredos.[17] However, because it was destroyed in about 1540 the object shown in the engraving and plan cannot have been the original shrine.[18] A 1245 inventory appears to describe the shrines of Erkenwald and Mellitus when it says 'these two are side-by-side with the high altar'.[19] Its proximity to the high altar did not prevent it having an altar of its own, as in 1211 Ralph de Cornehill spent 12d. on lights at an altar of St Erkenwald.[20] After the shrine was moved in 1326 the route prescribed for those censing the church during the *Magnificat* proves that the shrine continued to possess its own altar and that censors could move all the way around it. Together these facts seem to show that before Erkenwald's translation in 1326 his shrine flanked the high altar and afterward was some distance behind. At both times the shrine was not connected to the high altar or reredos.[21]

The physical abutment of major shrine and high altar had certain practical disadvantages. In greater churches it would have hindered movement, both of the priest circumambulating the high altar in order to asperse it from all sides and of pilgrims gathering around the shrine.[22] Furthermore, it made a separate shrine altar (which was highly desirable from a devotional perspective) impossible. The absence of concrete examples in cathedrals, and occasional evidence to the contrary, makes it unlikely that their shrines and high altars were commonly attached in post-Conquest England, although the spatial relationship was no doubt closer in the eleventh and twelfth centuries than it was in the fourteenth and fifteenth.

If the shrine was not connected to the high altar, where was it? The location of free-standing shrines in Anglo-Saxon churches was far from uniform, positions in

ante omnia, decorum domus Dei cupiens, feretrum Sancti Regis et Martyris Oswini, altari majori connexum, dimovit a loco, et in loco quo modo stat fecit magnifice collocari): Walsingham, *Gesta Abbatum*, vol. 2, pp. 379–80.

[15] A priest, hoping for a miracle, took up a position 'ante Sancti altare', from which he moved to the eastern end of the shrine where there was an image of the saint. From the twelfth-century *Vita Oswini*, p. 33.

[16] *Miracula Erkenwaldi*, p. 64.

[17] Dugdale, *St Paul's*, p. 114, plan between pp. 134–5. Dugdale states that it is based on a fifteenth-century design for the railings around the shrine (p. 24).

[18] In his plan Cook places the post-1326 shrine in the usual position away from the reredos and aligned east-west: Cook, *Old St Paul's*, p. 46.

[19] 'Haec duo sunt collateralia in magno altari': 'Two Inventories of St Paul's', p. 470.

[20] *Early Charters of the Cathedral Church of St. Paul, London*, ed. M. Gibbs (Camden Soc., 3rd ser., vol. 58, 1939), p. 187.

[21] *Registrum Statutorum et Consuetudinum Ecclesiae Cathedralis Sancti Pauli Londinensis*, ed. W.S. Simpson (London, 1873), pp. 81–2.

[22] Bond, *English Church Architecture*, vol. 1, pp. 29–30.

the nave, choir or even chapels beyond the walls of the church being possible.[23] Nevertheless, certain arrangements were becoming dominant. In the time of Bede the place to the south of an altar had the highest status and was the most common for major shrines. A position east of the altar, normal in Gaul by the seventh century, may have been neglected in England because the altar itself was often against or near the east wall.[24] By the Norman period, however, the position of sainted relics in English churches was less varied. As we have seen, most translations resulted in the shrine being situated in the east end, and especially the sanctuary, which was the holiest and most secure part of the church. When trying to locate a shrine more precisely, it is usually possible to describe a shrine's position through reference to its spatial relationship with the high altar: beside, in front or behind.

In the vast majority of post-Conquest cases the shrine was behind the altar. 'As to the position which the Feretory of the great local saint should occupy, there could be little doubt. Of the whole church the vicinity of the High altar was the most sacred, and it was near this that the Saint's chapel was built; not in front of it but behind.'[25] When the new Norman cathedrals were built, eight had major shrines. Of these, five (Ely, Winchester, Durham, London and Lichfield) had their main shrine behind the high altar. Many shrines in churches other than cathedrals were also placed behind the high altar. An extreme example of this preference, St Augustine's Abbey at Canterbury, has already been mentioned. The Norman configuration there had the shrine of St Augustine in the axial chapel flanked by the shrines of Sts Lawrence and Mellitus, while the ambulatory and eastern chapels held Sts Justus, Deusdedit, Honorius, Theodore, Adrian and Mildrid. A late medieval manuscript shows the same layout but includes more shrines in the western part of the ambulatory, namely Sts Nothelm and Lambert in the north, Sts Brihtwold and Tatwine in the south, and St Ethelbert directly behind the high altar on the reredos.[26] Obviously clerics were willing to put up with considerable crowding of their ritual space in order to place shrines east of the high altar.

The problem of precedence arising when a church possessed two saints of nearly equal virtue could be elegantly solved by erecting shrines on either side of the presbytery, usually in front of and flanking the high altar. Sts Dunstan and Alphege are good examples of this. They are first described in the eleventh-century manual for the instruction of novices (the *Instructio Noviciorum*), wherein novices entering the choir of Christ Church in the morning were instructed to kneel consecutively before the high altar, the altars of Alphege a little to the left ('*modicum versus sinistrum*'), and the altar of Dunstan on the right.[27] Although

---

[23] See Biddle, 'Architecture and the Cult of Saints', esp. pp. 11–13.

[24] C.A.R. Radford, 'Two Scottish Shrines: Jedburgh and St. Andrews', *Arch. J.*, vol. 112 (1956), p. 57.

[25] Bond, *English Church Architecture*, vol. 1, pp. 90–1.

[26] See plate in R.D.H. Gem, 'The Significance of the 11th-century Rebuilding of Christ Church and St. Augustine's, Canterbury, in the Development of Romanesque Architecture', in *Medieval Art and Architecture at Canterbury before 1220 (BAACT*, vol. 5, 1982), p. 8.

[27] *Decreta Lanfranci: Lanfranc's Monastic Constitutions*, ed. D. Knowles (London, 1951),

these shrines were removed because of the fire of 1174, they were returned in 1180 and were still described as being on the north and south sides of the high altar in a sixteenth-century list.[28] Their exact position on the east-west axis is not certain. Archbishop Winchelsey's statutes of 1298 define the two altars of Alphege and Dunstan as the 'nearer altars', suggesting that they were somewhat to the west of the high altar.[29] However, during the enthronement ceremony of Stafford in 1443 the archbishop reached the throne by passing 'by the high altar and the altar of St Alphege', and returned 'between the high altar and the altar of St Dunstan'.[30] For Stafford to be described as passing between the saints' altars and the high altar these sites could not have been separated by any great distance. Therefore the shrines themselves were probably in line with the high altar, making their altars further west and thus 'nearer' to observers in the choir.

There are other examples of flanking shrines. In the same cathedral, Sts Wilfrid and Odo were moved to the north and south of the Corona altar after the completion of the Trinity Chapel.[31] At Glastonbury, St Patrick was to the right of the high altar and St Indract to the left.[32] In 1302 the archbishop of Canterbury wrote that in a recent visitation to Worcester he found an offensive tomb which the bishop of Worcester had erected for himself close to the great altar and 'above' the site of the shrine of St Oswald, thereby blocking light to the high altar and occupying the place where the sedilia ought to have been.[33] Oswald's shrine must therefore have been to the south and west of the high altar. Because King John was described as buried between Oswald and Wulfstan, the latter was probably in the analogous position to the north.[34] By the late fourteenth century there was a beam for the shrines, for which forty wooden discs were bought in 1390/1 to catch wax dripping from candles.[35] The two shrines must still have been aligned for one beam to serve for both. If they were close enough to the high altar then this beam may have doubled as the beam for it too.

p. 137. This work is known from a manuscript of the end of the thirteenth century, but is based on Lanfranc's late eleventh-century Constitutions.

[28] Gervase of Canterbury, *Chronicle*, p. 22; Hope and Legg, *Inventories of Christchurch*, p. 40.

[29] 'At the two nearer altars, that is to say of Sts Dunstan and Alphege' (Duobus altaribus vicinioribus, videlicet sanctorum Dunstani et Alphegi): *Concilia*, vol. 2, p. 248.

[30] Stone, *Chronicle*, p. 34; According to Willis, the shrines were on the same platform as the high altar but slightly to the west: Willis, *Architectural History of Canterbury*, p. 102. More elaborate sections of the screen around the choir have been incorrectly claimed as part of the enclosures for the shrines. See discussions in Ramsay and Sparks, 'The Cult of St Dunstan at Christ Church', pp. 317–18.

[31] Steps under the windows still mark their places: Hope and Legg, *Inventories of Christchurch*, pp. 34–5.

[32] J.P. Carley, *Glastonbury Abbey: The Holy House at the Head of the Moors Adventurous* (Woodbridge, 1988), pp. 103–8.

[33] Wilson, 'John de Wyke, Prior of Worcester, 1301–17. Some Glimpses of the Early Years of his Priorate from the "Liber Albus" ', *Ass. Architectural Socs Reports and Papers*, vol. 34, pt 1 (1917), p. 141.

[34] See Gem, 'Wulfstan II and Worcester', p. 27; see also plate 8.

[35] WCA, MS C.457.

A single shrine (as opposed to two flanking shrines) could also be positioned beside an altar. The third translation of William of Norwich was from the chapter house to a place south of the high altar, and at about the same time St Erkenwald appeared in a vision giving directions to his temporary shrine: 'my sepulchre is on the right side of the altar of St Faith, virgin and martyr'.[36] The great shrine of St Chad may have been removed by Bishop Roger de Norburgh (1322–59) to a sepulchre south of the high altar.[37] The body of St Neot, Abbot and Confessor, was given to Crowland, 'and they placed it honourably in the northern part beside the altar of Saint Mary mother of God'.[38]

On the rare occasions when major shrines were not placed near the high altar the transepts could be used. William of Perth's tomb in Rochester cathedral, if not his shrine, was almost certainly in the middle of the north transept otherwise known as St William's Chapel, perhaps because the shrine of St Paulinus held the spot behind the high altar.[39] The base of the first shrine of St Thomas Cantilupe still remains in the north transept at Hereford, from whence he was later promoted to the Lady Chapel. A more novel but temporary placement was that of Sts Bregwin, Wilfrid and several others on the triforium level terminal bridges of Lanfranc's transepts at Canterbury.[40]

An abundance of shrines created problems of spacing which resulted in some shrines being relegated to places of lesser dignity. Glastonbury possessed major shrines for more than twelve saints, and these were placed throughout the quire.[41] Winchester held numerous relics of uncanonised but holy kings which, along with the ancient bishops that had been translated from the old church, were moved into lead caskets placed around the apse in 1158.[42] These were replaced in the early sixteenth century with wooden caskets set above the screens to each side of the presbytery, four of which can be seen today along with two added in 1661 to

---

36   Thomas of Monmouth, *Life of St William*, p. 221; *Miracula Erkenwaldi*, p. 159.

37   A.R. Dufty, 'Lichfield Cathedral', *Arch. J.*, vol. 120 (1963), p. 294.

38   'Et iuxta altare sanctæ Dei genitricis Mariæ in aquilonali parte honorabiliter collocauerunt': Orderic Vitalis, *The Ecclesiastical History of Orderic Vitalis*, ed. M. Chibnall (Oxford, 1969), vol. 2, p. 342.

39   'In that same year died Walter Merton, bishop of Rochester, and was buried honourably in that same church in the north part next to the tomb of St William' (Eodem anno [1278] obiit Walterus de Mertone, episcopus Roffensis, et sepultus est honorifice in ecclesia eadem in parte boriali juxta sepulchrum sancti Willelmi): *Flores Historiarum*, ed. H.R. Luard (RS, vol. 95, 1890).

40   Eadmer, 'Eadmer's Life of Bregwine, Archbishop of Canterbury, 761–764', ed. B.W. Scholtz, *Traditio*, vol. 22 (1966), pp. 145, 147; Willis, *Architectural History of Canterbury*, pp. 16–17; A.W. Klukas, 'The Architectural Implications of the *Decreta Lanfranci*', in *Anglo-Norman Studies*, ed. R.A. Brown (Woodbridge, 1984), vol. 6, p. 149; Gem, 'Significance of the 11th-century Rebuilding of Christ Church and St Augustine's', p. 2.

41   Carley, *Glastonbury Abbey*, p. 121. See William of Malmesbury, *The Chronicle of Glastonbury Abbey*, ed. J.P. Carley (Woodbridge, 1985), *passim*.

42   These kings were Kinegilsus, Kinewaldus, Kinewophus, Egburtus, Ethelwolphus, Edredus, Canute and Hardecanute: Crook, 'Romanesque Winchester', p. 19; *Anglia Sacra*, ed. H. Wharton (London, 1691), vol. 1, p. 194.

replace those lost in the civil war.[43] In summary, it can be said that the position of the high altar was favoured for shrines, but other locales and altars could also be used, especially for lesser shrines and relics or when space became limited.

It has often been asserted that the preferred position of early shrines was in the crypt.[44] The late Roman practice of building churches over the pre-existing tombs of martyrs resulted on the Continent in a continuing relationship between the crypt and the tomb. The reconversion of England in the seventh century, however, produced a situation that was different in two important ways. Firstly, because churches were built shortly after conversion they predated almost all domestic saints. Secondly, the canon law requiring saints' bodies to be left *in situ* had lost its force by the seventh century, so that it was possible to translate relics from their first site of burial into new churches. As a result the great majority of early English saints were either buried in or quickly translated to a church, and there is no solid evidence for the existence of shrines in early Anglo-Saxon crypts.[45]

While the structure of both churches and shrines from the ninth through the eleventh centuries was diverse, only two of the cathedrals holding remains of Anglo-Saxon saints have any evidence of major crypt shrines at the time of the Conquest. The Anglo-Saxon crypt at Canterbury was expressly modelled upon the *confessio* of St Peter's, and so had the plan of a true shrine crypt. However, the only pre-Conquest relic known to be in that crypt was the head of St Furseus, and that was apparently placed inside the main crypt altar.[46] In any case, the arrangement was changed after the fire of 1067. In the other instance, relics of St Swithun were discovered 'under the altar' at Winchester.[47] However, because Swithun's main shrine was in the nave area in the eleventh century these were probably lesser relics used to consecrate the altar. Certainly, they had been forgotten and were not used as a shrine by the time the old church was demolished. Thus, there is no evidence that post-Conquest English churches inherited a tradition of having shrines in crypts.

After the Conquest all English cathedrals were rebuilt. While crypts became prominent features they were not used for the cult of relics. The Norman

---

[43] G.H. Blore, *Notes on the Monuments of Winchester Cathedral* (Winchester, 1935), p. 14. See plate 16.

[44] 'The bodies of saints were first interred in crypts, as we have seen with Becket at Canterbury': Batsford and Fry, *Greater English Church*, p. 60; the crypt's purpose 'was for the burial of distinguished ecclesiastics, who upon their decease rose rapidly to the status of saints': F.H. Crossley, *English Church Design 1040–1540 A.D.* (London, 1945), p. 85. Other examples abound.

[45] Rollason, *Saints and Relics*, esp. pp. 34, 41, 49, 54; see also C. Thomas, *Bede, Archaeology, and the Cult of Relics* (Jarrow, 1973), p. 8.

[46] 'In imitation of the church of the blessed Peter, chief of the apostles' (Ad imitationem aecclesiae beati apostorum principis Petri): Eadmer, 'Opuscula', p. 365. It has occasionally been argued that the shrine of St Dunstan was accessible from the eleventh-century crypt (for example by Woodman, *Architectural History of Canterbury Cathedral*, pp. 18–20), based on a particular interpretation of Eadmer.

[47] 'sub altari veteris monasterii': *Annales de Wintonia*, p. 38; R.N. Quirk, 'Winchester Cathedral in the Tenth Century', *Arch. J.*, vol. 114 (1957), pp. 42–3, 56–7.

undercrofts never followed the typical plan of a shrine crypt (*martyrium* or *confessio*), but rather conformed in plan to the presbytery above. Sometimes the absence of shrines from crypts is striking. When the Norman abbot Scotland rebuilt St Augustine's Abbey, Canterbury, shortly after 1073 none of the fourteen or more abbey saints were placed in the new crypt. All were packed into the area east of the high altar even though it became severely crowded as a result.[48] Nevertheless, it has often been thought that Anglo-Norman shrines were generally found in crypts. According to F. Bond, for example, 'In the end, probably because the pilgrims to the more noted shrines, e.g. to that of St Thomas the Martyr at Canterbury, passed beyond what even the very largest crypts could contain, the more important shrines were removed from the crypt and placed on the pavement of the presbytery.'[49]

There are several reasons why the famous siting of the relics of St Thomas, in the crypt at Canterbury from 1170 to 1220, is a misleading example. The Canterbury monks found themselves with the body of an obvious martyr and enemy of the king. Their motives for placing the body in the undercroft were explicitly stated: 'The fierce threats of Becket's enemies induced the monks to carry his body, in haste, from the High Altar down to the remotest chapel of the crypt, for safety, within twelve hours after the murder.'[50] The threat to the body became so great that it was hidden for a time behind the altar of St Mary.[51] The original placement in the crypt was thus due to fear and expedience, not fitting and proper reverence.

Thomas's subterranean tomb was not, strictly speaking, a shrine. It functioned as a centre of devotion and pilgrimage, but there had been no elevation, nor was there a reliquary chest. It would have been unseemly (and in this case politically dangerous) to create a shrine without waiting for canonisation or miracles. Indeed, the monument in the crypt was consistently referred to as a 'tomb'. When the political pressure eased,[52] the chapter immediately determined to translate St Thomas to a newly built chapel above the high altar. The new Trinity Chapel was

---

[48] R.U. Potts, 'The Latest Excavations at St. Augustine's Abbey', *Arch. Cant.*, vol. 35 (1921), pp. 118–20. The tombs of several abbots and the remains of three altars were discovered in the crypt during the excavations of 1900–2, but no shrines: Gem, 'Significance of the 11th-century Rebuilding of Christ Church and St. Augustine's', p. 8; T. Tatton-Brown, 'The Buildings and Topography of St Augustine's Abbey, Canterbury', *JBAA*, vol. 144 (1991), pp. 62–6; Goscelin, 'Historia Translationis S. Augustini', pp. 24–5.

[49] F.B. Bond, *Gothic Architecture in England* (London, 1905), pp. 193–4. He gives the example of St Denis translated in 1144. Crossley's theory that the size of Norman crypts was required for the accommodation of pilgrims, but that shrines were moved to ground level over the period 1140–1240 so that all could view them, seems unfounded: Crossley, *Church Design*, pp. 89–90. Cook claimed that the translation above the crypt at Canterbury initiated a fashion: G.H. Cook, *English Monasteries in the Middle Ages* (London, 1961), p. 129.

[50] *Materials for a History of Becket*, vol. 5, pp. 521–2; W.A.S. Robertson, 'The Crypt of Canterbury Cathedral', *Arch. Cant.*, vol. 13 (1880), p. 53.

[51] *Materials for a History of Becket*, vol. 2, pp. 16–17, 77.

[52] The desecration caused by the spilling of blood forced the church to be closed until 1172, in which year 'God worked great miracles for St Thomas the martyr of Canterbury': *Annales de Wigornia*, p. 383.

begun by 1179, and some sort of feretory chapel was almost certainly planned five years earlier by the architect William of Sens.[53] 'In the meantime, a wooden chapel, proper enough for the time and place, was prepared over and round his tomb.'[54] Thus, within four years of Thomas's death and two years after the reopening of the church, steps were being taken to move his relics out of the crypt. It was only because unforeseen conditions prevented an earlier translation that Thomas was allowed to remain in the undercroft until 1220. It is thus clear that Becket's tomb in the Christ Church crypt cannot be considered the archetype of the Anglo-Norman shrine, since its location there was largely unintentional.

There is only one other example of a major saints' shrine in a post-Conquest crypt, and it too is an exception which proves the rule. The shrine of St Erkenwald survived but was made homeless by a fire that destroyed St Paul's in 1087. Bishop Maurice hastily housed Erkenwald in the first part of the new church to be completed, which was the crypt. In 1148, while the construction of the east end of the cathedral was still incomplete, Erkenwald was translated to a place behind the high altar.[55] In this instance there was at first no alternative to the crypt, but when one appeared the shrine was moved at the earliest opportunity. In the cases of both St Erkenwald and St Thomas the crypt was therefore an emergency and temporary location. No other evidence for saints' shrines in post-Conquest cathedral crypts has emerged.[56]

There were many sensible reasons for shunning crypts as shrine locales. They often lacked light, space, and ease of access. Some were prone to inconvenient flooding. The crypt at Canterbury is known to have flooded in 1271 and 1467, causing inconvenience to the tomb there, while the crypt at Winchester still floods every winter.[57] In both places the clergy attempted to raise the floors of their crypts above the high water table.[58] While flooding may have proved a problem, it did

---

53   Gervase of Canterbury, *Chronicle*, vol. 1, p. 26, translated in Willis, *Architectural History of Canterbury*, p. 51; P. Draper, 'William of Sens and the Original Design of the Choir Termination of Canterbury Cathedral 1175–79', *J. of the Soc. of Architectural Historians*, vol. 42 (1983), pp. 245–7.

54   Gervase of Canterbury, *Burning and Repair*, p. 17.

55   *Miracula Erkenwaldi*, p. 128; Paris, *Chronica Majora*, vol. 2, p. 183.

56   There is a very slight possibility that the relics of St Swithun, or some of the lesser Winchester saints, were originally placed in the Norman crypt and only moved behind the high altar in the twelfth century. However, 'It is unlikely that Swithun's relics were ever relegated to the crypt of Walkelin's church, having been so prominently displayed within the body of the old minster; and there is good archaeological and documentary evidence that from the mid twelfth century his remains were normally situated on the platform in the apse hemicycle behind the high altar': Crook, 'Romanesque Winchester', p. 19.

57   C.E. Woodruff, 'The Chapel of Our Lady in the Crypt of Canterbury Cathedral', *Arch. Cant.*, vol. 38 (1926), p. 154; Stone remarked on the inconveniences caused by flooding to shrines in the crypt: Stone, *Chronicle*, p. 102. Concerning Winchester, 'It is inconceivable that the Anglo-Norman builders intended that the crypt should flood annually; the cathedral was probably built at a time when the water happened to be at a low point in a major cyclical variation': Crook, 'Romanesque Winchester', p. 18.

58   At Canterbury a dirt floor (now removed) was installed before the late fourteenth century. Effects of flooding were perhaps felt at Winchester as early as 1200, when de Lucy's Lady

not make crypts useless as pilgrimage sites. The tomb of St Thomas, for example, remained a permanent attraction of the Canterbury undercroft. Perhaps the greatest problem for crypts as shrine sights was that they were symbolically unsuitable. The crypt, by definition subterranean, was too lowly for a shrine.

The purpose of Anglo-Norman crypts is slightly mysterious: 'The construction of these early crypts appears to have been in no instance necessitated by a fall in the ground towards the east, as was the case at the Trinité at Caen, and it can only be supposed that the Anglo-Norman builders designed them either for the multiplication of chapels or for some other definite reason.'[59] Five out of the seven English cathedrals with Norman crypts also possessed major saint shrines in the Norman period. Of the cathedrals without crypts only three out of twelve (Durham, Ely and Lichfield) had prominent shrines. Cathedrals with shrines were therefore more likely to have crypts than those without. But since the Anglo-Normans avoided placing their shrines in the crypt itself, we have to ask what other relationship existed between the two structures. One possibility is that crypts were used to elevate the floor of the shrine along with the presbytery. This theory is supported by the fact that Durham seems to make up for its lack of a crypt by having a high presbytery platform. However, since there is no consistent pattern (some cathedrals with crypts having no shrine and vice versa) this would be a difficult thesis to prove. A stronger possibility is simply that churches with shrines tended to be wealthier and more prestigious than those without, and thus could afford architectural elaborations. Whatever the reason, after 1220 there is no longer any question of major shrines in crypts, although they remained appropriate locations for minor relics, altars and tombs.[60] The crypt's role in saints' cults and shrines in post-Conquest England was therefore minimal.

Shrines and Romanesque architectural plans

While eccentric positions for shrines remained possible, use of the area behind the high altar was the most common. In light of this, what effect did the shrine have on church architecture? In particular, were church plans modified to accommodate the shrine or pilgrims? The eastern projections of the earliest Anglo-Norman churches were of two basic plans: 'triapsidal' or 'periapsidal'. Both types appeared in England almost simultaneously, having been developed in France prior to 1066, and seem to have been distributed equally.[61]

In the triapsidal plan the quire ended in an apse flanked by the apsidal endings

---

Chapel crypt was built with a floor 20–30cm. higher than the main crypt: Woodruff, 'The Chapel of Our Lady, Canterbury', p. 153; Crook, 'Romanesque Winchester', p. 20.

[59] A.W. Clapham, *English Romanesque Architecture After the Conquest* (Oxford, 1934), p. 66.
[60] The fashion for building crypts itself was short lived. They were rarely built after the early twelfth century, with the exception of York and those places where a crypt was structurally necessary: A.W. Clapham, *Romanesque in Western Europe* (Oxford, 1936), pp. 146–7; Clapham, *English Romanesque Architecture After the Conquest*, p. 67.
[61] Clapham, *English Romanesque Architecture After the Conquest*, p. 20.

of the two aisles (fig. 1). If, as often occurred, the transepts also had eastern apses then the plan took on the appearance of five apses in echelon (hence the alternative names of 'apse echelon' and 'parallel apse' for this design). The high altar was invariably on the chord of the main apse, at the far east end of the church. Notable examples include Canterbury (Lanfranc's Cathedral), Old Sarum, Lincoln and Durham.[62]

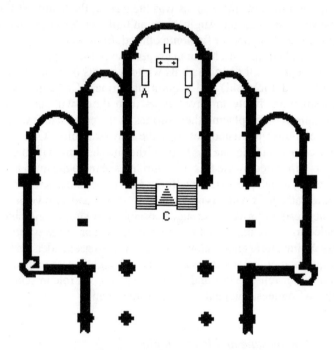

Fig. 1. A Triapsidal plan with elongated transeptual apses, based on Canterbury. The high altar is at H, the stairs to the crypt and presbytery at C, and the proposed site of the shrines of Sts Anselm and Dunstan at A and D.

Because it was the only part of the church east of the high altar, the main apse was the most appropriate place for a major shrine in this design. The apse tended to contain and seclude the shrine and readily gave it the character of an inner sanctum. Yet, because the apse was only a few yards long, it could be very cramped. The apse behind the high altar at Ely, for example, had the shrines of St Etheldreda and her three abbess companions all packed within it. The triapsidal plan also hindered circulation, as pilgrims had to pass through the presbytery to reach the apse. The fact that no English triapsidal quire survived the later middle ages suggests that it proved unsatisfactory in the long term.

The other Romanesque plan differed in one major respect: the aisles were

[62] Clapham, *Romanesque in Western Europe*, pp. 141–3.

curved around the main apse until they joined in a half-circle. This aisle (the ambulatory) separated the apse from the exterior wall and elegantly provided a processional way around and behind the high altar. Three or more radiating chapels were adjoined to the outside of the ambulatory, creating what is called the 'chevet', 'ambulatory', or 'periapsidal' plan (see fig. 2). Some have speculated that the chevet had its origin in the plan of ancient *martyria* crypts, which was preserved when the relics were moved into the choir above.[63] Even if this is true, however, crypt shrines were practically non-existent in England and so the periapsidal plan must have been borrowed directly from Continental examples rather than developed from indigenous crypts.

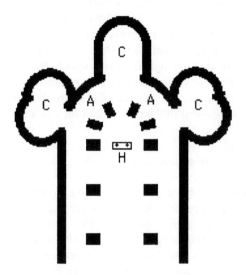

Fig. 2. The chevet plan, based on Norwich.
Radiating chapels are marked C, the
ambulatory A and the high altar H.

The curvature of the ambulatory preserved the apse in the form of a semicircular space between the easternmost arcade piers and the high altar. This space was, in theory, perfectly suitable for a shrine in that it was potentially open to view and access from all sides while it remained the architectural focus of the building. On the other hand, the curving ambulatory made it difficult to align the altars of the radiating chapels towards true east, a consideration about which the English were purists.[64] Nevertheless, the ambulatory plan proved more successful than its competitor. Norwich's periapsidal quire is the only Norman east end to survive in a cathedral, suggesting that the Norwich monks found it adequate in the face of

---

[63] See K.J. Conant, *Carolingian and Romanesque Architecture 800 to 1200* (3rd edn, Harmondworth, 1973), pp. 79–80.
[64] Bond, *English Church Architecture*, p. 128.

later fashions. Even more indicative of its superiority is that both Canterbury and Lincoln were rebuilt from a triapsidal to an ambulatory design in the twelfth century.

This plan, much more so than the triapsidal, is often associated with shrines. R.G. Calkins, for example, stated that 'Indeed, the invention and elaboration of the radial apsidal plan was rooted in the growing cult of relics.'[65] However, the seeming advantages of the ambulatory plan for shrine chapels were ignored by most of the greater shrine churches of England. The distribution of the two types of Norman termination among churches both with and without greater shrines was about equal. In addition, three of the greatest shrine churches (Ely, Durham and Canterbury) were originally triapsidal structures, while the periapsidal churches of Norwich and Lincoln (St Hugh's church) were both planned when they had a notable lack of saints. Three of the greatest periapsidal cathedrals (Worcester, London and Anselm's quire at Canterbury) had their major shrines in the presbytery, making the area behind the high altar irrelevant to the shrine. The only major cathedral shrine known to have been located in a periapsidal axial chapel was that of St Swithun at Winchester. The choice of plan by the first wave of Norman builders was thus independent of the presence or lack of a major shrine.

Shrines and post-Norman square-ended plans

Historians have also claimed that shrines had an important role in the Gothic style of architecture which succeeded the Romanesque in England. From the late twelfth to the fourteenth century one quire after another was torn down in an almost universal desire to beautify and enlarge. Although the new designs came in too many varieties to examine in depth this work, certain basic characteristics fundamentally altered the surroundings of the shrine. This section will examine these to see if any one form of Gothic plan was preferred by cathedrals and churches possessing greater shrines.[66]

The chevet, in an advanced Gothic form, went on to become the standard cathedral termination in France. Those at the abbeys of Canterbury and Westminster, ever open to foreign influence, were later rebuilt as Gothic chevets containing major shrines. This style was also used in several abbeys. Hayles, for example, had five radiating polygonal chapels, two concentric ambulatories and the shrine of the Holy Blood in the central apse.[67] However, despite its architectural advantages and success on the Continent, the Gothic chevet was rare in England, where

---

[65] R.G. Calkins, *Monuments of Medieval Art* (New York, 1979), p. 88.

[66] For an argument against any connection between relics and the Gothic style itself, see P. Frankl, *The Gothic: Literary Sources and Interpretations through Eight Centuries* (Princeton, 1960), pp. 210–11.

[67] W. Bazeley, 'The Abbey of St. Mary, Hayles', *Trans. of the Bristol and Gloucestershire Archaeological Soc.*, vol. 22 (1899), p. 267.

apsidal plans were almost completely replaced by square-ended designs: 'one of the most distinctive creations of English medieval architecture'.[68]

The earliest square ends were created by turning the aisles at right angles behind the high altar, forming a rectangular version of the ambulatory. Eventually the eastern bays, including the ambulatory and eastern chapels, were raised to heights at or approaching the main vault to create what is called a 'retrochoir'. Because the high altar was no longer restricted to the chord of the apse, the space between it and the ambulatory could be increased to two or more bays. An alternative to the retrochoir was an axial chapel, lower and narrower than the quire, projecting past the east wall. These are often called Lady Chapels because their popularity was related to developments in the cult of the Virgin. Most cathedrals had some form of Lady Chapel, retrochoir or both, resulting in much more space behind the high altar than existed in Romanesque plans. If used to accommodate a feretory chapel the spaciousness of both designs gave honour and grandeur to the shrine and provided abundant room for the burial of illustrious dead near the saint.[69]

The retrochoir has been linked to shrines more than any other architectural development. Venables was among the first to hold this opinion: 'In one great church after another we find the same process of eastern extension undertaken, not always exactly in the same mode, but always with the same object, viz., to obtain greater shrine-room.'[70] According to Batsford and Fry, the widespread development was 'due to the growing cult of the veneration of saints and their relics and the wish to attract great concourses of pilgrims and their offerings'.[71] The most recent exponent of this view is P. Draper, who has devoted several scholarly articles to the subject.[72] However, there is reason to believe that this theory is not as well grounded as is generally thought.

The problem of charting the relationship between shrine and architectural plan is much more complex for Gothic than for Romanesque terminations. Building took place over a greater length of time and there were many more factors involved, including quire space, translations of relics, the distance from the high altar to the ambulatory and the presence of eastern transepts and axial chapels. Some retrochoirs were undoubtedly created with the primary object of housing a shrine: the huge Trinity Chapel at Canterbury was expressly built to surround the shrine of St Thomas. Other examples are less clear. Draper believed that the reconstruction at Durham was done on behalf of St Cuthbert because an indulgence stated that the new work in which his body was to lie ought to be equally

---

[68] M.F. Hearn, 'The Rectangular Ambulatory in English Mediaeval Architecture', *J. of the Soc. of Architectural Historians*, vol. 30 (1971), p. 187.

[69] Cheney, 'Church Building in the Middle Ages', p. 25. See plates 9 and 10.

[70] Venables, 'Some Account of the Recent Discovery of the Foundations of the Eastern Termination of Lincoln Minster, as Erected by St. Hugh', *Arch. J.*, vol. 44 (1887), p. 195.

[71] Batsford and Fry, *Greater English Church*, p. 47.

[72] See especially Draper, 'Northwold and Etheldreda', and 'The Sequence and Dating of the Decorated Work at Wells', in *Medieval Art and Architecture at Wells and Glastonbury* (*BAACT*, vol. 4, 1981), pp. 18–29.

saᴄ and honourable.[73] However, the document clearly states that the work was about to be undertaken because the vault was 'now full of fissures and cracks'. It therefore seems likely that the reconstruction was performed primarily to avoid collapse rather than to provide Cuthbert with an improved location, especially since the extension provided little extra room for the shrine.

A saint occasionally appears in dedications or popular names for a retrochoir. In 1331, for example, the walls of Lincoln castle were described as extending from the east gate 'and thence to the eastern end of the shrine [feretri] of St Hugh in the monastery of Lincoln'.[74] This suggests that even the exterior of the Lincoln retrochoir was known as 'the shrine'. While it was natural for the medieval clergy to dedicate their new edifices to their patron, whose shrine was usually the most notable object they contained, it would be rash to conclude from this alone that the shrine was the overriding consideration in the choice of design. Other cathedrals, with equally prominent retrochoirs and shrines, ignored the presence of the saint when referring to the quire. The 1314 dedication of the new retrochoir at London, for example, was referred to as the 'new work of St Mary', ignoring the presence of St Erkenwald.[75]

Of the seventeen main cathedrals all but two were extended after 1200. Of the cathedrals with major shrines, six built at various times (Ely, Lincoln, London, Worcester, Winchester and York) are noted for large retrochoirs, while four (Chichester, Hereford, Lichfield and Salisbury) had two bays of retrochoir plus a large eastern chapel. Two other major cathedrals with shrines did not possess standard retrochoirs: Canterbury had a long Gothic chevet, while problems with difficult terrain were solved at Durham by a transeptual extension. Because both increased space east of the high altar these two examples will be included with retrochoirs in this study. The only two cathedrals without major extensions were Norwich, which was given a somewhat elongated axial chapel but was otherwise left unchanged, and Rochester, which was reconstructed with its high altar jammed into an eastern chapel with only two narrow bays behind it.

There was thus a total of twelve out of the fourteen cathedrals with shrines that also had eastern extensions, and the two which did not were among those possessing lesser shrines. On the face of it, then, there would appear to be a strong connection between retrochoirs and shrines. This appearance is deceptive. Many of the shrines can be shown to have had no direct relationship with the retrochoir of their cathedral. At Hereford, for example, the extension was built long before the cathedral came into possession of the relics of St Thomas. At Winchester, although the retrochoir was begun in 1200, the shrine of St Swithun remained on the site of the old feretory chapel until 1476, and therefore the extension cannot have been planned to hold the shrine.[76]

73 An Indulgence of Bishop Northwold in *Rites of Durham*, pp. 149–50; Draper, 'Northwold and Etheldreda', p. 10.

74 *Calendar of Close Rolls, Edward III, A.D. 1330–33*, ed. H.C.M. Lyte (London, 1898), p. 255.

75 W.R. Lethaby, 'Old St Paul's', *The Builder*, vol. 139 (1930), p. 193.

76 See Crook, 'Swithun of Winchester', pp. 57–68; Crook's findings disprove Draper's

These examples alone ought to prove that retrochoirs were not restricted to shrine chapels. However, a retrochoir without a shrine is often used as proof either that evidence of a shrine is lost or that the retrochoir was planned in the hope of a canonisation which failed to come about. This circular argument has been applied to Worcester, Salisbury, Exeter and Wells. Perhaps the only extended cathedral which has not been linked to a saint is Carlisle. The arguments for a siting of Sts Oswald and Wulfstan in the spacious Worcester retrochoir are based on very slight evidence, there being little information on the position of the shrines in the later middle ages. Draper concluded that the failure of the attempted canonisation of St Osmund in 1228 ruined plans for a translation into the rebuilt cathedral at Salisbury.[77] Yet not only was the area behind the high altar extremely narrow if intended for a shrine, but when Osmund was finally translated he was placed in the Lady Chapel, not the retrochoir.[78] The hoped-for canonisation of Bishop William de Marchia has been pointed to as a motive for the construction of the retrochoir at Wells.[79] The hopes of the medieval canons of Wells will remain a mystery, but they must have known that Bishop William's canonisation was far from certain yet extended their choir regardless.

In fact, less than half of the total number of greater shrines were in retrochoirs. At least eight cathedrals possessing retrochoirs either did not have major relics at the time of construction or did not enshrine them east of the high altar. In addition, the fashion for eastern extension of churches can be explained without recourse to shrines. Other reasons for their construction include the requirements of processional ritual, an increase in devotion to the Virgin Mary, the need for multiple altars for canons and monks in priest's orders, and the simple desire for prestige and space. The liturgical choir, entirely outside the short eastern limb of Romanesque plans, was often moved east of the crossing after reconstruction, thrusting the sanctuary even farther east. The pulpitum, or choir screen, was replaced in the eastern tower arch, leaving the now spacious nave (and in secular churches the crossing) open to the laity. This trend began in 1090–1115 when the monks' stalls at Canterbury were moved from the nave to the quire. 'This was a tremendous innovation, and completely turned the direction of the planning of the English Greater Churches.'[80] It also necessitated the reconstruction of the quire.

A second important reason for the increase in size and elaboration of a church was the steady increase in the number of altars. The first church at Cluny did not have more than two or three altars, but the second had thirteen and the third, built in the eleventh century, had at least twice as many again.[81] 'In the sixth century, when a monastery might expect to have only one priest, and some had none at all,

arguments to the contrary: P. Draper, 'The Retrochoir of Winchester Cathedral: Evidence and Interpretation', *Architectural History*, vol. 21 (1978), pp. 6–12. See plate 9.
77 Draper, 'The Retrochoir of Winchester', pp. 9–10.
78 The evidence for this is outlined in *Ceremonies and Processions of Salisbury*, p. 281.
79 First proposed by Bond, *English Church Architecture*, p. 92, later elaborated by Draper in 'Decorated Work at Wells', pp. 18–29.
80 Bond, *English Church Architecture*, p. 34.
81 Cheney, 'Church Building in the middle ages', p. 27.

so many altars would have collected the dust. The end of the process did not come till the twelfth century, when it came to be assumed that all choir monks would ultimately be priests and daily celebration of mass became the norm.'[82] Because the only available time for a monk to say mass was from nine to eleven in the morning, a community with thirty priests would need at least ten altars.[83] The inflation in the numbers of chantries and private masses must have produced a similar effect in secular cathedrals. Retrochoirs provided space for additional altars to meet this need.

Another ritual requirement was a wide path for processions east of the high altar. Always popular in Britain, processions changed little in form over the centuries while their frequency steadily increased.[84] They generally began at the high altar, exited from the north door of the choir, followed the ambulatory around the east end and thence moved down the south aisle to the nave. While usually limited in width to three abreast, the need for thurifers and bearers of crosses, candles, standards, reliquaries and even silk canopies on poles could make a procession wider.[85] As a result, all cathedrals (with the exception of Rochester) ultimately boasted a wide ambulatory, and this benefited from a retrochoir.

Architecturally, there was nothing to distinguish the shrine sites, since 'an accessible area behind the high altar for a shrine . . . does not amount to an architectural specification'.[86] The ornament surrounding the shrine chapel only rarely differed from that elsewhere. The north transept of Whitchurch Canonicorum in Dorset, built c.1220, is in a more elaborate fashion than the rest of the church, presumably because it housed the shrine of St Candida.[87] The retrochoir at Lincoln is a more certain example: 'In general terms the architect of the Angel Choir may be said to have produced an interior which resembled the exterior of an enlarged metalwork reliquary.'[88] Westminster Abbey has been said to show influence from the Ste Chapelle in Paris, admired by contemporaries for its lavishly decorated interior, also resembling the surface of a reliquary.[89] Nevertheless, the quality of ornamentation is a dubious and problematical method of associating buildings with shrines, especially since reliquaries often imitated architectural designs.

---

[82] C.N.L. Brooke, 'Religious Sentiment and Church Design in the Later Middle Ages', in *Medieval Church and Society* (London, 1971), p. 172.

[83] Klukas, 'The Architectural Implications of the *Decreta Lanfranci*', p. 149.

[84] Batsford and Fry, *Greater English Church*, p. 52. See T. Bailey, *The Processions of Sarum and the Western Church* (Toronto, 1971), pp. 62–76, 100–2; Bond, *English Church Architecture*, p. 100.

[85] As suggested by an interesting series of woodcuts made for sixteenth-century printed editions of the *Use of Sarum*, printed in Bailey, *Processions of Sarum*, pp. 180–93.

[86] C. Wilson, *The Gothic Cathedral* (London, 1990), p. 9.

[87] Prideaux, 'Notes on the Church of St. Candida', p. 137.

[88] Wilson, *Gothic Cathedral*, pp. 9–10; V. Glenn, 'The Sculpture of the Angel Choir at Lincoln', in *Medieval Art and Architecture at Lincoln Cathedral (BAACT*, vol. 8, 1986), p. 102.

[89] R. Branner, 'Westminster Abbey and the French Court Style', *J. of the Soc. of Architectural Historians*, vol. 23 (1964), pp. 16–18.

Cathedrals were rebuilt whether they had a shrine or not. Although often holding the principal spot of honour, the shrine was incorporated into the larger design without disruption. Typical of this is Hereford, where the popular shrine of St Thomas Cantilupe was first in the north transept and then in the Lady Chapel, the latter fulfilling its new function perfectly well despite being erected long before. Even in some of the grander retrochoirs, such as that at St Paul's, the shrine took up no more than one bay behind the high altar. As a result, the feretory chapel was only slightly more imposing in its demands on the architecture than any other chapel. There is thus no need to assume that shrines were entirely responsible for enlargements. The need for a wider processional path and more altars in eastern chapels could in itself account for two or more bays of retrochoir, while prestige and grandeur were equal but unmeasurable reasons for wanting a bigger church. Indeed, the form of a new church probably relied more on available funds and architectural fashion than relics: cathedrals with high, expensive retrochoirs tend to be among the wealthiest. The fact that church wealth and the possession of a shrine also tend to go together obscures the connection between shrines and large architectural projects, whether crypts or retrochoirs. Indeed, the relationship between income from shrines and the scope of new building projects deserves a degree of inquiry that cannot be provided here.

The problem of shrine vistas

The visibility of cathedral shrines from outside the feretory chapel could suggest a great deal about the theological and practical aspects of sanctity, as well as the architectural and social history of cathedrals. The orthodox opinion is that shrines were intended to be visible from afar: 'The reliquary, when not concealed by a canopy, could be seen from the main body of the church, above and behind the high altar.'[90] It has also been argued that the vista had an exceptional place in the planning of greater churches: 'The view as planned down the long nave approach was all-important.'[91] The necessity of a long-range view of the feretrum has been employed to establish architectural facts. For example, Radford cited it as the main reason why bishops' thrones were moved from an axial position, where they blocked the view, to the south side of the choir.[92] More commonly, the necessity of shrine visibility is used to argue that a particular shrine was in a certain position. The fact that the floor of the retrochoir at Worcester, for example, is several feet lower than the high altar has been used to suggest that a shrine there 'would have been inconspicuous', which therefore 'clearly demonstrates that Wulfstan's shrine was never intended to be placed behind the high altar'.[93]

90 Coldstream, 'Shrine Bases', p. 16.
91 O'Neilly, 'The Shrine of Edward', p. 136.
92 C.A.R. Radford, 'The Bishop's Throne in Norwich Cathedral', *Arch. J.*, vol. 116 (1961), p. 129.
93 B. Singleton, 'The Remodelling of the East End of Worcester Cathedral in the Earlier Part of the Thirteenth Century', in *Medieval Art and Architecture at Worcester Cathedral*

Arguments for shrine visibility are based primarily on prestige, and assume that shrines could not be properly venerated unless they visually dominated all else. For example, it has been suggested that bishops turned from their usual custom of facing west while celebrating mass when a shrine appeared behind the high altar at Canterbury: 'the archbishop could not celebrate facing west . . . except by turning his back on the saint and even appearing to exhibit himself as a rival object of interest'.[94] Coldstream suggested that St William's shrine may have been on the top of the wooden reredos at York because the traditional place behind the screen 'would not have been visible above the high altar, and a church as important as York would not have concealed its chief reliquary, particularly with knowledge of the arrangement at Canterbury; local pride would not have allowed it'.[95] While I will not seek to prove that no shrine could ever be seen from afar, I will attempt to prove that visibility cannot be assumed and was not an important factor in church arrangement.

Contemporary writers did not make direct statements about cathedral vistas. One argument for shrine visibility, however, is based on an oft-repeated comparison of a shrine to a candle, derived from Jesus' saying that 'no man, when he hath lighted a candle, putteth it in a secret place, neither under a bushel, but on a candlestick, that they which come in may see the light' (Math. 5:15). This was frequently paraphrased in sermons and accounts of translations, both as a justification for elevation and as an admonition to do so.[96] It was particularly popular with proponents of Edward the Confessor. In 1138 Osbert de Clare demanded that Edward be set up as a lamp, and at his translation in 1163 Ailred of Rievaulx preached on the text 'The glorious lantern was put on a candlestick in the hopes of the Lord so that all who come in may see the light and be illuminated by it.'[97] Thomas Wykes described the elevation of Edward's relics with a strong allusion to the same verse.[98]

The symbolic nature of this phrase is illustrated in the records of St Thomas of Hereford. A request for his canonisation used the hidden candle reference to mean both that the entire Catholic church would be illuminated by his sanctity and that

(*BAACT*, vol. 1, 1978), pp. 109–10. P. Draper combined this belief with an assumption about the interrelationship between retrochoirs and shrines when he wrote that the creation of the great reredos at Winchester 'coincides with the period when most of the other major shrines were being elevated on elaborate new bases and made increasingly visible to the faithful. It would be strange if Winchester had gone so decisively against this trend, for the existence of the screen negated the original purpose of the retrochoir which was closely associated with the shrine': Draper, 'The Retrochoir of Winchester', p. 13.

94 C.S. Phillips, 'The Archbishop's Three Seats in Canterbury Cathedral', *Ant. J.*, vol. 29 (1949), p. 27.

95 Coldstream, 'Shrine Bases', p. 23.

96 Barlow, *Edward the Confessor*, p. 281.

97 E. Carpenter, *House of Kings* (London, 1966), p. 20; Barlow, *Edward the Confessor*, p. 283.

98 *Chronicon T. Wykes*, p. 226; translated in Perkins, *Westminster Abbey*, vol. 2, p. 36, as 'The King, grieved that the relics of Saint Edward were poorly enshrined and lowly, resolved that so great a luminary should not lie buried, but be placed high as on a candle-stick, to enlighten the church.'

'those who shall enter the house of the Church, on seeing his light will the more devoutly glorify our Father in heaven'.[99] The 1320 bull implied that the canonisation announcement alone, not any structural improvement to his tomb, had made him a 'candle' of faith.[100] In any case, neither of these statements could possibly mean that entrants to the cathedral were literally able to see Thomas's shrine from afar. They were made at a time when his shrine was in the north transept, invisible to the rest of the church. Even when finally translated he was placed far behind the high altar in the Lady Chapel, where there was no hope of seeing his shrine from west of the high altar. The symbolic meaning, that proper honouring of the saint spiritually illuminated worshippers, is plainly the main, if not only, intent of this usage.

I have found only one relevant contemporary description of the interior of a church. Erasmus in his *Colloquia* describes the view at Canterbury in 1513 from the western end of the nave, which was made through an iron screen. Vallance believed that this passage made it clear that 'the reason for the open grate instead of a close screen was, while insuring the requisite seclusion for the monastic community beyond, to enable the visitor immediately he should have set foot in the nave, to obtain a glimpse of the venerated martyr's shrine, which reared its lofty summit away in the distance behind the high altar'.[101] However, Erasmus clearly describes a view of the crossing alone (the bars 'permit a view of that space which is between the end of the quire') and does not mention the shrine.[102]

Medieval illustrations are no more helpful, and I have seen none which appear to influence this argument either way. The long perspective views which one would need are just not in existence. If anything, the profound silence from medieval documentary and art historical evidence suggests that the view was not important, but also means that it is probably impossible to directly assess the medieval view on church vistas. The most promising way to determine visibility is to examine the physical arrangement of medieval English churches. In particular, the visibility of specific shrines can be tested by examining the height and opacity of possible obstacles between them and potential viewers.

The most daunting obstacles to the sighting of a shrine were tall reredoses, or altar screens, erected behind the high altar. The high altar was placed near or against the western face of these screens, with a door on either side. The shrine was placed some distance from the other side of the reredos to allow space for the shrine altar and a passage for the priest and his servers moving behind the high altar. Screens have often been destroyed, and records can be rare. The only

99 'Now lest this bright light of her life placed on a candlestick of God's house should be hidden . . . let us, for the benefit of our hearers, relate a few of the many of his blessed habits and doings': *Extracts from the Cathedral Registers, A.D. 1275–1535*, trans. E.N. Dew (Hereford, 1932), pp. 31–2.

100 *Extracts from the Cathedral Registers*, p. 50.

101 A. Vallance, *Greater English Church Screens* (London, 1947), pp. 29–30.

102 'Cancelli ferrei sic arcent ingressum at conspectum admittant ejus spatii quod est inter extremum eidem chori, quem vocant locum': in Woodman, *Architectural History of Canterbury Cathedral*, p. 222.

memorial of the reredos of 'goodly stone work' at London, for example, is the notice in a chronicle that it was 'plucked down' in 1552.[103] We are only slightly more fortunate with the reredos at Lichfield destroyed by Wyatt in 1795, which was noted in a plan by B. Willis and whose surviving foundations indicate that it was a substantial structure.[104] A foundation trench also survives for a reredos behind the high altar built by Abbot Monington (1342–75) at Glastonbury.[105] Wooden reredoses, such as that removed from York in 1726, do not even leave a foundation.[106] The overall impression of the evidence, however, is that reredoses were once common.

In the later middle ages the reredos was tall enough to block the view completely. The reredos at Beverley forms 'a perfect background to the high altar, though blocking the view of all but the superstructure of the eastern part of the church'.[107] Most later reredoses were built in one of two versions: a tall and solid wall topped by a flat horizontal cornice, or a low wall surmounted by tall canopies and pinnacles.[108] The wall type of reredos was the ultimate barrier. The earliest surviving example, at Ottery St Mary, is from 1340–50.[109] Particularly massive examples, each over forty feet tall, survive at Winchester and St Albans.[110] These screens are large and solid enough to provide structural support for the nearby piers, a fact which may have saved them from destruction at the hands of reformers. A drawing of c.1532 shows how the wall reredos of Westminster Abbey, completed in 1441, originally looked.[111] Although it is now only slightly over fourteen feet high, it once supported a gallery with life-size statues of Sts Peter and Paul flanking an altar. A tester was suspended above the gallery altar from a double beam which also supported a massive rood, complete with statues of Sts Mary, John and two angels. The whole assembly reached higher than the capitals of the arcade piers.[112]

---

[103] Lethaby, 'Old St Paul's', pt 5, p. 234; A tall structure in a seventeenth-century choir view may not be the original reredos. See Dugdale, *St Paul's*, plate between pp. 134–5.

[104] Willis, 'Foundations of Early Buildings in Lichfield', pp. 3–22.

[105] C.A.R. Radford, 'The Excavations at Glastonbury Abbey, 1951–5', *Somerset and Dorset Notes and Queries*, vol. 27 (1955–6), p. 72.

[106] E. Gee, 'The Topography of Altars, Chantries and Shrines in York Minster', *Ant. J.*, vol. 64 (1984), p. 342.

[107] Batsford and Fry, *Greater English Church*, p. 108.

[108] C. Wilson, 'The Neville Screen', in *Medieval Art and Architecture at Durham Cathedral* (*BAACT*, vol. 3, 1980), p. 91.

[109] Wilson, 'Neville Screen', p. 91.

[110] G.W. Kitchin, *The Great Screen of Winchester Cathedral* (3rd edn, London, 1899), p. 7. See plate 11.

[111] The Islip Roll, Soc. of Antiquaries MS Roll 36, reproduced in Hope, *English Altars*, pl. xiii. It is a line drawing included in the mortuary roll of Abbot John Islip (d.1532), showing his coffin lying in state before the high altar.

[112] The statues and the rood are mentioned in the 1445/6 sacrist's roll, which recorded the purchase of a linen cloth to cover them: WAM, MS 19695; O'Neilly, 'The Shrine of Edward', p. 136. The construction of this reredos has offended one modern commentator. 'The high altar was henceforth completely divorced from its time-honoured connexion with St Edward's Shrine, thus contradicting the original ideals which had placed the two in close

The canopy type of reredos was no less an obstruction. The oldest standing example is the Neville Screen completed at Durham in 1380.[113] Although the solid wall forming its base is only about seven feet high, its tightly clustered and once statuary-filled pinnacles tower over twenty-five feet, effectively obscuring the site of the shrine beyond.[114] While the date of this type of screen's first introduction is uncertain, architectural remnants on the pier behind the high altar at Exeter show that the reredos begun by 1315 was of the canopy type and completely opaque to twenty feet with pinnacles rising at least another ten.[115] C. Wilson believes that this form was introduced in c.1300, and may have had antecedents as far back as 1269.[116]

From the early fourteenth century, then, tall screens began to block the area behind the high altar. While it is agreed by all parties that later reredoses formed an effective barrier, it is usually asserted that earlier shrines were entirely visible and that concealment only came as part of a tendency to enclose the chancel 'in the course of the fourteenth century'.[117] However, there is no positive evidence to this effect for an English cathedral. It is also uncertain exactly what obstructions to the view existed around high altars before this time. There was certainly a substantial beam which usually passed from pier to pier across the presbytery above the high altar. The beam set up at St Alban's by Abbot William of Trumpington, for example, was painted with the history of St Alban.[118] At Old Sarum a beam supporting a rood and relics stood in front of the high altar.[119] The great beam at Canterbury was, predictably, even more elaborate. It was supported on the capitals of two wooden columns at the east corners of the high altar. On top stood a majesty, images of Sts Alphege and Dunstan, and seven chests filled with diverse relics.[120] This assemblage could certainly block the view of St Thomas's shrine depending on the angles of sight.

It is quite probable that a retable, in the form of a wooden backdrop, rose three feet or so behind the high altars of most greater churches. Appearing in the

---

juxtaposition': Perkins, *Westminster Abbey*, vol. 1, p. 42. By erecting the reredos at Westminster the builders were accused by Perkins of 'flouting the customs and traditions of many generations', 'the rough handling of a venerable tradition', 'rude destruction', 'a tragedy of the first order' and 'an act of unhistorical and unprincipled vandalism': *ibid.*, vol. 1, p. 119, vol. 2, pp. 66–7.

[113] *Historiæ Dunelmensis Scriptores Tres*, ed. J. Raine (SS, vol. 9, 1839), p. 136.

[114] See Wilson, 'Neville Screen', plate xii.

[115] P. Morris, 'Exeter Cathedral: A Conjectural Restoration of the Fourteenth-Century Altar Screen', *Ant. J.*, vol. 23 (1943), p. 141. Morris's artistic reconstruction is not solidly based on evidence, but the height is certain from traces left on nearby piers: Wilson, 'Neville Screen', p. 93.

[116] Wilson, 'Neville Screen', p. 93.

[117] A good description of the development is in R. and C. Brooke, *Popular Religion in the Middle Ages* (London, 1984), pp. 88–9; Brooke, 'Religious Sentiment and Church Design', p. 175.

[118] Walsingham, *Gesta Abbatum*, vol. 1, p. 203.

[119] W. St John Hope, 'The Sarum Consuetudinary and its Relation to the Cathedral Church of Old Sarum', *Archaeologia*, vol. 68 (1917), p. 116.

[120] Gervase of Canterbury, *Chronicle*, vol. 1, p. 13.

eleventh century, the retable may have developed into the reredos by growing progressively larger and more ornate.[121] Some retables were probably of significant size, including the *'nova tabula magni altaris'* which was given great prominence in a list of works built by Prior Eastry at Canterbury.[122] What obstacle these posed to the view of the shorter shrines in existence in the thirteenth century and earlier is difficult to guess. Shrines may have only been visible from the choir by looking through the space between the retable and the beam over the high altar, if at all.

The liturgical choir and presbytery were the sole domain of the clergy. If commoners and pilgrims were to see the shrine without going to the shrine chapel then they would have to see it from the nave. However, screens that were earlier and more substantial than the reredos shut out the masses from the choir (see plate 12). The principal barrier was the choir screen or pulpitum, which was joined in monastic churches by a second, very similar screen called the rood screen. Besides acting as dividing walls, these screens had liturgical uses as processional stations or platforms from which to read the gospel. For example, the Chichester ordinance of 1197 that 'The cross should be borne before the Gospel [book] when the Gospel is read from the loft' refers to the loft of the pulpitum.[123] Later choir screens were high, solid structures. Surviving pulpita are invariably near or over fourteen feet tall, and usually consist of two walls supporting a loft and enclosing an inner space pierced by a central door.

In monastic cathedrals there was also a rood screen, situated one or two bays west of the pulpitum, which separated monks from the laymen in the nave and was invariably surmounted by a large cross.[124] It was similar in construction and height to the choir screen, but had two doors in place of one. A clear view east through the passages of both screens was thus impossible, even if they were open. At Canterbury Archbishop Winchelsey's statutes of 1298 called for doors to be put in the choir and rood screens, and these to be kept locked and closed except when necessary.[125] Occasionally the two screens were joined by a single loft, as at Ely where the whole assembly comprised three stone walls.[126] Almost all surviving, intact choir screens were made in the fourteenth and later centuries. Secular examples include those at Chichester, Lincoln, Exeter, Wells, York and Hereford, all but the latter originally under the eastern arch of the crossing, while fifteenth-century monastic pulpita survive *in situ* at Canterbury, Norwich, Carlisle and Rochester.[127] When monastic cathedrals were converted to secular ones at the

121 O'Connell, *Church Building and Furnishing*, p. 129; For a discussion of the early development of choir screens see Wilson, 'Neville Screen', pp. 93–4.
122 CCA, MS Reg. K, f. 220.
123 *The Chartulary of the High Church of Chichester*, ed. W.D. Peckham (Sussex Record Soc., vol. 46, 1942 and 1943), p. 47.
124 For example, see the description of the screen built by Walter of Colchester, Sacrist of St Albans: Paris, *Chronicles*, p. 49.
125 *Concilia*, vol. 2, p. 249.
126 Plan in Willis, *Survey of Lincoln, etc.*, between pp. 332 and 333.
127 Hereford's pulpitum was only moved under the eastern arch in modern times by Gilbert

time of the Dissolution their rood screens were no longer necessary, and therefore very few survive. The rood screen at Westminster Abbey, for example, was
pulled down in the sixteenth century.[128]

'The whole question of the early history of screens is very obscure. We may
be sure that from the late thirteenth century onwards they tended to grow higher
and more opaque; but so far as I know no recent study has been made of the very
slender evidence as to the nature and height of eleventh and twelfth-century
screens. None survives in this country.'[129] This fact has caused some scholars to
conclude that the twelfth-century cathedral had an open vista, often pointing to
surviving twelfth-century screens on the Continent, especially that in the Church
of San Clemente in Rome, which have very low and open arcades.[130] However,
mere absence of evidence is not proof of non-existence.

As with reredoses, it is difficult to say exactly when significant choir screens
appeared. They probably developed from a number of features, such as veils or
low colonnades, that delineated the chancel and nave of the earliest Christian
churches.[131] The evidence for Anglo-Saxon arrangements, however, is practically non-existent. Eadmer's description of pre-Conquest Canterbury suggests a
very substantial screen of stone slabs: 'The choir of the singers was extended
westward into the body of the church, and shut out from the multitude by a
proper enclosure.'[132] However, there is evidence to suggest that English choir
screens were tall and solid from early Anglo-Norman times. The monk Gervase
described the screen surrounding the choir of Canterbury before the great fire of
1174: 'At the base of the pillars was a wall made of marble slabs; which, surrounding Ernulph's choir and presbytery (built 1096–1115), divided the church
from its sides, which are called *alae*.'[133] It took eight steps to reach the throne of
the archbishop set on the top of this wall, and the presbytery itself was three
steps higher than the aisles, making it uncertain that people in the ambulatory
could see into the sanctuary. This wall, dividing the presbytery from the aisles,
was undoubtedly lower than the more important choir screen, which had to guard
the choir from the noise and turbulence of the nave and crossing.

Other screens are known to have existed by the late-eleventh century under the

Scott: F.B. Bond, *Screens and Galleries in English Churches* (London, 1908), pp. 151,
160. The Arundel Screen at Chichester, built in 1459–78, was removed in 1859 but has
now been replaced: Clarke, *Chichester Cathedral in the Nineteenth Century*, pp. 3–4.

[128] Perkins, *Westminster Abbey*, vol. 2, p. 2.

[129] Brooke, 'Religious Sentiment and Church Design', p. 166.

[130] F.B. Bond, *Gothic Architecture in England*, pp. 181–2; Brooke, 'Religious Sentiment and
Church Design', p. 167.

[131] There has been some dispute over this amongst scholars. See Bond, *Screens and Galleries*,
pp. 5–11; F.B. Bond, 'Medieval Screens and Rood-Lofts', *Trans. of the St. Paul's
Ecclesiological Soc.*, vol. 5 (1905), pp. 197–201.

[132] 'Inde ad occidentum chorus psallentium in aulum aecclesiae porrigebatur, decenti fabrica a
frequentia turbae seclusus': Eadmer, 'Opuscula', p. 365.

[133] 'Ad bases pilariorum murus erat tabulis marmoreis compositus, qui, chorum cingens et
presbiterium, corpus ecclesiæ a suis lateribus quæ alæ vocantur dividebat': Gervase of
Canterbury, *Chronicle*, p. 13; translation from Bond, *Gothic Architecture*, p. 182.

western crossing arches at Lincoln, Old Sarum, Lichfield, Southwell, Hereford and Winchester, and 'foundations of several of these structures have been uncovered'.[134] For example, the substantial foundations of the pulpitum built at Old Sarum sometime before 1139 indicate a heavy, fourteen-foot wide stone structure supporting a loft reached by stairs. It probably had two separate walls containing an internal chamber over fourteen feet wide, just like later pulpita.[135]

Slightly more is known about the choir screen at Ely, erected in the early part of the episcopate of Nigel (1133–69) and surviving until destroyed by James Essex in 1770. The pulpitum originally occupied a full bay with a loft, but the eastern half was destroyed in the 1321/2 fall of the tower and was later replaced.[136] Sketches by Essex show a fourteen and a half foot tall screen pierced with spaces surmounted by round-headed arches forming what was probably a partially open arcade.[137] However, when the foundations were excavated they indicated that the screen was solid except for three open arches, the central of which was probably a niche for the nave altar. A plan made by B. Willis in 1730 shows that the rebuilt screen was mostly solid except for three large gaps for the above mentioned doors.[138]

The shrine of St Etheldreda could not have been seen over or through this pulpitum. Even if both walls of the Norman screen were made of partially open arcades, the view east would have been obstructed unless the two walls were of roughly the same design and observed head-on. Other perspectives would result in the structure of the rear screen blocking the view through the apertures of the first. Even a direct line of sight would not guarantee that the holes lined up with the shrine of Etheldreda. None of this proves that the shrine could not be seen from the nave, but it does clearly demonstrate that the view was unimportant.

Pulpita were both numerous and substantial in secular churches by the thirteenth century. The east face of the wooden pulpitum at Rochester, built c.1227, is the only existing thirteenth-century example *in situ*, yet records show that there were several others.[139] The pulpitum at Durham, for example, built 1153–95 and rebuilt by Prior Wessington, must have been at least thirteen feet tall as described in the *Rites of Durham*.[140] The remains of a thirteenth-century choir screen at Salisbury were taken down by Wyatt in 1789.[141] In 1345 Prior Eastry built a new choir screen at Canterbury over the top of one built by William the Englishman in

134 Hope, 'Quire Screens', pp. 51, 88; Bond, *Gothic Architecture*, p. 149.

135 Hope, 'Quire Screens', p. 54; Hope, 'Sarum Consuetudinary', p. 114, pl. xxi.

136 Hope, 'Quire Screens', pp. 43, 85–7.

137 This is Rosalind and Christopher Brooke's interpretation of the drawings: *Popular Religion*, p. 89.

138 Willis, *Survey of Lincoln, etc.*, plan opposite p. 332.

139 W. St John Hope, 'Quire Screens in English Churches, with Special Reference to the Twelfth-Century Quire Screen Formerly in the Cathedral Church of Ely', *Archaeologia*, vol. 68 (1917), pp. 43–110, esp. p. 80.

140 *Rites of Durham*, pp. 32–4.

141 A. Clapham, 'Salisbury Cathedral: Churches and Religious Building, Monuments and Sculpture', *Arch. J.*, vol. 104 (1947), p. 145.

c.1180.[142] It is probable then that large screens were in existence from earliest Norman England, and this probability increases with each century.

Let us look at one example in detail. The idea that a shrine was meant to be visible from afar seems to have been largely inspired by Canterbury cathedral, where an early thirteenth-century shrine was raised on an elevated chapel behind the high altar. Canterbury was often exceptional, but I hope to prove that even there a shrine vista from the nave was impossible, and from the choir unlikely. The question of visibility does not really arise until after the fire of 1174, when plans were made to rebuild the quire and move St Thomas out of the crypt. Pier bases show that the original plan of the architect William of Sens was to have the Trinity Chapel behind and at a lower level than the high altar.[143] From that position it could never have been seen from the west: 'The shrine itself would surely have been raised on a base with steps, but unless that base was to have been of inordinate height it is hard to imagine that it was ever intended to be seen above the raised platform of the high altar.'[144] This alone suggests that visibility was not crucial.

Although the design was changed to its present configuration before completion, it still cannot be assumed that the shrine was ultimately visible. Besides the beam, there were two obstacles behind the altar. Firstly, there was a tall iron railing called the 'Hake' at the top of the stairs, shown in an oil painting of 1657 to have reached to within about a yard of the pier capitals.[145] Although once topped by a wooden cornice, it was relatively transparent but did obscure sight to some degree.[146] An early reredos existed, which was replaced by Prior Eastry in 1320–30, and again replaced or modified by a silver-gilt 'tabula' begun in 1394/5.[147] The uniquely lofty steps above the high altar, however, render the

---

[142] This was in turn obscured by construction in the mid-fifteenth century. There is some confusion over the choir and rood screens: Woodman, *Architectural History of Canterbury Cathedral*, pp. 143, 188–91; 'In the year 1345, repaired the whole choir with three new doors and a new pulpit' (Anno m.ccc.iiij et quinto. Reperacione totius chori cum tribus novis ostijs et novo pulpito) CCA, MS Reg. K, f. 220. See plate 12, and for the more open Arundel Screen at Chichester see plate 13.

[143] Woodman, *Architectural History of Canterbury Cathedral*, p. 115.

[144] Draper, 'Choir Termination', pp. 240, 245–6. Draper assumes that the choir was redesigned in order to correct this fault: 'There are good reasons for associating this change with the decision to raise the floor level of the Trinity Chapel in order to set the shrine in a more ostentatious position where it would serve as the focus for the church': p. 246. See also Woodman, *Architectural History of Canterbury Cathedral*, p. 115.

[145] Although the screen was removed in 1750, the hooks which fastened it to nearby piers remain. In 1464 the convent 'passed through the hake to the shrine of St Thomas' (transierunt per le hake ad feretrum sancti Thome): Stone, *Chronicle*, p. 90; C.S. Phillips, *Canterbury Cathedral in the Middle Ages* (London, 1949), p. 10 n. 4; W.D. Caröe, 'Canterbury Cathedral Choir during the Commonwealth and After, with Special Reference to Two Oil Paintings', *Archaeologia*, vol. 62, pt 2 (1911), plate xl.

[146] Caröe, 'Canterbury during the Commonwealth', p. 358.

[147] 'A Monastic Chronicle Lately Discovered at Christ Church, Canterbury: with Introduction and Notes', ed. C.E. Woodruff, *Arch. Cant.*, vol. 29 (1911), p. 71; Hope and Legg, *Inventories of Christchurch*, pp. 109–10.

reredos a less important obstacle than in most churches since they raise the base of the shrine chapel to an unusual height. Nevertheless, even if the shrine were on a ten foot tall base then a reredos of only seven and a half feet would have obscured the view from the high altar. From further west the angles of view improved, but even from the rear choir stalls (over 180 feet from the shrine) sight would have been blocked by a twelve-foot reredos or beam. Because the shrine of St Thomas probably rested on a base less than eight feet tall (rather than the ten feet assumed above), visibility from all parts of the choir was unlikely.

It can be demonstrated that the choir screen built in 1180 must have been high enough to obstruct the view from the nave. At Canterbury a tall pilgrim standing in the middle of the nave could not have seen a shrine standing on even a twelve-foot base if the choir screen were any taller than three feet, which was certainly the case.[148] This is because the tall flight of stairs leading up from the nave to the choir are themselves an effective obstacle and served to increase the height of any screen set at their top. Because Christ Church was a monastery the observer would have had to see past a rood screen as well, at least until c.1500 when it was replaced by an open iron-work screen.[149] The evidence therefore suggests that St Thomas's feretrum was probably not visible from the choir, and certainly not from the nave, from the foundation of the shrine to its destruction. Thus, even for the most prestigious English shrine visibility was not important.

A probable history of the cathedral vista from the Norman Conquest to the Dissolution can now be re-constructed. The evidence of the screens at Ely and Sarum makes it reasonably certain that the nave was separated from the rest of the church by tall pulpita or rood screens by the early twelfth century, thus preventing the shrine from being visible to the mass of church-goers and pilgrims in the nave from that date forward. In addition, there was certainly no concern for a view of the shrine from the choir or presbytery from c.1300, when large reredoses began to be erected. Just when the shrines were becoming more conspicuous by virtue of their height the reredos rose to block them off. It cannot be said that no shrines were ever visible from the west. As we have seen, the twelfth and thirteenth-century situation in the choir must have forced the high altar and shrine into close proximity, and some shrines must have been visible from the choir at that time. However, any such visibility, if it occurred, was probably incidental in the vast majority of cases.

There were good reasons for shutting the shrine away. Screens separated the services in the choir from the host of pilgrims at the shrine and in the nave, with tall reredoses providing 'an additional barrier against the unwashed and suffering crowd of common humanity'.[150] The shrine of St Frideswide was supposedly

[148] See plate 12.
[149] Although itself pulled down in 1748 or 1750, the iron grille can still be seen in an engraving of 1726: J. Dart, *The History and Antiquities of the Cathedral Church of Canterbury* (London, 1726), p. 28; Vallance, *Church Screens*, p. 30.
[150] Kitchin, 'Winchester Screen', p. 12.

enclosed with a partition in 1180 to protect it 'from the sight of the vulgar'.[151] Because the shrine was usually on the far side of the choir from the layman's part of the church (the nave) any attempt at separation of clergy and laity would have ruined the shrine vista. There also may have been a gradual mystification of the shrine area. With time it became less public and more mysterious, an inner sanctum which one could only reach by passing through successive barriers. It has even been suggested that shrines were concealed in order 'to stimulate a curiosity which would certainly endeavour to secure its gratification, even though it involved the payment of a price'.[152]

On account of the fate of shrines in the sixteenth century their physical aspects are a difficult subject to be conclusive about. However, it is time that some assumptions about shrines were challenged. In particular, it is certain that post-Conquest shrines were never associated with crypts, which were only used as emergency storage places while more suitable parts of the church were under construction. After the Conquest the principal free-standing English shrines began to be consistently placed behind the high altar in feretory chapels. The design of churches affected the shape of these chapels, but the choice of cathedral plan was not greatly influenced by the existence of a shrine, if at all. Finally, the evidence does not show that the medieval designers cared whether the shrines, even elevated on high, were visible from outside their immediate vicinity.

---

[151] A. Wood, 'Survey of the Antiquities of the City of Oxford' Composed in 1661–6 by Anthony Wood, ed. Andrew Clark (Oxford, 1890), vol. 2, p. 165. Unfortunately, I could not find the original source for this.

[152] Perkins, Westminster Abbey, vol. 1, p. 44.

4

Pilgrims and the Shrine

There were two ways in which a contemporary could experience a medieval shrine: as an insider, from the privileged position of the clergy, or from the outside, as a pilgrim or tourist. While there was no clear division between these two perspectives (the clergy, for example, could become pilgrims through devotion and offerings at the shrine) a distinction between the two is helpful when analysing the activities at the shrine. This chapter will view the shrine through the eyes of pilgrims, examining their activities within the cathedral but ignoring other important aspects of pilgrimage, such as making vows or the journey itself, for which arrival at the shrine was the climax.

The sources of information on pilgrims' activities are diverse. Cathedral financial records are of some use, but they naturally ignore the pilgrim except when his or her reception involved money. More emphasis must be placed on the accounts of miracles, or *miracula*, which have the advantage of often being pilgrims' own stories (as written down by the keeper of the shrine records) and thus provide a valuable insight into the mentality and behaviour of common pilgrims. Nevertheless, the information these sources give about medieval pilgrim practices is small compared to the total quantity of hagiographic literature. *Miracula* are generally limited to the twelfth and thirteenth centuries, and are much more concerned with details of a malady and its miraculous cure than in details of how the pilgrim gave thanks at the shrine. Many other and very different types of document can shed smaller amounts of light on pilgrim activities, two of the more useful sources being bishops' registers and chronicles. Despite the variety of sources, the amount of information contained in any one is small. For example, it is rare to find even a single mention of a shrine in a bishop's register. In general, the medieval view seems to have been that everyone knew what happened at a shrine, and therefore it needed no description. Not so for us.

The pilgrim in the city and cathedral

The pilgrim's first involvement with the cathedral often occurred before his or her entry into the church itself. The influence of the shrine was felt in its host city through special fairs which were often granted to a cathedral on the major festival of its saint. At Canterbury, for example, one of the four fairs administered by the sacrists occurred on the feast of the translation of St Thomas.[1] Usually a fair of this type lasted about a week. At Ely a similar fair occurred on the Translation Feast of St Etheldreda and the three days before and after.[2] Henry I granted St Augustine's Abbey, Canterbury, a fair lasting five days before the feast of the Translation of St Augustine and two days after.[3] A more remarkable example is the fair instituted by Henry III in 1248 to commemorate the arrival of the Holy Blood at Westminster Abbey. It was to last a fortnight starting on the Translation Feast of Edward the Confessor, during which all other markets were forbidden. 'As a result, a vast crowd of people flocked there as if to the most famous fair, and so the translation of the blessed Edward and the blood of Christ was amazingly venerated by the people assembled there.'[4] Matthew Paris claimed that the Westminster fair competed unfairly with that at Ely, whose bishop complained without success.[5] Although fairs were an additional attraction to pilgrims, they were mercantile in nature and their association with shrines was almost entirely due to the fact that they occurred simultaneously with the feast of the saint.

Having negotiated the town, pilgrims could proceed directly to the cathedral. How did they get in? There is a tradition common to several cathedrals that pilgrims entered the church by way of a special door in the north. For example, Atkinson held that the north transept door at Ely was for the use of pilgrims, and was perhaps later replaced by doors in the north quire aisle.[6] It has also been assumed that pilgrims to Westminster and Winchester entered via doors in the north transepts.[7] In at least one case a door in the north of a cathedral was named after the shrine saint: the north door of the nave at Winchester, located in the west most bay of the north aisle, is known as St Swithun's Door, probably because it opens towards Swithun's original grave site.[8] Nevertheless, hard evidence that pilgrims entered any cathedral exclusively from the north, or from any other direction, is non-existent. One might expect pilgrims to be given a more

---

[1] This fair was granted by Richard II in 1383 and was held on 7 July: Woodruff, 'The Sacrist's Rolls of Christ Church', pp. 40–1. It was not particularly valuable to the priory.

[2] The charter granting the fair is printed in Bentham, *The History and Antiquities of Ely*, appendix, p. 18.

[3] I.e. from 8 to 13 September: Thomas of Elmham, *Historia Monasterii S. Augustini Cantuariensis*, ed. C. Hardwick (RS, vol. 8, 1858), p. 358.

[4] Paris, *Chronicles*, p. 149.

[5] Paris, *Chronica Majora*, vol. 5, p. 29.

[6] T.D. Atkinson, *An Architectural History of the Benedictine Monastery of Saint Etheldreda at Ely* (2 vols, Cambridge, 1933), vol. 1, p. 28.

[7] 'They would probably enter the north transept by the small doorway of the western aisle, which we may call the Pilgrims' doorway': Bond, *Westminster Abbey*, p. 67. Kitchin claimed that pilgrims to St Swithun were not allowed in the choir, nave or south transept: *Compotus Rolls of the Obedientiaries of St Swithun's Priory, Winchester*, ed. G.W. Kitchin (London, 1892), p. 44.

[8] C.R. Peers and H. Brakspear, 'Architectural Description of Winchester Cathedral', *VCH: Hampshire and the Isle of Wight*, vol. 5, ed. W. Page (Folkstone, 1912), p. 58. At Rochester there was a 'St William's Gate' opposite the north transept, although this was presumably a gate in the close: Richardson, 'Saint William of Perth', p. 125.

impressive entry through the large west doors, but perhaps these were reserved for special occasions.

In any case, pilgrims probably entered the nave first, since it was the public part of the church and the only area where lay people could gather to loiter or join in services. Admission to the nave was easy, since it was open during regular daylight hours. The sites of lesser and unofficial cults, such as miracle-working images or tombs with saintly occupants like that of Archbishop Robert Winchelsey at Canterbury, were often there. The only likely obstacle between pilgrims and these shrines would have been the iron grill or fence which surrounded most tombs in the later middle ages, although more popular nave shrines, like the tomb of St William in York or the statue of St Mary in Christ Church Canterbury, had a clerk to watch over them. In the case of greater shrines, the really big attractions, the pilgrim needed to penetrate further into the cathedral, passing a series of screens one by one and entering the domain largely reserved to the clergy. Indeed, the status of laymen beyond the choir screen is uncertain. There is evidence that secular cathedrals allowed lay people limited access to choir services and to the quire aisles and altars.[9] Lincoln records state that on ordinary Sundays the presiding cleric should, 'after aspersing the clerics, he should then asperse the laity who stand in either side of the presbytery'.[10]

Benedictine cathedrals were more restrictive, and in theory laity were not normally allowed in the choir since it was part of the convent. 'The most essential aspect of the monastic house was its privacy. The services in the splendid choirs were entirely limited to the professed monks and novices, the public being rigidly restricted to the nave.'[11] Benedictine chapter statutes of 1444, for example, state that outsiders should not pass through any part of the convent, and that doors should be closed and seculars kept out during breakfast and dinner, when the monks were absent.[12] The Ordinal of St Mary's, York, however, mentions the presence of people standing outside the north door of the presbytery hoping to be aspersed during high mass.[13] Cathedral priories were perhaps more open to laity than other monasteries, and early *miracula* suggest that shrines were open at all times no matter where in the church they were. Thus, a man spent a vigil at the shrine of Etheldreda, right behind the high altar, 'all night and day'.[14]

Monastic cathedrals certainly restricted the entrance of women to a greater degree than men. St Cuthbert's supposed aversion to women, and their resultant restriction to the Galilee chapel and points west of a line drawn on the nave floor

9   Hope, 'Quire Screens', p. 44.
10 'Post aspersionem clericorum, laicos in presbiterio hinc inde stantes aspergat': *Ceremonies and Processions of Salisbury*, p. 20.
11 H. Braun, *English Abbeys* (London, 1971), p. 97.
12 *Documents Illustrating the Activities of the General and Provincial Chapters of the English Black Monks, 1215–1540*, ed. W.A. Pantin (3 vols, Camden Soc., 3rd ser., vol. 45, 47 and 54, 1931–7), vol. 2, p. 208.
13 *Ordinal and Customary of the Abbey of Saint Mary, York*, eds The Abbess of Stanbrook and J.B.L. Tolhurst (Henry Bradshaw Soc., vol. 73, 1936), p. 89.
14 'totaque nocte et die': *Liber Eliensis*, p. 306.

of Durham cathedral, is well known.[15] Presumably, this denied women access to the shrine of St Cuthbert far to the east of that demarcation, yet eleven are still mentioned as givers of gifts, and some even as pilgrims, in a pair of shrine inventories from 1397 and 1401.[16] At Ely a statute of Bishop Ralph of Walpole issued in 1300 placed the cathedral choir, and thus St Etheldreda's shrine behind the high altar, off limits to women except on special occasions.[17] Of course, this could be taken to mean that women were frequenting the shrine freely beforehand. A partition was ordered to be erected in the south quire aisle of the same cathedral 'lest the frequent approach of lay people and especially women hinder the contemplation of the monks'.[18]

In at least one instance the presence of female pilgrims in an abbey was lamented. After a rood placed in the convert's choir of the abbey of Meaux in 1339 resulted in miracles the Cistercian abbey sought licence to admit women. The passage that describes this is illustrative of a conservative monastic view of women's place in a church:

> It was then thought that if women had access to the said cross the devotion of the community would be augmented, and would redound with many advantages to our monastery. Concerning which the Abbot of the Cistercian Order, having been asked by us, gave us license so that honest men and women could approach the said cross, although women would not be permitted to enter through the cloister and dormitory or other office, unless they were a foundatrix, wife or daughter [of a founder], or wife of a son of a founder; the which would also not be permitted either to stay over night within the limits of the abbey, nor to linger before prime or after compline. And also if we have them among us, then he will revoke the aforementioned license. On account of this license, to our misfortune, women often came to the said cross, but in them devotion is particularly cool and they came as much to get a look at the inside of the church, and our wealth was spent in their hospitality.[19]

The monks' hopes that admitting women would increase local devotion had not turned out according to plan. Again, in practice women were probably granted

---

[15] Bishop Hugh made the chapel, so that women have some consolation at Durham: Geoffrey of Coldingham, in *Historiæ Dunelmensis Scriptores Tres*, p. 11. See also Reginald of Durham, *Libellus de Admirandis Beati Cuthberti*, pp. 152–3. H. Colgrave stated that 'The legendary dislike of women which was later attributed to [Cuthbert] belonged to the Norman period, when the belief in the inferiority and impurity of women caused admirers of the saint to bestow on him the fashionable prejudice': H. Colgrave, *St Cuthbert of Durham* (Durham, 1947), p. 15. V. Tudor believed that the Benedictines introduced the belief shortly after their arrival in order to strengthen their position against the married clergy they replaced: V. Tudor, 'The Misogyny of St. Cuthbert', *Archaeologia Aeliana*, 5th ser., vol. 12 (1984), pp. 158–64.

[16] DDCA, 'Feretrars' Rolls', 1397, 1401. See Chapter 7.

[17] *Ely Chapter Ordinances and Visitation Records, 1241–1515*, ed. S.J.A. Evans, in *Camden Miscellany*, vol. 17 (Camden Soc., 3rd ser., vol. 64, 1940), p. 11.

[18] 'Ne frequens accessus secularium et maxime mulierum contemplationem impediat monachorum': *Ely Chapter Ordinances*, p. 23.

[19] Burton, *Chronica Monasterii de Melsa*, vol. 3, pp. 35–6.

much freer access to shrines than the statutes ordain. Miracle stories in particular seem to show that women could come and go at all hours. For example, an ill woman entered Reading Abbey while the monks were singing matins and, throwing herself to the pavement, writhed all night at the shrine before being healed after a bout of vomiting.[20] It should be remembered that the fact of its being recorded in the *miracula* shows that this type of behaviour was not only tolerated but celebrated in at least some circles.

While the *miracula* suggest little regulation of pilgrims, later sources seem to indicate that viewings were more controlled. Access to the shrine through the quire was generally organised under the supervision of the shrine-keeper and his clerk or servants acting as guides. Erasmus was given a personal tour of Canterbury by the prior, but such a high-ranking escort must have been a rare privilege. Shrines were generally closed during mass or when the guardians were obliged to be absent, but their opening was announced in some way.[21] At Durham this was by bells attached to the rope suspending the cover of the shrine which would ring when it was lifted.[22] At Ely the almonry schoolboys were given 3s. to call pilgrims, while some Lincoln servants were paid for 'arousing the people'.[23] Before the morning mass at the shrine of Thomas Becket the temporal guardian opened the doors of the church and rang a bell three times to tell pilgrims and travellers that the service was about to begin. The Canterbury shrine was then closed for lunch, during which time the junior clerk was to attend to any pilgrims at 'the doors in the forward part of the church' (probably at the rood screen). After noon the doors were again opened, and the feretrarians received pilgrims and ensured that all showed proper reverence.[24] The time after matins was apparently also the most popular time for pilgrims to assemble at the tomb of St Hugh.[25] More careful organisation, even segregation of pilgrims according to class, was possible. The *Tale of Beryn* (a continuation of Chaucer's *Tales*) has the pilgrims heading to the church after arranging their lodging. At the church door a question of courtesy arises, which is settled by the Knight putting the Parson and Friar to the fore. Once in and having been aspersed by a monk, the Knight hurries to the shrine while the others stop to gaze at stained glass windows.[26] In general, it appears that

---

[20] 'The Miracles of the Hand of St James', trans. B. Kemp, *The Berks. Archaeological J.*, vol. 65 (1970), p. 7. The situation was more pronounced in secular cathedrals. At Lincoln a group of matrons of the city appear to have been in the habit of holding vigils together at the tomb of St Hugh shortly after 1200: Giraldus Cambrensis, *Vita S. Hugonis*, pp. 132, 133.

[21] This may have been less true in the twelfth and thirteenth centuries. A pilgrim approached the shrine of St Cuthbert while Bishop Hugh de Puiset was saying mass at the high altar: Reginald of Durham, *Libellus de Admirandis Beati Cuthberti*, p. 209.

[22] The bells were six, and of silver: *Rites of Durham*, p. 4.

[23] For example, in 1425/6, 'For four scholars' helping in the time of the fair, for calling pilgrims and minding wax- 2s': CUL, MS EDC. 5/12, Feretrar's Roll 4; At Lincoln, 'Duobus exitantibus populum .xij.d.', 'Capellano custodi inferiori excitandi populum sicut superius': *Liber Niger*, pp. 336–7.

[24] 'Customary of the Shrine of St Thomas', ff. 1, 2 and 4.

[25] Giraldus Cambrensis, *Vita S. Hugonis*, p. 133.

[26] *The Tale of Beryn*, eds F.J. Furnivall and W.G. Stone (London, 1887), pp. 5–6.

fourteenth-century and later pilgrims assembled in the nave and were summoned forward at an appropriate time. Of course, those of particularly high status could command the opening of the shrine. At Durham the clerk of the shrine, as soon as 'any man of honor or worshippe' wished to see the shrine, was to rush to the feretrar. The latter then brought the keys and oversaw the clerk unlocking and uncovering the shrine.[27]

As we have seen, shrines were usually surrounded with stone screens or iron fencing. Since most feretory chapels were therefore limited in space, pilgrims seeking access to the shrine would have had to file in one entrance and out the other in order to view the various relics and marvels, all the while under the supervision of the clerk. Alternatively, they might have been marshalled in groups, each one consecutively assembled before the shrine and given a dissertation, much as with modern tours for sightseers and as seems to have been the case when Erasmus toured Canterbury. Indeed, the only time the Westminster sacrist was supposedly allowed speak in church was to draw a layman's attention to relics.[28] In summary, *miracula* suggest frenetic activity around shrines that were relatively free of access in the twelfth and thirteenth centuries. Other later and more worldly sources suggest a more sober and controlled atmosphere.

Before going on to discuss what occurred at the shrine, I would like to discuss the route that pilgrims took from the nave to a shrine behind the high altar. Local historians have occasionally discussed this in reference to particular cathedrals. The most probable path usually involved passing through the choir and/or rood screens, going through the crossing and then moving down the north or south quire aisle before entering the shrine chapel from the side. To take one specific case, we have more information on the pilgrim route at Canterbury than anywhere else. From an analysis of the *Decreta Lanfranci*, A. Klukas has posited that eleventh-century pilgrims to Canterbury entered the cathedral by the west door, passed through gates in the aisle south of the rood and choir screens, and then moved down to the crypt by way of axial stairways situated just before the presbytery.[29] Although his theoretical route is probably correct in its basics, there were at that time no significant shrines in the crypt.

The route taken by dignitaries and monks for their offerings at the 1420 Jubilee was probably typical: they went first to the nearest shrine, that of the Martyrdom in the north transept, then to the tomb and the altar of St Mary in the crypt. They returned to the transept and passed through the choir, moving progressively farther east, visiting the high altar and the main shrine before arriving at the far east end, the Corona chapel. Finally, they returned to the presbytery to visit the relic collection and the tombs of Alphege, Blaise and Dunstan.[30] The route through Canterbury cathedral taken by Erasmus in the early sixteenth century was

---

27 *Rites of Durham*, p. 94.
28 Westlake, *Westminster Abbey*, vol. 2, p. 291, with no original source cited.
29 Klukas, 'The Architectural Implications of the *Decreta Lanfranci*', p. 148.
30 Contained in the treatise on the jubilee, printed in Foreville, *Le Jubilé*, pp. 140–1. See plate 14.

very similar. He left the nave by doors in the south aisle, then passed through the tunnel under the choir steps to the Martyrdom in the north transept. From there he entered the crypt before ascending to the choir where he visited the high altar, Corona and main shrine of St Thomas. Finally, he descended into the crypt for a second time to see the altar and shrine of St Mary in the undercroft.[31] While it is by no means certain that Erasmus, a very distinguished visitor, was taken on the usual tour (he was certainly shown things not seen by ordinary pilgrims), the main pattern of his visit was probably typical. Pilgrims began in the nave and made their way to the closest shrine: in the case of Canterbury this was the Martyrdom. Next, they descended the nearby steps to the crypt, returned by the same route and probably reached the main shrine by passing the high altar via the north quire aisle or by taking the ambulatory to the Corona and then the shrine.

In the fourteenth century pilgrims proceeded (or should have proceeded) to the shrine of St Thomas at least occasionally by way of the north choir aisle because in 1392 Prior Chillendon caused to be rebuilt 'the rooms of the three petty sacristans which then were in the north aisle of the Church, obstructing in very unseemly fashion the way, that is to say the passage leading to the shrine of St Thomas'.[32] While few churches had as many shrines as did Canterbury, in most pilgrims also appear to have moved down the north quire aisle.[33] Architectural remains at Norwich show that the south quire aisle was effectively blocked by a number of chapels.[34] Draper claims that the north aisle of the quire at Ely was kept clear of tombs for the benefit of pilgrims approaching the feretory of St Etheldreda.[35] However, the Ely aisle may have been blocked by a series of chapels, called the Three Altars, which have been proposed as running from the fourth to the sixth bays west of the eastern termination of the north aisle.[36] In these instances, as perhaps elsewhere, the pilgrims must have left the same way they came.

Once the area behind the high altar was reached, entrance into the feretory chapel depended on its precise situation. A shrine in a retrochoir, especially one at or near the height of the surrounding aisles, was most easily entered through a gate in the encircling fence or screen. This was certainly the case at Ely, where an iron grating was penetrated by a door in the north.[37] The grate around the shrine

31 Erasmus, *Pilgrimages to Saint Mary and Saint Thomas*, pp. 42–50.
32 'Et cameras trium parvorum sacristarum, que tunc in ala boriali ecclesie in via viz. qua itur ad fferetrum Sci Thome multum inhoneste dictum viam accloyantes . . .': 'A Monastic Chronicle at Christ Church', pp. 62, 65.
33 As for example at St Albans, discussed in Klukas, 'The Architectural Implications of the *Decreta Lanfranci*', p. 159.
34 'From the cuts in the walls it is clear that the aisle was crossed by a number of screens': W. St John Hope and W.T. Bensly, 'Recent Discoveries in the Cathedral Church of Norwich', *Norfolk Archaeology*, vol. 14 (1901), p. 111.
35 Draper, 'Northwold and Etheldreda', p. 13.
36 Plan in Ladds, *Monastery of Ely*, insert.
37 The sacrist roll for 1349/50 mentions a door in the feretory fence at Ely: 'Item for one pair of hinges for the wicket across from the shrine' (Item in j pare garnet pro le Wyket versus feretrum): E.M. Hampson and T.D. Atkinson. 'The City of Ely', in *VCH: Cambridge and*

at St Paul's cathedral also had locking doors which, if the representation in Dugdale is correct, were on the east side.[38] If a shrine chapel was raised on a platform above the level of the ambulatory then steps of some sort would be needed. The shrine platform at Chichester, for example, was apparently reached by a flight of stairs to either side.[39]

In a few instances the barriers around shrines suggest that some shrines were approached by way of the presbytery, passing right by the high altar. A view of Canterbury's choir painted in 1657 shows clear abrasions in the pavement at the position of the two doors of the missing reredos, flanking the original position of the high altar and possibly caused by pilgrims going to and from the shrine.[40] At York, after the renovations of 1472, the shrine was almost certainly approached only by going past the high altar.[41] A 1728 plan by B. Willis, the earliest information we have for Durham, does not show any steps to the north or south of the feretory platform.[42] It is therefore highly possible that medieval access was restricted to the two doors in the reredos. There are examples of this means of access from outside England as well. At St Andrews, after the reconstruction sometime prior to 1443, the shrine was reached solely by going through the reredos doors.[43] Perhaps a shrine was made holier by virtue of its only being accessible by passing the high altar. This would accentuate the *sanctum sanctorum* aspect of later shrines and give the process of entry an added degree of solemnity. This necessitated the closure of shrines during mass but, as we shall, this was probably the case anyway.

The pilgrim's devotions

The objective of pilgrimage was to adore the saint, and the pilgrim's goal was to get as close to the relics as possible. By the later middle ages the golden feretrum itself was just out of reach, and even if it were not the vigilant clergy would have prevented anyone from touching it. Therefore, the only tangible part of the shrine was the shrine base. Pilgrims caressed, kissed and pressed against the stonework, sometimes prying or scraping pieces off for use in healing.[44] Without exception,

---

the Isle of Ely, vol. 4, ed. R.B. Pugh (1953), p. 70 ('Garnet' is given as a hinge p. 70 n.15) and an undated feretrar's roll which places his chamber 'opposite the doors of the shrine of St Etheldreda in the north part' (opposito hostii feretri S. Ethaldr' ex parte boreali). Note that the latter (CUL, MS EDC 5/12/6) is not a regular feretrar's account but appears to be a fabric roll for that officer's various tenements and buildings.

[38] Dugdale, St Paul's, p. 114.
[39] 'Early Statutes of Chichester', p. 173.
[40] Caroë, 'Canterbury During the Commonwealth', p. 359.
[41] Wilson, Shrines of St William, pp. 19–20.
[42] Willis, A Survey of the Cathedrals of York, etc., p. 223.
[43] D. McRoberts, 'The Glorious House of St. Andrew', in The Medieval Church of St Andrews, ed. D. McRoberts (Glasgow, 1976), p. 67.
[44] Scrapings from the tomb of St William of Norwich were reportedly a commonly used cure, see Thomas of Monmouth, Life of St William, miracles on pp. 135–6, 150, 162, 190. Dust

shrine bases were provided with niches in which pilgrims could kneel, an accommodation towards what seems to have been a fervent desire to be virtually *inside* the shrine.

An unusual case is the low tunnel known as the 'Holy Hole' which leads under the feretory platform at Winchester.[45] It has been proposed that this passage 'allowed pilgrims to crawl beneath the platform, presumably in order to absorb the holy radiance emanating from Swithun's relics'.[46] However, it could just as likely have been used as 4a sort of relic aumbry. The inscription above the doorway seems to state as much: 'The bodies of the saints are here entombed in peace, out of whose merits miracles flow.'[47] The hole would have been a very convenient and secure place for Winchester's abundance of relics, while at the same time mirroring the Anglo-Saxon arrangement whereby relics were under the high altar.[48]

Whether ensconced in a niche or gazing up at the golden feretrum, the pilgrim prayed to the saint for intercession or thanked him for help already given. In the prologue to the *Tale of Beryn* the pilgrims kneeled down before the shrine and prayed.[49] In the *miracula* stories some pilgrims appear to have given very brief thanks while others remained for days: one blind woman is said to have stayed near the tomb of St Hugh for a year.[50] Yet, the shrine was more than just a convenient spot to honour the powers of a saint. It was also a space to experience that power, a holy place where miraculous healings took place. Some pilgrims came to the shrine specifically to be healed. Perhaps the most common method of accomplishing this was through the process familiar to all pilgrims of praying, offering and departing in hope. This method did not really make use of the numinous qualities of a shrine, but rather expected help through the saint's intercession with God. However, it was also believed that intimate contact with a shrine could bring about healing of a more thaumaturgic nature. For example, touching one's head to the place of the first burial of St Etheldreda was said to cure maladies of the eyes.[51]

The offering, particularly if it was of a votive nature, was crucial to any miracle of healing. A vivid illustration of the variety and number of votive objects can be

scraped with a knife from the mortar of the tomb of St Hugh was used as a healing plaster: Giraldus Cambrensis, *Vita S. Hugonis*, p. 141. At York a piece of the tomb of St William, broken off by a man to take home for his sick wife, turned into bread while crossing Ousebridge: *Miracula Sancti Willelmi*, in *Historians of the Church of York*, vol. 2, p. 539.

45 See plates 9 and 15.

46 Crook, 'Romanesque Winchester', p. 19.

47 'Corpora Sanctorum hic sunt in pace sepulta, ex meritis quorum fulgant miracula multa': Draper, 'The Retrochoir of Winchester', p. 12.

48 'Sub altari': *Annales Monasterii Wintonia*, p. 38.

49 *Tale of Beryn*, p. 6.

50 Giraldus Cambrensis, *Vita S. Hugonis*, p. 139.

51 'Any who pray while laying their head on that little place will soon have sickness or cataracts removed from their eyes' (Qui cum suum caput eidem loculo apponentes orassent, mox doloris sive caliginis incommodum ab oculis amoverunt): Richard of Cirencester, *Speculum Historiale de Gestis Regum Angliæ*, vol. 1, p. 209.

seen in an inventory of the non-monetary offerings collected at the shrine-tomb of Thomas Cantilupe at Hereford. Made in 1307 by the commissioners investigating Thomas' canonisation, the inventory's contents include:

170 ships in silver and 41 in wax
129 images of men or their limbs in silver, 1,424 in wax
77 images of animals and birds of diverse species
108 crutches
3 vehicles in wood and 1 in wax, left by cured cripples
97 night-gowns
116 gold and silver rings and brooches
38 garments of gold thread and silk[52]

The number of wax eyes, breasts and ears could not be counted due to their 'multitude', and there were also many chains, anchors, lances and arrows. Despite the number of listed objects, the investigators were told that the wax offerings were only a small fraction of the total, the rest having been sold or having deteriorated with age. Some offerings were collected even as the commissioners were counting, including eighty-five of wax and one of silver, while two silver ships and one of wax were brought by a group of Irish sailors.[53] Two similar lists, one for just those items newly acquired during the office of treasurer Robert Langton, exist for the tomb of Richard Scrope in York Minster, including whole bodies, heads, hands, arms, legs, feet, hearts, breasts, teeth, eyes, rings, crosses, buckles, anchors, oars, belts, sheep, sixty ships, two bulls, an arrow and a horse, all of silver.[54]

These gifts were symbolic of the miracle sought or obtained. The night-gowns (*camisiae*) mentioned at Hereford were given by formerly infertile women who had been granted a child.[55] Crutches were left at the shrine, as at Lourdes today, and were found when the shrine of St Mary at Caversham was pulled down in 1538.[56] A gift could also be left in the hope of a cure not yet worked, usually in the form of a wax image of whatever needed the miraculous attentions of the saint. As we have seen at Hereford, limbs, eyes and whole figures of people were common.[57] Sometimes such votive gifts were made by moulding wax to an ailing body part. Two examples were left at the shrine of St William of Norwich, including wax boots which had covered a man's swollen feet and the wax left by a woman after she had applied it to her afflicted breast.[58]

---

[52] *Acta Sanctorum, Oct.*, vol. 1, pp. 594–5.

[53] *Acta Sanctorum, Oct.*, vol. 1, pp. 594–5.

[54] *Historians of the Church of York*, vol. 3, pp. 389–90.

[55] *Acta Sanctorum, Oct.*, vol. 1, p. 595.

[56] In a letter to Cromwell Dr London reported: 'I have also pullyd down the place sche stode in, with all other ceremonyes, as lightes, schrowdes, crowchys, and imagies of wex, hangyng abowt the chapell': *Three Chapters of Letters Relating to the Suppression of Monasteries*, p. 221.

[57] For a general discussion of votives see Finucane, *Miracles and Pilgrims*, pp. 96–9.

[58] Thomas of Monmouth, *Life of St William*, pp. 196, 266–7.

An interesting case study for votive offerings is the tale of John Combe, recorded in 1414. During a sporting dispute John was struck with a large stick so that his head was broken open and his shoulder blade smashed. Made deaf and blind, he had been bedridden for three months when a vision of a man in shining white told him to make a head and shoulders of wax and give them the same wounds as his, then go to the tomb of Bishop Osmund at Salisbury where he was to pray and offer the image. Combe obeyed the instructions and was cured.[59] Edward I employed the same cure for his gerfalcons, an image of one being offered at the shrine of St Thomas at a cost of 4s. 8d. (in addition to 4d. in monetary offering).[60] Wax images were often left on the tomb or shrine, or hung from a beam like that over the high altar.[61] At Richard Scrope's tomb these offerings seem to have been placed on rods (marked A through F) or attached to three cloths hanging nearby.[62] Some votive images offered to the tomb of Bishop Edmund Lacy at Exeter were found walled into a screen. All were made in moulds (suggesting that they were made and marketed in quantity) and show signs of having been hung by wick-like threads.[63]

A more symbolic method of representation in wax was 'measuring', in which a candle was made to match in some way the proportions of an invalid.[64] There are many examples of this in *miracula* and other records. For Hereford we are lucky to have the personal account of a devotee of Thomas Cantilupe, given as testimony in the canonisation investigation of 1307. Hugh le Barber, who had been barber to Thomas while the bishop was alive, appealed to his deceased master when his eyesight left him in old age, sending two wax eyes to Hereford, twice making and sending his measurements (presumably converted into wax) and finally going there on pilgrimage. With each donation his eyesight improved until he was able to play chess and read the pips on dice.[65] As with wax images, kings were not adverse to following the common practice, although in an uncommon luxuriance: in 1245 Henry III spent £51 13s. 6d. for fifteen candles 'of his size' (*cera ad xv. mensuras nostras*) placed around the shrine of Edward the Confessor.[66]

The details of how 'measuring' was carried out are not absolutely clear. An

---

59 *Canonization of St Osmund*, pp. 171–2.

60 *Records of the Wardrobe and Household, 1285–1286*, ed. B.F. Byerly and C.R. Byerly (London, 1977), no. 368, p. 2239.

61 Two separate wax arms were left on the tomb of St Hugh: Giraldus Cambrensis, *Vita S. Hugonis*, pp. 138, 143.

62 *Historians of the Church of York*, vol. 3, pp. 389–90.

63 U.M. Radford, 'Wax Images Found in Exeter Cathedral', *Ant. J.*, vol. 29 (1929), p. 164.

64 For a fuller description of this practice see Finucane, *Miracles and Pilgrims*, pp. 95–6.

65 See the testimony of Hugh in E.M. Jancey, 'A Servant Speaks of his Master: Hugh le Barber's Evidence in 1307', in *St. Thomas Cantilupe, Bishop of Hereford; Essays in his Honour* (Hereford, 1982), pp. 200–1.

66 *Liberate Rolls*, vol. 2, p. 306. Presumably this was for fifteen candles which were continually replaced. If this was for fifteen large candles, then, at the price of 5½d. per pound (the price paid by the king in the last determinable wax purchase in 1241) each candle weighed slightly more than 150 pounds

invalid (usually unable to visit the shrine in person) was measured with a piece of string, sometimes in both length and breadth, sometimes wound about the body or afflicted member in a spiral.[67] For example, one man ordered 'a candle made to his measurement in length and width'.[68] If the descriptions are literally correct, and a candle of the height of a man was made (perhaps with the string used as a wick), then the candle would of necessity have been over five feet tall, which seems unlikely. In one example a man surrounded his sick oxen with a thread and offered a candle of the thread's length ('*ad fili mensuram*') to the tomb of St William of Norwich.[69] Obviously, the candle was not as long as the circumference of a herd of oxen. 'The normal practice was to use the measuring thread (sometimes doubled back on itself) to form the wick of a candle of standard proportions; or alternatively to coat it thinly with wax and twist it into a 'trindle', a coil shaped like a Catherine wheel.[70] An example of the former is a candle offered to the shrine of St Cuthbert made of sixty-six folded threads.[71] A candle of the coiled type is depicted sitting on St Thomas's tomb in one Canterbury stained glass window and being offered in another.[72] However, the only roughly contemporary use of the word 'trindle' in this sense is in the injunctions of Edward VI forbidding 'Candlestickes, tryndilles or rolles of waxe' as superstitious objects.[73] 'Trindle' generally meant 'wheel' or 'roll' and so is an appropriate, but not specific, term for these objects.[74] An apparently unique offering was the *'candela in rota'*, a taper wound around a drum which was renewed and donated to the shrine of St Thomas at Canterbury each year by the city of Dover, 'whose length will contain the circuit or border of the said city'.[75] This candle was lit during the mass of St Thomas and on other occasions of note in the shrine chapel, and lengths were cut from it to supply tapers for the funerals of Canterbury paupers.

On occasion a candle or image was said to be of the same weight as an invalid. In 1443, for example, some wax images made to the weight of John Paston were

67 See discussion in J. Fowler, 'On a Window Representing the Life and Miracles of S. William of York, at the North End of the Eastern Transept, York Minster', *Yorkshire Archaeological and Topographical J.*, vol. 3 (1875), pp. 304–6. In one example the candle is made to the length of the Saint's tomb: Thomas of Monmouth, *Life of St William*, p. 151.

68 'Ad longitudinis et latitudinis sue mensuram fieri candelam': Thomas of Monmouth, *Life of St William*, p. 210.

69 Thomas of Monmouth, *Life of St William*, pp. 153–4.

70 'Miracles of St Osmund', ed. D. Stroud, *Hatcher Rev.*, vol. 23 (1987), pp. 112–13. See also Finucane, *Miracles and Pilgrims*, p. 95.

71 Reginald of Durham, *Libellus de Admirandis Beati Cuthberti*, p. 134.

72 See plates XIV and XV in M.D. Anderson, *A Saint at Stake* (London, 1964).

73 'Also, that they shall take awaie, utterly extincte, and destroye, all shrines, coueryng of shrines, all tables, candelstickes, tryndilles or rolles of waxe, pictures, paintynges, and all other monumentes of fained miracles, pilgremages, Idolatry and superstition': Edward VI, *Iniunccions geuen by the moste exellente Prince, Edwarde the .vi.* (London, 1547), §28, p. 18.

74 *Oxford English Dictionary 2 on CD ROM* (version 1.00, Oxford, 1992).

75 'Cuius longitudo continebit ambitum siue circuitum dicte ville': 'Customary of the Shrine of St Thomas', f. 9.

sent to Walsingham by his mother-in-law when he was ill.[76] This type of offering would have been affordable only for the wealthy. Most cathedrals paid about 6d. per pound for wax, at which rate an image or candle made to the weight of an average man would have cost over £4. Nevertheless, we know that candles approaching this weight were occasionally made. Henry, duke of Lancaster, willed that his funeral should be 'nothing vain or extravagant' yet should include five candles weighing one hundred pounds each.[77] While the exact nature of these wax offerings remains a mystery, their use is clear; both wax images and measured candles had very potent symbolic and magical aspects. It is possible that burning the offering was symbolically equated with the disappearance of the disease.[78] Certainly, sympathetic magic using wax images could be employed in other contexts to curse or harm as well as heal.[79]

If healing did not happen instantaneously, then a sick pilgrim was usually prepared to remain within the holy emanations of the shrine as long as permitted. Vigils at the shrine extended into lengthy residences and could lead to the permanent presence of pilgrims day and night, in monastic as well as secular churches. The waiting pilgrims' constant presence 'made it necessary for the monastic wardens of the shrine to sleep alongside of their charge'.[80] Pilgrims, nestled in the niches and holes of the shrine base, often (according to the *miracula*) received healing visions in their sleep. The mentally deranged had to be chained to the shrine by well-wishers and relatives. What effect a screaming, chain-rattling demoniac had on the other pilgrims, or indeed on the services at the nearby high altar, is worth wondering.[81]

If pilgrims were not healed by the shrine then they could resort to other relics presented by the cathedral clergy for that purpose. Saint's water, most famously that of St Thomas Becket, was a healing potion as was the oil which occasionally flowed from tombs. The oil from the tomb of St William of York, for example,

---

[76] 'My moder hat be-hestyd a-noder ymmage of wax of [th]e weytte of yow to Oyur Lady of Walsyngham': *Paston Letters and Papers of the Fifteenth Century*, ed. N. Davis (Oxford, 1971), vol. 1, p. 218.

[77] 'Issint q'il ny ait chose voine ne de bobaunce': *A Collection of All the Wills, Now Known to be Extant, of the Kings and Queens of England*, ed. J. Nichols (London, 1780), p. 84.

[78] Anderson, *Saint at Stake*, p. 188.

[79] See C. Hole, 'Some Instances of Image-Magic in Great Britain', in *The Witch Figure*, ed. V. Newall (London, 1973), pp. 83–8. For continental examples and a general discussion of candles used in the cult of saints, see D.R. Dendy, *The Use of Lights in Christian Worship* (London, 1959), pp. 108–19.

[80] D. Knowles, *The Monastic Order in England* (2nd edn, Cambridge, 1963), p. 481. He cites miracle stories including that of a soldier, cured during a vigil, who woke up the monks there, in *Memorials of St. Edmund's Abbey*, vol. 1, p. 78.

[81] A demoniac who was not chained down tore off his clothes and terrified other worshippers at the tomb of St William: Thomas of Monmouth, *Life of St William*, p. 225. Another was chained at the tomb of St Hugh for a week: Giraldus Cambrensis, *Vita S. Hugonis*, p. 127; Some writers have enjoyed evoking scenes of this sort. To take a rather florid example: 'Lunatics were driven forward, bound and beaten, to wake the echoes of the great churches with their eldritch screams.' M.D. Anderson, *History and Imagery in British Churches* (London, 1971), p. 207.

cured several pilgrims in the early fourteenth century.[82] The cathedral clergy occasionally fêted a genuine recipient of a miracle. An interesting case from Canterbury seems to indicate money being given to a poor recipient of a miraculous cure: *'Dat' cuidam pauperi in Elemosina miraculose sanato iiis. iiijd.'*[83] A woman whose cure at Lincoln was judged to be a true miracle was led in procession to the tomb of St Hugh.[84]

The offering

By no means all offerings were votive. An offering was an indispensable part of any pilgrimage regardless of whether or not a miracle was sought. Although a gift was probably not mandatory, later shrine-keepers no doubt exerted considerable pressure on visitors to pay. At Walsingham Erasmus noted that a priest stood and watched and, although no force was employed, he believed that 'a kind of pious shame' caused some to give more than they otherwise would.[85] One standard type of gift was a wax candle or taper similar to those seen in some saints' shrines at the present day. These were sometimes on sale to pilgrims in the cathedral; the offerings to the relics at Ely were recorded by the feretrar together with candles sold to pilgrims.[86] Although Ely seems to have sold its wax at 4d. per pound, elsewhere candles often cost 6d. or 7d. Prior William More, for example, spent 13d. on renewing two tapers at St Wulfstan's shrine in 1528.[87] The high cost was partly due to the Church's insistence that tapers be made only of expensive beeswax, which was fragrant and given mystic significance by the supposed death of the bee during its labour.[88] The volume of candles and wax votive offerings both offered and burnt made wax a sort of currency at shrines, with the clerks sometimes making two accounts: one for money and one for wax.

Offerings in money, however, were the most common and best recorded. In the twelfth and thirteenth centuries it was probably common to place coins directly on the altar or shrine top, and in some places this continued. The early fifteenth-century 'Customary of the Shrine of St Thomas' advises that the paraphernalia for mass at the shrine altar be tidied up promptly so that pilgrims could quickly give their offerings.[89] In most instances, however, one or more strong boxes, or pyxes, were eventually used. By the fifteenth century the usual description of money

[82] *Miracula Sancti Willelmi*, in *Historians of the Church of York*, vol. 2, pp. 282, 284, 537–40. A less well known water was that of Wulfstan: *Miracula Wulfstani*, appended to William of Malmesbury, *The Vita Wulfstani*, pp. 127–8.

[83] C.E. Woodruff, 'Notes on the Inner Life and Domestic Economy of the Priory of Christ Church, Canterbury, in the Fifteenth Century', *Arch. Cant.*, vol. 53 (1940), p. 14.

[84] Giraldus Cambrensis, *Vita S. Hugonis*, p. 126.

[85] Erasmus, *Pilgrimages to Saint Mary and Saint Thomas*, pp. 14–15.

[86] For example, the Feretrar's roll for 1422/3: CUL, EDC 5/12, Feretrar's Roll 1.

[87] WCA, 'Prior William More's Journal', f. 106.

[88] Anderson, *Saint at Stake*, p. 184.

[89] 'Customary of the Shrine of St Thomas', ff. 1–2.

from an offering site was, for example, *de pyxide*.[90] Canterbury cathedral had many offering boxes even besides those connected with St Thomas; the Sacrist's rolls of the late fifteenth century mention boxes in the nave and crypt, at Sts Sythe and Appollonia, and the shrines of Sts Dunstan and Alphege.[91] Both the chests themselves and the keys were frequent items of expense in the shrine accounts. For example, 4d. was paid towards making a pyx in the Canterbury crypt in 1487/8.[92] All the offering pyxes that survive (universally from the fifteenth century and none known to have been from a shrine) are of oak, except one of iron at St George's chapel, Windsor.[93] Those in great shrines might be of more precious materials: a 1520 relic list from Westminster Abbey mentions 'a lytle box of sylver enamelyd to putt in the offryng money'.[94] Iron bound and provided with coin slots and locks, a pyx had an obvious advantage for security over offerings left on an altar. It also might be fixed in place, as was the iron box attached to the pillar below the image of the Virgin in the nave of St Paul's.[95]

Cathedral accounts occasionally tell us of the types of coins, sometimes rare, sometimes illegal, used by pilgrims. In the Durham accounts various non-sterling coins were usually recorded in a separate sum, presumably because they were jointly disposed of by being sold to a money-changer or silver-smith. Sometimes, however, the different types of coin were itemised separately. Scottish money was the most frequent, appearing from 1417/8 to 1431/2. In 1418/9 it was worth 27s. 9d., but after it was banned from England in 1423 the receipt of Scottish money was much reduced, usually to about 2s.[96] A sharp rise in the receipts in 1428/9 suggests that the Scots and their money were again current in the north of England. In 1432/3, however, the receipts were suddenly zero again, this time with the explanation that they were given to a brother. An identical entry the next year is the last time it appears. Possibly, all Scots money was thenceforward given away to monks as part of their payments without being accounted.

Coins from France also feature at Durham. They included the Anglo-Gallic gyan, first minted by the lieutenant of Guienne in 1412 and appearing in the shrine box five years later.[97] Coins called 'crowns' are presumably to be identified with the French crown worth 3s. 4d., since no English coin of that name was minted until 1526.[98] A final type of coin, mentioned only in 1428/9, was the French blaunky or blank, so called from its whitish colour. Blanks were of impure silver

90 DDCA, Feretrar's roll 1381–2.
91 CCA, MS DCc/MA 7, ff. 36r, 69, 92r, among other references.
92 CCA, MS DCc/MA 7, f. 69.
93 J.C. Cox and A. Harvey, *English Church Furniture* (London, 1907), p. 240.
94 Westlake, *Westminster Abbey*, vol. 2, p. 500.
95 Dugdale, *St Paul's*, p. 21.
96 Raine, *St. Cuthbert*, p. 148n.† It is unlikely that Raine was right that the 1423/4 entry recording 'mulkyn' of Scottish money was a fine (mulct) imposed on the feretrar for possession of the newly illegalised coinage, since the 8s. 2d. is a receipt.
97 Raine, *St. Cuthbert*, p. 148n.†
98 For the English crowns, see C.H.V. Sutherland, *English Coinage 600–1900* (London, 1973), p. 127.

and, like Scottish money, were banned by parliament in 1423.[99] It is evident that some pilgrims did not have the interests of the Durham monks uppermost in their minds, since they fulfilled their vows and obligations to St Cuthbert by unloading inconvenient currency.

A form of receipt listed along with coins in several shrine accounts is *pecunia fracta* (or more rarely *argenta fracta*). This entry occurred six times between 1419 and 1442 at Durham, where it averaged about 13½s. At Hereford the fabric account for 1291 received 3s. 'for broken silver sold', and five of the clavigers' accounts (most from the early sixteenth century) have an identical heading ranging in value from 1s. to 7s. Broken silver was also sold at Canterbury, where the sacrist received 36s. for 18 oz. of broken silver in 1392/3.[100] In 1423/4 the Worcester sacrist received 13s 4d for the same thing.[101] This type of income was therefore widely spread over time and place, and seems to have been connected with offerings at shrines.

Broken money or silver could be one or a combination of three things. Firstly, it could represent the remains of coins halved or quartered to make small change, and so damaged or cut that they were no longer passable currency.[102] Secondly, it might signify coins that had been bent or folded to dedicate them to a saint, a reasonably common practice.[103] This or similar mutilation, such as piercing holes in a coin, could accompany a vow of pilgrimage and so ensure that the promised money was not spent before it was offered.[104] Thirdly, *pecunia fracta* could represent silver gifts or shrine paraphernalia that were not fine or whole enough to preserve at the shrine or sell as an item. At Durham in 1433/4 some silver spoons were sold at the same time as *pecunia fracta* and to the same person, which suggests that they were similar but different enough to deserve separate mention.[105] In each of these cases the silver was no longer usable in its original form and had to be sold by weight.

Gold coins were another variant and somewhat rare offering. Before they became common circulation in England gold coins were generally reserved for shrine offerings. Their earliest record in England comes from 1171, when Muslim Spanish coins found their way to the shrine of St Lawrence in London.[106]

---

[99] Raine, *St. Cuthbert*, p. 148n.†

[100] CCA, DCc/Sacrist 11.

[101] *Compotus Rolls of the Priory of Worcester of the XIVth and XVth Centuries*, trans. S.G. Hamilton (Oxford, 1910), p. 64.

[102] Raine, *St. Cuthbert*, p. 149n.†

[103] See Finucane, 'Use and Abuse of Medieval Miracles', p. 1 n. 5; Finucane, *Miracles and Pilgrims*, pp. 94–5. For an example, see Reginald of Durham, *Libellus de Admirandis Beati Cuthberti*, p. 231.

[104] E. Duffy, *The Stripping of the Altars: Traditional Religion in England, c. 1400 – c. 1580* (London, 1992), pp. 183–4.

[105] 'And concerning 25s. received from Thomas Nesbytt for "broken money" and two spoons' (Et de 25s. rec. de Thome Nesbytt pro fracta pecunia et duobus coclearibus): DDCA, Feretrar's Roll 1433–4.

[106] Spufford, *Money and Its Use*, p. 185.

Just as in France, a certain amount of gold coin was available in England in the mid thirteenth century, and, as in France, it was treated as a commodity and not yet as a part of the currency. Instead it was used for such strictly uncommercial purposes as prestigious alms-giving by the king. Those gold coins that were used as royal alms at once ceased even to be objects of commerce. They were given on the great festivals of the Church and ended up, along with similar offerings by other great men, in the treasuries of monasteries and cathedrals, or attached to shrines, such as that of St. Thomas of Canterbury, or those of St. Lawrence and St. Ethelbert in London. They remained there until they were melted down and turned into ornamental goldsmith's work.[107]

Gold coins of Arabic origin were often called 'obols of musca', a late example being the £12 collected at Westminster in the six years previous to 1476.[108] D.A. Carpenter has made an argument that the Wardrobe under Henry III at first acquired gold coins (the bulk in *oboli de musc*) for no other purpose than to fund royal offerings, especially to the shrine of Edward the Confessor.[109]

In 1456, by which time gold and larger silver coins had become relatively common as English currency, a *Cista Osmundi* contained 37s. 4d. in gold, £9 in groats, £2 in half groats and £6 6s. 8d. in pennies (a proportion that was not necessarily the same as that received at the shrine since larger and more valuable coins were no doubt retained preferentially).[110]

This state of affairs held true until gold became a standard component of English currency in the middle of the fifteenth century and therefore began to be recorded in the accounts. In 1456, for example, a chest of St Osmund contained 37s. 4d. in gold, £9 in groats, £2 in half groats and £6 6s. 8d. in pennies (a proportion that was not necessarily the same as that received at the shrine since larger and more valuable coins were no doubt retained preferentially).[111] The Lincoln *aperturæ* of the fifteenth and early sixteenth century occasionally have separate reckonings for gold in the possession of the shrine, including florins, angels and Portuguese cruzados.[112] As early as 1341, for example, the shrine had two gold florins.[113] The same coin can sometimes be followed through several accounts as it remained in the possession of the shrine keepers. A particularly

---

107 Spufford, *Money and Its Use*, p. 183.

108 WAM, MS 19723.

109 'The story of Henry III's gold treasure begins on his return from Gascony in September 1243. Before that, the Wardrobe only acquired gold to fund the king's pious oblations': D.A. Carpenter, 'The Gold Treasure of Henry III', in *Thirteenth Century England I*, eds P.R. Coss and S.D. Lloyd (Woodbridge, 1986), pp. 62, 71.

110 *Canonization of St Osmund*, p. 174. This may have been a chest kept towards the canonisation of the saint, since the preceeding record in the register concerns the repayment of a loan from a Florentine merchant made to procure the bulls of canonisation.

111 *Canonization of St Osmund*, p. 174.

112 I have assumed that the 'crusidors' mentioned were Portuguese cruzados, minted after 1457 from African gold obtained by Henry the Navigator. Portugal was, at that time, the most important source of gold for England: Spufford, *Money and Its Use*, pp. 321–2, 370.

113 LCA, D&C, Bj/5/16/1, f. 50.

long-lasting example was the 10s. double cruzado which survived five accounts.[114]

The most valuable of offerings were gifts of jewellery, among which rings played a special role. In 1441, for example, the widow Joan Denys willed to the shrine of St Thomas her profession ring (*anulum de professione mea*) and to the shrine of St Augustine her wedding ring (*anulum nuptiale*).[115] Bishops seem to have been partial to willing their pontifical rings to shrines. For example, the bequests of Archbishop Walter Reynold included:

> Item, I leave one great pontifical ring with a precious sapphire stone which once was St Wulfstan's, impressed for ornament in the circumference with emeralds to the shrine of the glorious martyr Thomas. Item, I leave to the same shrine a gold ring with a sapphire stone insculpted in the manner of a lion which I wish to be fixed to the shrine of the glorious martyr aforesaid between the other jewels which I bought and gave over to the same shrine in times gone by.[116]

Bishop Lewis Charleton (d.1369) left sundry rings to St Thomas of Hereford's shrine, and in 1436 Bishop Robert Fitzhugh left his pontifical ring 'which I will to be fixed on the case of St Erkenwald and there to remain in perpetuity'.[117] Edward I paid for gold attachments to fix eight brooches to the shrine of 'St Quitere'.[118] Rings and jewellery were frequently fixed to the surface of a shrine, as above, or even placed inside. A Lichfield inventory of 1345 states that there was 'Also one morse [clasp] of pure gold and two gold rings, which were offered that they may be placed in the shrine of St. Chad, by Dan Thomas de Berkeley and his wife, and one other (ring), as catalogued above, replaced in the coffer; and Richard, the Sacrist, now says that they are in the shrine of St. Chad'.[119]

Gifts in kind were rare but continued to be made until late in the middle ages. At Hereford cathedral in 1490/1, for example, 8s. were received as the *precia j. bouis* given to the shrine and sold.[120] The *Valor Ecclesiasticus* records £6 6s.

---

114 LCA Bj/5/16/2b, ff. 6–7.
115 'Some Early Kentish Wills', ed. C.E. Woodruff, *Arch. Cant.*, vol. 46 (1934), p. 34.
116 Charlton gave another ring to the shrine of St Edmund of Pontigny: *Sede Vacante Wills*, p. 68.
117 'Quem super Capsam Sancti Erkenwaldi figi et ibidem remanare in perpetuum volo': J.W.F. Hill, *Medieval Lincoln* (Cambridge, 1948), p. 75, from Lambeth, Reg. Whittlesey, f. 102; *Registrum Statutorum Londiniensis*, p. 398.
118 Admittedly the proper translation of *firmacula* in this case might be something closer to 'little fasteners', but they are still seemingly an ornamental afterthought and might have any number of purposes. 'For attachments for gold brooches to Henry Goldsmith of London for attaching eight gold brooches on the case of the head of St Quentin, 20d. sterling' (Attachimenta firmaculorum auri Henrico aurifabro London' pro attachimentis factis ad adtachianda octo firmacula auri super casum capitis Sancte Quitere, xx d. sterlingorum): *Records of the Wardrobe and Household, 1286–1289*, ed. B.F. Byerly and C.R. Byerly (London, 1986), no. 560, p. 69.
119 The entry concludes that 'it is well to enquire of John, his predecessor, as to the truth of this': 'Sacrist's Roll of Lichfield', pp. 208–9.
120 'Clavigers' Accounts', HCA, MS R585, f. 22.

received for wool given to St Kenelm at Winchcombe.[121] Other, rarer offerings might be in the same category. For example, gifts from shipwreck survivors to St John of Beverley included a silk cloth, possibly part of the rescued cargo, which the writer of the late twelfth-century *Miracula S. Johannis* saw among the relics.[122]

Other activities

Their offering at the shrine completed, pilgrims could avail themselves of various religious services in the cathedral. The most important of these were masses, often celebrated at the shrine altar. One of the two Canterbury shrine-keepers was dedicated to performing mass at the shrine of St Thomas.[123] Sometimes specific chantries were set up. For example, there were chantries at both the head and altar of St Richard of Chichester, and in 1311 Bishop Ralph Baldock founded a chantry at the altar attached to the shrine of St Erkenwald of London.[124] Chantry masses might have been watched, if not attended, by pilgrims. One woman was cured at the tomb of St Hugh while mass was performed at the nearby altar of St John the Baptist, with others present *tam clerici tam laici*.[125] It was only on rare occasions that sermons were preached. At the 1420 jubilee of St Thomas an Augustinian doctor of theology gave a sermon on the theme of *'Annus Jubileus est'*, which he had to repeat three times because those who could not hear the earlier performances demanded it.[126] Sermons might also be given in the event of a miracle, such as that delivered at Lincoln after the cure of a woman at Hugh's tomb.[127]

In the later middle ages one of the major attractions of a shrine was the indulgences attached to it. In 1215 Innocent III limited the indulgence power of bishops to forty days for most occasions, one hundred if for the dedication of a church.[128] However, indulgences were cumulative, and often many bishops would grant indulgences to the same shrine, especially if they were present on the translation of the saint. The pope could grant further and much more potent indulgences. In 1472–3, for example, Sixtus IV granted twelve years and twelve quadragesimas of penance to those who visited Salisbury cathedral on the obit and translation of St Osmund.[129] The subject of indulgences is a complex and detailed

---

121 *Valor Ecclesiasticus, Tempore Henrici VIII*, ed. J. Caley (London, 1814), vol. 2, p. 461.
122 *Miracula Sancti Johannis*, pp. 319–20.
123 'Customary of the Shrine of St Thomas', f. 1.
124 *Chartulary of Chichester*, p. 308; Cook, *Old St Paul's*, p. 54.
125 Giraldus Cambrensis, *Vita S. Hugonis*, p. 123.
126 Foreville, *Le Jubilé*, p. 142.
127 'And so the precentor William, who a little afterwards was made bishop of Lincoln, that same Palm Sunday, in his sermon to the people, solemnly promulgated this miracle' (Unde et præcentor Willelmus, qui paulo post episcopus Lincolniensis effectus est, eodem palmarum die, in sermone suo ad populum, solemniter hoc miraculum promulgavit): Giraldus Cambrensis, *Vita S. Hugonis*, p. 122.
128 This was canon 61 of Lateran IV: Foreville, *Le Jubilé*, p. 36.
129 *Ceremonies and Processions of Salisbury*, p. 43.

one for which there is much evidence of a legal nature. The process by which they were sought and obtained by churches has been examined by Foreville and others, and does not need to be dealt with here. However, the means by which indulgences were 'promoted' by the local clergy and granted to pilgrims are much less clear and more within the scope of this book.

I know of at least two instances of direct advertisement of an English indulgence outside the church it was intended for. In the Westminster sacrist's accounts of 1364/5 a monk was paid 2s. for riding to London to proclaim an indulgence on the day of the relics and St Peter.[130] There was also some effort to advertise the 1420 Jubilee of St Thomas and its plenary indulgence. The author of the treatise on the Jubilee saw poems proclaiming the jubilee and letters with schedules of indulgences nailed to church doors, including St Paul's, London, and the church of the Domus Dei in Ospringe, Kent, on the pilgrim route from London to Canterbury.[131] It is hard to imagine that the existence of most shrine indulgences was not frequently advertised in a similar manner. If not, then pilgrims had to rely on word of mouth for their information.

If a pilgrim knew the power of remission granted to a shrine then he or she might consider it received merely by performing the usual devotions. It might be expected, however, that pilgrims would have sought some confirmation of the blessing, and certainly conditions were attached to most indulgences. The pilgrim often had to visit the shrine at a required time and leave offerings, and always had to be properly contrite, confessed and absolved. For example, indulgences were given to those who celebrated the first feast of St Thomas of Hereford in October.[132] Two letters granting indulgences from Popes Nicholas IV (1291) and John XXII (1328) to Canterbury order that confession be made, while the indulgence granted to the shrines of Canterbury by Boniface IX in 1395 was only for certain feast days and only on condition that gifts were made to the fabric of the church.[133] Canterbury needed special provisions for confession by large numbers of pilgrims. In a letter of Martin V to Christ Church in 1426 the priory was granted the right to ordain monks at a younger age than usual in order to minister to the frequent pilgrims.[134] To make up for the inconvenience, an indulgence was another source of revenue: offerings at the three chief altars at Norwich increased greatly in 1400 due to the seven-year indulgence of Boniface IX.[135] During the three fiscal years 1399–1402 an indulgence for Trinity Sunday increased offerings to the high altar by £49 to £85 per year.[136]

The last act of a pilgrim in a great church, like that of today's tourist, was often to obtain a souvenir, of which pilgrimage badges are the best known. In the *Tale*

---

[130] WAM, MS 19630.
[131] Printed in Foreville, *Le Jubilé*, p. 129–36.
[132] *Registrum Ade de Orleton*, pp. 142–3.
[133] Printed in Foreville, *Le Jubilé*, pp. 172–4.
[134] Printed in Foreville, *Le Jubilé*, pp. 182–3.
[135] Saunders, *Introduction to the Rolls of Norwich*, p. 103.
[136] N.P. Tanner, *The Church in Late Medieval Norwich 1370–1532*, Studies and Texts 66 (Toronto, 1984), p. 88.

of Beryn the pilgrims all bought badges 'ffor men of contre shuld[e] know whom [th]ey had[de] sou[gh]te', except for the miller and pardoner who filled their pockets with stolen brooches.[137] Despite being made of fragile lead or pewter about 1,300 have been found in England, indicating that they were once exceedingly numerous, especially since only three pairs out of ninety surviving badges showing the mitred head of St Thomas are from the same mould.[138] Of the badges found in London, most date from the period 1340–1400 with the quantity, quality and size steadily deteriorating during the fifteenth century.[139] They generally carry an image of the saint, the shrine or instruments of martyrdom, and once had their open-work design set off by a background of coloured parchment, paper, or mirror attached to the back of the badge, plus clips or pins for fixing them to the traditional pilgrim's hat.[140]

At many shrines pilgrims could also obtain a small lead ampulla filled with holy water or oil from many shrines. A sealed ampulla found in Yorkshire was found to contain an infusion of aromatic herbs and spices.[141] The earliest surviving ampullæ, from the thirteenth century, are large and adorned with images. For example, a surviving ampulla of St Wulfstan is a wide-mouthed vessel surrounded by a narrow circular band and having on one side a figure of Wulfstan, on the other St Mary.[142] Later ampullæ lost their pictorial role to badges and became smaller so that they could be stitched on a hat rather than worn suspended from the neck.[143]

Paper or parchment souvenirs may have been on sale at some shrines, but only one possible example survives: a vellum 'postcard' from Bromholm showing an image of the sacred cross over prayers that were probably meant for recitation in front of the relic.[144] If it was necessary to prove that one had performed a pilgrimage then a document could be obtained for that purpose. A certificate dated 1312 and sealed by Prior Eastry affirmed that someone with the initials N. de L. had gone on pilgrimage (*'causa peregrinationis'*) to the lights of St Thomas of Canterbury and other sanctuaries which he personally visited.[145] Other souvenirs were specific to the shrine. At Ely a pilgrim could purchase brightly coloured silken necklaces called 'Etheldreda's Chains' during the fair.[146] Stubbs claimed,

---

137 *Tale of Beryn*, p. 7.
138 There is written evidence of badges made of precious metals. B. Spencer, 'Medieval Pilgrim Badges', *Rotterdam Papers*, vol. 1 (1968), pp. 137, 139.
139 B. Spencer, 'Pilgrim Souvenirs', in *Medieval Waterfront Development at Trig Lane, London*, eds G. and C. Milne, London and Middlesex Archaeological Soc. Special Paper no. 5 (London, 1982), p. 304.
140 Spencer, 'Pilgrim Badges', p. 138. See also *Tale of Beryn*, p. 7.
141 Spencer, 'Pilgrim Badges', p. 139.
142 B. Spencer, 'A Thirteenth-Century Pilgrim's Ampulla from Worcester', *Trans. of the Worcester Archaeological Soc.*, 3rd ser., vol. 9 (1984), p. 7.
143 B. Spencer, 'Two Leaden Ampullae from Leicestershire', *Trans. Leicestershire Archaeological and Historical Soc.*, vol. 55 (1979–80), pp. 88–9.
144 F. Wormald, 'The Rood of Bromholm', *J. of the Warburg Institute*, vol. 1 (1937–8), p. 34.
145 Foreville, *Le Jubilé*, p. 171.
146 Stewart, *On the Architectural History of Ely Cathedral*, p. 190; 'Our women of England

on what authority I do not know, that the monks originally gave out tiny shackles of iron, in commemoration of a famous miracle, and only later replaced them with plaited ribbands.[147]

Except in the case of the ribbons sold at Ely, which show up as sales of silk in the feretrar's rolls, income from badges and other souvenirs does not appear in cathedral accounts. Perhaps the common practice was for cathedrals to lease a stall in the cathedral close to a private merchant. In any case, the cathedral did not have a monopoly on souvenirs, as badges were often sold in town shops. The duke of Norfolk bought badges from a Bury townsman in 1483 and others are known to have been displayed in shops outside the gates of Canterbury cathedral in the fifteenth century.[148]

Pilgrim numbers and patterns

The above describes in brief what pilgrims did at a great shrine. Our impression of the conditions at a shrine is not complete, however, without an indication of how many pilgrims were there. *Miracula* give the impression of great crowds. The tomb of St Erkenwald, for example, was said to be surrounded by a *'turba innumerabilis'*.[149] After a miracle of Milburga in 1101 the sick were reported hardly to fit in the church and cemetery.[150] Certain other sources give equally grand impressions. The Worcester Chronicler declared that in 1201 fifteen to sixteen people were being miraculously cured by St Wulfstan each day, suggesting that the total number of pilgrims was much higher.[151] Pilgrims at Canterbury were said to number over one hundred thousand.[152] At the 1420 jubilee of St Thomas numbers were so great that they almost filled the nave 'because the lower part of the church was almost entirely full'. While the doors were opened private mass could only be said at the shrine with difficulty, and solemn mass with singing not at all, because the confluence of people was so great.[153] A process-verbal of 1420 from the records of the City of Canterbury reports that 'the people, in estimate, then arrived to the number of one hundred thousand men and women as much English as foreigners from outside, that is to say Irishmen, Welsh, Scots, French, Normans, [Garnisientium, Gernisentium?] to that city'.[154] Hugh Latimer wrote of

are accustomed to bear on the neck a certain necklace, bound and subtly made of silk, which they call the necklace of Etheldreda' (Solent Angliæ nostræ mulieres torquem quendam tenui et subtili serico confectum collo gestare, quem Etheldredæ torquem appellamus): Nicholas Harpsfield, *Historia Anglicana Ecclesiastica*, ed. E. Campion (London, 1622), p. 86.

[147] C.W. Stubbs, *Historical Memorials of Ely Cathedral* (London, 1897), p. xiii.
[148] Spencer, 'Pilgrim Badges', p. 141.
[149] *Miracula Erkenwaldi*, p. 134.
[150] Odo of Ostia, 'Translation of St. Milburga', p. 146.
[151] *Annales de Wigornia*, p. 391.
[152] Heath, *Steps of the Pilgrims*, p. 21, no reference.
[153] Quod pene posterior pars ecclesie totaliter est replita: Foreville, *Le Jubilé*, p. 142.
[154] 'Because the church was totally full, almost to the back' (Qui quidem populus, ut

another pilgrimage in a letter of 1533: 'I dwell within a mile of the Fossway, and you would wonder to see how they come by flocks out of the West Country to many images, but chiefly to the Blood of Hayles.'[155] All of the above are valuable contemporary statements, but as estimations of special events they could be extreme exaggerations of the numbers of pilgrims that could usually be expected.

There is a simple exercise that I have used to estimate the number of pilgrims based on the theory that one coin, usually a penny sterling, was the standard and indeed traditional offering to an English shrine. If this is true, then the number of coins ought to roughly equal the number of pilgrims. At Lincoln for the account of 1335 we can estimate the number of coins offered because it accounts for obols and farthings separately from the rest of the income, namely £28 3s. 10d. plus 13s. 9d. in *ob. et quad,* smaller coin in halfpennies and farthings.[156] The sum of the income is left blank in the accounts of the next few years, although the remainder continues to be divided as above.[157] By the time sums are again entered the accounting practice has changed, so that 1335 is the only full year for this purpose. A shrine box was sometimes used by cathedrals as a convenient source of rare small change. At Durham the feretrar gave an average of 7s. per year towards 'the prior's obols', which were probably a gift of small coins, perhaps literally half penny pieces, to the prior for his almsgiving. There was a shortage of small-denomination coins for charity giving in England in the later middle ages, a situation described as injurious to beggars and other recipients.[158]

The unique accounting at Lincoln in 1335 allows us to calculate that obols and farthings made up only 3.2% of total offerings. Virtually all the rest of the oblations must have been in sterling pennies, for at that time larger coinage was not in common use. If half of the small change at Lincoln was obols and half farthings, and all the other money was in pennies, then the number of individual coins received by the shrine of St Hugh in 1335 was 7,936. If one makes the normally unjustified assumption that the few pilgrims who got away without paying cancelled out the effect of those who gave more than one coin at the shrine, then about 8,000 can be taken as a basic estimate of the number of pilgrims to the Lincoln shrine in the accounting year 1334/5. This works out to a daily average of about twenty-two pilgrims. The same exercise performed using the part term account of 1409, which includes the feast of the Translation of St Hugh and

---

aestimabatur, ad tunc attingebant ad numerum centum millium hominum et mulierum tam Angligenum quam alienigenum exterorum, videlicet Hibernicorum, Wallicorum, Scotticorum, Francorum, Normannorum, Garnisientium, et Gernisentium, ad eandem civitatem): Foreville, *Le Jubilé,* p. 180. From the City Archives, Reg. 1, pt 1, f. 34v.

155 *Letters and Papers Foreign and Domestic of the Reign of Henry VIII,* ed. J. Gairdner (London, 1893), vol. 6, p. 113.

156 I have added the two aperturae for the year. LCA, D&C, Bj/5/16/1, f. 46.

157 LCA, D&C, Bj/5/16/1, ff. 46v–50.

158 P. Spufford, *Money and its Use in Medieval Europe* (Cambridge, 1988), p. 331.

records 3s. in *oboles*, results in 408 pilgrims, or about twelve per day for that period.[159]

The Lincoln numbers show that coinage other than pennies was rare. Therefore, if Lincoln in 1335 was representative, each pound of yearly offerings to a shrine represents about 240 pilgrims. Thus a small income of £5 yearly required about 1,200 pilgrims, while £100 was produced by 24,000. I readily confess that these figures are only a very rough estimate. They would be greatly reduced if more than a few pilgrims gave more than one penny, or increased if there were hordes of non-offering pilgrims or tourists. However, I hope they do at least indicate the correct order of magnitude. They show, for example, that the claims of Canterbury to have hosted over one hundred thousand pilgrims on special occasions are probably not gross exaggerations, yet also that a shrine like Lincoln's was not exactly thronged by pilgrims on an average day in the four-teenth century.

These average numbers, however, changed greatly depending on the time of year. An indication of seasonal fluctuation can be derived from the accounts of Ely, Hereford, Durham and the Shrine of the Martyrdom at Canterbury, all of which record incomes for fractions of a year. The accounts of William Tylney, feretrar of the shrine of St Etheldreda at Ely from 1464 to 1477, divide the yearly offerings into five terms plus the time of the indulgence. These show that late spring and early summer saw about 3d. to 4d. per day. The autumn was much more profitable, at 22d. per day, but this was due to its including the fair and the feast of the Translation of St Etheldreda on 17 October. From Christmas to Easter the shrine only received about ½d. per day.

In the late fourteenth century the Durham shrine box was emptied at intervals by the feretrar's colleague (*socius*) and the money recorded in a receipt indenture. While only nineteen of these pyx indentures survive, most of the feretrar's accounts state that the yearly offerings were 'as shown by indentures', and so they once must have been at least as numerous as the account rolls. Each indenture covered an irregular period of two weeks to a year in length, recording multiple and apparently random dates of collection. Dividing the amount contained in each receipt by the days between collections results in an average daily income, which in turn can be averaged between indentures to give a rough estimate of how much money could be expected on any one day of the year.

Three or four days accounted for one third to one half of the yearly income to St Cuthbert's shrine. The most profitable was the feast of the Translation on 4 September which was not only the major festival of the saint but also the time when all tenants holding land under St Cuthbert were bound to come to Durham cathedral. The other exceptional days were the Deposition of St Cuthbert, Pente-cost and Corpus Christi. The latter two, during which a great procession passed through the feretory chapel of St Cuthbert,[160] fall so closely together that it is difficult to separate their effects using the method described above. Movable

[159] 30 Sept. to 2 Nov. 1409: LCA, D&C, Bj/5/16/1, f. 95.
[160] *Rites of Durham*, pp. 107–8.

feasts, they could occur on any date between 17 May and 24 June. The usual income on any one of the main offering days was £4, compared to an average of about 1s. per day in summer and half that in winter. The period from Christmas to late January was unseasonably profitable, often over 10d. per day. The periods immediately after the main feast days were also above average; for example, the offerings after the translation feast remained higher than average well into October.

A similar study can be made for Hereford, where accounts include sub-entries for terms of slightly variable length. The daily average is small; from late November to early March only 1.23d. was received per day, climbing through Spring to 3.02d. in June. For July to early October it is more difficult to obtain an accurate daily average. While the receipts appear to rise steadily, in fact offerings would have been concentrated around the feast of St Thomas on 2 Oct. In a term lasting from 24 Aug. to 10 Oct., for example, the saint's feast near the end of the term would raise the daily average of shrine receipts for the entire period. The concentration of income around the feast day was extreme. In 1479 only 25s. were put in the box from 30 May to 2 Oct., but £12 17s. 4d. was discovered on the tenth of that same month. Most pilgrims to Canterbury also appear to have arrived on the feast days: the feretrarians were sent extra food and coal for attending pilgrims on the day and night of the Passion of St Thomas.[161]

In only one instance do we have a direct record of income by day. This occurs in the accounts of the Martyrdom at Canterbury cathedral for the years 1500 and following.[162] Although not itself a saint's shrine of the type we have been discussing, the Martyrdom probably experienced a pilgrimage pattern directly related to that of the main shrine of St Thomas, since pilgrims to St Thomas can be expected to have visited both sites. I have taken the accounting year running from July 1503 to September 1504 as an example.[163] This account is divided into five quarters, with separate entries for each week and the weeks in turn subdivided into individual days if the money received was plentiful. For example, the shrine receipts for the week from the first Sunday in August 1503 were 8s. 6d. Two days in that week have special entries: on Tuesday 3d. was received in oblations plus 2s. from a visiting abbot, and on Thursday the oblations were 2s. 8d. plus 4d. from the bishop of Winchester.[164] The daily average for that week, not counting the offerings of dignitaries, was 10½d.

The averages of the Martyrdom accounts show that the main period of offerings was from March to September, when incomes were generally over 1s. per week. The most profitable week included the Translation of St Thomas in August. The vigil and the day of the Translation itself accounted for 11s. 4d. in 1503 and 9s. 8d. in 1504 out of weekly totals of 12s. 4d. and 11s. 4d. respectively. November

---

161 'Customary of the Shrine of St Thomas', f. 6.

162 CCA, Lit MS C11, ff. 26 on.

163 CCA, Lit MS C11, f. 38.

164 It is possible that the clerk accidentally reversed the amounts for that day, since 2s. 8d. is high for a daily receipt at that time, while 4d. is low for the offerings of a bishop.

to February were the off season, never receiving more than an average of 3½d. per week, although the week of Christmas was unusual in that 10d. arrived in oblations.

The records of Ely, Hereford, Durham and Canterbury generally match, and show, not surprisingly, that offerings to shrines were subject to seasonal variation. This weakly suggests that the bulk of the money came from pilgrims travelling from out of town, since they would have been more influenced by weather and travelling conditions than would townsmen or cathedral clerics. The fact that December, and not January or February, was the least profitable month suggests that available daylight played a greater limiting role than did temperature. The accounts also show that activity centred strongly around the feasts of the saints as well as Pentecost and Corpus Christi. Combining these facts with my theory on pilgrim numbers given above, it is conceivable that only three or four pilgrims arrived on an average day at shrines like that of St Hugh of Lincoln, but that many hundreds arrived on the days close to major feasts. It is important to remember that this is for established shrines in the fourteenth and fifteenth centuries. Newer, earlier cults certainly attracted much more attention.

Using the records of the Martyrdom, we can also average the receipts of each weekday. For this purpose I have disregarded the rare days when incomes were over 2s. because a special feast day or the visit of a generous dignitary happening to fall on that day would disturb the overall result. This exercise shows that Sunday was the most profitable day with an average income of a little over 3d. Although 60% better than the income of Saturdays, Sundays averaged only 0.3d., or under 10%, ahead of Thursdays (the second most profitable day), a difference that is noticeable but not dramatic. This again suggests that most of the offerings were coming from travelling pilgrims who offered on the day they arrived, rather than from locals who might be expected to visit the cathedral on Sunday, their only regular day off.

Royal, noble and ecclesiastical pilgrims

So far we have mostly discussed ordinary pilgrims. However, chroniclers were always proud to describe the attentions paid to their churches by illustrious devotees, particularly royal visitors. As a result, the known pilgrimages of English kings are too numerous to mention in detail. The earliest visit by foreign royalty occurred in 1179, when Louis VII of France visited the tomb of St Thomas seeking a cure for his son Philip. He placed gold on the altar and granted the priory an

---

[165] Louis's visit is mentioned in several chronicles, for example in *Chronicon T. Wykes*, pp. 38–9; Johannes de Oxenedes, *Chronica*, p. 68. The charter is copied into CCA, DCc Reg. E, f. 34. Several letters and charters concerning this wine are printed in *Literæ Cantuarienses*, ed. J.B. Sheppard (3 vols, RS, vol. 85, 1887–9), vol. 1, pp. 62, 158–61, vol. 2, pp. 480–2, vol. 3, p. 293. The wine, grown at the same latitude as Paris, would not travel, and so in later times it was sold and the money used to buy better Gascon wines: Woodruff,

annual income of 1,600 gallons of wine, which grant was confirmed by Philip the next year.[165]

Royalty visited shrines for the same reasons as other pilgrims, including the fulfilment of a vow of pilgrimage. Henry I calmed a stormy sea by vowing a pilgrimage to Bury St Edmunds in 1130.[166] King John, for example, fulfilled his own vow to St Edmund by visiting the shrine at Bury immediately after his coronation, and in 1343 Edward III went to Canterbury, Walsingham and Gloucester 'after many vows' given before surviving a shipwreck.[167] Kings sometimes sought aid in battle from shrines. For example, a fifteenth-century tradition had Richard I venerating the tomb of St Thomas on leaving and returning from crusade.[168] In 1283 Edward I gave thanks for subjugating Wales at the shrine of St Wulfstan, 'because he had a special love for it'.[169] Before leaving for France he sent gold necklaces to the shrine at Worcester where the monks performed three weekly masses of St Wulfstan until his safe return in 1297, after which he sent the shrine another necklace, nine candles and 14s.[170] Henry V prayed, kissed the relics and made an offering at both Canterbury and St Paul's on his return from Agincourt.[171] At least one royal act of thanksgiving was related to marital rather than martial success. Henry III put an image of a queen on the shrine of Edward the Confessor to commemorate his wedding in 1236.[172] The Confessor's shrine often benefited from coronations in Westminster Abbey, as in 1400 when it received £16 in gold during the coronation of Henry IV.[173]

Although performed for the same general purposes as a regular pilgrimage, a royal visit understandably received much more attention. The 1447 visit by Margaret of Anjou to Canterbury, when she was only sixteen years old, exemplifies the great planning and solemnity involved. The queen was met by the prior at the entrance to the cathedral, then waited on her knees in the nave while the choir sang verses. When the antiphon *Rogamus Te* began she set out for the presbytery, and when she reached the high altar the prior said a collect. After the queen made

'Notes on the Inner Life of Christ Church', p. 3. A common entry in the treasurer's rolls, about the same amount every year, is 'De vino Regis francie – £6 6s. 8d': CCA, DCc/MA1, f. 56 (Treasurer's account 1214/5). The grant was tranferred to Touraine by Louis XI.

166 John of Worcester, *The Chronicle of John of Worcester, 1118–1140*, ed. J.R.H. Weaver (Oxford, 1908), p. 34.

167 John came 'dragged by vows and devotion' (voto et deuocione tractus): Jocelin of Brakelond, *Chronicle*, p. 116; *Adae Murimuth Continuatio Chronicorum*, ed. E.M. Thompson (RS, vol. 93, 1889), p. 135.

168 H.E.J. Cowdrey, 'An Early Record of the Export of Becket's Relics', *Bulletin of the Institute of Historical Research*, vol. 54 (1981), p. 253; He was certainly in Canterbury: *Chronicles and Memorials of the Reign of Richard I*, ed. W. Stubbs (RS, vol. 38, 1864), vol. 1, p. 145.

169 'Erga quem amorem habuit specialem': *Annales de Wigornia*, p. 488.

170 *Annales de Wigornia*, pp. 514, 536.

171 Jehan de Waurin, *Recueil des Croniques et Anchiennes Istoiries de la Grant Bretaigne, a Presente Nomme Engleterre*, ed. W. Hardy (RS, vol. 39, 1868), vol. 2 (1399–1422), pp. 223–4.

172 *Calendar of Close Rolls of the Reign of Henry III, A.D. 1234–1237*, ed. H.C. Maxwell-Lyte (London, 1908), p. 278.

173 WAM, MS 19659.

an offering at the altar the precentor began the antiphon *Pastor Cesus*, and the convent processed with her to the shrine. There the prior said a second collect, and the queen offered first at the shrine altar and then at the Corona. Finally, she went down to the palace through the cloister.[174]

By the fifteenth century major ecclesiastics were treated in much the same way as kings and queens, although with correspondingly less pomp and excitement. When Archbishop Chichele arrived unexpectedly at Canterbury cathedral he was ceremoniously brought into the church and taken to the choir during mass. At the response of St Thomas he went to the shrine where the prior said a collect while the archbishop prayed. When finished, the Archbishop gave his blessing, received amen and went on to the Corona.[175] When Chichele arrived again in Rogation Week 1439 he joined the convent in a procession past the shrine.[176] According to Stone, the archbishop of York came to Canterbury in 1469 and made a pilgrimage to Sts Thomas and Augustine, but caused a dispute when he at first refused to give a jewel to the shrine of St Thomas as a sign of his obedience.[177]

The royal and wealthy had several advantages not available to other pilgrims, one being the ability to perform pilgrimage by proxy. In 1502 Elizabeth of York sent two men on round-robin pilgrimages. The first, a priest, was gone twenty-seven days and distributed 48s. 4d. to many shrines including those at Windsor, Reading, Hayles, Tewkesbury, Worcester and Walsingham, for which labour he received 10d. per day. The other man was gone thirteen days to seven places including Canterbury and London.[178] Powerful individuals could also ask for relics. In 1315 a letter from Archbishop Walter Reynalds to Prior Eastry warned of Queen Isabelle's imminent arrival. She had specially asked the archbishop whether she could have any particle (*aliquam particulam*) of St Thomas's bones, which Reynalds ordered the convent to give her when she arrived.[179]

Royal and noble offerings were, of course, much greater than others in value. In 1285 Edward I gave 'Four images and two boats of pure gold, and also brooches [bosses?] adorned with both priceless gold and precious gems' to the shrine of St Thomas, these being images of Edward the Confessor, St George, St George's horse and a pilgrim costing a total of £355 10s. 11½d.[180] Cloth of gold

174 William Glastynbury, 'The Chronicle of William of Glastynbury, Monk of the Priory of Christ Church, Canterbury, 1419–1448', ed. C.E. Woodruff, *Arch. Cant.*, vol. 37 (1925), pp. 126–7.

175 'Chronicle', p. 130. I am uncertain that Glastynbury's use of the term 'response' is technically correct.

176 William Glastynbury, 'Chronicle', p. 134.

177 Stone, *Chronicle*, pp. 109, 111.

178 *Privy Purse Expenses of Elizabeth of York*, ed. N.H. Nicolas (London, 1830), pp. 3–4.

179 Printed in Foreville, *Le Jubilé*, pp. 171–2. From Lambeth, Register of Walter Reynolds, f. 64.

180 'Quatuor imaginibus & duabus navibus de puro auro, ac etiam firmaculis et inestimabilibus aureis et lapidibus preciosis ornatis': C.E. Woodruff, 'The Financial Aspect of the Cult of St. Thomas of Canterbury', *Arch. Cant.*, vol. 44 (1932), p. 29 n. 1. A.J. Taylor, 'Edward I and the Shrine of St Thomas of Canterbury', *JBAA*, vol. 132 (1979), pp. 24–5.

was frequently used as a royal gift, as for example by Edward I to the shrine of St Richard at Chichester in 1299.[181] There are even some instance of spoils of war being offered at a shrine. The Crown of Llewelyn II was offered to the shrine of St Edward at Westminster by Prince Alphonse in 1285, two years after it was surrendered to his father.[182] Richard I gave the banner of the emperor of Cyprus, taken in 1192, to the shrine of St Edmund.[183] Finally, Edward I gave a 'jewel' made out of a 'vase' captured at Edinburgh in 1294 to the shrine at Chichester.[184]

The most common form of offering made by kings was gold coins. Edward I, for example, placed gold florins on the shrine altar at Canterbury for 'the foetus then existing in the queen's belly' in 1300.[185] The adoption of gold coins as real currency did not stop their traditional use as a royal gift. In the Pentecost *aperturæ* at Lincoln cathedral in 1484/5 the keeper of the shrine had in his possession 'a certain gold Noble fixed to the head of St Hugh by Richard III king of England'.[186]

Royal offerings were often formalised. For example, when Edward I and his family visited Canterbury in 1285 the cost of an offering, whether by the king, his wife or his children, was consistently 7s.[187] The king made twelve separate donations in the cathedral worth a total of £4 4s., while three offerings by the queen came to 21s. This price of a royal offering prevails in other wardrobe accounts as well.[188] No single coin in general usage or multiple thereof was worth exactly 7s. It is possible that this was a token value assigned to a special coin used for royal oblations. The *Liber Regie Capelle* records that Henry VI daily offered in his chapel a special gold talent equivalent to five nobles in weight that was redeemed each time by the clerk of the jewels for 7d.[189] In the

181 Walcott, *Memorials of Chichester*, p. 174.
182 E.M.R. Ditmas, 'The Cult of Arthurian Relics', *Folklore*, vol. 75 (1964), p. 28; *Annales de Wigornia*, p. 490.
183 W.T. Mitchell, 'The Shrines of English Saints in Wartime before the Reformation', *Pax*, vol. 30 (1940), p. 79.
184 'Early Statutes of Chichester', p. 174.
185 M. Prestwich, 'The Piety of Edward I', in *England in the Thirteenth Century*, ed. W.M. Ormrod (Woodbridge, 1985), p. 124.
186 'A certain gold Noble fixed by Richard III, King of England, on the head of St Hugh' (Quadam nobile Auri per Ricardem tercium Regem Anglie Applicate super capitem sancti hugonis): LCA Bj/5/16/1, f. 36.
187 Taylor, 'Edward I and the Shrine', pp. 22–3.
188 For example, the Wardrobe Accounts for 25 Edward I (1296/7), BL Add. MS 7965.
189 'However, the king offered for himself one talent of gold weighing five Nobles. On one side of which is described the image of the holy Trinity, with an inscription in the margin: *Suscipe, sancta Trinitas, hanc oblacionem, quam offero in honore tuo*. On the other side is described the Salutation of the Blessed Mary with an inscription in the margin: *Ac beate Marie et omnium sanctorum tuorum*. This talent is redeemable by the king on any day he pleases for seven pence sterling' (Offert autem Rex pro se unum talentum auri ponderis quinque nobilium. In cuius una parte describitur ymago sancte Trinitas, cum superscriptione in margine *Suscipe, sancta Trinitas, hanc oblacionem, quam offero in honore tuo*. In alia uero parte describitur salutacio beate Marie cum superscriptione in margine *Ac beate Marie et omnium sanctorum tuorum*. Quod talentum quolibet die redemitur a Rege pro septem denariis sterlingorum.) The queen's talent was redeemed for

late thirteenth century one of the king's oblations in France was described as 'and regarding the King's offering at the High Mass that he heard at St Eutrope's: for his great penny, 7d. sterling'.[190] Similarly, in 1286 the wardrobe paid 'for the price of the great penny of the King 7d.'.[191] The 'great penny' of Edward I may have been equivalent to the special gold talent of Henry VI. If so, then perhaps the frequent oblations worth 7s. represent a traditional offering of twelve such talents, which were later redeemed by the king's clerks so that the same offering could be given again at the next shrine. Alternatively, the one coin could sometimes have been redeemed at 7s. rather than 7d., since its value was arbitrary anyway.

The pilgrim's experience at a cathedral or great abbey shrine was complex, involving many layers of social, spiritual and economic interaction. It is important to note that these activities were governed not by law or theology, but by tradition and custom. Many of the practices, such as bending pennies or using prayer niches, have much to do with magic and medieval perceptions of the universe that today are easy to label as superstitious. The substance of these beliefs did not change with social status, only the scale and style with which they were acted out. Thus the actions of a king, whether visiting a shrine with his court or offering a wax image of his falcon, were directed with the same hopes and expectations as the average supplicant. The cathedral clergy, the best educated class in medieval England, was involved in the shrines as heavily as anyone else. It is their perspective on the shrine that will be examined next.

4d.: *Liber Regie Capelle*, ed. W. Ullmann (Henry Bradshaw Soc., vol. 92, 1961), pp. 61, 63; B. Wolffe, *Henry VI* (London, 1981), p. 11.

[190] 'Et in oblacione regis in magna missa sua quam audivit apud Sanctum Eutropium pro magno denario suo, vij d. sterlingorum': *Records of the Wardrobe and Household, 1286–1289*, no. 2532, p. 288.

[191] 'Pro precio magni denarii Regie *vij d.* summa 7s. 7d': 'Wardrobe Accounts for 25 Edward I', BL Add. MS 7965, f. 6.

5

Cathedral and Shrine

The power of sanctity

The cathedral clergy had a more complex and perpetual involvement with shrines than did common pilgrims. For the local clerics the shrine was not only a holy place, but also an institution, a material part of their church, a financial resource, a focus of worship and an earthly dwelling of a mighty celestial patron. Saintly patronage could be personal. At the Fourth Lateran Council William of Trumpington, abbot of St Alban's, obtained the right for those 'who are known to have in our churches the body of some saint' to invoke their names as intercessors in private masses.[1] The saint was also a patron in a more general sense. Thus, an indulgence to those helping a poor hermit at Chichester trusted in the merits of 'the most blessed confessor St Richard, our patron'.[2] The easiest way for clergy to proclaim their patron was to include his or her name in the dedication of their church. Lichfield, for example, was dedicated to St Chad by the time of the Domesday Book, while Ely's dedication was changed to include St Etheldreda in 1252.[3] Sometimes the dedication was unofficial, as in the common but inaccurate late medieval reference to Christ Church Canterbury as the Church of St Thomas.[4]

The possession of a saint was a matter of great prestige, and cathedral clergy lacking great relics sometimes expressed a feeling of deprivation. Bishop Robert de Bethune of Hereford was forced to write to Abbot Suger asking for relics of St Denis, since his new Romanesque cathedral at Hereford had nothing to use as a focus for the cult of saints.[5] When the relics of St Petroc were stolen from Bodmin Priory in 1177, it was said to be done 'so that our house, thus destitute of its patron, might be utterly ruined'.[6] Some gave the possession of special relics exaggerated

---

[1] Paris, *Chronicles*, p. 40; Walsingham, *Gesta Abbatum*, vol. 1, pp. 261–2.
[2] *The Episcopal Register of Robert Rede, Ordinis Predicatorum, Lord Bishop of Chichester, 1397–1415*, ed. C. Deedes (Sussex Record Soc., vols 8 and 11, 1908 and 1910), vol. 1, p. 55.
[3] A.J. Kettle and D.A. Johnson, 'The Cathedral of Lichfield', in *VCH: Stafford*, vol. 3, ed. M.W. Greenslade (London, 1970), p. 140; 'Chronicon Ecclesiae Eliensis', f. 37.
[4] See, for example, *A Relation of the Island of England*, p. 29, written about 1500.
[5] G.M. Hills, 'The Architectural History of Hereford Cathedral', *JBAA*, vol. 27 (1871), pp. 58–9.
[6] Robert de Tautona, 'The Relics of St Petroc', trans. C.G.H. Doble, *Antiquity*, vol. 13 (1939), p. 405.

importance. Bishop Antony Bek called Chester-le-street the pre-eminent church in the diocese after Durham cathedral on account of the 115 years that St Cuthbert's body had lain there.[7] Even among churches with shrines there was competition for status, seen expressed in *Miracula* stories boasting the superiority of one saint over another. Among many examples, a woman planning to take a candle to Salisbury was told in a vision to go to Reading instead, and in another Reading story a cripple coming to Canterbury was told by a vision of St James that she would only be cured at Reading, thus asserting the miraculous predominance of the hand of St James over the shrines of Sts Thomas and Osmund.[8]

The belief that saints offered supernatural aid to their home churches and districts was strong throughout the middle ages. In 1361 the bishop of Lichfield wrote to the archdeacon of Coventry asking for special prayers to God, trusting in the merits of Mary, Peter and Paul, the glorious confessor St Chad and all the saints because plague had not yet come to the diocese.[9] In 1470/1 over 8s. in candles were burnt at Canterbury 'in honour of God and St Ouen at the High Altar because of a pestilence'.[10] Clergy considered it a saint's duty to protect his church. Prior Roland of Tynemouth admonished St Oswin for not preserving their monastery from fire, exclaiming 'if you will not save your monastery, save your body'.[11] A man who saw St Wulfstan in a vision asked him why he cured others and not one born and bred on the land of his church.[12]

Those violating the church were believed to merit and receive the saint's wrath, and any misfortune which befell them could be ascribed to the workings of saintly vengeance. In 1372 the earl of Pembroke was captured by the Spaniards and was poisoned a few years later, both events falling on the feast of St Etheldreda. This coincidence was ascribed to the fact that he did not support her church in a dispute with Bury St Edmunds.[13] Punishment did not have to be immediate. A rapacious captain named Fawkes, having plundered the city of St Albans, 'provoked the holy martyr Alban to take the sternest revenge for these injuries to him, and the angry martyr reserved this revenge until the Last Judgement, which made it more to be feared'.[14] Fawkes came to a late but unpleasant end and all his followers were hanged. Monks gloated over these victories. Robert FitzWalter, another persecutor of St Albans, quickly desisted from his acts as 'He was very much afraid of such an enormous breach of conscience as well as of the stern vengeance of the martyr Alban, for he had heard how his accomplice in the perpetration of

---

7   *Records of Antony Bek, Bishop and Patriarch, 1283–1311*, ed. C.M. Fraser (SS, vol. 162, 1953), p. 7.
8   'Miracles of the Hand of St James', pp. 11, 15.
9   *The Register of Bishop Robert de Stretton, A.D. 1360–1385*, ed. R.A. Wilson (Collections for a History of Staffordshire, n.s. vol. 8, 1905), vol. 2, p. 99.
10 CCA, DCc Sacrist 50.
11 'Si monasterio tuo non parcis, parce corpori tuo.': *Vita Oswini*, p. 37.
12 William of Malmesbury, *Vita Wulfstani*, p. 135.
13 Thomas Walsingham, *Historia Anglicana*, ed. H.T. Riley (RS, vol. 28, 1863), vol. 1, pp. 314, 320.
14 Paris, *Chronicles*, pp. 43–4.

the fraud, William Pigun, struck down by the Lord, had ended his miserable life horribly.'[15] In return for safeguarding its liberties, a church protected the reputation of its saint. A certain Matthew de Ludlow, having uttered blasphemous words against St Thomas of Hereford, was made to perform a public confession and would have suffered greater punishment if not for the intercession of his brother on his behalf.[16]

Shrines even protected churches in time of war. Richard of Hexham believed that his church's shrines gave divine help around the time of the Battle of the Standard: 'In this raging and tempestuous period, that noble monastery of Hexham . . . on account of the renowned merits of its tutelary saints, Andrew the apostle, and Wilfrid, bishop and martyr, and of its other patrons, Saints Acca, Alcmund, and Eata, bishops and confessors, and the other saints who reposed within that church, offered the most tranquil security to its people and those who took refuge in it.'[17] Similarly, William of Malmesbury believed that the relics of the passion given to his abbey by Athelstan preserved it from harm.[18] Some claims were more spectacular: according to a life of St Werburg written late in the middle ages, her shrine, carried onto the walls of Chester, smote attackers with blindness and madness during sieges by both the Welsh and Scots.[19]

The spiritual authority and protection of a saint's shrine translated into worldly effects. One of these was sanctuary, the legal power of some shrines to protect fugitives from their pursuers as long as they were in the precincts of the shrine. This was more than a right conferred by earthly authorities and was actually thought to be a divine attribute of the shrine understood even by animals. For example, a dove hit in its wing by an arrow instinctively sought sanctuary at the shrine of St Oswin: 'and as though seeking sanctuary, it hid itself under the shrine of the holy martyr'.[20] The sanctuary at Durham was miraculously confirmed by a vision of St Cuthbert, in which he claimed thirty-seven days and nights of peace to whomever fled to his shrine.[21] It was thus he, and not the temporal authorities, who pronounced the law on this subject. Any shrine could be used as a refuge in an emergency. For example, there are two records of persons fleeing to St William of York, even though his shrine was not well known as a sanctuary. One of these

---

[15] Paris, *Chronicles*, p. 19.

[16] *Registrum Ade de Orleton*, pp. 189–90.

[17] *Chronicles of the Reigns of Stephen, Henry II, and Richard I*, ed. R. Howlett (RS, vol. 82, 1884), vol. 3, p. 153. Translated in *English Historical Documents, 1042–1189*, p. 315.

[18] William of Malmesbury, *De Gestis Regum Anglorum*, ed. W. Stubbs (RS, vol. 90, 1887), vol. 1, p. 151; L.H. Loomis, 'The Holy Relics of Charlemagne and King Athelstan: The Lances of Longinus and St Mauricius', *Speculum*, vol. 25 (1950), p. 438.

[19] *The Holy Lyfe and History of Saynt Werburge, Very Frutefull for all Christen People to Rede*, ed. E. Hawkins (Chetham Soc., vol. 15, 1845), pp. 160, 162–3.

[20] 'Et quasi refugium quaerens, sub scrinio Sancti Martyris se occultavit': *Vita Oswini*, p. 40–41. In an interesting series of miracles, a stag gained benefit of sanctuary in a church dedicated to St Cuthbert: Reginald of Durham, *Libellus de Admirandis Beati Cuthberti*, pp. 181–5.

[21] Symeon, *Historia Ecclesiæ Dunhelmensis*, p. 69.

was the treasurer of the cathedral, who 'fled to the tomb of St William'.[22] The other was a woman accused of homicide whom twelve knights wanted to drag away from the tomb even though a miracle had acquitted her of the crime. Fortunately 'the priest in charge of the tomb was unwilling to permit her to be abducted, who had been cured by a miracle of St William'.[23] Nevertheless, the sanctuary of a shrine was not always respected. In 1381 the mob of London paid little heed to St Edward's sanctuary: 'Sir Richard Imworth, Steward of the Marshalsea, who had fled for safety to the church of Westminster, was clinging to the columns of the shrine when he was forcibly dragged away from that holy spot, to be later beheaded.'[24] Sanctuary was a criminal's last resort. Even at Durham, where the authority of sanctuary was strong and sanctioned by tradition and worldly authorities, the fugitive had to make a full confession and swear to leave the country forever.[25] By the fifteenth century the practice of sanctuary was becoming unpopular, largely because of abuses.[26]

Belief in the divine protection provided by a church's patron was also used as leverage in legal struggles. In a late twelfth-century dispute with the archbishop of Canterbury, the abbot of Bury swore to defend his cause 'with the help of St. Edmund whose rights are attested by our charters'.[27] The identification of monastic communities with their patron saints was particularly strong. 'An assault on the persons and possessions of the Durham monks was *ipso facto* an act of aggression against the greatest of the northern saints.'[28] The writer of a memorandum for the admission of John Oll as prior of Coldingham (claimed by Durham) in 1441, for example, complained that the abbot of Dunfermline and others were 'about to spoyll and exclude saynt Cuthbert and the said Priour and covent of thair auld possession'.[29] The monks of St Albans sought the speedy granting of the right to install their new abbot by daily processing barefoot before the shrine of St Alban singing psalms and collects. Eventually the prior and sub-prior presented the elect to God and St Alban at the high altar, at which time tapers were lit around the high altar and the shrine was uncovered. The shrine of St Alban was also used in the Abbey's rite of excommunication, during which stoles were placed on the feretory.[30]

---

22 Walter of Coventry, *Collections*, vol. 1, p. 390.
23 'Noluit sacerdos custos tumbæ permittere eam abduci, quæ curata fuit per miraculum Beati Willelmi': *Miracula Sancti Willelmi*, in *Historians of the Church of York*, pp. 542–3.
24 *The Westminster Chronicle, 1381–1394*, eds L.C. Hector and B.F. Harvey (Oxford, 1982), p. 9.
25 *Sanctuarium Dunelmense et Sanctuarium Beverlacense*, ed. J. Raine (SS, vol. 5, 1837), pp. xvi–xvii, with a good example pp. 30–1.
26 See J.C. Cox, *The Sanctuaries and Sanctuary Seekers of Medieval England* (London, 1911), pp. 319–33; P.I. Kaufman, 'Henry VII and Sanctuary', *Church History*, vol. 53 (1984), p. 472.
27 *English Historical Documents, 1042–1189*, p. 458.
28 R.B. Dobson, *Durham Priory 1400–1450* (Cambridge, 1973), p. 11.
29 *The Correspondence, Inventories, Account Rolls, and Law Proceedings of the Priory of Coldingham*, ed. J. Raine, (SS, vol. 12, 1841), p. 130.
30 *An Account of the Altars, Monuments, and Tombs Existing A.D. 1428 in Saint Alban's*

The shrine saint was often the recipient of charters and grants. One example is from about 1189, when Philip of Hardres gave land to God, St Thomas and the monks at the tomb of Thomas on the day he took the cross from the sub-prior.[31] The estate of Doccombe was given by William de Tracy 'in pure and perpetual alms for the dead St Thomas'.[32] Less directly, grants could be made to a church out of pious intent towards its patron, as in 1303 when Edward I restored a franchise to Durham 'out of devotion to St Cuthbert and of good will to the bishop'.[33] The liberties of the church were particularly connected with the saint. St Etheldreda was appealed to as patroness and 'holy queen' in a 1080 plea respecting liberties of Ely in Suffolk.[34] Archbishop Thomas of York, after he was cured of a fever following a vigil at the shrine of St Cuthbert, granted a charter conferring certain rights to the bishops of Durham by placing it on the shrine.[35]

Shrines became involved in regular legal transactions. In 1523 Bishop Robert Sherbourne of Chichester granted freedom to John Holden, 'nief' of his manor of Stretam, and all his children in return for everlasting fealty to Robert and his successors, 'and each of his descendants shall, at the age of twenty-six years, do the same, and shall make an offering of 12d. to the shrine of St. Richard'.[36] The shrine of St Cuthbert was involved in the consecration ritual of bishops of Durham, and their broken seals were offered there upon their deaths.[37] In these cases the shrines did not bring about the transactions, but were used as convenient symbols of the authority of the church. While a shrine could be important to the self image of a church it was not always crucial. Many examples have been presented showing devotion to shrines, while ignoring the vast number of cases which show less regard. At a visitation of Chichester by Archbishop Winchelsey in 1299, for example, St Richard's feretory played no part in the intricately described reception ceremonies.[38] In addition, many of the references to the saint

---

Abbey, trans. R. Lloyd (Saint Albans, 1873), pp. 34–5; Walsingham, *Gesta Abbatum*, vol. 1, p. 317.

[31] W. Urry, *Canterbury under the Angevin Kings* (London, 1967), p. 430; the charter is written in full in CCA, DCc/Reg. H., fol. 31.

[32] 'En pure et perpetuele almoigne pur la mort Saint Thomas.' Referred to in a letter of 1322: *Literæ Cantuarienses*, vol. 1, pp. 68–70.

[33] *Records of Antony Bek*, pp. 92–3.

[34] *English Historical Documents, 1042–1189*, p. 452.

[35] The charter is printed and translated in Raine, *St Cuthbert*, p. 69 n. *.

[36] *Chapter Acts of the Dean and Chapter of the Cathedral Church of Chichester, 1472–1544 (The White Act Book)*, ed. W.D. Peckham (Sussex Record Soc., vol. 52, 1951–2), p. 15.

[37] C.M. Fraser, *A History of Antony Bek* (Oxford, 1957), p. 43. See also a public instrument of 1333 concerning Bishop Ludowic: 'Two silver seals with silver chains, which the said lord bishop had the use of, while he lived, were borne to the shrine of St Cuthbert, as the custom is from antiquity. – Which certain seals were broken into pieces after the death of the said father' (duo sigilla argentea cum cathenis argenteis, quibus dictus dominus Episcopus usus fuerat, dum vixit, optulit feretro Sancto Cuthberti, prout moris est ab antiquo. – Quæ quidem sigilla fracta fuerunt per particulas, post obitum dicti patris): *Historiæ Dunelmensis Scriptores Tres*, p. cxxviii.

[38] *The History and Constitution of a Cathedral of the Old Foundation*, ed. C.A. Swainson (London, 1880), p. 49.

in legal and political documents are purely formal, and may not have been made out of any real devotion. It is thus easy to exaggerate, and impossible to measure, the symbolic and prestige value of a saint's cult to a church.

We can be more certain of how possession of a shrine altered a church's ceremonial. The shrine's altar was used for certain masses, as at Chichester where Chancellor Burwell left 16d. for a mass 'at the altar near the shrine of St Richard' in 1488.[39] Proper worship of the saint created additional services for the church, particularly on his feast days. Indeed, the bulk of the 'Customary of the Shrine of St Thomas' is devoted to the form of mass and procession to be performed there on various feast days, in addition to the daily mass held in the morning.[40] In monastic communities a saint was commemorated on his appointed day with a mass-set of four prayers: *collecta, secreta, praefatio* and *postcommunio*. Commemoration in office would begin at vespers on the vigil, which required a collect and hymn. On the feast day itself, beginning at matins, lections were needed.[41] In addition, the shrine-keeper was expected to conduct semi-private masses at the shrine. For example, it is known that in 1426 the chaplain of St Chad at Lichfield said his mass at the sixth hour.[42] The shrine chapel was also a convenient place to set up a chantry. In the later middle ages a chantry existed at the altar of St Richard of Chichester, and in 1311 Bishop Ralph Baldock founded a chantry at the altar attached to the shrine of St Erkenwald.[43] Three chantries were set up at the shrine of St Chad for the souls of Canon John de Morton, Bishop Alexander and Dean Collingwood.[44] Chantries do not appear to have made special use of the shrine itself, but only the convenient and prestigious altar and chapel. In this sense the shrine altar was little different from the other altars of the church.

The saint's feast could be quite a celebration. The church was cleaned for the occasion, Edward the Confessor's translation feast being one of the occasions on which new rushes were bought to cover the choir floor of Westminster Abbey.[45] As well as additional services, minstrels were sometimes hired, such as those costing the prior of Canterbury 6s. 8d. on the day of St Thomas and 20s. on the day of his translation, or the minstrel that sang at St Richard's shrine in 1297.[46] At Canterbury the Jubilee celebrations lasted a fortnight beginning at midnight on the vigil of the Feast of the Translation of St Thomas, and included a play of his passion performed on a pageant wagon.[47] Because several feasts of local

---

[39] 'Early Statutes of Chichester', p. 173.

[40] 'Customary of the Shrine of St Thomas', ff. 1–9. The daily mass was foregone on Tuesdays, when the conventual mass was said 'in fferetro': f. 3.

[41] Wulfstan of Winchester, *The Life of St Æthelwold*, eds M. Lapidge and M. Winterbottom (Oxford, 1991), pp. cxii–cxiii.

[42] LJRO, 'Chapter Act Book I', f. 113.

[43] *Chartulary of Chichester*, p. 308; Cook, *Old St Paul's*, p. 54.

[44] LJRO, 'Chapter Act Book I', f. 22, 76, Book III, f. 34, Book IV, f. 10; LJRO, A9.

[45] WAM, MS 19631.

[46] Prior's account draft for 1446/7, CCA, DCc/MA 4, ff. 142, 144, 227v; 'Early Statutes of Chichester', p. 174.

[47] Stanley, 'Shrine of St Thomas', p. 219. The expenses on the play appear in the city archives,

importance fell around Easter an almost continuous festival occurred during the time when Chaucer says that pilgrims were most likely to travel.[48] The saint's feast was also an occasion for charity. A bequest of Aethelstan in 1015 left land with an income sufficient to supply one day's bread to all the brethren of Ely, give 100d. to the monastery, and to feed one hundred poor souls on St Etheldreda's mass day.[49] There were also special alms to the poor at Worcester on St Wulfstan's day: 'much monastic charity served liturgical purposes, one aim being to assemble a large crowd'.[50] However, the local saint's feast was not always so important an event. The feast of St Erkenwald became so neglected that in 1386 Bishop Robert Braybrooke of London had to remind his diocese of its existence and order it held as a highest festival.[51]

Staff and organisation

There are several reasons why shrines needed to be incorporated within the organisation of a church. The precious metals and gems of the feretrum, not to mention the other valuables in and about a shrine, could form a significant proportion of a religious community's total wealth and clearly required guarding and managing. Offerings and rents had to be fitted into the financial structure of the church, as did the inevitable expenses incurred by the shrine. Activities taking place in the feretory chapel also needed monitoring and organisation; people had to be found to watch and guide pilgrims, while the ceremonies performed in the shrine chapel required priests to officiate and oversee. There was no set form for how a shrine should be governed, each church deciding on its own system based on custom and need, and changing over time as the situation demanded. However, common conditions and the observation of trend-setting precedents at other shrines resulted in somewhat similar organisations, with a slight difference between secular and Benedictine churches.

The shrine naturally belonged to that part of the church hierarchy concerned with altars and ornaments since it possessed both. The treasurer was responsible for the bulk of the income and property in a secular church, and was often directly accountable for altar cloths, lights and other such ecclesiastical equipment. At Chichester, some statutes of 1232 went so far as to specifically state the exact number of candles that the treasurer had to provide and where they were to be placed. For example, seven wax candles weighing two pounds each were to be kept at the high altar, 'and above the painted beam which carries the crucifix eight

---

and include the use of gunpowder: T. Wright, 'On the Municipal Archives of the City of Canterbury', *Archaeologia*, vol. 31 (1846), pp. 208–9.

[48] Phillips, *Canterbury in the Middle Ages*, p. 24.

[49] *Sede Vacante Wills*, p. 60.

[50] C. Dyer, *Standards of Living in the Middle Ages; Social Change in England c.1200–1520* (Cambridge, 1989), p. 240.

[51] Dugdale, *St Paul's*, p. 23.

of the same weight'.[52] The ornaments of the church itself were the specific responsibility of the sacrist. It was his duty that nothing was lacking for the performance of divine service or any other ceremony. In secular cathedrals sacrists were in positions more or less subordinate to the treasurer. At York, for example, the treasurer had three sacrists serving under him, as well as a subtreasurer and clerks of the vestibule, while the Chichester treasurer had two sacristans in 1481.[53] Most monastic churches, however, lacked a treasurer altogether, the sacrist being an independent and important obedientiary. At Bury St Edmunds the sacrist was unusually powerful, being in charge of building operations, church repairs and the abbey's interests in the town.[54] An exception was Canterbury, where, although a sacrist existed and kept separate accounts, the priory finances were heavily centralised first under a treasurer and later under the prior himself.

As a result of his responsibility for ornaments, altars and precious objects, the treasurer or sacrist was given overall authority over shrines. However, managing a large church was a difficult task, and so lesser officials were recruited from among the monks, canons, hired priests of the cathedral, or even laymen. In some places these officials were assistants with general duties, while in others they were assigned to a particular post. For example, at Christ Church Canterbury the sacrist had under him not only a subsacrist, three petty sacrists and various servants, but also two feretrarians of St Thomas' shrine, single keepers of both Dunstan and Alphege's shrines, two clerks each at St Mary's chapel in the crypt, Mary in the Nave and the tomb of St Thomas, and single keepers with clerks to assist at both the Corona and Martyrdom of St Thomas.[55] *Custodes* (guardians or wardens) could be created to serve new demands. At Lincoln the tomb of Bishop Robert Grosseteste so attracted pilgrims that by 1300 it was given its own chaplain and was later assigned an additional *custos* from among the canons.[56] If a shrine was of relatively little importance then its management was subsumed within the regular duties of the treasurer or sacrist and their subordinates. Examples of shrines without a separate officer include those of St William of York, under the overall authority of a secular treasurer, and St William of Norwich, which was subsumed within the duties of a monastic sacrist. A similar arrangement probably existed at Rochester.[57]

---

52 *Statutes and Constitutions of the Cathedral Church of Chichester*, eds F.G. Bennett, R.H. Codrington and C. Deedes (Chichester, 1904), pp. 4–5.

53 *Statutes of Lincoln*, vol. 2, p. 97; *Statutes and Constitutions of Chichester*, p. 20.

54 Jocelin of Brakelond, *Chronicle*, pp. xxv, xxvii.

55 There is some confusion concerning the exact situation. See Woodruff, 'Sacrist's Rolls of Canterbury', p. 39, for one assessment.

56 The earliest notice of a chaplain is in c.1295: *Registrum Antiquissimum*, vol. 2, pp. 304–5.

57 We know little about the operation of William of York's shrine, but in the later middle ages the treasurer was responsible for offerings of wax at the shrine of St William and for finding wax at its altar: *Statutes of Lincoln*, vol. 2, p. 98. Concerning the shrine of William of Perth: 'There is no evidence to suggest that any special officer was appointed to deal with the moneys and gifts offered at the tomb. The only reference to it is in the deed relating to John de Sheppey's chantry which was nearby': A.M. Oakley, 'The Cathedral Church of St Andrew, Rochester', *Arch. Cant.*, vol. 91 (1975), p. 58.

A popular shrine needed its own official, a position which could have evolved naturally out of the practice of setting persons to watch the earlier tomb. This process probably occurred at Lincoln, where a chaplain is known to have had custody of the tomb of St Hugh both before and after his canonisation.[58] The most usual name for the official at a shrine was *custos feretri* (shrine-keeper) or, in monastic cathedrals, *feretrarius* ('feretrar' or 'feretrarian'). Christ Church Canterbury, Westminster Abbey, Ely and Durham all had feretrars. At Winchester the relevant official, only mentioned once in the records of the later middle ages, was the *custodus scrinium* (shrine-keeper).[59] The shrine-keeper at Worcester was called several things: in the late thirteenth century he was 'the keeper of the feretories of Sts Oswald and Wulfstan', but by 1308 he was referred to as the *custos tumborum*.[60] From 1375 there are financial accounts of an officer called the *tumbarius*, who is described in the first account as the guardian of the shrines of Sts Oswald and Wulfstan.[61] Other names for shrine officials were possible: at Hayles it was an *altararius* who displayed the Holy Blood to pilgrims at appointed times.[62]

In monastic cathedrals there was usually a single feretrar, although at Canterbury there was both a 'spiritual' and a 'temporal' feretrarian.[63] At Durham the feretrar had a *consocius*, also a monk, who was a subordinate. The level of responsibility held by shrine-keepers varied. The most important were those monastic obedientiaries, such as the feretrars at Durham and Ely, who presented their own financial accounts and were largely independent of the sacrists. At Durham, however, the feretrar could not dispose of the shrine's possessions without permission from the convent; thus the feretrar's trade in 1411/12 of 8s. and a girdle for a new cross was described as 'by consent of the prior and convent'.[64] In places such as Canterbury and Westminster the shrine-keepers

---

58 A chaplain described as 'Philip chaplain of the tomb of St Hugh' (Philippo de Tumba sancti Hugonis capellanis) existed from about 1200 to at least 1240: *Registrum Antiquissimum*, vol. 4, pp. 60, 65, 51, vol. 8, p. 172. A 'custodibus tumbæ' was also mentioned: Giraldus Cambrensis, *Vita S. Hugonis*, p. 128.

59 *Documents Relating to the Foundation of the Chapter of Winchester, A.D. 1541–1547*, eds G.W. Kitchin and F.T. Madge (London, 1889), p. 24.

60 From grants of a light at the shrines of Oswald and Wulfstan, which last until the late fourteenth century (WCA, MSS B936, B1039, B1089, B1135, B1214, B1299 and B1549). In 1308 Bishop Walter Reynolds gave leave, *hac vice*, for the prior and chapter to nominate a suitable *custos tumborum*: *The Liber Albus of the Priory of Worcester*, ed. J.M. Wilson (London, 1919), p. 25.

61 WCA, MS C453

62 St C. Baddeley, 'The Holy Blood of Hayles', *Transactions of the Bristol and Gloucestershire Archaeological Soc.*, vol. 23 (1900), p. 278.

63 'One is called spiritual and he shall be the chaplain in all services . . . and the other [is called] temporal' (Unius dicitur spiritualis et hic erit capellanus in omni servicie . . . .et alter temporalis': 'Customary of the Shrine of St Thomas), f. 1.

64 'Item ad excambium nove crucis deliberavi zonam datam per Nicholaum Bacar ad valorem 32s., quia tantum ponderabat et in argento 8s., de consensu d'ni et conventus': D.C.A., 'Feretrar's Roll', 1411–12; *Extracts from the Account Rolls of the Abbey of Durham, from the Original MSS*, ed. Fowler (SS, vols 99, 100, 103, 1898–1900), vol. 2, p. 458.

presented tallies to their sacrist, who then documented the proceeds, but were otherwise wholly responsible for the shrine.

Feretrars could usually hold other obedientiary offices simultaneously, and their position appears to have been of neither high nor low prestige, nor was it undertaken in any particular order with regard to other dignities. The excellent Durham accounts allow us to examine the monastic career of twenty-four feretrars.[65] Judging by the feretrars whose ordinations are given in Thomas Langley's register, a period of about thirty years was usual between ordination and accepting the position of feretrar.[66] The most successful of these monks, John Burnby, became feretrar only sixteen years after ordination and eventually became prior in 1456. On average, however, most feretrars must have been about fifty years of age upon taking office and had about as much seniority and experience as most other obedientiaries. Their period of office ranged from one to sixteen years and averaged four and a half. Of the feretrars between 1375 and 1461 only twelve are known to have ever held other offices, yet gaps in the record and the fact that eleven priory positions kept no accounts probably mean that the real total was higher.[67] The only office which appears to have had a consistent relationship to that of feretrar was the third or deece prior, who acted in place of the subprior if necessary. Feretrars held the position of third prior at least eight times, seven of those while acting as shrine-keeper. I know of no reason for this conjunction, but do believe that the importance of the shrine-keeper in the church hierarchy of other monastic cathedrals was roughly similar to the situation at Durham.

Shrine officials in secular cathedrals were usually chaplains. Some questions raised and tabulated during a visitation of about 1340 suggest concerns which the Chichester clergy had about the duties of their shrine chaplain: '29. Item, whether all the relics of the saints that are exhibited in the church should be venerated by Catholics. 30. Item, concerning oblations which are offered in honour of St Richard and others in the church, and to what uses they are put.'[68] Most shrines in secular cathedrals were organised in this simple manner, and probably had their wardens installed in the same way as the Lichfield chaplain, who was presented to the altar of St Chad.[69] At Lincoln and Salisbury the chaplain was overseen by a canon, who of course was superior to the chaplain but not as involved in day to day activities. At Salisbury the two men were often

---

[65] Valuable assistance here was obtained from A. Piper's 'Typescript List of Feretrar's and their colleagues' in the DDCA.

[66] *The Register of Thomas Langley, Bishop of Durham*, 1406–1437, ed. R.L. Storey (SS, vols 164, 166, 169, 170, 177, 182, 1956–67), *passim*.

[67] Dobson, *Durham Priory*, p. 67.

[68] '28. Item feretri et reliquiarum custodia, sit viro idoneo et honesto commissa. 29. Item an sanctorum sint omnes reliquiae quae in ecclesia exhibentur a catholicis venerandae. 30. Item de oblationibus quae in honore sancti Ricardi et aliorum in ecclesia offeruntur, et in usus quorum convertuntur': *History and Constitution of a Cathedral*, p. 61.

[69] LJRO, 'Chapter Act Book I', f. 145. Other notices of a change in the chaplaincy occur in 1386, 1408, 1434 and 1540: Chapter Act Book I, ff. 11, 76, 145, Book IV, f. 124.

installed together, as in 1470 when Richard Whitby and W. Crowton, who was a canon residentiary, were sworn in as 'wardens of offerings and jewles and things pertaining to the shrine of St Osmund'.[70] Hereford was unique in that the shrine finances were the responsibility of claivigers, officers with duties similar to those of sacrists at other secular churches. There was also a custodian of the shrine in 1287 at the latest, when Gilbert de Chevininge, who was present at the first miracle of St Thomas and later served as a proctor in the case for canonisation, held that post.[71]

Lincoln, with the best series of accounts of any secular cathedral, presents a useful example of shrine organisation and how it adapted to changing conditions. The first shrine-keeper at Lincoln was the chaplain of the tomb of Bishop Hugh, who after the canonisation in 1220 was joined by a chaplain of the feretory.[72] A warden of the altar of St Hugh was also mentioned in mid-thirteenth-century records of legal battles.[73] A 1322 statement of those who were to receive payments out of the offerings at the shrine of St Hugh shows considerable expansion in the officers of the shrine. There were to be two principal shrine-keepers, who were canons, and three lesser keepers, who were not, two of the latter apparently being night wardens. There was also to be a smaller group of officials serving at the tomb of Robert Grosseteste, comprising a canon as keeper, a chaplain, and at least one clerk.[74] For both shrines there was a host of payments for deacons, sub-deacons and singers for celebrating mass, as well as various servants. Records of *aperturæ* show that this basic arrangement was maintained.[75] By the sixteenth century the senior custodian was elected yearly from among the canons of the major residence.[76]

Whether in a secular or monastic cathedral, the shrine-keeper was usually assigned at least one secular clerk.[77] He was probably the busiest official at the shrine. Besides assisting the chaplain or monk when he officiated at the shrine, the clerk had charge of keeping the place clean and assuring that pilgrims did not

[70] SCA, 'Machon Register', fol. 24. Changes in office-holders occur regularly in the same register.

[71] R.C. Finucane, 'Cantilupe as Thaumaturge: Pilgrims and their Miracles', in *St Thomas Cantilupe, Bishop of Hereford: Essays in his Honour*, ed. M. Jancey (Hereford, 1982), p. 138.

[72] 'Phillip of the tomb' appears occasionally as a witness before 1220. See various notices in *Registrum Antiquissimum*, vol. 6. 'Adam de feretro Sancti Hugonis' begins to appear from 1220 (vol. 4, p. 62).

[73] For example, in 1248 Geoffrey of Banbury, 'custodem altaris beati Hugonis', won a case against the rector of Riseholme concerning a yearly payment due by the latter to the altar of St Hugh of two and a half marks. Geoffrey was involved in a similar dispute in 1253. *Registrum Antiquissimum*, vol. 2, p. 61.

[74] A gift of 2s. was stipulated for each clerk celebrating at the tomb: *Liber Niger*, p. 337.

[75] For example, the account of 1402 pays two principal custodians, a day custodian and two night custodians: LCA, D&C Bj/5/16/1, f. 90.

[76] *Chapter Acts of the Cathedral Church of St. Mary of Lincoln, A.D. 1520–1536*, ed. R.E.G. Cole (Lincoln Record Soc., vols 12 and 13, 1915–17), vol. 12, p. xiv.

[77] At Canterbury the two feretrarians shared two secular clerks: 'Customary of the Shrine of St Thomas', f. 4.

walk off with the more portable treasures. In many cases he personally collected the offerings. The clerks at Canterbury had to swear to preserve three things: faithfulness, counsel and the honour of the church. They also had to surrender all offerings they found to the feretrarians and never leave the shrine unless the feretrarians knew and consented, and 'by calling, addressing and answering pilgrims with constant and thorough gentleness, friendliness, and discretion'.[78] The Durham clerk's duties included unlocking and lifting the shrine canopy and helping to carry the banner of St Cuthbert.[79] The officials were also aided by various servants paid out of the shrine's account. At Lincoln stipends were to be given to practically everyone at the cathedral, from 5s. to the sacrist ('because he works hard on many things') down to the sweepers, candle makers and bell ringers, while anyone who had special duties connected with the shrine received 6d. for wine. All these payments amounted to about £4 13s. 4d.[80]

A good example of the organisation of a monastic shrine is Westminster Abbey, where the shrine of Edward the Confessor was in the general charge of a sacrist who kept the account of offerings and payments made there. Beneath the sacrist was a *custos feretri* who was paid 20s. per year in the early fourteenth century (although after 1373 he and his servants were given a combined stipend first of 33s. 4d. and later 40s.).[81] From the late fourteenth century the feretrar's servant also customarily received a robe worth 10s., brethren recruited during the time of the fair to handle the relics were given 4s. each, and the 'candelar' received a variable amount per term for making candles around the shrine and elsewhere.[82] The sacrist had a further four permanent servants who were probably recruited for occasional duties connected with the shrine, each receiving 16s. per annum in early years but 11s. after 1354.[83]

The responsibilities of a feretrar seem to have been straightforward. His first duty upon taking office was to take stock of the shrine's possessions. By the fifteenth century, if not before, this entailed an indentured inventory between the incoming and outgoing officers. For example, in a Westminster indenture of 1467 Thomas Arundell, late keeper of the shrine of Edward the Confessor and of the relics, delivered to his successor, Richard Tedyngton, the vestments, cloths, relics and jewels in his charge.[84] Once in place, a feretrar's responsibilities were essentially to watch over the treasures and relics and to say mass at the shrine altar. In the prologue to the *Tale of Beryn* the pilgrims kissed relics which were named by 'a goodly monk'.[85] The duties of the two feretrarians as explained in the

---

78 'Semper et omnino peregrinos cum omni mansuetudine, affabilitate et morositate convocando alloquendo respondendo': 'Customary of the Shrine of St Thomas', f. 4.

79 *Rites of Durham*, pp. 94, 96.

80 *Liber Niger*, pp. 335–7.

81 WAM, MSS 19622, 19637, 19720, 19628.

82 For example W.A.M., MSS 19622, 19626.

83 WAM, MSS 19618, 19623.

84 21 Dec., 1467: *Report of the Royal Commission on Historical Manuscripts* (London, 1874), vol. 1, p. 96.

85 *Tale of Beryn*, p. 6.

'Customary of the Shrine of St Thomas' mostly involved security measures and the performance of mass at the shrine altar.[86] In the *Rites of Durham* the feretrar's main duty was described as bringing the keys of the shrine whenever it needed to be opened.[87]

The shrine as a source of revenue.

As institutions, shrines had a legal existence and could thus own property. A shrine often received payments of rent from properties owned in its city, such as the many town rents bestowed on the shrines of Sts Alphege, Dunstan and Blaise at Canterbury.[88] Sometimes gifts of land were made for the direct use of the shrine. In 1301 Sir Robert de Arcy granted to God, Mary and St Thomas Becket 'to the work of his shrine' an annual rent of 10s., chargeable on the grantor's lands near Lincoln.[89] Shrines could also be used in customary or legal payments. In 1233 the rectory of Great Paxton was instituted to a certain Rainald of Bath with the proviso that he pay twenty marks yearly to the altar of St Hugh at Lincoln.[90] In the royal subsidy of 1526 John Parkyn, a vicar choral and holder of the chantry of Roger Fitz-Benedict, declared 30s. which he had paid to St Hugh's head as a deduction.[91] Unfortunately, in most shrine accounts the origin of various properties, whether from purchases or pious donations, is impossible to distinguish.

The bulk of a shrine's income was not from properties, but from pilgrims' offerings. These were entirely incorporated within the finances of the cathedral, except in the case of Worcester where the bishop claimed half the shrine offerings as well as the right to appoint a keeper of the shrine. This claim was resolved in a late thirteenth-century composition between the bishop and convent which declared that 'of the proceeds of the tomb and shrine of St Wulfstan . . . half should go to the bishop, and half to the convent, and for the guardianship of the same the bishop for his part, and the convent for its part, will choose to their liking honest clerics or monks as custodians'.[92] Worcester also saw internal disputes over the offerings. In 1302 the prior, *sede vacante*, appealed to

---

86 'Customary of the Shrine of St Thomas', ff. 1–11.
87 *Rites of Durham*, p. 94.
88 CCA, DCc/Reg. A., ff. 355–61; 59 charters to 'the bodies of the saints' are recorded in Reg. E. Most are to Dunstan, such as the first, which is a messuage with 8½d. rent for ornamenting his shrine: CCA, DCc/Reg. E, f. 145.
89 CCA, DCc/Reg. E., ff. 127–8; Woodruff, 'Financial Aspect', pp. 31–2.
90 *Registrum Antiquissimum*, vol. 3, nos 830–1, pp. 172–4.
91 *Chapter Acts of Lincoln*, vol. 12, p. 210.
92 'De proventibus autem tumbae et feretrorum beati Wlstani ita statuerunt, ut medietas eorum de cetero spectat ad Episcopum, medietas ad conventum, et ad custodiam illam Episcopus pro parte sua, et conventus pro parte sua, quos voluerint custodes honestos clericos vel monachos deputabit.' The bishop frequently ceded his right to choose shrine-keepers to the cathedral prior, as for example did Bishop Walter Maydestone in 1313–17: *Liber Ecclesiae Wigorniensis: A Letter Book of the Priors of Worcester*, ed. J.H. Bloom (London, 1912), pp. 29, 33; *Liber Albus of Worcester*, p. 64; In 1302 Edward I

the chancellor against the custos of the temporalities for claiming half of the offerings to Oswald and Wulfstan even though they were spiritualities.[93]

As we have seen, the volume of offerings of wax could be significant. If a large number of candles were unconsumed at day's end, they could be collected for use by the cathedral at large. For example, candles offered to the image of the Blessed Virgin Mary in the nave of St Paul's cathedral were apparently taken by the bell-ringer and chamberlains to a room below the chapter house where they were melted down for the general use of the dean and chapter.[94] At York the treasurer received the candles offered to St William in compensation for maintaining lights at his altar during mass.[95] The great value of offered wax sometimes led to disputes. In 1279 the income from tapers at the shrine of St Richard of Chichester, contested between the treasurer and the dean and chapter, was awarded to the latter (although they were also given responsibility for the costs of the shrine).[96] At Hereford, according to the taxation of 1291, income from wax was equal to £13 6s. 8d.[97] Offerings of candles there became less numerous with time, until the tax assessment was reduced by Pope Benedict XII in 1336 when the yearly income from wax offerings fell to just slightly over £6.[98]

We already know that there was often a difference between the collector of the offerings and the accountant. At Westminster, for example, the oblations were collected by the feretrar and recorded on a tally (a wooden stick marked with notches) which was presented to the sacrist.[99] In many places tallies were replaced by written indentures, notably at Durham where several of the latter (between the *socius feretrarii* and the feretrar) survive.[100] The responsibility for offerings could change over time. The oblations at the tombs of Oswald and Wulfstan were received by the Worcester sacrist in 1423/4 but in 1505/6, in the sacrist's account under *Oblaciones peregrinorum* (offerings of pilgrims), the sacrist received £23 6s. from the pyx of St Mary and additional money from wax and other gifts but none from the main shrines.[101] By 1515/6 the tumbarius was receiving a mark in

granted the convent the bishop's portion of the offerings 'to the shrine and at his tomb' during all future vacancies: *Patent Rolls, 1301–1307*, p. 28.

93   *Liber Albus of Worcester*, p. 9.
94   Dugdale, *St Paul's*, p. 21.
95   *Statutes of Lincoln*, vol. 2, p. 98. From the late medieval statutes of York.
96   *Chartulary of Chichester*, no. 713, pp. 184–5; *Registrum Ricardi de Swinfield, Episcopi Herefordensis*, ed. W.W. Capes (Canterbury and York Soc., vol. 6, 1909), pp. 230, 297.
97   *Taxatio Ecclesiastica Angliœ et Walliœ Auctoritate P. Nicholai VI*, Record Commission (London, 1802), pp. 157–8.
98   Morgan, 'Effect of the Pilgrim Cult on Hereford', p. 151; *Calendar of Entries in the Papal Registers Relating to Great Britain and Ireland, Papal Letters*, vol. 2, ed. W.H. Bliss (London, 1895), p. 531.
99   Clear examples of the wording are in the Sacrist's accounts for 1373/4 (WAM, MS 19634) and 1422/3 (MS 19663).
100   The Durham indentures are kept in the archives of the Dean and Chapter among the feretrar's rolls. Indentures also existed at Worcester between the subsacrist and the sacrist: WCA, MS C427.
101   WCA, MS C 427.

oblations from the 'tombs' of Oswald and Wulfstan.[102] Therefore, sometime between 1424 and 1505 the reception of the offerings at Worcester shrines may have switched from the sacrist to the tumbarius (see Chapter 6).

The first responsibility of these officials was to see that the shrine was properly maintained. When a shrine was being built or reconstructed the offerings often went towards its fabric. Income received from the Corona in 1221 and 1222, for example, was not entered into the Canterbury treasurers' accounts because it was earmarked for the shrine of St Thomas.[103] Very occasionally the expenses mention repairs carried out on a shrine or its accoutrements. In 1377/8, for instance, some of the relics at Westminster were repaired for 23s., a reliquary for 16d. and a silver tabula at the altar of St Edward for 20s.[104] The Canterbury treasurer's account of 1314 shows £115 12s. spent on gold and precious stones for adorning the 'new crown' of St Thomas.[105] After their initial construction, however, shrines were durable objects requiring little attention other than cleaning. Expenses on construction, or new ornamentation for the shrine, were rare.

A much greater percentage of the offerings went towards stipends for various officials attending the shrine. The feretrar himself received between 20s. and 40s., usually paid out of the offerings. The Winchester *custodus scrinium*, for example, was paid 26s. 8d. for his yearly work.[106] In 1469 Walter Luffekyn was given 40s. as *custos* of the altar and shrine of St Osmund.[107] The shrine-keeper at Chichester was maintained by giving him a chantry at the shrine, worth eight marks, in 1294.[108] Clerks of the shrine were usually paid about half of the feretrar's salary. The two clerks of the tomb of St Thomas were relatively well paid, each receiving 1d. per day plus bread and ale. When the clerk of Thomas's tomb carried the holy water in processions, he also received one portion of monk's food from the refectory.[109] The night wardens of the shrine of St Hugh were apparently paid the relatively high sum of 40s. yearly, perhaps because of their difficult hours of work.[110]

Wax played as large a part in shrine expenses as it did in receipts, particularly as shrine-keepers were often in charge of lighting the entire cathedral. In 1468/9 the Canterbury sacrist, for example, had to pay £62 13s. 4d. for 2,311 pounds of wax which he obtained through the feretrarians.[111] A more usual cost of lighting a cathedral for a year can be seen at Norwich, where the sacrist spent an average of £30 for ten to twelve hundredweight of wax and its conversion into candles out

[102] WCA, MS AXII, 'Miscellaneous Volume', f. 41.

[103] CCA, DDc/MA1, ff. 65, 66.

[104] WAM, MS 19637.

[105] CCA, DCc/MA1, f. 52; Woodruff, 'Financial Aspect', p. 18.

[106] *Documents Relating to the Foundation of Winchester*, p. 24.

[107] SCA, 'Machon Register', f. 17.

[108] *Chartulary of Chichester*, p. 65.

[109] A list of wages and allowances from Register J. is printed in Woodruff, 'Sacrist's Rolls of Canterbury', p. 76.

[110] *Liber Niger*, p. 337.

[111] CCA, DCc/Sac. 47; Sacrist's account for 1524/5: CCA, DCc/MA 30, f. 152.

of an annual budget of £50.[112] A payment by Henry VI in 1422/3 of £9 for 450 pounds of wax gives an indication of the possible rate of wax consumption around a shrine. This was stated to have supplied four candles burning continuously for 297 days about the tomb of Henry's father.[113] This seems conservative at only one and a half pounds of wax per day, but at Bury 66s. 8d. was spent on four candles burning continuously about St Edmund. At 6d./lb. this would amount to 133 pounds of wax, or about 33 pounds per taper for the whole year.[114] From the records of Canterbury we can see that a single light burning for one year cost anywhere from about a mark (13s. 8d.) to 25s. In 1284 a certain Richard, once clerk of exchange at Canterbury, gave Andrew of Bregge, clerk of the shrine, 50s. to maintain two tapers burning continuously at the shrine 'as the other lights around the said shrine do', the lights to be renewed four times per year.[115] A candle burning night and day seems to have cost 50s. while one burning just when mass was said cost only 3s.[116] These prices show that even a modest number of lights burning regularly could be expensive, not surprisingly since wax usually cost between 5d. and 7d. per pound when bought in bulk by the cathedral. This was recognised by contemporary church-goers, who occasionally granted rents to support lights at a shrine. For example, a rent of 12d. given for lights before St Erkenwald's altar appears in a pre-1211 charter.[117] Several thirteenth-century and later grants to the shrine-keepers at Worcester survive for lights at the shrines of Oswald and Wulfstan.[118] Henry III was a frequent and generous donor of candles to shrines. In 1238 he gave both Bury St Edmunds and Canterbury no less than 300 one-pound candles to burn about the shrines on the feast days of their respective saints.[119] In 1246 he gave four candles worth £100 each to the shrine of St Thomas at Canterbury, and the same to St Edmund at Bury.[120] It is a mystery what made such candles so valuable, since, at the usual cost of 6d. per pound, £100 could have purchased 4,000 pounds of wax (and they certainly were not that big).

Once the shrine and its expenses were paid for, the chapter was free to spend the money from offerings on whatever it pleased. Building projects were one

---

112 Saunders, *Introduction to the Rolls of Norwich*, p. 105.

113 WAM, MS 19663.

114 'Four tapers burn daily around the tomb of St Edmund in honour of God [and] St Edmund by custom from ancient time' (iiijor tapurris cotidiane ardent circa tumbam Sancti Edmundi in honore Dei Sancti Edmundi ex antiquo tempore usitate): *Valor Ecclesiasticus*, vol. 3, p. 465.

115 'Videlicet quemlibet de octo libris cere ardentes ibidem sicut alii faciunt circa feretrum.' Candles were to be renewed at the feasts of St Michael, Christmas, Easter and the Nativity of St John the Baptist: CCA, Reg. E, f. 143.

116 CCA, Reg. E, f. 143.

117 *Early Charters of the Cathedral Church of St. Paul*, p. 187.

118 WCA, MSS B936, B1039, B1089, B1135, B1214, B1299, B1549. The Worcester monks were also granted licence to appropriate the church of Lyndrugg, in the diocese of Hereford, in order to augment their number by three monks and to find two wax-lights to burn continually before the shrine of St Wulfstan: *Patent Rolls, 1301–1307*, p. 523.

119 This cost him £7 16s. 6d. in the case of Canterbury: *Liberate Rolls*, vol. 1, pp. 356–7.

120 *Liberate Rolls*, vol. 3, p. 93.

possibility, a well documented case occurring at Hereford during the first thirty years of St Thomas Cantilupe's cult when the tomb-shrine funded a significant reconstruction of the church. Before Cantilupe's death the only income to the fabric fund had been one canon's share of the common fund and the sporadic benefits of indulgences, mortuary dues, legacies and gifts.[121] The fabric roll of 1290/1, however, shows £178 10s. 7d. (plus 3s. in broken silver) being received from the tomb of the blessed Thomas, constituting over sixty per cent of the fund's total receipts.[122] Although the details and dating of the construction work in the cathedral are obscure, it is possible that the south transept, nave aisles, north porch, main tower and even the western tower were all rebuilt at this time. Witnesses in the canonisation investigation at Hereford in 1307 stated that the Great Tower and much of the rest of the church had been rebuilt from the proceeds of the tomb.[123] What is certain is that there was a burst of building activity after 1282.[124] Thus the time of greatest income from the shrine fortunately coincided with the time of greatest need in the building program of the church.

That the shrine of St Thomas had a very powerful effect on the income and building programs of Hereford, and that the decline of the oblations was acutely felt, is shown by the great difficulties faced by the Hereford fabric fund beginning in the early thirteenth century. New work on the nave and choir aisles and the eastern transepts was ruined when the foundations began to give way in 1219, causing the chapter to appeal to the Pope for financial aid claiming that 20,000 marks had been spent already.[125] Further quests for more sources of income such as indulgences, donations and the selling of church assets in the fourteenth-century show 'how desperate was the need for money . . . It is no exaggeration to say that the cult of St Thomas Cantilupe had an enormous effect on Hereford Cathedral. Without the resulting financial aid there would never have been sufficient money for as much rebuilding and enhancement, for ever since that time the chapter has had great difficulty in finding funds to keep the fabric in repair.'[126] The late fourteenth-century fabric rolls graphically illustrate the decline, as income to the fund from the shrine was down to £2 13s. 4d. in 1383/4 and dropped to 26s. 8d. three years later.[127]

There are scattered references to the funding of church construction by other shrines. Offerings to St William of Perth at Rochester are said to have helped rebuild the choir in 1220 and the north transept 'against the gate of St William'

---

[121] Morgan, 'Effect of the Pilgrim Cult on Hereford', p. 146.

[122] HCA, MS 2368; W.N. Yates, 'The Fabric Rolls of Hereford Cathedral, 1290/1 and 1386/7', *The National Library of Wales J.*, vol. 18 (1973–74), p. 79.

[123] *Acta Sanctorum, October*, vol. 1, p. 595.

[124] Morgan, 'Effect of the Pilgrim Cult on Hereford', p. 149.

[125] *Charters and Records of Hereford*, pp. 184–5. Hereford's poverty is also attributed to the expenses incurred in the canonisation of St Thomas: Morgan, 'Effect of the Pilgrim Cult on Hereford', p. 149. Morgan also gives a summary of differing opinions as to the order and dating of building works at Hereford around this time: *ibid.*, pp. 146–7.

[126] Morgan, 'Effect of the Pilgrim Cult on Hereford', pp. 151–2.

[127] HCA, MSS R.621, 2371.

from c.1235.[128] An attempt by the dean and chapter of Lincoln to raise funds for the repair of the Minster after it was severely damaged in 1185 had little success without the attraction of a popular saint's relics.[129] Honorius III allowed one quarter of the offerings for the Jubilee indulgence at Canterbury in 1220 to be diverted towards rebuilding the cathedral chevet until its completion.[130] A St Paul's Chapter ordinance of 1300 stipulated that any oblations to the Crux Borealis or elsewhere were to be converted towards the building of the London retrochoir until it was finished, while in 1483 the chapter of Lichfield ordered that offerings to the images of Christ and St Anne, after deductions for the chaplain and clerk, be used first to ornament the altar there, then pay for the fabric of the church.[131] Despite the above examples, a shrine's revenue was rarely diverted towards building work. In none of the surviving series of shrine accounts is there a regular entry for transferring offerings to the fabric fund.

In monastic cathedrals funds were sometimes transferred from the shrine to other, unrelated obedientiaries. For example, in the 1477/8 Worcester kitchener roll, under 'outside receipts' (*recepta forinsecus*), 40s. were supposed to be received from the tombs of Oswald and Wulfstan, but were written off.[132] A customary payment from the offerings to the Worcester pittancer also seems to have been in arrears.[133] These sorts of transfers, however, were not common.

Much of the income of any shrine went into subsidies for the resident clergy. At Lincoln this was set at 6s. 8d. to canons of the major residence, 3s. 4d. if they failed to be present at the shrine on the feast of St Hugh.[134] At Salisbury the subsidy amounted to only 4d. per canon, but this was at a time when a great deal of money was being spent on the uncompleted shrine itself.[135] Payments to the Durham monks ranged from 65% of the total shrine income in the decade 1400-1409 up to 96% in the 1430s. This money was paid out to the monks over five terms, each getting between 18d. and 4s., although 6s. 8d. went to the sub-prior and 20s. to the prior. Since there were usually only about forty monks in the convent at any one time, if all received a share of the payment then they would have averaged 12s. per year from St Cuthbert.[136] The fact that offerings to the shrine went mostly to the local clergy may have contributed to the fifteenth-century drop in offerings. Besides general Lollard criticisms of priestly avarice, Richard Fitzralph, archbishop of Armagh, in a 1356 sermon 'criticised the avarice

---

[128] 'Versus portam beati Willelmi': Richardson, 'Saint William of Perth', p. 124. He does not give a reference.

[129] Peter Kidson, 'St. Hugh's Choir', in *Medieval Art and Architecture at Lincoln* (*BAACT*, vol. 8, 1986), p. 30.

[130] Foreville, *Le Jubilé*, p. 7. The letter is printed on p. 165.

[131] *Registrum Statutorum Londiniensis*, p. 91; LJRO, 'Chapter Act Book II', f. 8.

[132] *Compotus Rolls of Worcester*, pp. 27, 30.

[133] From a 1483/4 pittancer account: *Compotus Rolls of Worcester*, p. 38.

[134] *Liber Niger*, p. 336.

[135] SCA, 'Account of the Warden of the Shrine of St Osmund, 1493/4'.

[136] DDCA, 'Feretrars' Rolls', by year, especially 1407/8 and 1410/1 which list the payments in full.

of the keepers of shrines, who fabricated miracles for their own enrichment'.[137] This could have disinclined pilgrims to generosity (see Chapter 7).

Any surplus income from the shrine was generally stored in a chest or 'treasury'. The wardens of the shrine of St Osmund, for example, put their arrears in 'St Osmund's chest'.[138] The contents of a shrine treasury could be lent to other offices. In 1307 the Lincoln cathedral treasurer, Robert de Lacy, borrowed £40 from the chest of St Hugh and £26 13s. 4d. from that of Robert Grosseteste, and the next year the vicars choral borrowed another ten marks.[139] In 1280 the king repaid Chichester cathedral £583 4d., which according to a political and pious fiction was lent by St Richard to Henry III but was in fact income outstanding from a vacancy of 1244–6.[140] In the same year that St Osmund was translated £26 were borrowed from his offerings by the keeper of the fabric at Salisbury to pay for repairs of lead.[141]

The shrine was a useful storehouse for jewels and precious metal, being continually in want of ornament and being well watched and protected. In 1489/90 two silver patens were made for oblations at the high altar of Westminster using twelve ounces of silver taken out of the stores of the feretory and vestibule, and the next year another twenty-four ounces of silver were obtained from the feretory stores for candelabras.[142] This suggests that the feretory kept a supply of raw or old metal. In 1266/7 Henry III borrowed jewels belonging to the shrine of St Edward which he promised to return within a year from Michaelmas.[143] In more serious instances of financial crisis the feretrum itself was stripped to help the church. In 1144 Bishop Nigel required the priory of Ely to lend him two hundred marks as part of a fine to the king, much of which they procured by stripping silver from the shrine of St Etheldreda. In return, Nigel gave them a manor by charter, specifically for the repair and ornamenting of the shrine.[144] Shrines throughout England were stripped to help pay for the ransom of Richard I, but sometimes a saint's reputation preserved his shrine: the judges of the Exchequer wanted to strip the shrine of St Edmund but dared not approach it.[145] The hand of St James at

---

[137] He called the miracles 'fabricated and false' (fabricata ac ficta): W.R. Jones, 'Lollards and Images: The Defense of Religious Art in Later Medieval England', *J. of the History of Ideas*, vol. 34 (1973), pp. 29, 33 n. 30.

[138] On 16 Oct. 1456 it contained £19 5s. There was also a *sacculo Osmundi*, which appears to have had no less than £164 5s. on 10 Nov. 1456: *Canonization of St Osmund*, p. 175.

[139] Venables, 'Shrine and Head of St Hugh', p. 60.

[140] Jones, 'Cult of St. Richard', p. 81.

[141] *Canonization of St Osmund*, pp. 172–3.

[142] WAM, MSS 19737, 19739.

[143] *Report of the Royal Commission on Historical Manuscripts*, vol. 1, p. 96.

[144] 'He took also from the feretrum of St Etheldreda 74 marks of silver and from the front 25 marks' (Cepit itaque de feretro sancte Æ[th]eldre[th]e lxxiiiior marcas argenti, et de fronte xxv marcas): *Liber Eliensis*, pp. 290, 335; Bentham, *The History and Antiquities of Ely*, p. 140.

[145] 'For the fury of St. Edmund can reach those who are absent and far away; much more will it strike those who are present and strip his shirt from off him': Jocelin of Brakelond, *Chronicle*, p. 97.

Reading was less fortunate, being stripped of gold plate to settle the abbey's debts with the same king.[146]

The collected treasure of a shrine attracted unscrupulous but talented thieves.[147] An interesting mid eleventh-century story from Evesham describes the theft of relics out of the feretrum of St Egwin. Aldith, a 'very noble matron' (*matronæ nobilissimæ*), convinced two brothers to hide in church and open the shrine by night. Although she was supposedly struck blind as a result, the relics were not regained by the monastery until the 1070s.[148] When St Erkenwald was in the crypt of London cathedral several men tried to break in to steal the shrine but were scared off by a youthful watcher. The translation of 1140 was described as a security measure intended to foil further attempts.[149] Despite night watchmen the reliquary of St Hugh's Head was stolen from Lincoln in 1364. Stripped by the thieves, the head itself was thrown away and only recovered, so it was said, by the miraculous help of a guardian crow. Shortly after selling their spoils for twenty marks the robbers were caught, confessed, and hanged. Edward III, now the legal possessor of the head through judicial forfeiture, returned it to Lincoln as an act of special favour to the Blessed Virgin, her church in Lincoln, and the body of the holy confessor.[150] In 1324 robbers stole a large golden cross, said to have been the gift of King Edgar, from the shrine at Ely. The custodian of the shrine followed the thieves to London and recovered the treasures.[151] Other thefts from shrines occurred at Chichester in 1280 and a second time at Ely in 1385.[152] Monasteries even had to fear their own monks. In two separate instances Canterbury monks stole from the Martyrdom of St Thomas: in 1176 a certain Benedict, finding the monastery empty, stole some flagstones, two vials of blood and parts of a vestment, all relics which he took back to Peterborough where he had become abbot, while a certain Roger, keeper of the Martyrdom, was successfully induced

[146] King John helped to restore the hand with an annual gift of 1 mark in gold bestowed in 1200: *Reading Abbey Cartularies*, ed. B.R. Kemp (Camden Soc., 4th ser. vol. 31, 1986), vol. 1, pp. 71–2.

[147] See C. Oman, 'Security in English Churches, A.D. 1000–1548', *Arch. J.*, vol. 136 (1979), pp. 90–8.

[148] *Chronicon Abbatiæ de Evesham*, pp. 45–6, 94.

[149] *Miracula Erkenwaldi*, pp. 150–3.

[150] Henry Knighton, *Chronicon Henrici Knighton*, ed. J.R. Lumby (RS, vol. 92, 1895), vol. 2, pp. 120–121.

[151] 'Item to Father Robert de Richling form go ing to London to look for the silver stolen from the feretrum' (Item Fratri Roberto de Richelyngge eunti apud London pro argento furato de feretro querend): *The Sacrist Rolls of Ely*, ed. F.R. Chapman (2 vols, Cambridge, 1907), p. 31.

[152] *History and Constitution of a Cathedral*, p. 47. The bishop and dean and chapter of Chichester were reluctant to replace the recovered jewels until ordered to do so by Edward I, who considered their return miraculous: *Patent Rolls, 1272–81*, p. 363. The Latin original is printed in 'Early Statutes of Chichester', p. 174. The thieves at Ely removed the wooden capsa, broke the locks and removed rings and other jewels, for which they were excommunicated in absentia: 'The Register of Bishop Thomas Arundell', CUL, MS G/1/2, f. 54.

by an offer of the position of abbot to take a portion of the skull of St Thomas to St Augustine's Abbey.[153]

A number of measures were taken to augment security. As we have seen in Chapter 2, watching chambers could be built and the shrine barricaded with gates and fences. The shrine, as at Canterbury, could then be closed and locked when the tonsured guardians were away.[154] Special watchmen were also employed, especially at night. An Ely dean and chapter statute of 1314, for example, ordered that two trustworthy servants of the sacrist were to watch the cathedral day and night.[155] At Lincoln the church was searched after the ringing of the bells by the night watchman, the lay-sacrist and the candle-lighter, who ate their supper in a wooden chamber in the north-east aisle within sight of the feretory. The night watchman then stayed awake while the other two slept.[156] At Canterbury the two feretrarians slept in the shrine precincts, rising at six in winter and autumn, and at five in spring and summer.[157] After high mass the senior clerk 'with some instrument of attack or defence should make diligent search of each dark place and suspect corner in which anyone of pernicious intent could lie concealed to perpetrate a theft which should not occur, or in which any mad or rabid dog might lie hidden'.[158] The sanctity and heavy protection of a shrine often led to its being used as a secure vault. At Durham in 1195 the keys of the castle were hung over the feretrum of St Cuthbert.[159] From 1389 the king had use of a ruby-studded coronation ring when in England, but when abroad had to place it on the shrine of St Edward.[160] In 1529 the common seal of Lincoln cathedral was ordered returned to a triple-locked chest near the chest of St Hugh.[161] These instances testify to the relative security of the shrine chapel.

The importance of a shrine to a cathedral and its clergy was manifold. It provided a spiritual point of reference for their existence and a divine patron who continuously affirmed their authority and history. The shrine was an efficient institution assimilated into the ceremonial and organisational life of the cathedral to the extent that it had little effect on the overall structure; a shrine was an addition to rather than a change of cathedral life. Financial benefits were more concrete,

---

153 Stanley, 'Shrine of St Thomas', p. 201.
154 'Customary of the Shrine of St Thomas', f. 2.
155 This followed a visitation ruling of 1300: *Ely Chapter Ordinances*, pp. 22–3, 42.
156 C. Wordsworth, *Notes on Medieval Services in England, with an Index of Lincoln Ceremonies* (London, 1898), pp. 51–2.
157 'Customary of the Shrine of St Thomas', f. 1.
158 'Cum aliquo instrumento invasino vel defensino scrutinium diligenter faciet in singulis locis obscuris et angulis suspectis in quibus aliquis perniciosi ingenij latrocinium quod absit operaturus clandestine latere posset vel in quibus aliquis canis velictus seu rabidus se latenter occultaret': 'Customary of the Shrine of St Thomas', f. 2.
159 'And the keys of the castle he hung over the feretrum of St Cuthbert' (Et claves castelli suspendit supra feretrum Sancti Cuthberti): Walter of Coventry, *Collections*, vol. 2, p. 83.
160 *Report of the Royal Commission on Historical Manuscripts*, vol. 1, p. 96.
161 *Chapter Acts of Lincoln*, vol. 12, p. 117.

with most of the income being channelled towards the clergy. Nevertheless, the wealth from offerings was incorporated seamlessly into the finances of a cathedral except when those offerings were exceptionally high. The importance of these offerings will be examined in the following two chapters.

6

Shrine Accounts and Offerings

Historians have often made much of the wealth generated by medieval shrines. However, no concerted effort has been made to determine the importance of offerings to church finances, how the income fluctuated, or how those fluctuations may have reflected trends in popular piety.[1] This neglect has largely been the result of various deficiencies of the sources themselves. The rolls and registers containing the financial records of any one shrine are imperfectly preserved, with the result that a historian studying one cathedral can come to feel that the evidence is not sufficiently abundant or trustworthy to justify careful analysis. Even in studies involving more than one church, the offerings and the way they were recorded varied greatly from shrine to shrine, making direct comparisons difficult.

Nevertheless, the unique nature of these sources justifies the time and care they require. As financial records, the accounts of shrine income were intended to be read only by the clergy responsible for the administration of a particular religious house and thus are relatively free from the exaggeration, hagiographic convention and attempts at cult promotion that affect material like *vitæ* or *miracula*. The fact that they were subject to internal audit also helps to ensure that they held to a reasonable degree of accuracy. In addition, the accounts are a rare source of quantifiable information on an aspect of medieval popular religion. Expressing worship in numerical terms may seem impossible or a contradiction in terms, but shrine offerings were at least directly related to the number of pilgrims. The accounts, if examined carefully, thus provide a crucial check on evidence derived from other, arguably more subjective sources and can provide new insights into the religious sentiment of the middle ages.

Obtaining such information is essentially a mechanical task, involving the study of enough documents to supply a reliable statistical sample. More serious difficulties arise from interpretation, for although the records may be unbiased they are invariably cryptic. The restriction of the intended readership to clergy within the cathedral helps to ensure that the information is accurate, but also results in a series of bald figures accompanied by very little explanation. The complexities of cathedral administration are left invisible behind single entries because the reader was assumed to be already familiar with local practices. In order to discover the underlying situation the accounts must be analysed both in detail and in quantities. Only after the reliability and content of the records have

---

1 An exception is Woodruff, 'Financial Aspect', pp. 13–32.

been determined can they then be subjected to quantitative and statistical analysis. Such a process elicits all sorts of new problems, but is nevertheless the best of very few means of studying the changing patterns of devotion to the cult of relics in a manner approaching objectivity. It is these patterns and trends which will be the primary focus of the last part of this book.

Significant series of accounts recording the receipts of shrine offerings survive for six cathedrals (Canterbury, Durham, Hereford, Ely, Lincoln and Norwich) and one abbey (Westminster). The archives of a few other cathedrals, such as York and Worcester, have one or two useful references to offerings but do not possess a sufficiently complete series to supply an adequate statistical sample. They can be used, however, to elucidate practices found elsewhere. The more complete series of accounts usually begin sometime in the fourteenth century and continue until a few years before the Dissolution. None of the records go back to the origins of a saint's cult, although those at Canterbury do include references to the creation of the actual shrine of St Thomas in 1220 (as opposed to the erection of the original tomb in 1170).

The problems involved in interpreting shrine accounts are many. Firstly, the amount of information given for any one year is often very small. In most cases, it comprises only the isolated and unexplained sum of the money offered at the shrine. The proportion of the total real income received that this figure represents is uncertain, a problem that is exacerbated by the administrative routines whereby the receipts were recorded. Usually the money had passed through one or more sets of hands before being recorded. At Durham, for example, we know from the receipt indentures that the shrine clerk was actually in charge of receiving the oblations from the pilgrims. The offerings were accounted for, however, in the rolls of the feretrars, who were the immediate supervisors of the shrine clerks. The accounting at the shrine of St Cuthbert was therefore one administrative level removed from the actual collection of the offering. Except for the above mentioned indentures, and the unusual situation at Lincoln (see below), this is the closest that the records get to the act of giving itself. The accounting was removed still further from the shrine by being placed in the hands of the sacrist at Ely, Westminster and Norwich, and at Canterbury where it was given over to the treasurer. In the fifteenth century the reorganisation of Canterbury's finances, giving ultimate authority for shrine accounts to the prior, placed yet another level of bureaucracy between record and event. At worst, therefore, the information available to the modern historian records the offerings only after they have passed through three levels of cathedral administration.

There are two major ways in which the figures in the extant accounts might differ from the amount actually offered to the shrine: they could be smaller if some of the money was diverted prior to the making of the account and therefore not recorded, or larger if non-oblationary income was included in the total. Several situations could result in offerings being diverted prior to accounting. Customary expenses of the shrine, such as buying wax or paying an official, could have been paid directly out of the money box. Since these expenses were necessary and out of the control of the shrine-keeper (wages and candle consumption, for example, being relatively fixed), it might have been considered unnecessary to document them. It is also possible that these expenses were accounted for by lesser officials whose documents were not preserved. In some places functionaries or offices unrelated to the shrine, such as the fabric fund, had rights to certain kinds of gifts or offerings which might not have been recorded or recorded under other headings. Occasionally the offerings were rounded down to an even sum before inclusion in an account, with the remainder apparently given away in charity or used as petty cash (see below).

The second major form of error possible in the accounts, the inclusion of non-devotional income, would tend to make the receipts appear larger than they were and is potentially more serious for the analyst. Such items could include rents from holdings attached to the shrine or fees involuntarily presented to the shrine as a form of tax or duty. An extreme example is the granting to St Edmund in 1296 of the fines and forfeitures exacted whenever the king's ministers of the market passed through Bury St Edmunds. These sums went towards the decoration of the tomb.[2] These might have been grouped together with offerings under one sum for the purpose of easier accounting, as there was little theoretical and no practical difference between these incomes for the medieval accountant. Everything could be construed as income due to the saint. Fortunately, however, rents almost always have their own and often very detailed section in the receipts, a practice which should eliminate the most serious possible error of this sort.

There are a few ways to check the reliability of accounts, none of them conclusive. One is by assessing the comprehensiveness of the account: the more detailed the record of expenses, the more certain one can be that nothing was diverted. For example, if the accounts record the shrine-keeper's yearly stipend then we can discount the possibility that he received his fee directly out of the offerings before they appeared in the receipts. Also, the recorded total of offerings becomes more trustworthy the more irregular it is since fluctuations are to be expected in this kind of offering. In the same way, a shrine receipt showing a sum with individual shillings and pence, or even farthings, is more believable than a suspiciously even number, such as one that shows only pounds or is easily divisible into marks. A series of even numbers, one year after the next, is even more dubious, suggesting that the receiver is handing over a set or round sum to the accountant rather than the full amount, the small change, if not more substantial moneys, having been removed first. For example, in all but one year the shrine income at Canterbury over the decade 1291 to 1300[3] is recorded in even pounds, and in eight of these years the sum was rounded to the nearest tens digit. In both

---

2 *Patent Rolls, 1292–1301*, p. 183.
3 The financial year was usually from Michaelmas (29 September) to Michaelmas the year following. The full, formal indication of any complete accounting year should therefore be in the form 1290/1 or 1290–1 (the former being preferred here). Those accounts not covering the usual span of time are noted in the tables in the appendices.

1291/2 and 1292/3 the shrine was recorded as receiving an even £200.[4] One inevitably suspects that an even sum was paid to the treasurer after some money had been diverted. On the other hand, the receipts at Norwich were almost always noted down to the last farthing. Obviously, judging the validity of a record by its variability is not rigorously scientific. However, it does help when no other tools are available.

Most problems of accuracy in the shrine accounts can be minimised if we remember not to place too much trust in the absolute value of the money involved (i.e. the raw recorded number) or its value relative to other shrines. While both have their interest, the most substantial insights can be achieved only by studying the value of the offerings from year to year in the same series of records. Not only do the offerings then take on statistical significance, but when the relative yearly change becomes the most significant factor then possible divergence between the recorded sum and the actual offerings are less serious. The history of the income before it was recorded does not matter greatly as long as the accounts are consistent in themselves. The real danger in such analysis is confined to changes in accounting procedure. For example, if the offerings at a shrine are recorded separately for a time, but then placed together with a second source of income, it will disturb our perception of the underlying trend. A change in the administrative level at which income was recorded might have a similar effect. Only careful study of the accounts can even partially guard against this kind of threat. It is not unreasonable to hope that the comparison of several cathedrals over long periods of time will allow us to spot irregularities and show any important trends common to all shrines. But first we must examine the individual shrine accounts in systematic detail.

Canterbury

The earliest and most complete set of shrine accounts derives from the cult of St Thomas Becket at Canterbury Cathedral Priory. Almost all priory receipts were concentrated at first in the hands of the treasurer, whose surviving accounts begin in 1198/9 and continue very consistently until 1384/5 (see table 2 and graph 1). Two significant gaps in the record occur from 1207 to 1213 (when the Canterbury monks were in exile) and from 1338 to 1369 (for which only the accounts for 1350/1 and 1351/2 survive).[5] The treasurers' accounts cease abruptly in 1385, and although they eventually reappear in a very reduced form they no longer contain references to St Thomas's shrine, since the function of centralised financial

---

4   CCA, DCc/MA 1, ff. 178, 185. The chance of a random sum being evenly in pounds is 1 in 240. The odds of it randomly occurring ten times in a row is one in 6.34×10^{23}.

5   The treasurers' accounts can be found in the CCA DCc/Lit MS D4 (1198–1206); DCc/MA 1 (1206–1307); DCc/MA 2 (1307–82, 1384/5); DCc/Treasurer 26, 27 (1382–4, 1350–2). Reference other than the year usually will not be made to these or following documents unless a direct quotation is made, since in most cases the source is unambiguous.

receiver was transferred to the office of prior in 1391 as part of the great concentration of priory finances under Prior Thomas Chillendon.[6] Compared to the earlier series of treasurer's accounts these later records are disappointing. Only eighteen priors' accounts survive over the period from 1395/6 to 1473/4, and these are inconsistent and ambiguous in their documentation of the shrine.[7] There is also one feretrarians' account and a list of customary expenses at the back of the 'Customary of the Shrine of St Thomas'.[8]

The period between 1198 and the monks' exile in 1207 already shows significant offerings to the cult of St Thomas. The average income from all offerings, including the high altar, was £426, of which the tomb of St Thomas made up £309, the Martyrdom £27 and the Corona £40. The most profitable of these years, perhaps because King John and his queen were crowned in the cathedral that year, was 1200/1201, when £620 4s. were received from all offerings.[9] Nor did the exile of the monks stop the faithful from visiting the tomb. The prior of Dover, who had been entrusted with the care of the shrine in the convent's absence, handed £245 10s. in offerings over to the monks on their return. This was but a fraction of what would normally have been received over the six years, no doubt one reason why King John paid the convent £1,000 in compensation for the exile.[10]

The period from 1213 until the translation of St Thomas's relics in 1220 saw the recorded income at the tomb range widely from a low of £65 13s. 9d. in 1215/16 to a high of £300 in 1213/14. The translation, of course, brought about a great change. From receiving £275 9s. in 1219/20 the now empty tomb dropped to £31 3s. 3d. in 1220/1 and only received between £5 and £10 for most of the next century and a half. By the time of the treasurer's last surviving account as general receiver in 1384/5 the recorded income at the tomb had been zero for four consecutive years. The priors' accounts which followed do not always record tomb receipts. The tomb received £23 in the jubilee year of 1420, but only £2 in 1436/7, the last time it appears.[11]

The Corona and Martyrdom had independent incomes, hovering around £35 and £10 respectively over their entire history. Both sites recorded offerings below average in the 1320s and 1330s (down to about £25 and £5), but when accounts resumed in the 1370s their incomes were abnormally high, averaging £62 for the Corona and £14 for the Martyrdom. The last decade of the treasurers' rolls, the 1380s, saw incomes average close to what they had been in the thirteenth century. In the priors' accounts the Martyrdom is only mentioned in 1410/11 (10s.), 1411 (6s. 8d., an incomplete year) and the jubilee year of 1419/20 (£23).[12] The Corona income was more enduring. It amounted to no less than £150 in 1419/20, and

6   See R.A.L. Smith, *Canterbury Cathedral Priory* (2nd edn, Cambridge, 1969), pp. 190–1.
7   Found in CCA, DCc/Prior 1–15; DCc/MA 4 (Drafts for 1444–9).
8   CCA, DCc/Feretrarian 1; 'Customary of the Shrine of St Thomas', BL, Add. MS 59616.
9   CCA, Lit. MS D4, f. 8; Woodruff, 'Financial Aspect', p. 16.
10 CCA, DCc/MA 1, f. 53.
11 CCA, DCc/Prior 7.
12 CCA, DCc/Prior 2, 1; DCc/Reg. H, f. 102.

averaged about £20 until the last two recorded years (1472/3 and 1473/4), when it received £6 13s. 4d. and £7 respectively (see graph 2).

We are fortunate in being able to follow the offerings at the main shrine of St Thomas from its creation in 1220 throughout the duration of the treasurers' accounts. However, because the treasurer had two subordinate feretrarians, who in turn oversaw clerks of the shrine, the administrative level of this information is somewhat removed from the act of oblation. Nevertheless, the accounts seem to be consistent in their methods.

The main shrine of St Thomas outshone all other English saints' shrines in its attraction to pilgrims. In 1219/20, the first year of its existence, the income was no less than £702, the highest recorded for any English shrine. The long term trends for the period covered by the treasurers' accounts can be followed in a graph of the yearly income (see graph 1). What stands out is a low point reached in the 1250s and 1260s, a subsequent recovery followed by a second but less significant decline in the early fourteenth century and, finally, a massive increase occurring by 1351. Unfortunately, the period 1338–70 is represented by only two accounts, so we cannot be sure when after 1338 the increase began or whether the revenues in the 1350/1 and 1351/2 accounts were typical of the 1350s.[13] The income was still high in the 1370s, although it may already have begun to decline at that time.

The priors' rolls continue roughly from when the treasurers' end. However, the shrine income was now described as being 'from the feretrarians', and is therefore even more ambiguous than the treasurers' rolls had been. It begins with a receipt of over £396 in 1395/6 and continues for a while to be high, if apparently declining.[14] In the years 1409/10 and 1419/20, for example, the shrine received £221 15s. and £360 respectively. The next surviving account of 1436/7 records only £30 15s. received, and the six accounts of the 1440s show amounts of £10 to £15. The sums decrease still further after 1446, to £1 6s. 8d. in 1472/3. A roll that no longer has a visible date, but has a modern label giving 1467/8, specifically states that nothing was received from the shrine, tomb, Martyrdom or the chapel of St Mary Undercroft.[15] The last prior's roll of 1473/4 also lacks an entry for the shrine. The final record of the offerings to St Thomas, or any other site at Canterbury, appears in the sacrist's account for 1531/2, the only one to mention oblations to the main shrine:

> And in offerings to various altars in the church, namely to the altars of the shrine, corona of St Thomas, in the private chapel to the north, to the altar of blessed Mary in the crypt, to the tomb of St Thomas, to the Martyrdom of St Thomas, and in the same place to the chapel of St Mary, and to all other altars in the church except the high altar, and the altar of the holy cross in the nave of the church which pertains to the care of the high altar, the sum of £13 13s. 3d.[16]

---

[13] CCA, DCc/Treasurer 27, ff. 2, 5.
[14] CCA, DCc/Prior 4 (these rolls are not numbered in strict chronological order).
[15] CCA, DCc/Prior 11.
[16] CCA, DCc/MA 16, f. 1; Woodruff, 'Financial Aspect', p. 25 n. 1.

This total is less than one fiftieth what the shrine alone received in 1220.

Despite doubts as to their absolute accuracy, the treasurers' accounts seem to be reasonably consistent. The priors' rolls, on the other hand, are so confusing and irregular that they cannot be considered a straightforward record of the offerings to St Thomas. For example, the only offering to the shrine listed in 1454/5 was 20s. from the king. Since it is unlikely that the king was the only pilgrim that year something is probably missing. A particularly vexing question is why the receipts from offerings dropped so dramatically in the early fifteenth century. If we discount 1419/20 as a jubilee year, and therefore not representative, then the difference between the £211 15s. received in 1410 and the £30 15s. received in 1436/7 is a drop of 85% in just twenty-seven years, a sudden and unusual change. This is dissimilar to the patterns of the offerings to the Corona as recorded in the priors' rolls over the same period. One would expect the Corona to continue to mirror the fortunes of the main shrine as it did in the earlier treasurers' accounts, yet the Corona offerings not only declined at the beginning of the fifteenth century at a reasonably smooth and consistent rate but remained constant for the rest of the century. In most of the priors' accounts the Corona is actually recorded as having received more in offerings than the shrine itself. This is unusual in that the Corona was, of course, a lesser site of the same cult as the shrine of St Thomas. A reversal in the order of popularity between the two stations during the fifteenth century is not supported by other evidence, and in all writings the shrine of St Thomas is referred to as the main object of attraction at Canterbury. As we have seen, the standard pilgrimage route within the cathedral took the devotee to the shrine and Corona in quick succession.

There is little doubt that the income of the shrine continued to decline after 1420, and the fall may have been dramatic. The final sacrist's account seems to suggest this. It is unlikely, however, that the decline was as severe or as early as the priors' accounts seem to indicate. It is not credible that the shrine of St Thomas, which we know from other sources to have maintained considerable popularity, should have sunk so quickly as to receive under £2 per year in the 1470s. As we shall see, this is far below the contemporary receipts of offerings at less famous shrines such as those of Sts Etheldreda, Cuthbert or even Thomas of Hereford (see below).

There is certainly evidence that the shrine continued to attract numerous pilgrims. A considerable amount of money was obtained from the jubilee indulgence of 1470. In the account of 1472/3 the Prior only records oblations worth two marks from the shrine, but another notice declares that £85 were received out of oblations in the year of the indulgence.[17] The next year the prior received another £13 6s. 8d. from the same source. How this money was being delivered, and why it appears years after the time it was apparently received, is unknown. However, it is clear that offerings from the jubilee were making an impact on priory revenues

---

[17] 'But he received of £85 8s. 1d. received from the part remaining of the offerings in the year of the indulgence' (Sed recepit de lxxxv li. viijs. jd. receptis de parte remanent' oblacionum Anni indulgencie): CCA, DCc/Prior 12.

as long as three years after the event, proving that the shrine was still a considerable attraction for pilgrims, at least in combination with a plenary indulgence. It also shows that the priory was sensible in making a considerable effort to obtain a similar indulgence for 1520.[18]

The single surviving feretrarians' account of 1398/9 and the 'Customary of the Shrine of St Thomas' suggest that the offerings were considerable in the late fourteenth and early fifteenth centuries. It is possible that the feretrarians were newly, and perhaps temporarily, required to enrol accounts in 1398 as part of the general reorganisation of the priory finances in the late fourteenth century. A problem arises when trying to explain the difference between the shrine income recorded by the feretrarians and that recorded by the priors. The feretrarians' account contains only two receipts: £21 6s. 9d. from the previous year's remainder and £249 19s. 7d. *de anima*. There was a long list of expenses, of which surprisingly little was actually spent on the shrine. Most went to various officers (cellarer, chamberlain, third and fourth priors, subclerk of the shrine etc.), but with no obvious payment of offerings to the treasurer or prior. Because a remainder of £21 9s. 10d. was carried over to the next year, we cannot explain the priors' income from the shrine as the feretrarians' surplus.

The most likely explanation for the feretrarians' receipts is that they consisted of offerings made to the altar at the shrine after the special daily mass said there by the spiritual feretrarian, for which the phrase *de anima* ('for souls') is a suitable description. The 'Customary' states that the feretrarians were to clear the altar quickly after mass so that the pilgrims could make their offerings.[19] The temporal feretrarian was to make an account on Sunday of receipts for the week, out of which the stipends and expenses were to be paid.[20] This income from the altar is probably the same as appears in the feretrarians' account. Since this seems to be independent of that received by the priors, the real total of offerings to the shrine might have been the sum of the priors' and feretrars' oblationary receipts. If so, then the shrine would have been worth well over £600 *per annum* to the priory at the close of the fourteenth century. There is no way at present to be certain of this.

Large sums of money belonging to the feretrarians were left out of the priors' accounts. Evidence for this exists even within the priors' rolls themselves. In 1453/4 they record 60s. at the shrine, plus £7 'received from the feretrarians by the hand of the chaplain for making wicks'.[21] The same amount was spent in 1456, although this entry was later crossed out, and it appears in the 'Customary' as a standard annual payment to the prior's chaplain. The feretrars thus had an independent budget sufficiently large to be able to spend more than twice as much on this relatively minor item as they gave to the prior outright.[22] Because no payments to the feretrarians exist in either the treasurers' or priors' accounts it can be

[18] See letters concerning this matter in *Literæ Cantuarienses*, vol. 3, pp. 340–3, 345–7.
[19] 'Customary of the Shrine of St Thomas', ff. 1–2.
[20] 'Customary of the Shrine of St Thomas', f. 2.
[21] CCA, DCc/Prior 9.
[22] For example, £7 was received for wicks in 1453/4: CCA, DCc/Prior 9.

assumed that normal expenses of the shrine, such as the feretrarians' stipends, were deducted from the amount passed to the controlling financial office, thus saving the administrative trouble of handing the money back and forth. This is confirmed by the 'Customary', which outlines annual payments to various officers in the cathedral of at least £240 plus various obligatory gifts of wine and food and the annual expenditure on wax.[23] The feretrarians' own considerable expenses were thus certainly deducted before any money reached the prior's office.

By 1420 the office of the feretrarians was burdened with extra duties and direct payments, resulting in them delivering a suddenly much smaller sum to the prior. There is some indication of this in the priors' rolls. In 1409/10 the prior made a payment to the chaplain 'beyond £11 assigned from the shrine of St Thomas'.[24] The prior also occasionally described his payments to the chamberlain as money beyond that given by the feretrarians and the almoner. In 1468 the same transfer payment is described as being in addition to 100s. given to the chamberlain in part payment of £20 by the feretrar (the same amount that is stipulated by the 'Customary').[25] It is clear then that the feretrarians were expected to give the chamberlains £20 yearly, even if they were unable to meet this obligation by 1467/8.

In the fifteenth century the feretrarians were also paying for the wax consumed in the cathedral. Every year the sacrist received about £30 from the prior 'by the hands of the feretrar', designated for and spent on wax. The sacrist kept a separate record of the wax acquired and burnt according to its equivalent value in money. In 1488/9, for example, the sacrist burnt 1,356 pounds of wax at 46s. 8d. per hundredweight.[26] The 'Customary' confirms this, stipulating that feretrarians not only had to purchase wax for their own and the sacrist's use, but had to provide for its carriage by ship from London to Faversham, and by wagon from there to Canterbury.[27] In the feretrarians' roll the act of buying the wax was performed by the prior in London but was paid for by the feretrarians, who then gave 1,000 pounds of wax to the sacrist and kept 900 pounds for themselves.

Between payments to other officers and expenses for wax and other necessities of the shrine, it seems clear that a great deal of the shrine income was not reaching the prior's accounts in the fifteenth century. An increase in these diversions of funds could therefore account for the sudden decline in recorded shrine receipts in about 1520. In any case, if the priors' income from the shrine was only a form of surplus after deduction, then any reduction in income would appear more serious than it was since it would affect the surplus first.

Information on offerings to less famous shrines at Canterbury can be found in the sacrists' accounts. First appearing in 1341/2, they exist in roll form to 1474/5

---

23 'Customary of the Shrine of St Thomas', ff. 10–1.
24 CCA, DCc/Prior 2.
25 CCA, DCc/Prior 7, 9 and 10; 'Customary of the Shrine of St Thomas', f. 10.
26 CCA, DCc/MA 7, f. 67. This calculates to 5d. per pound, which is about the average price for bulk purchases of wax.
27 'Customary of the Shrine of St Thomas', f. 11.

and in book form from 1491/2 to 1531/2.[28] The early rolls contain a receipt entitled 'offerings', without distinction between types or sources. However, the rolls of 1383/4 and 1385/6 (neither recording a full accounting year) have instead two separate accounts at the bottom of the roll, one for altars and the other for offerings to 'the bodies of saints' (*de reddito corporum sanctorum*). The latter is divided into rents and oblations. A similar account of 1392/3 records £9 14s. 11½d. 'to the bodies', of which only 36s. 11d. is in oblations, 10s. in sales and the rest in rents. This dramatically demonstrates the lack of distinction that could exist between the revenues accruing from the holdings of a shrine and the offerings of pilgrims. If there had been no separate account for those years, the rents would have been invisibly included in the sum of receipts from 'the bodies of the saints' yet would in fact have made up the great bulk of the 'offerings'.

Fortunately, each property is listed individually in the sacrist's account of 1390/1, starting with the Hall of St Dunstan at a rent of 61s. 8d. In 1409/10, after the administrative reorganisation of priory finances was complete, they were removed from the accounting 'of the bodies of the saints' and placed with the other properties of the sacrist's office. In later accounts the only way to tell which rents were once the property of the saints from those which were always attached directly to the sacristy is to compare their descriptions with those in the 1390/1 roll. The holdings of the shrines, once theoretically belonging to the saint, now belonged to the church. This distinction was of no practical importance but perhaps demonstrates a change in attitude towards saints' property, specifically that a saint's possessions were synonymous with those of the church.

Although not involved with the cult of St Thomas, the sacrist received oblations at a variety of altars, pyxes and shrines. Before 1170 the most prestigious shrine at Canterbury was that of St Dunstan.[29] However, offerings to Dunstan do not appear in the records until 1507/8, the year his shrine was opened and his head separately enshrined. The offerings were to a money box described at first as 'at the head' and later 'at the shrine of St Dunstan'.[30] They usually amounted to between 6d. and 9d. and sometimes included the offerings at St Ælphege's nearby shrine. Another Canterbury saint, Anselm, received two special gifts at his altar before offerings to him were regularly accounted; 3s. 4d. was given by Prince Peter of Portugal in 1425/6 and 2s. from the countess of Stafford in 1441/2. In the early sixteenth century his tomb began to record the occasional offering, such as 10d. in 1520/1. This occurred during a general rebirth in Anselm's popularity resulting in his canonisation in the late fifteenth century. To these saints' shrines the sacrist added various lesser offering sites. Annual income from 'money boxes', 'diverse boxes', 'boxes wherever' and boxes in the nave and crypt varied from a few pence to 33s. 10d. The only direct connection of any of these items

28 CCA, DCc/Sacrists 7–73; DCc/MA 7, 9, 10, 11, 30.
29 For an interesting discussion of Dunstan's early cult see A. Thacker, 'Cults at Canterbury: Relics and Reform under Dunstan and his Successors', in *St Dunstan: His Life, Times and Cult*, eds N. Ramsay, M. Sparks and T. Tatton-Brown (Woodbridge, 1992), pp. 221–45.
30 CCA, DCc/MA 11, ff. 71, 102, DCc/Sacrist 72, 73.

with the cult of St Thomas was a vestment of the archbishop, which received 6d. in 1511/12.

Offerings to St Mary were more significant. The Marian chapel in the nave, under the authority of the treasurer, regularly received about £2 in the late fourteenth century. The chapel of St Mary in the Undercroft was also popular with pilgrims, partly because it was on the way to St Thomas' tomb. Offerings there on the feast of the Purification of St Mary, a regular entry throughout the fifteenth century, were about 6s. 6d. per year. Unfortunately, most of the offerings listed in the sacrists' accounts are too small and irregular to be useful as statistical data.

A particularly interesting cult at Canterbury was that of Archbishop Robert of Winchelsey, who died in 1313. His tomb, once in the south transept, was destroyed along with other shrines in 1539 despite the fact that he was never officially canonised. Because the offerings there were recorded in the treasurers' accounts we have an opportunity to study the finances of a popular and apparently unpromoted cult from its beginnings (see graph 3). In 1312/13 and for the next two years the income was £50. This is a suspiciously even sum, and we can suppose the real total to have been somewhat greater. The income was no less than £90 in 1319/20, and was still £50 in 1323/4. By the break in regular accounts in 1337, however, the offerings were only £3, and had fallen to 11s. in 1350/1 and 18d. in 1371/2. For the next three years Winchelsey's tomb received a similar sum, then disappeared from the accounts. In summary, the cult attracted high offerings for only ten years, but managed to survive in the records for about sixty. It is unfortunate that the sums for the early years of this cult are apparently untrustworthy, as it would be interesting to know whether the offerings were highest in the year of Winchelsey's death or if the cult took a few years to reach its peak. However, it does appear that a real decline had begun within at least six years of Winchelsey's death, indicating a meteoric rise and fall of his cult.

Ely

The relevant records surviving from Ely Priory include twenty-four feretrars' accounts dating from 1420/1 to 1498/9 and a series of sacrists' rolls extending from 1291/2 to 1535/6 (see tables 3 and 4, graph 4).[31] Tragically, all these documents are written on paper and are deteriorating. Of the sacrists' rolls only thirty-one contain a legible receipt of offerings at the shrine of St Etheldreda, since many potentially interesting rolls now lack the portion that once contained the receipts. In some cases I did not dare even to open a roll for fear of causing its total destruction. Both series of accounts itemise most possible types of income and expense, and therefore appear to be relatively straightforward. The feretrars' rolls are more exacting, taking the income to the half penny and, in later examples, noting the receipts of offerings to the relics under five seasonal terms.

The shrine of St Etheldreda was a considerable source of profit, if not as

31 CUL, EDC 5/10 1–44; EDC 5/11, 1–10.

lucrative as that of St Thomas of Canterbury. When it first appears in the sacrists' accounts in 1302/3 the shrine brought in an even £11, but income ranged between £21 and £34 in the 1320s and 1330s. By the 1350s the average rose to about £40, and then increased more rapidly from £41 4s. in 1371/2 to £86 19s. 3d. in 1387. The next reliable receipt year is not until 1408/9, when the income had risen to a recorded high of £94 9s. 10d. From then until 1477/8 we have only four accounts, but those seem to show that the oblations declined at an even rate over that period. In its final stages the income remained in the range of £30 to £40. Indeed, the penultimate account of 1516/17 shows a shrine receipt of £36 17s. 8d., a very healthy income for an account written well within Henry VIII's reign. Only with the last account, written on the very eve of destruction in 1535/6, does the sum drop considerably (to £4 13s. 8d.). In the sacrists' accounts the wording of the entry for the offerings shows that the offerings were to the shrine and were recorded on tallies from a feretrar: a commonly used phrase is 'to the shrine of St Etheldreda by tally'.[32]

The Ely sacrists' rolls are not consistent or numerous enough to provide data for an exact model of the fluctuating fortunes of the shrine of St Etheldreda. However, they are sufficiently evenly spaced to reveal the general trends with some degree of certainty. From a stable or slightly increasing trend in the early fourteenth century the shrine offerings experienced a marked rise in value a generation or two after the Black Death, reaching a high point of around £100 at or a little later than 1400. Offerings then declined steadily before remaining stable at £30 or £40 from the mid-fifteenth century until shortly before the destruction of the shrine.

The feretrar's accounts begin in 1420/1 and survive to 1428/9 without loss. There is then a gap until a piped roll containing all the accounts from 1464/5 to 1476/7. Finally, three more accounts exist, the last being for 1498/9. The feretrar did not account for the offerings to the shrine proper, all of which went to the sacrist. The oblations that they were able to keep were mostly to 'the relics', presumably those in the chapel in the south choir.[33] The offerings to the relics for 1420–9 averaged £14 12s. 11½d., but the average for 1464–7 was only £8 6s. The last roll records £5 9s. ½d., so it appears that the offerings to the relics were declining steadily but slowly in the fifteenth century.

Three other sources of offerings were recorded by the feretrars. Wax was sold to pilgrims for about £2 per year. After 1475/6 'silk' was sold for over £10 in each of the last three accounts, presumably in the form of 'St Audrey's chains': coloured necklaces sold to pilgrims at the fair held on Etheldreda's feast day and the reputed origin of the word 'tawdry' (from 'St Audrey').[34] C.W. Stubbs claimed that the plaited ribbon replaced tiny shackles of iron which had originally

---

[32] For example 'to the shrine of St Etheldreda by tally against brother Simon of Banham', taken from the sacrist's roll for 1372: CUL, EDC 5/10, roll 18.

[33] See E.M. Hampson and T.D. Atkinson, 'The City of Ely', in *VCH: Cambridge and the Isle of Ely*, vol. 4, ed. R.B. Pugh (1953), p. 72.

[34] Stewart, *On the Architectural History of Ely Cathedral*, p. 190. See chapter 4, p. 151, n. 145.

been sold by the monks as pilgrim souvenirs in memory of a famous relic (see below).[35] The final category of offerings, worth about £7 *per annum*, were those collected from all shrines for the indulgence of forty days granted by Innocent IV and offered over the Feast of the Dedication.[36] This entry probably included offerings to the shrine of St Etheldreda, while the selling of wax and silk was probably also connected with her cult. Therefore, the total revenue generated by the main shrine was at least slightly higher than the figures given in the sacrists' rolls.

Besides the shrine of St Etheldreda, the Ely sacrists' rolls record offerings to two crosses (the High or Great Cross and the Cross at the Fountain), the fetters (a famous votive object left by a pilgrim to St Etheldreda and thus a secondary object of her cult)[37] and, in the early sixteenth century, Bishop Alcock's Chapel (see graphs 4 and 5). The fetters and the Cross at the Fountain were combined in the receipts after 1407/8, and are last mentioned in 1458/9. After an early increase over the first two account rolls, the entry for the Cross at the Fountain declined steadily from £9 5s. 4d. in 1291/2 to £1 6s. in 1374/5. Offerings to Alcock's Chapel, recorded as receiving £5 18s. 1d. in 1509/10, £4 7s. 2½d. in 1517, and nothing in 1535/6, were in a straightforward decline. The income at the High Cross was irregular, showing no particular trends.

Norwich

The Norwich archives contain over 126 sacrists' rolls dating from 1272/3 to 1535/6 (see table 5, graph 6).[38] The sacrist collected offerings from money boxes at a rich assortment of relics, bishops' tombs, crosses, altars, and several images. In 1367, for example, there were fifteen separate items named in the oblations section of the receipts. Perhaps it is not a coincidence that the shrine of St William, Norwich cathedral's one truly indigenous saint, never achieved great popularity. There was no separate officer for his shrine, it being tended by the sacrist and his servants.

Despite the excellent survival rate of the accounts, the fortunes of St William's shrine are difficult to trace because the offerings were so small that they were not always separately itemised. From 1272/3 to 1300/1 the sacrists' accounts do not differentiate between most sources of offerings, mentioning only the altar of the Blessed Virgin Mary, the high altar (including the shrine of St William) and 'from chests (*de Trunciis*)'.[39] Later, as the accounts became more detailed, the offerings at the shrine were mentioned more frequently, but were often grouped under a

---

35 Stubbs, *Historical Memorials of Ely Cathedral*, p. xiii.
36 *Ely Chapter Ordinances*, p. 39 n.
37 This miracle is in *Liber Eliensis*, pp. 266–9.
38 NCA, DCN 1/4/1–125 (Sacrists' rolls 1 to 125); MC 136/1 (1366/7). For discussions of the finances of the Norwich sacrists see Saunders, *Introduction to the Rolls of Norwich*, pp. 102–10, and Tanner, *The Church in Late Medieval Norwich*, pp. 85–9.
39 NCA, DCN 1/4/1, Sacrist's Roll 1.

single figure with offerings at other places of devotion, such as the New Cross or the altar of St Stephen. When St William's shrine is first mentioned as a distinct source of income in 1304/5 it received a mere nine pence, and although the offerings were 21s. 5½d. in 1314 they had sunk again to only 2d. by 1363/4. From the brink of extinction the offerings made a dramatic recovery. In 1368/9 the box at his shrine held 4¾s., and in 1385/6 no less than £19 13s. 5½d., or about 3,600 times what the oblations had been twenty-two years previously. The decline which inevitably followed was just as steady and swift, with the proceeds of William's shrine permanently dropping to below £1 after 1419/20. From 1439/40 to the last individual record in 1521/2, when the accounting style changed so that the income from St William's shrine was for evermore subsumed in other entries, it varied from 5s. 7½d down to 9d. Some of the offerings, as at Canterbury, may have been given to other obedientiaries. The communar roll of 1288/9 records a receipt of 8s. 5d. 'for the tomb of St William'.[40] This is the only such entry in all the numerous communar rolls, but other transfer payments may have been subsumed within the donations from the sacrist that are sometimes mentioned.

For most of its history the income at the shrine of St William was so small that the gift of a shilling or even a few pence by a single pilgrim could have dramatically changed one year's total. For this reason statistical analysis is not worthwhile for much of the period. It suffices to say that the total of the offerings was very small overall but remarkably persistent over long periods of time. Other offering sites rarely recovered after income fell below 1s., yet St William's name and memory never faded completely. The one obvious variation in the general trend of oblations was the enormous and sudden increase in offerings in the 1460s. William, almost forgotten a few years before, seems to have suddenly found a relatively large number of generous pilgrims. This new-found popularity may have been related to William's adoption in 1476 by the peltiers' guild of Norwich, whose members were bound to make an annual procession with offerings to the tomb.[41] The offerings to his shrine had a definite and pronounced peak, but did not fade out entirely for at least another sixty years.

Although it is unnecessary to follow closely the fortunes of the entire host of images, crosses and other sites of devotion at Norwich, we can briefly look at the income at three of the more interesting minor sources of oblations (see graphs 7–9). The offerings placed in the chest at Bishop Walter's tomb (*trunco Walteri*) show a pattern very similar to that seen at Canterbury for Archbishop Winchelsey, although not as pronounced. Offerings reached a recorded peak of £4 thirteen years after they began in 1283/4, and sank to below 1s. in 1363/4. They then persisted for another twenty-seven years before vanishing entirely from the

---

[40] *The Early Communar and Pittancer Rolls of Norwich Cathedral Priory, with an Account of the Building of the Cloister*, eds E.C. Fernie and A.B. Whittingham (Norfolk Record Soc., vol. 41, 1972), p. 51.

[41] J.R. Shinners, 'The Veneration of Saints at Norwich Cathedral in the Fourteenth Century', *Norfolk Archaeology*, vol. 40 (1988), p. 136. Shinners suggests that the peltiers' involvement actually caused the surge in popularity, but it is at least as likely that St William's new fame convinced the peltiers to adopt William as their patron.

sacrists' rolls. The cult was thus on the increase for thirteen years, faded within fifty, but took another ninety-seven to disappear completely. Offerings to the relics and the cross at Norwich display different patterns. They had slower rates of increase and were longer lasting, in the case of the relics maintaining a reasonable income from 1400 onwards. Note that all these offering sites, when graphed, show pronounced peaks of highest income occurring at different times: the tomb of Walter in about 1290, the relics in 1320, the cross in 1360, and St William in about 1385. This is in contrast to the more consistent patterns seen at greater saints' shrines.

Lincoln

The main pilgrimage destination at the secular cathedral of Lincoln was the shrine of St Hugh. The earliest record of money possibly belonging to St Hugh is from 1307, when the cathedral treasurer, Robert de Lacy, borrowed £40 from 'the chest of St Hugh'.[42] We know that St Hugh's treasury survived at least until 1528/9, when the chapter decided to put the common seal of the cathedral in a triple-locked chest described as nearby.[43] Regular accounts of the offerings survive from 1334/5, and record openings of the shrine's money box during twice yearly events called 'openings' (*aperturae*, see table 7 and graph 10).[44] These took place at Pentecost and the Translation of St Hugh in the presence of several canon dignitaries, as in 1452/3 when the chest was opened in the presence of the precentor, the masters of the head and shrine of St Hugh, and the archdeacon of Bedford.[45] The shrine-keepers were severely limited by statute in their control over the proceeds and expenses of the shrine and seem to have had no operating budget between *aperturæ*. Accounts were apparently made on the spot at the opening, with the money discovered in the boxes distributed (mostly in the form of stipends and payments for wax) and the remainder locked away until the next *apertura*. With minor alterations this procedure was followed until the accounts ceased two centuries later in 1531/2.

The *aperturæ* system was either instituted or re-established in an ordinance of 1321–2 which complained that the 'chilling of men's devotion' had caused the offerings to be only a third of what was paid out.

> Memorandum, that with the chilling of men's devotion towards the church and the saints and the works of god in this, and also because the adversities and pressures of this age, which increase daily, work against this devotion, the offerings to the head and shrine of the glorious confessor blessed Hugh, and the tomb of blessed Robert in the church of Lincoln, which usually are abundantly made, are so much diminished that the distributions that were customarily made

42 Venables, 'The Shrine and Head of St. Hugh', p. 60.
43 *Chapter Acts of Lincoln*, vol. 12, p. 117.
44 LCA, D&C Bj/5/16/1, 2.
45 LCA, D&C Bj/5/16/1, f. 3.

to the canons, vicars, and other ministers of the said church are so little able to suffice that they scarcely extend to the third part of what they used to. Thus it happens that the distributions in this manner, as much to canons as to vicars and other ministers aforesaid, are totally dragged down.[46]

Apparently there was an older budget whose customary payments were too high for the current shrine income, forcing the cathedral chapter to set out a new schedule of expenses. This indicates that the offerings once amounted to more than appears in the earliest surviving *aperturæ* accounts.

After the mandatory payments any remainder at Pentecost was kept 'in the little red shrine where the head of St Hugh is adored'.[47] It was held there until the shrine's year-end account, occurring on the Feast of the Translation of St Hugh, when the balance was calculated. If the remainder at that time was sufficiently large then it was added to the treasure chest of St Hugh. In 1449/50, for example, the remainder was 64s., 'which they placed in the treasury of St Hugh'.[48] If expenses exceeded receipts, then money could be withdrawn from the same source. The total holdings of this chest were periodically assessed but were never a great fortune, their highest level recorded in the *aperturæ* being £24 4s. 7d. in 1342/3. This is another indication that the income from the shrine was declining: if £40 could be borrowed from the chest in 1306/7 then its holding must have decreased.

The accounts of the *aperturæ* invite questions about the chapter's 1321–2 lamentations concerning 'chilling devotion'. If we look at a graph of yearly offerings (the sum of the two *aperturæ* of each accounting year), we can see that income was actually climbing from the 1330s, when our data begins, until it reached its highest level in 1364 at about double that first recorded. The amount of offerings plunged at the end of the fourteenth century before levelling out over the fifteenth century into a very shallow decline. From the late 1420s until 1494 (when a break occurs in the data) the income, while very irregular, cannot be said to have been declining seriously. By 1491, however, the cumulative effect of the decline was such that 47s. 8d. had to be drawn out of the treasury to meet expenses 'which the offerings provided during the said time were not sufficient to support'.[49] The value of the offerings for the 1510s and 1520s, however, was still reasonably high, higher in fact than in the early 1490s.

---

46 'Memorandum, quod cum frigescente hominum deuocione, erga ecclesiam et sanctos dei operantibus eciam ad hoc huius seculi aduersitatibus et pressuris que indies augmentantur oblaciones ad caput et feretrum gloriosi confessoris beati Hugonis, ac tumbam beati Roberti in ecclesia Lincolñ, que solent fieri habundanter, in tantum essent diminute, quod ad distribuciones fieri consuetas Canonicis, vicarijs, et alijs Ministris dicte ecclesie minime sufficere potuerunt. vtpote que vix se extendebant ad terciam partem illius quod solebant; Vnde euenit, quod distribuciones huiusmodi, tam Canonicis, quam Vicarijs et ceteris Ministris predictis totaliter subtrahebantur': *Liber Niger*, p. 335.
47 LCA, D&C Bj/5/16/1, f. 129.
48 LCA, D&C Bj/5/16/1, f. 1.
49 'recepta de thesauro sci hugonis existens in thesauraria et sibi liberate pro sustentationem onerum dicti sancti, eo quod oblaciones dicto tempore provenientes non sufficiebant ad

With the Lincoln accounts we can be more certain than usual that we are dealing with the real income at the shrine. The very name *aperturæ* tells us that the recorded income is what was actually found in the offering box, and is unlikely to have been combined with any other rents or incomes. This is supported by the variable yet precise numbers in which the revenue is recorded. The possibility that money was deducted before the making of the account is minimised by the detail of the expenses, eliminating possible recipients of such funds. Finally, the accounts usually tell us what was done with the remainder, i.e. whether it was put to some use, kept for the next account, or put in a treasury. These factors combine to make Lincoln's the most reliable of English shrine accounts.

Hereford

The cult of St Thomas Cantilupe at Hereford was very profitable when it commenced at the end of the thirteenth century. Worcester found its income increase by £10 just from being on the pilgrim route to Hereford, and in 1291 the value of wax tapers offered to Thomas were reported to be £20 above what was burnt at his tomb.[50] The rights to the wax revenue were disputed between the treasurer and the dean and chapter, the latter eventually (1293) getting one third of the profits after the expenses of the cathedral lights were defrayed.[51] The first surviving account of shrine proceeds is a fabric roll of 1291, made while the cult was still at its height just nine years after Cantilupe's death. The master of the fabric received 'from the tomb of St Thomas' no less than £178 10s.[52]

The two surviving fabric accounts of the late fourteenth century show somewhat lower receipts from the custodian of the shrine: 53s. 4d. (4 marks) in 1384 and 26s. 8d. (2 marks) in 1387.[53] Another roll from 1447 records nothing at all from the shrine of St Thomas, even though it includes oblations at an image of St Mary and 'from the box of the indulgence at the north door'.[54] The latter presumably held money paid for those indulgences authorised for the aid of the fabric. The decline in offerings is also reflected by the reduction in the papal tax assessment granted by Pope Benedict XII in 1336 when the yearly income from wax fell to barely £6.[55]

supportanda onera que denar. finorem et sibi liberate per Thes. et [Thomas] Hilt': LCA, D&C Bj/5/16/1, f. 41.

[50] *Acta Sanctorum, October*, vol. 1, p. 584; D.L. Douie, 'The Canonization of St. Thomas of Hereford', *Dublin Rev.*, vol. 229, no. 469 (1955), p. 276. Interestingly, the *Taxatio Ecclesiastica* of Nicholas gives only £13 6s. 8d. from wax: *Taxatio Ecclesiastica*, pp. 157–8.

[51] *Registrum Ricardi de Swinfield*, pp. 230, 297.

[52] Fabric rolls exist for 1291, 1384, 1387 and 1447; HCA, MSS 2368, R.621, 2371, 2370; The quote is from HCA, MS 2368. See also Yates, 'Fabric Rolls of Hereford Cathedral', p. 79. The building projects at Hereford have been discussed in Chapter 5.

[53] HCA, MSS 2371, R. 621.

[54] HCA, MS 2370.

[55] Morgan, 'Effect of the Pilgrim Cult on Hereford', p. 151.

The offerings presented to the fabric fund, certainly in the later period, probably represent only a portion of the total. The keeper of the fabric did not collect the shrine offerings himself but was assigned them on the basis of need; the less construction under way the less money was presumably allocated to him. The fact that the last two entries are in even numbers of marks also suggests a set payment. It is virtually certain that at least some of the offerings went to other causes, especially the administration of the shrine. In any case, there can be little doubt that the income dropped considerably between the two fabric rolls of 1291 and 1384.

The responsibility for the shrine eventually belonged to sacrist-like officers called clavigers who produced accounts in the late fifteenth and early sixteenth centuries. Only eight clavigers' accounts exist from 1478/9 to 1522/3, four of them in sequence from 1505 to 1509.[56] The receipts are described as 'from the pyx of St Thomas', and therefore must represent the contents of an offering box at the shrine. Other sources of income, including rents, are listed separately and in great detail in the receipts, further eliminating the possibility that shrine revenue is anything other than a record of devotional offerings. There are several sources of offerings listed, including boxes at the head of St Thomas and the relics, the 'Pyx of King Henry', sold wax, and 'broken silver'. Oblationary income is recorded for several terms in each account and varies from a total of £22 18s. 8d. per year in the first account to £8 6s. 11½d. in the last, of which the main shrine to St Thomas usually contributed over 90%. A graph of the offerings shows that receipts were dropping steeply and steadily over the period of surviving accounts, although the gaps in the data are large enough to allow doubt about the exact speed of decline.

Durham

Durham cathedral had over twenty altars and many notable tombs, including the shrine of St Bede. For the most part these were the province of the sacrist, but the shrine of St Cuthbert had its own feretrar who, unlike Ely's, accounted for the offerings. The pyx at the shrine was the sole coin box allocated to the feretrar until 1455/6, when the prior assigned to him the oblations at the tomb of John Wharton in St Oswald's church. The feretrars' rolls extend from 1376 to 1461 in an almost continuous series of seventy-seven accounts, plus seven later accounts scattered over the period from 1480 until 1538 (table 8, graph 12).[57] As the longest and most complete body of feretrars' accounts for any cathedral, the Durham rolls are of great importance and are perhaps the most reliable accounts of this sort to be found in a monastic cathedral. The offerings are distinctly described as relating to a pyx of St Cuthbert, and we have receipt slips from the clerk to show how the money

56 HCA, MSS 369, 584–6. See table 6, graph 11.
57 DDCA, 'Feretrars' Rolls', by year. See also *Extracts from Account Rolls of Durham*, vol. 2, pp. 420–83.

was passed on and the administrative level at which it was recorded. Furthermore, all the expected rents, receipts and payments are clearly visible in the account.

The chronological pattern of the revenue is straightforward. The offerings climbed for the first few accounts, exhibiting an average of almost £38 at the end of the fourteenth century, then steadily declined to under £16 in the 1450s. If calculated as a straight line the rate of decline from the start of accounts in the 1380s to the end of the consistent series in the 1450s can be estimated at between 4s. and 6s., or about 1%, per year. Although later accounts are less numerous, it seems that this trend continued until the end in 1538. The accounts begin too late to be sure, but it is possible to fit this data into the pattern seen at Canterbury, Lincoln and Ely. In other words, the 1380s could have been the high point in offering and the fifteenth century a period of very gradual decline. The actual incomes varied widely about the average. The highest for a twelve-month period was £63 17s. 8d. in 1385/6 and the lowest was £4 7s. 5½d. in 1537/8.

We can also examine the offerings to Wharton's tomb, despite the fact that it was not actually within the cathedral. John Wharton was one of that host of lesser 'saints' whose cults achieved intense local popularity without the help of official sanction. He was never officially canonised or beatified, nor have I found any information concerning him outside of the feretrars' rolls.[58] Almost by definition, such unofficial cults do not receive the attention of biographers. Unless the object of a cult was famous for something other than his sanctity (which presumably Wharton was not) then there is little chance of our knowing much about them in the absence of hagiographic material. Wharton's cult already appears to have been in decline by the first record in 1455/6, because that was the largest receipt at £5 14s. 9½d., or a little under a third of what was received at St Cuthbert's tomb in the same year (see table 8 and graph 13).[59] By 1479/80 Wharton's receipts were under £1, and were only about 1s. by the beginning of the sixteenth century.

Westminster

Although not a cathedral, Westminster deserves to be included in this study by virtue of its excellent set of sacrists' accounts ranging from 1317/8 to 1531/2 (see table 10, graph 14).[60] Unfortunately, however, these rolls are somewhat removed from the activities at the shrine of St Edward the Confessor. Two feretrars supervised the shrine but surrendered the offerings to the sacrist with tallies, much as at Ely.[61] In the first three rolls (1317/18, 1318 and 1346/7) the shrine income, 'to the shrine of St Edward', is recorded separately. However, from 1354/5 until the mid-fifteenth century it was combined with the oblations to the relics. These had previously been recorded together with offerings to the high altar, the two

---

58 Raine, in *St. Cuthbert*, p. 162 n, also confesses ignorance.
59 DDCA, Feretrar's roll 1455–6.
60 WAM, MSS 19618 to 19807, many of which are duplicate rolls.
61 For an example, see the 1374 and 1423 rolls: WAM, MSS 19634 and 19663.

totalling £10 6d. in 1317/18 and £1 16s. 3d. in 1346/7 (when they were again mentioned separately). After 1342 the phrase used in the entry for offerings at the shrine became 'oblations to the shrine of St Edward and elsewhere inside and outside the church through the whole year'.[62] Some sources of offerings were still entered separately and were generally very low, and those not given their own entry in the account were probably still lower. While the accounts do not give a thoroughly reliable indication of the real shrine income, an approximation can be made by making the reasonable assumption that the vast majority of the money noted was received by the main shrine itself.

The expenses of the shrine are not detailed, but do include the feretrars' fees, their servants' wages, repairs and a wax account. It is thus doubtful that any but minute expenses were diverted. After 1355 the accounting procedure was consistent, and therefore the Westminster rolls are probably sufficiently reliable for constructing a pattern of shrine offerings. The trend revealed is the now familiar one seen at cathedrals. Offerings declined slightly in the first two good records, then shot up so that they were slightly over £100 in the 1470s. Decline was again well under way by the turn of the century, but a reasonably stable situation was maintained from the mid-fifteenth century until the Dissolution.

There were several lesser shrines of note at Westminster. The proceeds of the *Crux Borialis* or North Cross and the 'new pyx' are listed in table 7. Marian devotion had two objects at Westminster: a chapel 'outside the north door' from 1353/4, and from 1379/80 'the image of the blessed Mary called "le Puwe" ' (St Mary of the Pewe).[63] The offerings at both were significant in the late fourteenth century, but declined rapidly to relatively low levels by 1400. St Mary of the Pewe soon recovered, however, and had an amazing efflorescence in the 1470s and 1480s.[64]

York

Almost the only source for offerings to shrines at York Minster is the forty-five fabric accounts running from 1359/60 to 1543/4.[65] In general they hold little relevant information. There is, however, a receipts section entitled 'oblations' which is subdivided into terms, for some of which the money is described as *de truncis* and in others as *de oblacionibus*. There were probably two sources of these funds. One (from 'the oblations') perhaps represented offerings to the high altar, but was more probably the result of direct donations to the fabric fund, and the other ('from the chests') may have been a collection from lesser cult locations, such as crosses and images, where coin boxes had been stationed. Because all

---

62 The example is from the sacrist's roll for 1442: WAM, MS 19685.
63 The two starting years are recorded in WAM, MSS 19622, 19639.
64 The image received a fixed amount of 5s. from 1444/5 until 1470/1, when it began to increase to a recorded high of 76s. 11¾d. in 1481/2. It had shrunk back to about 5s. per year by about 1498: WAM, MSS 19694–19753.
65 YMLA, E/3/1–45; extracts are printed in *Fabric Rolls of York Minster*.

those sources of offerings are grouped under one heading, little can be done with them. By the 1432/3 roll most of the oblations were 'to the red chest', although guild offerings at the tomb of St William and money found in various trunks are still noted separately.[66] The 'red chest' might have been set up specifically to receive fabric fund donations.

An interesting entry in the rolls concerns the offerings on the feast of St William, which usually amounted to between 15s. and 30s., but were only 2s. 10d. in 1415/16.[67] There is no direct evidence that this income was connected to the cult of the saint except that it occurred on his feast day. The site of the offering is never mentioned. Two fraternities are described as giving money *ad tumbam S. Willelmi*, i.e. to the empty tomb in the nave of the church: the gild of St Christopher and the weavers' gild, each in the region of 10s.[68] The fluctuation of these receipts over the next century is evidence for the prosperity of these gilds but because the offerings were almost certainly mandatory payments rather than true offerings they probably have more to do with gild numbers than with devotion to St William.

The tomb of Richard le Scrope was much more popular than that of St William, at least in the early fifteenth century, and oblations there twice merited their own heading. In the 1415/16 fabric roll £73 8s. were received from Scrope's tomb, designated to pay for eight masons and one hundred fothers of stone. Because the uses of the money are clearly set out we can assume that this was not the total offerings but only a sum drawn from them for a specific purpose. What happened to the rest of the offerings is unknown, but the total must have been more than £73 8s. in 1414/15. Three years later the receipts at the tomb of Scrope were recorded as £150 *pro stipendis cementoriorum*.[69] Because the cult of Scrope was both new and officially discouraged it was neither bureaucratically nor politically wise to keep accounts for the tomb. Offerings to the executed archbishop were perhaps treated as a windfall, apportioned where and when the canons saw fit and without formalities. Fabric rolls continue, but no longer record oblations to specific tombs or shrines.

Worcester

As we have seen, Worcester was unique in that the bishop laid claim to the offerings at the shrines (see Chapter 5). The first concrete note of offerings at Worcester occurs in the earliest surviving sacrist's roll of 1423/4, when the

---

[66] YMLA, E/3/12.

[67] YMLA, E/3/7. Raine is in error here, leaving out the offerings on St William's day, and instead ascribing to him 100s. 8d. which was actually offered on Corpus Christi day: *Fabric Rolls of York Minster*, pp. 30–1.

[68] YMLA, E/3/12, Fabric Roll 1432/3. Only one of these is transcribed by Raine for the 1415/16 account.

[69] YMLA, E/3/8.

oblations were £38 15s. 1½d. besides 'from broken silver sold 13s 4d.'.[70] The next sacrists' accounts are much later and do not specifically include offerings at the twin saints' shrines. However, they do record the phenomenal offerings to the image of the Virgin Mary. The sum of money dropped in her pyx (collected by the subsacrist and delivered by indenture) was high for so late a period, being a little over £20 at the beginning of the sixteenth century and declining slowly thereafter to £11 7s. 2d. in 1522/3.[71] The value of the wax offered there was even more: £33 10s. in 1498/9, climbing to £44 5d. in 1507/8 and £49 9s. 11d. in 1522/3.[72] This wax is specifically described as 'received from the sale of wax offered by pilgrims to the image of St Mary'.[73] These receipts correspond with records in two other accounts, one of the receipts of the whole monastery for 1513 and another of sacrist receipts for 1515, both in a miscellaneous register. The 1513 record shows 'offerings made to to St Mary with others in the year ending £93 2s. 2d.' out of a total convent income of £1,219 6s. 6d.[74] The statue of St Mary therefore brought in almost 8% of the convent's income. The 1515 account includes two separate incomes from the statue: £15 7s. 1d. from offerings placed in the pyx of St Mary and £42 9s. from sales of wax offered to the image.[75] It thus seems that offerings to St Mary's statue, unlike saints' shrines, were not declining in the early sixteenth century if one includes the wax that made up at least three quarters of their value.

The accounts of the shrine-keeper (the *tumbarius*, described as the guardian of the shrines of Ss Oswald and Wulfstan) begin in 1375/6.[76] Although the expenses of the twin shrines seem to be included, the offerings at that time were apparently received by the sacrist.[77] In the accounts of 1515/16 and 1521/2, however, we see both receipts from the shrine ('received from the offerings to the tombs of saints Oswald and Wulfstan – 13s. 4d.') and payments ('to the lord prior for oblations to the pyx of St Wulfstan through the year 18d.' and 'for offerings to the head of Sts. Oswald and Wulfstan through the year 5s.') connected with it.[78] It seems that offerings to the tombs and heads of Sts Oswald and Wulfstan, if not to the shrines proper, were in the hands of the sixteenth-century *tumbarius*. In any case, the records of offerings at Worcester are too few to be statistically useful.

70 WCA, MS C.425; *Compotus Rolls of Worcester*, pp. 64, xxi.
71 WCA, MSS C.426–30.
72 WCA, MSS C.426–30.
73 'Recepta de proficuis cere oblata per peregrinorum ad Imaginem beate Marie': WCA, MS C.429.
74 'Oblaciones beate marie cum aliis perficiens anno £93 2s. 2d.': WCA, Misc. Vol. AXII, f. 30.
75 WCA, Misc. Vol. AXII, f. 35.
76 WCA, MSS C.453–72; Misc. Vol. AXII, f. 41 (1515/6).
77 *Compotus Rolls of Worcester*, p. xxv.
78 WCA, Misc. Vol. AXII, f. 41; *Accounts of the Priory of Worcester*, p. 25.

Other cathedrals

For several other cathedrals there is only the briefest reference to offerings at shrines. The only official notice of the receipt and use of shrine offerings at Chichester cathedral is due to a financial dispute between the treasurer and the dean and chapter over who received the offerings and who paid for the candles at the shrine. Bishop Stephen de Bersted resolved in 1279 that the 'offerings of tapers, candles, or lumps of wax' should go to the dean and chapter but that they also had to purchase the candles out of those funds, while the treasurer was to have nothing to do with either the offerings or the expense.[79] At Lichfield, St Chad's shrine is known to have been attracting pilgrims as late as 1536, but no more concrete records survive.[80] The same is true of Rochester, where we know little more than that offerings to St William of Perth were rumoured to have helped rebuild the choir in 1220 and the north transept 'opposite the gate of St William' shortly thereafter.[81] One sole treasurer's account for 1468/9 survives for St Augustine's Abbey, in which £15 8s. ¾d. was received in oblations at the bodies of the saints, over and above what was in the box of St Jambert, given to the sacrist by way of the two subsacrists and the *revestiarius*.[82]

At Salisbury the two canons with primary responsibility for the shrine of St Osmund were described in 1470 as 'the keepers of the offerings and jewels and things pertaining to the shrine of St Osmund'.[83] Two notices of 1456 show that offerings were being made to the shrine and money borrowed from it even before the next year's translation of St Osmund's relics.[84] Another note from 1456 mentions money in both a *cista* (chest) and a *saccula* (little sack) of St Osmund.[85] Finally, the Salisbury fabric accounts of the sixteenth century record two instances of pyx offerings in 1538: 15s. on 17 February, and £6 11s. 6d. on 11 July.[86] These records show that offerings to St Osmund were significant, but tell us little about their overall value or the organisation of the shrine finances.

I hope that the above sections provide a reasonably complete survey of the records of offerings at English medieval cathedrals. While some, like Winchester, have provided no financial documents at all the surviving sources are still reasonably

---

[79] *Chartulary of Chichester*, no. 713, pp. 184–5.

[80] *Letters and Papers of Henry VIII*, p. 137.

[81] Richardson, 'Saint William of Perth', p. 124.

[82] 'St Austin's Abbey, Canterbury. Treasurers' Accounts 1468–9, and Others', ed. C. Cotton, *Arch. Cant.*, vol. 51 (1940), p. 77.

[83] SCA, 'Machon Register', f. 24. Most of the interesting references to the shrine in the archives have been collected in S. Eward, 'St Osmund: The Building of the Shrine', *Salisbury Cathedral News*, no. 148 (April, 1952), pp. 5–7.

[84] Oblations were collected on 25 October and 29 July, the latter of £7 6s. 8d. More money was collected in March of the next year: *Canonization of St Osmund*, pp. 172–3.

[85] *Canonization of St Osmund*, pp. 174–5.

[86] SCA, MS 132, pp. 76–7.

numerous. The technical problems involved in document interpretation can usually be overcome, and most of the series of accounts appear to be sufficiently reliable for a general study. Only the priors' rolls at Canterbury have proved to be problematic, although the accounts of one or two other shrines, such as those of St William of Norwich or Oswald and Wulfstan at Worcester, either do not record enough money or are too few to illustrate any real and useful trend. In general, when shrine accounts have been shown to be misleading they have erred on the low side. We can usually demonstrate that at least some money was left out of the reckoning, whether in money diverted for fees or types of income that went unaccounted for. However, this was unlikely to have been a large proportion of the total. The records of offerings are accurate enough to begin a more serious analysis of larger trends.

7

The Offerings Examined

The information presented in the previous chapter can be used to broaden our understanding of shrines in general. It is dangerous to compare cathedrals directly, not only because of differences in accounting procedures but also due to varying local conditions. For example, a very popular shrine in one area might receive less money than a less popular shrine in a more populous or prosperous district. Even so, there is no harm and some advantage to be gained in making well-informed estimates about the nature and quantity of shrine offerings in general.

In the first part of the present chapter I will attempt to show a pattern in the fluctuations of shrine income in England as a whole over the period 1198 to 1538. The later two and a half centuries, which form the core of this study, are reasonably well documented, with series of accounts from two or more cathedrals which can be cross-checked against each other. The shrine of St Thomas, however, will have to stand alone as an example for the thirteenth century, even though its international status and extreme popularity probably makes it unrepresentative.[1]

Comparing the financial data for all shrines will result in a model for medieval shrine income showing how the financial aspect of devotion to saints changed over time. This model can be compared to what is known of the economic and demographic situation to see if those fluctuations in shrine income which were of a purely devotional nature can be isolated from those caused by non-religious factors. This chapter will conclude with a discussion of how profitable shrines were to cathedrals, an issue which will necessitate an examination of the evidence for those types of income generated by shrines which would not show up in the financial accounts.

A model of shrine income

Accurate information on shrine income begins at the very end of the twelfth century with the receipts from the tomb of St Thomas of Canterbury. We have seen that the Canterbury offerings maintained a reasonably constant average from 1199

---

[1] The international nature of the shrine is illustrated by some safe conducts issued to French knights, including Amaury de Montfort, constable of France, coming to the shrine with nine knights (1235), Arnold, count of Guisnes, coming with his wife and household (1255), and Mary, mother of the king of Scotland (1276): *Patent Rolls, 1225–1232*, p. 490, *1232–1247*, pp. 23, 45, 119, *1247–1258*, p. 404, *1272–1281*, p. 136.

until 1220. At that date the relics of St Thomas moved from the old tomb in the crypt to the new shrine in the choir and the offerings were accordingly transferred as well. The shrine proceeds were at a very high level at the translation, then declined fairly smoothly at a rate of about 5.2% per year to a low point of £46 in 1257/8.[2] A nine-year moving average calculated using this data shows that income continued to decline into the early 1260s, but then increased for the rest of the century. The graph shows that although the offerings fluctuated wildly in value over the short term, the trend of the latter half of the thirteenth century is steady and almost linear, amounting to an increase of about 3.1% per year.

The offerings to the shrine of St Thomas as described above indicate a fairly straightforward history of decline and recovery in the thirteenth century. There were, however, some outstanding conditions at Canterbury which prevent us from assuming that it was representative of other shrines. The first and most obvious is that the cult of St Thomas, still in its infancy, was abnormally famous and popular. As a result it must have been influenced by economic and devotional factors, such as offerings made by international pilgrims, that were not in operation at other shrines. Another peculiarity of the shrine at Canterbury was the 1220 translation and the fifty-year anniversaries of the martyrdom. The enormous income of 1220 was obviously due to offerings during the year of the translation. The rapid fall in income from 1220 until the late 1250s probably represents no more than a natural relaxation of pilgrimage at Canterbury to a more 'normal' level as the excitement of that spectacular event slowly dwindled in the public mind. In this respect it resembles the decline of other incipient cults which will be studied below. Therefore, we may need to exercise caution before assuming that the second quarter of the thirteenth century was a time of decreasing devotion to shrines as a whole.

The next two jubilees appear to have had little effect on the offerings. 1269/70 resulted in an income only slightly higher than the years before and after it, a difference insignificant compared with the generally upward trend then taking place and perhaps an indication that the second jubilee was not observed in practice.[3] The upward trend continued until 1319/20, when a drop in proceeds began. The income of 1319/20 is higher, at £500, than it had been for a hundred years, or indeed higher than it would be until the later fourteenth century. This would seem to indicate that the 1320 jubilee was more of a real event than that of 1270. However, the effect was minor, since the offerings of 1320 were not greatly above the average for the time. Although shrine proceeds fluctuated greatly, the trend had been upward and gradual since the early 1260s. It is inconceivable that the jubilee was anticipated, and influenced offerings, sixty years in advance. At

---

[2] Calculated from a logarithmic curve best fitting the data for 1220–58. All other growth rates expressed as percentages in this chapter were calculated in the same manner, except linear trends which were calculated using the method of least squares.

[3] CCA, DCc/MA1, f. 113. Jubilees are counted from St Thomas' passion in 1170, so that the first jubilee was the translation in 1220.

most offerings could be affected a few years before a jubilee, when the coming festivities began to be promoted. Therefore, the third jubilee may have contributed to the growth of offerings, and perhaps fixed their high point at 1320, but was not the cause.

From the commencement of the Ely sacrists' rolls in 1302/3 we have multiple records to support our conclusions. All offerings stagnated in the third and fourth decades of the fourteenth century. The Canterbury receipts were declining by about 1% per year, while the Ely accounts show an annual increase of about the same amount over 1323–46, both of which are much slower rates of change than the periods before or after. The 1322 reference to lowering receipts in the *Liber Niger* of Lincoln makes it likely that some decline had set in at Lincoln before accounts began in 1334/5 (see Chapter 6). The first surviving accounts, however, show a slight yearly increase. At Norwich we have only four records of the income at St William's shrine for this period, namely from 1305 (9d.), 1341 (5¾d.), 1343 (4d.), and 1364 (2d.). Although too dispersed and small in value to be used as primary evidence, they do not contradict the thesis of stagnation in the second quarter of the fourteenth century, and even show some decline. Records at Westminster are even more sparse, there only being two reliable accounts of receipts before the Black Death. Even there, however, the records do not contradict the pattern: the second account at £16 14s. in 1347 is lower than the £26 3s. 1d. reported in 1317/18. It seems reasonable to conclude, therefore, that offerings in general were stable or in slight decline from at least 1320 until the Black Death.

The accounts of the second half of the fourteenth century exhibit dramatic increases in offerings. The income at the shrine of St William of Norwich is perhaps the most extreme, increasing by 36.5% per year from 1364 to 1386. Elsewhere the rise in income began earlier, as at Lincoln where the increasing trend began by at least 1350 and climaxed in the early 1370s. At Canterbury the increase in offerings started sometime during the second major break in records, so that in 1350/1 the income was about double what it had been in 1336/7. The offerings there seem to have been declining again when regular records recommence in 1370; the rate from then to the end of the treasurers' accounts in 1384/5 was -3.1% per year, and therefore the high point in offerings occurred sometime over the period from 1337 to 1370. Recorded figures begin late at Durham but were climbing at the significantly positive rate of £1 6s. 2d. per year (2.6%) for the first decade from 1377 to 1386. At Westminster the increase had begun by 1354/5, and was fully under way by 1358/9. Offerings to Edward the Confessor were at their highest in the early 1370s, but were back down to their pre-plague levels by 1400. Ely shrine incomes also experienced a strong growth rate of over £1 per year from 1351/2 to 1386/7, and seem to have continued growing there after. The income in 1408/9 was even higher than 1386/7, at £94 9s. 10d., and that for 1419/20 remained high at £87 15s. 8d. Data for Ely is so sparse for this period that it is difficult to determine whether the peak in offerings occurred in the late fourteenth century or the first decade of the fifteenth. Even so, it is clear that Ely experienced the surge in offerings at roughly the same time as other cathedrals but that the high sums persisted much longer than was usual. In summary, it appears that offerings in general increased dramatically in the early 1350s, and continued to grow into the 1370s or later depending on locale.

After 1400, however, shrine offerings show a gradual decline. The least rapid was at Westminster, where the income was relatively stable from about 1430 to 1510, declining at only 0.3%, despite fluctuating greatly over the short term. Lincoln receipts also dropped slowly, at a rate of 0.7% per year throughout the fifteenth century, from £22 1s. 1d. in 1400 to £8 15s. 5d. in 1493/4. The annual decline at Ely from 1420 to 1517 (leaving out the unusually high and low accounts of 1408/9 and 1535/6, respectively) was 1.1%, while at Durham it was 1.2% from 1386 to the end of accounts. The Hereford clavigers' accounts finally make their appearance in the late fifteenth century, registering a decline of 2.2% until their end. The drop was slightly faster at Norwich (3.0% per year from 1386 to 1522). In most places the fall in income apparently accelerated as 1538 approached. Westminster, Ely, Durham and Hereford all received relatively insignificant sums from offerings after about 1510.

To summarise, the general model of offerings to shrines (graph 15) exhibits an early thirteenth-century high declining to a low in the 1260s. This is followed by a steady increase into the early fourteenth century culminating in about 1320, after which it declines, stagnates or slows depending on location. Offerings dramatically increase shortly after the Black Death, at least doubling in value by the time they reached their highest level in the 1370s or 1380s. By 1400 the values of all saints' shrine offerings, with the exception of the shrine of St Etheldreda at Ely, were back to pre-plague levels. This was followed by a long-term, relatively shallow deterioration of about 1% per year until the very end of accounts, when the decreasing trend became more serious.

Very few contemporary comments on the level of shrine offerings exist to supplement the accounting figures. The Lincoln statutes referring to the 'chilling of devotion', mentioned above, explicitly state that offerings had decreased and that payments customarily made from them were reduced as a result. It is noteworthy that this memorandum appeared not in the final, fifteenth-century decline but in the early fourteenth-century stagnation. Thus temporary declines, brief compared to the entire period under study but still several decades in duration, were a concern to the clerics who could not, after all, predict that offerings would eventually recover in value.

One would not expect large changes in income to go unnoticed by the clerical caretakers, and there is some indication of a reaction in the financial organisation, particularly to the lowering receipts encountered in the fifteenth century. The 1480/1 Durham feretrar's roll states that the prior gave the feretrar relief of £4, which he assigned from other cathedral offices. We know from later references and other obedientiaries' accounts that this money was contributed from the almoner, chamberlain, hostiller and the master of the infirmary beginning in 1471.[4] The Lincoln shrine-keeper reacted in the same period by regularly reducing expenses. The fall account for 1334, for example, noted £11 3s. 11d. in expenses,

---

[4] DDCA, 'Feretrar's roll' 1488/9; 'And paid to the feretrar in relief of his office by order of

while in 1450 this was down to £9 8s. and by 1490 expenses totalled only £4 10s. 7d.[5]

In analysing the income from shrines it becomes apparent that there were two levels or categories of saints, a distinction that affected the pattern of offerings being discussed here. Almost all saints' cults first relied on spontaneous popular fervour. However, some cults never received any official backing and were entirely a popular creation. More mercurial than official cults, they received high incomes immediately after the death of the saint, with the offerings then fading rapidly away. It seems that such cults relied absolutely on the personal reputation of the deceased and lasted only so long as personal memory of him or her persisted. After the last people to know the holy person died only a vague reputation for sanctity lingered, enough to coax no more than a few pence per year out of visitors to the cathedral or church in question. John Wharton at Durham and Archbishop Winchelsey at Canterbury seem to be in this category, since both cults lasted about fifty years before their offerings fell to under 1s. The pennies continued to trickle into Winchelsey's pyx after that, perhaps more because an offering box of any sort is always likely to attract one or two coins than because the archbishop retained a saintly and popular reputation. On the other hand, official recognition was not a guarantee of popularity. St William of Norwich had ceased to entice significant numbers of coins from pilgrims' purses by the time Norwich records begin in 1272/3, despite a *vita*. Even so, his 'official' status (although treated as a saint he was never canonised) did lay the foundations for the recovery of his cult in the late fourteenth century.

Saints' cults in the second category began in the same rush of popular enthusiasm but were also aided by official sponsorship and the active involvement of the clergy. They received periodic boosts to their popularity through secondary events such as jubilees and translations, were commemorated with at least one feast, had their memories kept alive through *vitæ* and *miracula*, and possessed a special lure for late medieval pilgrims in the form of indulgences granted for visits to the shrine. St Thomas of Canterbury is the ultimate English example of a pilgrimage saint, but almost all the other greater shrines commemorated saints of this type. When a saint reached a certain height of popularity, and had survived for long enough, he or she was no longer just a local phenomenon, but became part of the wider religious culture. Saints like Cuthbert and Etheldreda reached this state even before the Conquest. In a sense, they joined the universal saints of the Bible and Rome, and relied to a lesser degree than others on momentary enthusiasm. The proceeds from their shrines survived at significant levels for longer periods, moving up or down with contemporary trends.

---

the lord Prior' (Et sol. feretrario in relevamen officii sui ex ordinatione domini Prioris): *Extracts from the Account Rolls of Durham*, vol. 1, pp. 56, 245, 280.

5   LCA, D&C Bj/5/16/1, ff. 1, 41, 46.

Underlying influences on the level of shrine offerings

The vicissitudes in shrine offerings outlined above must have had underlying causes. Because offerings were made in money, it is prudent to consider possible economic reasons for the changes in shrine incomes. The main economic factors that are likely to have affected offerings are inflation and fluctuating wage-rates, each of which could have changed the value of a coin to the offerer. The gift of a penny, for example, would have been a much greater sacrifice to an early pilgrim than it was to his grandson if there had been significant inflation in the intervening years or if family income had improved. After all, devotion to a saint's cult might have been proven by the relative degree of sacrifice that a pilgrim was willing to offer.

Most analyses of prices show light inflation from about 1220 until the late fourteenth century.[6] Averaged for half-centuries and indexed by Lord Beveridge, the mean price of seven basic commodities climbed from an index value of 65 for 1200–49 to 119 in 1350–99, but dropped in 1400–49 to 104.[7] The Brown-Hopkins index is more detailed. It shows inflation in the price of consumables to about 1320, deflation to 1340, inflation again to about 1370, then a fairly gradual deflation until 1500, when costs climbed sharply (see graph 17).[8] Thus inflation roughly followed the same trend as shrine proceeds until 1500, although the changes were not nearly as severe. Prices could fluctuate greatly in the short term, but the long-term trend was one of stability. The change in prices over the fifteenth century was apparently no more than -0.096%, or effectively zero.

Brown and Hopkins have also constructed a matrix of average wage indices for England.[9] Because they based their study primarily on the accounts of two chantry priests with an income of £20 it tends to understate the improvement in real wages from the mid-fourteenth to mid-fifteenth centuries, but the main conclusions are valid.[10] A similar but more detailed and broadly based effort by D.L. Farmer produced similar results.[11] Wages remained very constant until the period immediately after the Black Death, when for a brief time it was significantly harder to earn enough to purchase a unit of grain. However, the purchasing power of labour soon increased, and by the mid-fifteenth century was over twice

6 There may have been high inflation previous to this. P. Harvey has postulated an inflation from 1180 to 1220 of as much as two or three times: P.D.A. Harvey, 'The English Inflation of 1180 to 1220', *Past and Present*, no. 61 (1973), pp. 3–31.

7 W. Beveridge, 'The Yield and Price of Corn in the Middle Ages', *Economic History*, vol. 1 (1926–9), p. 165. Also see summaries in D. Farmer, 'Prices and Wages, 1350–1500', in *The Agrarian History of England and Wales*, ed. J. Thirsk, vol. 3 (Cambridge, 1991), p. 501.

8 E.H.P. Brown and S.V. Hopkins, 'Seven Centuries of the Prices of Consumables, Compared with Builder's Wage Rates', *Economica*, vol. 23 (1956), pp. 311–13.

9 E.H.P. Brown and S.V. Hopkins, 'Wage Rates and Prices, Evidence for Population Pressure in the Sixteenth Century', *Economica*, ns vol. 24 (1957), p. 303.

10 Dyer, *Standards of Living*, pp. 220, 229.

11 Farmer, 'Prices and Wages', pp. 501–25.

its pre-plague worth.[12] In other words, a labourer would have had to work only half as long to earn a meal. Salaries remained high and steady until about 1500, when a severe decline set in. Wages seem less directly connected to shrine proceeds than inflation. They increased more slowly after the onset of plague, so that the period of highest wages occurred at least fifty years after the high point in shrine receipts, and stayed high for another fifty years. The early sixteenth century is the one time the two coincide significantly, with oblations and wages both declining rapidly.

The evidence suggests that there was no obvious correlation between shrine offerings and changes in prices and wages. Major shifts in both sometimes occurred at about the same time, but not always in the direction one would first expect and rarely to the same degree. Any correlation is probably the result of other forces acting upon both, rather than a simple case of cause and effect. Shrine proceeds were not solely economic. Although the favour of the saints was in some ways a service purchased with offerings, it was not subject to the usual market forces. The law of supply and demand, for example, did not apply since there was theoretically no limit to the supply of divine favour. Saints in heaven plainly had no need of a cash income, and therefore the faith and devotion that the act of offering itself showed probably counted for more than its monetary value. I have found no direct evidence that the clergy responsible for shrines overtly tried to increase pilgrim spending or relate the quality of the saints' aid to the amount of money spent. If the clergy can be accused of over-commercialisation, it is in the setting up of ever more numerous devotional stations, such as crosses and statues, in the hopes of attracting a separate offering for each.

While it might be assumed that the gift of a halfpenny from a pauper was considered more pious than a shilling from a rich man, there is some evidence that the offerings of pilgrims were not directly related to how much they could afford. Instead, it seems that a more symbolic donation of a single coin was made, one that was often dedicated to the shrine before the pilgrim left home. This is well illustrated in *miracula*, not only in references to offerings of one penny, but also the practice of bending pennies or hanging them about the neck to seal a vow of pilgrimage.[13] As we have seen, the vast majority of money in pyxes was in the form of pennies, with some farthings and obols. There is also the testimony of Robert of Gloucester who, when asked what pilgrims left at Worcester, said 'some leave the fourth part of a sterling penny, others half a penny, and others a whole penny'.[14] The placement of a coin on the altar or in the pyx may therefore have meant more as a ritual gesture signifying completion of a pilgrimage than as a payment or charitable donation. In light of this possibility, economic factors

---

[12] Farmer estimates an improvement of as much as 137% by assuming a more cereal-based diet than that postulated by Brown and Hopkins. See Farmer, 'Prices and Wages', pp. 493–4.

[13] See for example miracles in William of Malmesbury, *Vita Sancti Wulfstani*, pp. 124–6, 128; Duffy, *Stripping of the Altars*, pp. 183–4.

[14] 'Dixit, quod aliqui quartem partem unius denarii sterlingi, et alii medium sterlingorum, & alii unum sterlingorum': *Acta Sanctorum, October*, vol. 1, p. 584.

become largely irrelevant. It would not matter what the currency was worth in loaves of bread or hours of labour: a penny was the proper and traditional offering and token of faith. Obviously some pilgrims, certainly the richer individuals, offered a great deal more than one penny. But for most even one penny sterling, in England's relatively undebased currency, must have been a significant unit of wealth. The majority of pilgrims are therefore likely to have offered one coin each regardless of wage-rates or prices, with the poorest perhaps offering a halfpenny or farthing rather than a penny. Wage rates are also applicable only to wage earners. Wage payers, such as craftsmen or land owning farmers who employed workers, and who are likely to have been richer and therefore among those who offered more than the standard penny, would have been adversely affected by any increase in wages. The non-waged peasantry may not have been affected at all. For the above reasons, and with the economic trends showing only weak correlation, it can be said with reasonable confidence that monetary factors like inflation and wage rates were at best a secondary influence on the level of shrine offerings.

A greater correlation can be shown between offerings and population levels. If the proportion of the population that underwent pilgrimage remained constant, then the population level ought to have affected the number of pilgrims, and consequently the amount of their offerings, even if the level of devotion to saints and relics remained unchanged. We shall see that this hypothesis, while not entirely unreasonable, makes many assumptions.

While demographic trends are a contentious subject in the study of medieval English history,[15] this study does not require an examination of fluctuations in detail, but only the broadest and most long-term movements. The model of shrine offerings is so general, and covers such a broad period of time, that the differences between various theories of population change in medieval England are not usually relevant. Whether an increase or decrease in population occurred a few years or even a decade earlier or later will not greatly affect comparison with fluctuations of shrine income. In addition, we are not concerned in this context with the absolute number of people, but only with change and the approximate proportions of change.

Most historians agree that the medieval English population climbed until at least the early fourteenth century. Pressures due to over-population itself may have started a regression in numbers starting around or shortly after the time of the famines of 1315–18. Death rates were exceptionally high during the Black Death of 1348 and following years, reasonable estimates varying between 30% and 45% for the main epidemic alone.[16] Recurrent plagues kept the population in decline. When recovery came it was slow and gradual, making it difficult to pinpoint an exact time when the population began to recover. Most economic indicators, which might reflect population, do not show increased output until the later fifteenth century and were at a nadir in the 1450s and 1460s. 'Both schools of

---

[15] For a summary of the controversy to 1977, see J. Hatcher, *Plague, Population and the English Economy, 1348–1530* (London, 1977), chapter 1, pp. 11–20.

[16] Hatcher, *Plague, Population*, p. 25. The extreme estimates vary between 25 and 55%.

historians [medievalists and early modernists] have tended to agree that the origins of the demographic explosion of the sixteenth and early seventeenth centuries lay in the last quarter of the century, more especially in the decade 1475 to 1485.'[17] In any case, re-population was probably under way in the early sixteenth century. The above model of population change is basically the same as that first put forward by M. Postan in the 1950s.[18]

Comparing the model graph of income at English shrines (graph 15) with Hatcher's graph of national population estimates (graph 16), we notice that population was climbing steadily until at least 1300, while shrine income did not begin to rise until after 1250. We have already discussed how the information for early thirteenth-century shrines, derived only from the Canterbury evidence, could be misleading, and in fact offerings may on average have been increasing throughout the thirteenth century. We are on much more certain ground when both the shrine income and the population graphs show a decline or stagnation setting in before the Black Death. So far the graphs agree considerably, suggesting a direct relationship. However, at the time of the plague the two graphs move sharply in opposite directions; population down and shrine income up. While population continued to decline, but at a slower rate, the increase in shrine proceeds was much briefer and was followed by a swift decline. For the majority of the fifteenth century population and offerings were relatively stable, but by the sixteenth century the graphs again move in opposite directions, this time with shrine income down and population up.

Because population and shrine income followed the same pattern for most of the Middle Ages, it is at least possible that changes in the population level could have been responsible for most of the changes in offerings; in particular the thirteenth-century increase, the early fourteenth-century stagnation and the slow fifteenth-century decline. These were all periods of gradual change in both population and offerings. However, during times of more sudden population growth or decline, such as during the second half of the fourteenth century and the first part of the sixteenth, shrine proceeds moved sharply in the opposite direction. This suggests that those times saw even greater *per capita* change than the graphs suggest. For example, if the population halved between 1348 and 1380 while shrine income doubled, then the oblations must have increased fourfold compared to the population. Thus, if the amount of money given by each pilgrim remained constant, then people must have been four times as likely to go on pilgrimage. Alternatively, if the percentage of people who became pilgrims remained constant then each must have left four times as much money at the shrine as before. The reality may have been somewhere between these two extremes.

The three factors of wages, inflation and shrine proceeds were probably influenced more by population than by each other. However, the English economy did not react to changes in population as might at first be expected. In particular,

17 Hatcher, *Plague, Population*, pp. 36, 63.
18 Also summarised in M. M. Postan, *The Medieval Economy and Society: An Economic History of Britain in the middle ages* (London, 1972), pp. 35–9.

the period after 1349 has puzzled economic historians: 'In the first place the Black Death and the immediately ensuing waves of devastating epidemics which, as far as it is possible to judge at present, must have led to a reduction in population of at least a third and more probably almost a half, had few of the debilitating effects that one has been led to associate with the population decline of the later Middle Ages.'[19] The economic downturn resulting from the plague was very short lived and productivity soon increased. From all indications the economy boomed until late in the century, and did not decline until the late fourteenth or early fifteenth century depending on region or sector of the economy.[20]

This economic boom in the face of demographic collapse only makes sense if individuals behaved differently before and after the plague. 'The reduction in population must also have led to a sharp increase in *per capita* wealth and consumption. In simple terms, the survivors inherited the property of those who had perished and, when presented with a sudden increase of wealth at a time of recurrent plague and considerable uncertainty, it is not surprising that they chose to spend on a greater scale than their predecessors.'[21] Those most affected tended to be lower on the economic ladder: 'The increase in the spending power of the urban wage-earners and artisans after 1349 attracted a good deal of contemporary comment', as well as bringing about sumptuary laws in 1363.[22]

The same forces may have been at work on pilgrim behaviour. Inheriting the land and goods of the dead, the survivors were better off materially than their predecessors, but were under a real threat of early death. This may have resulted in a lessening of the incentive to save and in increased spending. Under these circumstances it is not surprising that shrines became more popular. A pilgrimage could be an expensive undertaking, more so in travel costs and absence from work than offerings. In that sense pilgrimage was a form of consumption (conspicuous consumption in the case of some of Chaucer's pilgrims). In addition, the miraculous aspects of shrines would have made pilgrimage an obvious choice for the insecure faithful as a refuge from the plague. In many ways the fifteenth century was a return to normal. The inheritance of wealth caused by the Black Death was a one-off occurrence, and the mood of the generation after the plague, with its attitude of 'spend now for we might not be here tomorrow', no longer existed. Those who grew up with high death rates and the threat of plague must have learned to live with them and even accept them as the norm. This seems to be one reason why shrine offerings declined as rapidly as they rose: the mass psychology supporting the increase lasted at most for one generation.[23]

For most of the fifteenth century shrine proceeds, although dropping gradually, can be said to have restabilised. This suggests that the influences causing the

---

19 Hatcher, *Plague, Population*, p. 31.
20 Hatcher, *Plague, Population*, p. 35.
21 Hatcher, *Plague, Population*, p. 33.
22 Dyer, *Standards of Living*, p. 207.
23 For an interesting account of the religious reaction to a much later pestilence, see R.J. Morris, *Cholera 1832: The Social Response to an Epidemic* (London, 1976), esp. pp. 144–55.

dramatic swings of the fourteenth century had ceased. What decline existed can largely be explained by two phenomena. The first is depopulation, which probably lasted at least until the 1470s and would have gradually reduced the number of potential pilgrims. The second is the fact that any individual cult tended to decline naturally after its period of initial popularity, whether or not pilgrimage or the cult of relics as a whole was being abandoned.[24] Saints' cults were victims of vagaries in fashion. With no new cathedral saints in the fifteenth century, the recorded offerings could be expected to dwindle gradually as people turned their attention to newer attractions, whether other saints' shrines, miraculous statues of Mary or holy crosses.[25] 'Transfer of allegiance from the older healers to the new seems to have been an explicit theme of some of the miracle stories associated with newer shrines.'[26] In the face of technical problems involving the evidence, the decline in offerings is therefore not severe enough to unequivocally signal a 'chilling of devotion' to the relics of the saints in the fifteenth century.

The accelerated decline occurring in the early sixteenth century requires more explanation. Since it was counter to the probable trend of increasing population, *per capita* shrine offerings must have declined at an even greater rate than is at first apparent. Perhaps this can be explained by the economic hardship created by rising prices and falling wages after 1500. If the standard of living dropped considerably, then it is not surprising that pilgrimage was forgone. These conditions are largely the reverse of those that caused the surge in offerings after the Black Death. Both the threat of early death and disposable income receded somewhat, making the 'consumption' of pilgrimage less attractive.

We have seen that population and standard of living probably had something to do with the amount of offerings received by English shrines. They are not enough, however, to explain everything about the trend, particularly the severity of change during times of economic and demographic crisis. Possible non-economic, non-statistical reasons for the changes in donations at various times are legion. One is the fifteenth-century tendency for relics to pass into private hands, which might have removed some of the incentive for the wealthy to go on pilgrimage.[27] This process was aided by the clergy themselves, as when the Durham monks gave relics to the king, the earl of Rutland and Countess Neville in 1401.[28] Relics were not given away without hope of profit to the church, but the practice must have diverted some devotion away from the greater shrines.

---

[24] For an argument in favour of a continuance of devotion to local shrines, see Finucane, *Miracles and Pilgrims*, pp. 193–5.

[25] For the evidence of a turning towards crosses and Marian shrines see Duffy, *Stripping of the Altars*, pp. 191, 195–6; Finucane, *Miracles and Pilgrims*, pp. 195–9. For images, see Duffy, *Stripping of the Altars*, pp. 156–68, especially p. 167: 'Where early medieval devotion to the saints was focused on their relics, late medieval devotion focused on images.'

[26] Duffy, *Stripping of the Altars*, p. 195.

[27] See C. Richmond, 'Religion and the Fifteenth-Century English Gentleman', in *Church, Politics and Patronage in the Fifteenth Century*, ed. B. Dobson (Gloucester, 1984), pp. 197–8.

[28] *Extracts from the Account Rolls of Durham*, pp. 450–4.

Since those able to afford their own relics were also the richest, the financial effect of personal relics on shrine income might have been out of proportion to their numbers.

The later medieval interest in chantries could also have created competition for shrines. However, the establishment of chantries resembled the founding of shrines much more than the sort of offerings that are recorded in the regular accounts. If a wealthy fifteenth-century person decided on a pious construction project, he was perhaps more likely to build a chantry chapel for himself than contribute, for example, to the construction of a new screen for a shrine, but it does not necessarily mean that his need for pilgrimage would diminish. Few shrines were in need of construction in any case.

J. Sumption believes that fourteenth- and fifteenth-century pilgrims were more numerous than ever before but were also increasingly lowly and poor, and thus required more in alms and support than they gave in offerings.[29] Leaving aside for the moment the expense of hospitality, poorer pilgrims may indeed have felt that they could avoid the usual coin offering. A flood of simpler people may also have scared away wealthier pilgrims, resulting in even less revenue. Unfortunately, we have too little information about the lower classes of pilgrim to be able to accurately judge their numbers, average wealth or how much they offered. Such pilgrims, by their very nature, would leave little evidence. However, a statute of Edward IV made in 1473 ordained that 'no person go in pilgrimage, not able to perform it without begging, unless he have letters testimonial under the great seal ordained for the same, testifying the causes of his going and the places whence he came and whither he shall go'.[30] This type of legal evidence can argue both for and against the frequency of the activity it forbids; the need for legislation may indicate that it was common, while the fact that it was legislated against argues that it was frowned upon and thus rare.

Shrines may also have been harmed by the ever increasing importance of indulgences. It was more difficult to obtain indulgences as a shrine aged, partly because the shrine lost novelty value but also because new competitors for indulgences were always springing up. At the same time the value of old indulgences lessened due to a kind of 'inflation' in effectiveness and years remitted, making new indulgences more powerful. The Papacy made matters worse by continually increasing the cost of this precious commodity, so that eventually Papal indulgences became practically unattainable. The legal correspondence of Canterbury Cathedral Priory shows how hard the convent and archbishop tried in vain to obtain an indulgence for the 1520 jubilee of St Thomas, and how severe a bargain the Pope was driving.[31] The fever for indulgences was intense, and without their attraction the potential pilgrim might go elsewhere than to the old, established cathedral shrines.

---

[29] Sumption, *Pilgrimage*, p. 165. It is unclear what Sumption's sources are for this.
[30] J.M. Theilmann, 'Communitas among Fifteenth-Century Pilgrims', *Historical Reflections*, vol. 11 (1984), p. 268; from *Calendar of Close Rolls, 1465–76*, p. 299.
[31] *Literæ Cantuarienses*, vol. 3, pp. 340–3, 345–7.

The most interesting alternative explanation for the eventual decline in offerings, in the light of later events, is a rise in antipathy toward the cult of relics and pilgrimage. This is a contentious issue, and requires a more thorough study than is possible here. In brief, however, changes in shrine offerings do coincide roughly with three of the best known reactions to pilgrimage. Firstly, the point of highest offerings was roughly contemporary with the writing of *The Canterbury Tales* in the 1380s. Sometimes called a critique of the late medieval decadence of pilgrimage, the *Tales* appear in this light as a sophisticated satire of a practice at the height of its popularity. Secondly, the collapse in offerings at the end of the fourteenth century was roughly synchronous with the arrival of the Lollard movement. It may be that this marks the start of a truly popular reaction against the cults of pilgrimage and relics.[32] Finally, the ultimate drop of the offerings in the early sixteenth century was of course at the same time as the beginnings of the Reformation which ultimately destroyed the shrines.

If the Black Death had a severe effect on offerings, then what about smaller epidemics and other disasters such as famine? Shrines were traditionally sought out by those in need, but did a catastrophe like a famine make people too weak to travel and too poor to give money away, and thus reduce donations at a shrine, or did it tend to make people more eager to seek the saints' aid for their deliverance, and therefore increase donations? Crop failure and resulting famine must have had a considerable impact on the agriculturally based society of the middle ages. Although irregular cycles of good and bad harvests were frequent, they are not clear enough in their effects to help us. Instead, we must look at the worst harvests in the expectation that their effects on the shrine receipts will be the most visible and unambiguous. 'In the later Middle Ages, two episodes stand out because of their concentration of bad years, including dearths: 1315–18 and 1437–40.'[33] To this might be added the harvest of 1290 which was 'catastrophically bad' due to wet weather.[34] Because it is uncertain how long it took the ill effects of a famine to strike, we will have to look at both the famine year and the year following. After all, it is likely that food supplies lasted long enough to delay the effects of famine until after the Michaelmas accounting period for any one year.

Canterbury is our only source for shrine offerings during the 1290 and 1315–17 famines. The treasurers' rolls show that the income for 1289/90 was somewhat high at £233 6s. 8d. Although part of an upward trend in shrine proceeds at the time, this was still the highest income until 1296/7. The next year the shrine received £190. The average income at Canterbury for the years 1315–18 was £322 10s., while the decade average was £360. Since this was probably the worst period for harvests in medieval England the difference is surprisingly small. While 1326 was 'a year of agricultural crisis' for Canterbury, during which many cattle and

---

[32] See Finucane, *Miracles and Pilgrims*, pp. 199–200. The events of the Reformation as regards shrines will be briefly summarised in the conclusion.

[33] Dyer, *Standards of Living*, p. 265.

[34] Postan, *Medieval Economy and Society*, p. 34.

sheep died of pestilence,[35] the account for 1325/6 was exactly on the decade average and the next year was only slightly above.

It is possible that the dearth of the late 1430s was the last serious medieval famine.[36] At Ely the account for 1438/9 survives and shows £64 15s. This is a high receipt for Ely, but is in accordance with the prevailing long-term trend. All the accounts for this period survive at Durham and Lincoln. At Durham the figure for 1436/7 was unusually high at £36 3s. 11d., the highest income in 36 years. However, the total for the next three years was unusually low, at a level not dropped to again until the 1450s. At Lincoln most years from 1437 to 1440 were nearly average. The total for 1438/9, however, was only a little over half the average for the decade at £6 17s. 7d.

Although the data for famines is sparse and unreliable it does show that the changes exhibited in shrine donations during famines were neither consistent nor pronounced. The shrine figures have such a high variation at all times that some high and low figures are to be expected. As a result, I can make only the very cautious suggestion that perhaps famines did not have an extreme effect on offerings one way or the other.

We can examine occurrences of plagues and contagious disease for their effects on donations in the same way as for famines, considering only a few of the greater epidemics. The Black Death itself is too major to be considered here (and is treated above as a long-term influence), but major epidemics of plague recurred in 1361–2, 1369, and 1375.[37] At Lincoln the receipts for 1362 were somewhat higher than the accounts before and after, but were very close to the average for that decade. 1369 and 1375 showed *aperturæ* proceeds within 10% of the accounting years both before and after. Ely accounts survive for the two later episodes, neither significantly higher than receipts in other years. At Canterbury we have only the 1374/5 account, which is average for the decade. Other shrine accounts are not useful for this purpose.

Other national epidemics as noted in chronicles and other sources occurred in 1400, 1430, 1433–5, 1438–9, 1463–5, 1467, 1471–3, 1479–80 and 1513.[38] An examination of the best records for the fifteenth century (Ely, Norwich, Durham, Westminster and Lincoln) produces no uniform pattern. The distribution of plague-year receipts above and below the average seems about equal. For example, accounts survive for 1400, 1433–5, 1439, 1463–5, 1467, 1471–2 and 1479 for Westminster. In those twelve years some incomes, particularly those in 1400 and 1439, are lower than those in adjacent years, while 1471–3 was a period of higher revenues than any year since 1424.

---

35 Smith, *Canterbury Cathedral Priory*, pp. 108–9.
36 C. Dyer, *Lords and Peasants in a Changing Society: The Estates of the Bishopric of Worcester, 680–1540* (Cambridge, 1980), p. 228.
37 Hatcher, *Plague, Population*, p. 25.
38 These dates are extracted from Dyer, *Lords and Peasants*, p. 225; R.S. Gottfried, *Epidemic Disease in Fifteenth-Century England* (1978), pp. 84–5; P.J.P. Goldberg, 'Mortality and Economic Change in the Diocese of York, 1390–1514', *Northern History*, vol. 24 (1988), pp. 44–8.

These results show that epidemics, like famines, did not have a noticeable effect on shrine income. However, it is a condition of the data that only very extreme changes in the receipts can be used as evidence for direct relationship, since offerings fluctuated greatly at all times. Therefore, I can only say that there is no evidence that epidemics, famines or other sharp increases in the death rate caused *great* changes in pilgrimage and shrine donation in the short term. It is possible that the forces operating on pilgrimage due to disasters may have cancelled out; desire for supernatural aid inhibited by fear of travel, for example. We have already seen that severely increased mortality (due for example to the Black Death) did have a long term effect on shrine income by way of changes in the standard of living and religious sentiment. Disasters of only one or two years duration, however, do not – on admittedly limited evidence – seem to have created the sort of panic mentality that we might have expected.

The importance of offerings to cathedral finances

We have examined how offerings to shrines changed over time, but what did this mean to the finances of a cathedral? Did fluctuations hurt church finances? Were shrines profitable? The shrine of St Thomas at Canterbury, which regularly attracted £50 to £500 per year, was in a league of its own. Of the other shrines under examination, only one, that of St Edward the Confessor at Westminster, received more than £100 in a regular obedientiary account, although fabric rolls show that both Archbishop Scrope's tomb at York and St Thomas' tomb at Hereford surpassed £100 during early stages of their cults.[39] Accounts generally began a considerable time after the foundation of the shrine, so that extrapolating backwards on the basis of known patterns of decline, and using the evidence of the above-mentioned fabric rolls, it is reasonable to estimate that most greater shrines generated offerings of over £100 per year in their opening phases but eventually dropped to a usual annual receipt of between £10 and £80. In the fifteenth century several shrines were still earning more than £20 yearly, but by the end of the century most had dropped to single digit receipts.

For most times in most places the shrine offerings were a noticeable if not crucial element of church revenue. The early income from St Thomas's shrine was, of course, extraordinary. Before the translation the shrines of St Thomas contributed 88% of all offerings and 28% of Canterbury cathedral's income from all sources. For the most important cathedral in England, this was a considerable proportion. With the exception of Canterbury, however, cathedrals rarely received more than 10% of their income from the shrine. The late fifteenth-century oblationary income from Hereford, for example, from all sources but primarily from Cantilupe's shrine, was between one-fifth and one-quarter of the clavigers' total receipts, the remainder being mostly rents, while the claviger was in turn a relatively minor official of the cathedral. The situation was similar at monastic

[39] WAM, MS 19633 (1372/3).

cathedrals. At Ely the account rolls show that the income of the priory averaged £1,198, with the sacrist's portion equalling about £200 and the feretrar's £24.[40] The shrine income averaged about £50, or about 4% of the total: large enough that its loss would hurt, but not so great that the church would be bankrupted. This seems to have been typical for England, but unlike the situation at some continental churches: St Gilles's Abbey in Provence was made destitute when pilgrims stopped coming.[41]

While cathedrals were not financially dependent on shrines, there is no question that the offerings in themselves were large. Given the size of a great church's revenue, 5% of that income was certainly worth notice. However, it is open to debate whether cathedrals made a profit on offerings or paid more in shrine-related expenses, especially in hospitality to pilgrims, than they received. We know that hospitality was a particularly expensive obligation when a monarch visited a cathedral, a burden which was accentuated by the giving of gifts. Christ Church gave £109 16s. worth of presents to Edward II and his queen on their arrival at Canterbury in 1330, while they offered only a little over £10 pounds at the shrines in return.[42] When Edward I arrived in Canterbury in 1301 his family gave the various shrines £7 4s. while the convent gave him £100 plus £66 to the prince.[43] Greater than normal attention was also given to dignitaries of the nobility and episcopate, although not to the same degree. These are all exceptional gifts; the more mundane costs of food and entertainment for such guests are not known.

In theory the *Rule of St Benedict* demanded that monastic cathedrals lodge pilgrims, and indeed all travellers, in an ample guest house: 'In the reception of poor men and pilgrims special attention should be shown, because in them is Christ more truly welcomed; for the fear which the rich inspire is enough to secure them honour.'[44] According to some monastic statutes, the usual period for free accommodation was two days and nights.[45] It is unclear how far this injunction was followed. Monasteries frequently complained about the burden of hospitality, but there is little evidence of direct expenditure. Beds within the cathedral precincts were certainly extended to wealthier guests, and there are a few, rare references to the lodging of visitors within cathedral precincts. For example, at Canterbury in 1444/5 one of the priory's seneschals was put up in the Crown Inn in the city, since 'due to the presence of strangers he could not be put up with us', but we cannot say who these 'strangers' were or whether they were staying free of charge.[46] In cathedral accounts such payments are usually hidden within the

[40] *Ely Chapter Ordinances*, p. xii.
[41] Sumption, *Pilgrimage*, p. 162.
[42] C.E. Woodruff and W. Danks, *Memorials of the Cathedral and Priory of Christ in Canterbury* (London, 1912), pp. 146–7.
[43] Woodruff, 'Financial Aspect', p. 28.
[44] 'Pauperum et Peregrinorum maxime susceptioni cura sollicite exhibeatur, quia in ispsis magis Christus suscipitur; nam divitum terror ipse sibi exigit honorem': *The Rule of St. Benedict*, ed. J. McCann (London, 1952), pp. 120–1.
[45] F.A. Gasquet, *English Monastic Life* (London, 1904), p. 32.
[46] 'Propter extraneos non potuit hospitare infra nos': CCA, DCc/MA4, f. 29; Woodruff

everyday expenses of the cellarers or hospitallars, and would be very difficult to reconstruct.

There is little evidence that cathedrals regularly extended free hospitality to non-noble pilgrims except on special occasions. A Canterbury historian has remarked that 'The Christ Church monks were at no period conspicuous for the liberality of their almsgiving, but in the fifteenth century their work in this direction nearly ceased altogether . . . All the evidence goes to show that they cared but little for their obligation to poor travellers and to the poor at the gate.'[47] Almshouses built to house pilgrims seem to have been separate from regular cathedral organisation, having their own lands and incomes. At Canterbury the Hospital of St Thomas the Martyr, founded by Archbishop Hubert Walter in 1193–1205, was sufficiently endowed to provide food and lodging for up to twelve pilgrims at a maximum cost of 4d. per person per day.[48] Hospitals were sometimes founded by non-ecclesiastical organisations. For example, a hostel with thirteen beds for poor men passing through the city of Coventry on pilgrimage, providing the services of a governor and cleaning woman at a cost of £10 yearly, was founded by a merchant gild.[49] These sorts of institutions seem to have satisfied the cathedral clergy's obligation of hospitality without their having to be involved with it themselves.

Those who were neither very rich nor very poor were probably expected to pay for their lodging, and by the fourteenth and fifteenth centuries pilgrim inns were common.[50] One of the most famous was the Chequers of the Hope at the corner of Mercery Lane in Canterbury, which is described in the prologue to *The Tale of Beryn*.[51] The Chequers, built by the priory over three years for a total cost of £867 14s. 4d., was said to have a dormitory with one hundred beds, its attraction to pilgrims enhanced by a subterranean gallery leading to the cathedral precincts.[52] Woodruff argued that 'the popularity of "the holy blissful martyr" declined during the fifteenth century, so that the great outlay incurred in rebuilding the inn was not a particularly good investment'.[53] On the contrary, however, the inn was built at a high point of pilgrimage to St Thomas and there were at least three decades of high offerings, and therefore numerous paying guests at the inn, to come. John Hales, a baron of the exchequer, wrote to Cromwell in 1538 asking him to give the city of Canterbury a mill once belonging to St Augustine's Abbey to make up

thought that the visitors were pilgrims: Woodruff, 'Notes on the Inner Life of Christ Church', p. 14.

47 Smith, *Canterbury Cathedral Priory*, p. 200.

48 Heath, *Steps of the Pilgrims*, p. 170.

49 H.F. Westlake, *The Parish Gilds of Medieval England* (London, 1919), p. 231.

50 Heath, *Steps of the Pilgrims*, pp. 220–3.

51 *Tale of Beryn*, p. 1.

52 'A Monastic Chronicle of Christ Church', pp. 62–8; the George, an inn at Glastonbury built for pilgrims in the fifteenth century, also had secret passages to the abbey. Heath, *Steps of the Pilgrims*, pp. 180–1. In fact the Chequers was finished a few years after the probable completion date of the original *Tales*, and so would not have been used by Chaucer if he had actually finished his work. See Smith, *Canterbury Cathedral Priory*, p. 200.

53 'A Monastic Chronicle of Christ Church', p. 66 n. 6.

for the loss of revenue which innkeepers and victuallers used to make out of pilgrims.[54] Keeping an inn for pilgrims was thus a profitable enterprise even in the mid-sixteenth century. This, and the fact that the priory built the Chequers of the Hope as an investment, not a charity, proves that most pilgrims could not expect free accommodation. The situation must have been more extreme at places like Walsingham, where a small priory received large numbers of visitors. Indeed, extortionate rates levied on pilgrims were rumoured to be the cause of an arsonous 1431 fire in four inns at Little Walsingham.[55] These factors combine to suggest that only a fraction of pilgrims, if any, were given free accommodation in monastic guest houses paid for out of regular priory funds. Others, probably the poorest, would have been put up in hospitals or other independently funded institutions. This made much more sense economically than the idealistic impracticality of being a free hotel as recommended in the *Rule of St Benedict*.

The subject of hospitality, like so much else in this chapter, is a controversial issue that deserves a thesis in its own right. It is appropriate, however, to make one point relating to shrine expenses. The profitability of shrines has been put into doubt by an oft-repeated comment made by C. Woodruff about the value of the shrine of St Thomas. At Canterbury the cellarers, like most functionaries, received their operating funds almost entirely from the treasurer. Woodruff noticed that in some cases an increase in shrine receipts coincided with an increase in cellarer's expenses and surmised that this was due to costs involved in extending hospitality to pilgrims. In the translation year of 1220, for example, the allowance made to the cellarer by the treasurer was £1,154 16s. 5d., up from £442 8s. in the previous year. Offerings, of course, were also at their highest that year. Again, in 1375/6 offerings totalled £692 4s. 7d. from all sources, but the expenditure of the treasurer's office still exceeded income by £486 18s., 'a result which was largely due to the abnormal demands made upon the cellarer's office'.[56]

This analysis does not stand up to investigation. One of the examples used by Woodruff was the very unrepresentative year 1219/20, which saw the translation of St Thomas and a lengthy and no doubt expensive stay by the king at Canterbury. The increase in cellarer's expenses from 1218/19 to 1219/20 was £692 7s. 11d., while the additional offerings to the various shrines of St Thomas amounted to £872 7d. Thus a net profit was made even when considering only the monetary proceeds revealed in the treasurers' accounts and assuming that all cellarers' expenses were shrine-related.

Let us assume for the moment that the cellarers at Canterbury were deeply involved with hospitality. If so, then their expenses should have had a direct relationship to shrine proceeds: increasing when they increase and falling when they fall. If we use standard statistical methods to determine the correlation,

---

54 G. Baskerville, *English Monks and the Suppression* (London, 1937), p. 23; *Letters and Papers of Henry VIII*, vol. 13, pt 2, no. 1142, p. 475.

55 John Amundesham, *Annales Monasterii S. Albani*, ed. H.T. Riley (RS, vol. 28, 1870–1), vol. 1, p. 62; J.C. Dickinson, *The Shrine of Our Lady of Walsingham* (Cambridge, 1956), p. 34.

56 Woodruff, 'Financial Aspect', pp. 18, 26.

however, we obtain an inconclusive result.[57] We need to examine consecutive years and compare changes. Of the 140 cases where there are accounts for two consecutive years of both cellarers' expenses and shrine receipts, the two changed in the same direction, that is both grew or both declined, on only seventy-seven occasions, or slightly more than half the time. The other sixty-three times the offerings fell when cellarers' expenses increased, or vice versa. Out of eighty-three years in which the shrine income changed by more than 10% the cellarers' expenses followed suit only forty-four times, or again a little over half. In forty-seven cases where the cellarers' expenses also changed by 10% or more, twenty-nine matched the movement of the shrine proceeds, while 18 changed in the opposite direction. Therefore there is no evidence in these accounts that the shrine of St Thomas greatly increased the cellarer's expenses in hospitality. This is striking, considering that both figures were indirectly connected in many ways, for example by the general population and economy. Increased shrine income would also allow the cellarer to spend more on food and drink without being a cause of that expenditure. These facts combine to make it unlikely that pilgrims significantly increased the cathedral's expenses.

We have already seen that the expenses of the shrine itself were not normally a great drain on cathedral resources. By far the most common costs were wax and stipends for shrine officials, both of which were usually met entirely out of the offerings even though they sometimes served the cathedral at large as well as the feretory chapel. The duties assigned to the canons and monks nominally responsible for the shrine were not onerous, leaving them free for other tasks while providing them with an income. The shrine thereby enabled the cathedral to support a larger staff. For example, the expenses of the shrine of Thomas Cantilupe were light, the only consistent entry being the 20s. paid yearly to the custodian of the shrine. Even at the end of the shrine's cult this could be paid easily out of the shrine's pyx receipts. The rest of the offerings were mostly spent on wax, fees for the officers of the shrine, and payments to the canons. At Durham only about 10% of the pyx income went towards the operation of the shrine. The other 90%, along with rents and other additional income, enriched firstly the monks themselves and secondly, through the feretrar's various obligatory payments, the priory administration as a whole.

A somewhat more complex example of receipt and expenditure is that of the shrine of St Hugh. At Lincoln the shrine takings were 100% of the income of the *aperturæ* and covered all the greatly fluctuating expenses. These were almost never spent on material or repairs for the shrine, the one exception being the regular payment of about £5 per year on wax. Lincoln had a great many more guardians and chaplains than Hereford, but still spent under £3 per term on stipends and payments in wine for those who had duties connected with the shrine.

---

57 The most common statistical method of establishing a relationship between two variables is to calculate the correlation coefficient. In this case the coefficient is 0.40838, which would normally indicate a slight correlation. However, it would be surprising if the coefficient were less than 0.4 because the two variables are indirectly related in many ways.

Some of these, such as the night watchmen, probably served the cathedral beyond the feretory chapel as well. The *aperturæ* also paid fees for individuals, such as 6s. 8d. to the clerk of the altar of St Peter, who, as far as we know, had little to do with St Hugh. The shrine was thus paying for more than its share of the staff of the cathedral, while all the expenses that might be attributed to the shrine amounted to no more than about £11 per year, or about half of the usual total. The rest went towards payments to the canons. As time went on and the *aperturæ* income decreased, the cathedral eliminated some of the expenses, and various servants and officials received reductions in pay (although the canons' take of the income was never reduced). By this means the shrine of St Hugh never became a financial burden. At Durham the shrine clerk suffered most from decreasing offerings. At the beginning of surviving accounts he was receiving 20s., but by 1411 this was down to 13s. 4d. and by 1457 it was only 10s. Feretrars' stipends, and payments to the monks, did not decrease to nearly the same extent.[58]

English cathedrals seem to have used the cash income from shrines as a kind of supplementary salary paid to their canons or monks. These payments took up the bulk of the offerings. Little was spent on other essentials of the church, such as building programmes, unless the offerings were unusually high. In those cases, the clergy appear to have recognised that the offerings were a temporary windfall, rather than a permanent income that could be relied upon, and therefore channelled the money into fabric funds.

There were many types of income that were not included in the records of offerings. Although often the more interesting gifts, they are not statistically analysable and therefore, in this context, do not clarify the estimate of the total real income of a shrine. Testamentary bequests, for example, were rarely included in the account rolls. The Canterbury treasurer's account of 1318/19 records £432 11s. 11d. in bequests made by pilgrims and collected by the shrine-keepers, quite separate from and almost as much as offerings collected at the shrine itself.[59] This is a unique entry, placed under the heading *obvenciones* instead of *oblaciones* (where all the different types of offerings were usually classified), so it is hard to know what to make of it. The executors of wills would presumably have wanted to present the money in their charge directly to the keepers of the shrine (and perhaps obtain a receipt) rather than place it anonymously in a coin box, thereby proving that they had fulfilled their legal duty. This would probably have resulted in the bequest being accounted separately, as at Canterbury. In general bequests to shrines were not recorded in the accounts and are rarely found in wills.

Also not included in the financial reckoning, but occasionally mentioned in the accounts, are the many and various precious objects, gems and jewels given to shrines. In Chapter 4 we discussed the gifts of royalty, but precious gifts were not entirely restricted to the higher classes. John Brun, the convent plumber at

---

[58] DDCA, 'Feretrars' Accounts', by year.
[59] CCA, DCc/MA1, f. 96; Woodruff, 'Financial Aspect', p. 18.

Canterbury, for example, offered gold trinkets to St Thomas.[60] Gifts also differed in type. They ranged from liturgical plate, including chalices, statues and crosses, to silver spoons.[61] Bishops seem to have been fond of leaving rings to shrines, such as the ring offered to the shrine of Thomas Becket by the archbishop of Rheims in 1445, the gold ring with a sapphire given by Bishop Bewforth to St Hugh in 1398/9 or the ring set with a diamond given to the same shrine ten years later by Bishop Philip.[62] Many of these gifts were, no doubt, among the jewels recorded in the inventories made at Christchurch and elsewhere.

Perhaps the most famous gift ever given to an English cathedral was the Regale of France, given by Louis VII to Becket's shrine. Although not exceedingly large, it was a jewel of exceptional beauty and clarity, and was considered priceless in the estimation of contemporaries.[63] The usual worth of non-monetary offerings is more difficult to estimate, but the value of some gifts to the shrine of St Cuthbert can be judged thanks to an inventory of shrine goods made in 1401.[64] The Durham inventory includes appraisals for a complete list of donations (except for the first five entries, which are illegible). The estimates were probably made by a London goldsmith brought from York to see the shrine by order of the bishop.[65] Three of the items in this inventory (or *status* in the Durham terminology) cannot be included in any generalisations about donations. The first is a group of five rings worth five marks that 'were in the custody of the feretrar', and therefore were not a gift from outside the shrine but a transfer from the pertinences of the feretrar to those of the shrine, the two apparently being separate in the monastic bureaucracy.[66] The second was a golden image of the blessed Virgin with the arms of the 'Lord of Durham' (presumably the bishop) which was acquired by the feretrar of the said lord in exchange for another statue and thus was also the result of a transaction rather than an oblation.[67] Finally, there was a precious stone called the

---

[60] 'Item given to the sgrine of St Thomas the Martyr one pair of beads [?] to the value of £10 of purest gold that is in the southern part near the Regale of France' (Item optulit ad feretrum sancti Thome martire unum par p'cum ad valorum .x.li. de auro purissimo vide in australi parte prope regalem francie): CCA, DCc/MA 1, f.1. This is a note in the volume of treasurers' accounts. The account on the dorse is from 1286, but Woodruff dates it to 1434. Woodruff, 'Financial Aspect', p. 18.

[61] For example, LCA, Bj/5/16/2a, f. 6.

[62] Stone, *Chronicle*, p. 38; LCA, Bj/5/16/1, ff. 89, 95.

[63] See Stanley, 'The Shrine of St. Thomas', pp. 233–4; it was described by a Venetian at Canterbury in about 1500 as a ruby the size of a thumbnail which shone in the dark: *A Relation of the Island of England*, pp. 30–1.

[64] *Extracts from the Account Rolls of Durham*, vol. 2, pp. 450–4.

[65] First mentioned in the 1400/1 account and still at work in the 1401 roll: DDCA, 'Feretrar's Roll' 1400–1, 1401.

[66] DDCA, 'Feretrar's Roll' 1401; *Extracts from the Account Rolls of Durham*, vol. 2, p. 454.

[67] This earlier statue was given as a fine by William Scrope 'pro quadam transgressione facta infra libertatem Dunelm': DDCA, 'Feretrar's Roll' 1401; *Extracts from the Account Rolls of Durham*, vol. 2, p. 451. In the previous status of 1397, however, the gift is recorded as an oblation: DDCA, 'Feretrar's Roll' 1397; *Extracts from the Account Rolls of Durham*, vol. 2, p. 444. The fall from favour and beheading of the same William Scrope in 1399 may have rendered that statue unsuitable for display. The bishop also left an image of Mary with the

'Emerald', which was conserved previously amongst the relics by the feretrar. This stone's worth was estimated at £3,000 in the text and £3,336 in the sum, the latter figure including the value of a chain with five rings. The Emerald was probably a true devotional gift, but for the purpose of estimating non-monetary offerings we must exclude it on two counts. Firstly, it was so obviously exceptional and extreme in value that it would distort the results. If it were to be accepted then the average worth of donations as calculated below should be many times higher. Secondly, the wording of the entry seems to suggest that it was offered to the Durham relic collection somewhat earlier than the period covered by the inventory, and only transferred to the shrine itself at this time.

The items in the inventory of 1401 were not included in an earlier *status* of 1397,[68] and therefore we can assume that they were received within the intervening four years, which was the term of office of the feretrar Thomas de Lythe. The total value of the thirty-five gifts in the 1401 *status*, not counting those excepted above, was £464 4s. 8d, for an average of about £13 each. The feretrar must have received at least nine such gifts per year over the period 1397 to 1401. There are several references to 'various other gifts' by pilgrims, plus a remark that, besides the above, 'diverse others were offered and attached to the feretrum in the time of the said Sir Thomas which for the time being do not occur to memory'.[69] As a result, it is likely that only the more valuable gifts were inventoried at this time. Obviously, it is hard to judge accurately the quantity and value of non-monetary donations from the imprecise *status* figures, but they can be used to make generalisations. If the 1401 *status* was representative of gifts to St Cuthbert's shrine in the later middle ages then the minimum average yearly value of non-monetary donations was about £117, or well more than three times the average pyx income for the same period.

However, the 1401 *status* seems to have covered an exceptional period. 1401 was a year of unusually high oblations, with over £56 having been put in the shrine box. Also, the *status* period included a royal pilgrimage worth £40 in jewels from the king alone, and a campaign against Scotland which would have brought large amounts of wealth and potential noble benefactors into the north. Finally, the 1397 inventory lists only nine gifts received in the term of the feretrar Roger Lancaster, averaging only a little more than one item per year. For these reasons it is unlikely that the later, high values of 1401 are truly representative. In fact, an inventory with detailed appraisals might have been necessary precisely because the offerings were so unusually lavish. How far above the average the 1401 *status* was is not easy to judge, but it is reasonable to estimate that gifts of jewels and plate were at least comparable in value to monetary offerings at that time.

prior on account of a debt to Lord Neville in 1388: *Historiæ Dunelmensis Scriptores Tres*, p. clviii.

[68] DDCA, 'Feretrar's Roll' 1401. Printed in full in *Extracts from the Account Rolls of Durham*, vol. 2, pp. 444–5. This *status* does not give the value of objects, so is of much less use.

[69] 'Diverse alia sunt ablata et affixa feretro tempore dicti domini thome que pro tempore non occurunt memorie': DDCA, 'Feretrar's Roll' 1401; *Extracts from the Account Rolls of Durham*, vol. 2, p. 452.

In Chapter 5 we saw that the expenses of shrines were low. The offerings, even in the fifteenth century, easily paid for the few necessities. The hidden expenses, especially those arising from hospitality to pilgrims, are hard to judge, but they have left little evidence and would have had to be great indeed to surpass the income. Therefore, even if the cash income alone is considered shrines must have been at least marginally profitable for most of the middle ages. If we include gifts and other forms of income that do not appear in the financial accounts yet were not negligible, we can see why shrines were considered so valuable by contemporaries. While it is difficult to be precise, it is reasonable to conclude that shrines were financially profitable throughout the middle ages, with the possible exception of the period after about 1510 when shrine incomes became very small. In better times, particularly the period shortly after the inauguration of a shrine or during the golden age of pilgrimage after the Black Death, the shrines of saints must have been extraordinarily lucrative.

Conclusion

The shrines of medieval England came to an abrupt and violent end. Although criticism of the entire practice of pilgrimage existed since the first Lollards at the end of the fourteenth century, and was later joined by 'humanist' critiques in the manner of Erasmus, the final attack came extremely suddenly.[1] Despite their previous devotion to shrines, Henry VIII and his ministers converted to a revulsion towards relics and greed towards the vast wealth of the shrines. Those involved in the destruction were aware that their motives might appear to be mixed: in a letter of 1538 to Thomas Cromwell, agents who had just defaced St Swithun's shrine declared that '. . . we entende, both at Hide and St. Maryes, to swepe away all the roten bones that be called reliques; which we may not omytt, lest it shuld be thought we cam more for the treasure thenne for avoiding of thabomynation of ydolatry'.[2] At least among a powerful clique, however, religious objections towards the 'ydolatry' of shrines seem to have been genuine. It has also been argued that, because the destruction of shrines sometimes preceded the dissolution of the monasteries by a year or more, 'the campaign for the destruction of relics and the putting down of pilgrimages was embarked upon initially on its own merits, and that only as the dissolution of the monasteries proceeded did the two operations tend to become linked'.[3]

Most of the shrines were destroyed between 1536 and 1540, beginning with the preliminary visitations of the abbeys. The royal agents making these inspections were eager to secure the shrines' treasures. When Dr Layton visited Christ Church cathedral priory on 25 October 1535 a fire in his lodgings caused him to take exceptional measures to protect the shrine from theft in the confusion, including tethering ferocious bandogs in the feretory chapel.[4] Shrines in abbeys were plundered along with most other monastic goods, and indeed sometimes earlier.

---

1   For some of the later attacks see those made by Latimer in 1534, John Bale in 1536 and Wilfrid Holme in 1537: *Three Chapters of Letters Relating to the Suppression*, p. 8; M. Aston, *Lollards and Reformers: Images and Literacy in Late Medieval Religion* (London, 1984), p. 235; A.G. Dickens, *Lollards and Protestants in the Diocese of York, 1509–1558* (London, 1982), pp. 114–25.

2   G.H. Cook, *Letters to Cromwell on the Suppression of the Monasteries* (London, 1965), p. 198.

3   G.W.O. Woodward, *The Dissolution of the Monasteries* (London, 1966), p. 53. 'The monastic visitors of 1535–6 seem to have concentrated their attention almost exclusively upon sexual irregularities and the retention and veneration of relics of the saints': *ibid.*, p. 51.

4   As soon as he set men to firefighting, Layton wrote that he went into the church and there 'tarried continually, and set 4 monks with bandogs to keep the shrine'. The abbot of St

Special commissions were also created to destroy those shrines in secular churches. The order for the commission to Chichester declared that the shrines were to be 'raysd and deffaced even to the very ground'.[5] The agents arrived on 14 November, 1538, and carried out their task six days later. The commissioners were in no great hurry and proceeded about their task at a leisurely pace: the shrines at Lincoln were ordered to be torn down no less than a year and a half later than those at Chichester.[6] Most shrines were destroyed in a business-like manner, with payments to the workmen recorded in the accounts of secular cathedrals.[7] The calm with which the proceedings appear to have been carried out may be illusory, the result of fear preventing open opposition. In fact the royal agents must have encountered some local hostility. A letter of John Kyngysmyll to Wriothesley (one of the commissioners at Winchester) complained that he had the bishop of Winchester's malice and that of the priests' because he 'ffeett' away the jewels of St Swithun.[8] Effective opposition, however, was non-existent.

The shrines' relics, gold and jewels, and sometimes the feretra themselves, were usually conveyed to the treasury in the Tower of London. The plunder was great. The commission arriving at Bury St Edmunds in the summer of 1536 wrote back to Cromwell: 'Pleasith it your lordship to be advertysed, that we have ben at saynt Edmondes Bury, where we founde a riche shrine whiche was very comber-ace [cumbersome] to deface. We have taken in the seyd monastery in golde and sylver ml.ml.ml.ml.ml. [5000] markes, and above, over and besydes a well and riche cross with emereddes [emeralds], as also dyvers and sundry stones of great value.'[9] The shrines of York, Durham, Wenlock, Beverley and Ripon together yielded no less than 24,163¾ ounces of silver.[10]

Sometimes the monument itself was left until long after the relics and gold were removed. For example, the shrine of St Werburg at Chester may not have been finally destroyed until 1549.[11] The original shrine of Thomas Cantilupe, without relics or a golden feretrum, remains relatively untouched to this day. The relics themselves were treated in a variety of ways, a few reburied honourably, some

---

Augustine's was also sent for, to take the shrine to his house should the fire threaten it: Cook, *Letters to Cromwell*, p. 58.

[5] 'Early Statutes of Chichester', p. 176.

[6] Lincoln was dealt with on 6 June, 1540: *Monasticon Anglicanum*, vol. 6, pt 3, p. 1286.

[7] Those involved in the destruction of St Osmund's shrine (then less than forty years old) at Salisbury, for example, are recorded in SCA, MS 132, pp. 83–9. In particular, John Sylvester was paid 2s. 8d., for working eight days with John Somer 'circa demolicione scrinii sci Osmundi' (p. 88). Somer and a 'famulus' worked for another fifteen days for which they received 20s., part of which was for tools broken on the job (p. 89).

[8] 31 March 1539: *Letters and Papers of Henry VIII*, vol. 14, pt 1, pp. 246–7.

[9] Wright, *Three Chapters of Letters Relating to the Suppression*, p. 144.

[10] John Williams, *Account of the Monastic Treasures Confiscated at the Dissolution of the Various Houses in England*, ed. W.B.D.D. Turnbull (Edinburgh, 1836), pp. 32–3.

[11] R.V.H. Burne, *Chester Cathedral, from its Founding by Henry VIII to the Accession of Queen Victoria* (London, 1958), p. 35.

sent to London, and others destroyed.[12] Seventeenth-century traditions and testimonials swore that the relics of St Thomas of Hereford were removed from the
shrine and kept hidden in the homes of Catholics, once even being carried in a
nocturnal procession through the streets in a successful seventeenth-century
attempt to avert a plague.[13] Some of the relics of St Chad were saved by a Lichfield
prebendary, four bones eventually making their way to Birmingham cathedral
where they are once again enshrined.[14] Edward the Confessor's body received the
kindest treatment of all English saints, being carefully reburied and then replaced
in his shrine during the reign of Queen Mary.

The ultimate demise of the cult of relics and shrines in England predisposes the
historian to look for its flaws and weaknesses. However, pilgrimage to shrines was
popular when the Normans arrived in England and remained so well into the
fifteenth century: at least a sizeable minority of the population remained devoted
to the worship of the saintly dead to the very end. Bishop Bothe, for example, was
inspired to bequeath several gifts to ornament the shrine of St Thomas of Hereford
in 1535, the same year that Dr Layton was inspecting Canterbury with a view to
pulling its shrine down.[15] Shrines underwent periods of greater and lesser popularity, the latest upswing in devotion occurring after the Black Death in the later
fourteenth century. We have seen that, given the nature of the sources, it is
impossible to declare that the cult of shrines was in serious decline much before
1500, and indeed seems to have been stable throughout the fifteenth century.

Until near the end of the middle ages in England it is evident that shrines were
playing a significant, albeit not central, role in the life of the cathedral. Indeed, it
is probable that what decline existed was not because shrines in general were no
longer vital, but that the cathedrals that many of them were in no longer had a
monopoly on religious attraction. Much of the devotion formerly directed towards
saints' shrines in cathedrals was now given to those in smaller churches and to
Marian shrines. Without new construction and new saints in the greater churches
it is not surprising that the older sites yielded to the newer. Thus the changes that
are evident are likely the result of the transformation of the religious sentiment
that led to pilgrimage, not its death.

What can we conclude from the information presented in this book about the
importance of shrines to cathedrals? Certainly the acquisition and possession of

---

[12] The fate of Becket's relics has long been debated: see Mason, *Bones of St Thomas, passim*.

[13] For a full account of the evidence and the later history of St Thomas's bones, see I. Barrett,
'The Relics of St Thomas Cantilupe', in *St. Thomas Cantilupe, Bishop of Hereford: Essays
in his Honour*, ed. M. Jancey (Hereford, 1982), pp. 181–8. The relics were eventually
dispersed. The skull was discovered in 1881 in a cupboard of the church of Lamspring in
Germany and is now kept at Downside, while a shinbone once kept by the Jesuits at
Holywell is now at Stoneyhurst: Barrett, 'Relics of Cantilupe', pp. 183–4; Jancey, *St.
Thomas of Hereford*, p. 19.

[14] Hewitt, 'The "Keeper of Saint Chad's Head" in Lichfield Cathedral', pp. 73–8.

[15] Jancey, *St. Thomas of Hereford*, p. 18.

shrines was psychologically and spiritually important to the clergy. The effort to which they would go to obtain a canonisation and the resources they would devote to the translations of their patron saints prove this. The translation of a saint was, in fact, one of the high points of a church's history. In terms of craftsmanship, precious materials and aesthetic splendour the shrines themselves were the most impressive objects in the church and, arguably, in all of England. The structures provided a symbolic focus for a church, yet their influence stopped short of greatly affecting English ecclesiastical architecture as a whole. Greater churches shared the same designs whether they possessed shrines or not. In England there were shrines in churches, but not 'shrine-churches'; that is to say the shrine never dominated a cathedral.

The shrine's influence was felt much more keenly through the presence of pilgrims, who provided a source of funds and prestige as well as altering the daily life of the cathedral through their presence. This influence varied greatly depending on the shrine, year and season, yet most shrines at most times could attract thousands of additional visitors to their cathedral every year. At Canterbury, and even at second-rank shrines like those at Durham and Ely, pilgrims must have been a constant and powerful influence on the daily monastic life. The influence on secular churches was probably little less.

The management of pilgrims and the shrine often comprised an important part of the cathedral bureaucracy and finances. However, as with the cathedral's architecture, the shrine was incorporated in the church's administrative structure with little overall disruption. The most concrete influence of a shrine was the revenue from offerings. Until at least the mid-fifteenth century these offerings were considerable and shrines in general were profitable. Only in the fifteenth century did the costs of canonisation perhaps begin to outweigh the potential benefits. Certainly, considering events that occurred only forty years later, the canonisation of St Osmund and the construction of his shrine at the end of the fifteenth century can be seen as a disastrous investment for Salisbury cathedral. Yet this is only with the benefit of hindsight, and the late fifteenth-century clergy of that cathedral obviously considered St Osmund's shrine a worthwhile project whether their motives were religious or financial. They were unable to predict the disappearance of shrines and expected theirs to last for centuries to come, and they can hardly be blamed for this since shrines in general were a valuable spiritual and economic resource almost to the 1530s.

Some of the above themes, at times too briefly, have been discussed in this book. However, there are many other aspects of the cult of shrines that could benefit from further exploration. In particular, the shrine as a work of art, the behaviour of pilgrims as recorded in *miracula* and other sources, and the destruction of the shrines and the influences leading up to their disappearance call for detailed studies of their own. It is hoped, however, that the present work provides an adequate overview of cathedral shrines and their operation, and can act as a platform from which other studies can proceed. The subject certainly merits such study, since the activity surrounding shrines is a fascinating window into medieval culture. It is one of the areas where the medieval world was markedly different from our own, so much so that understanding can be difficult. These very areas are exactly those that need to be rescued from the ghetto of strangness and absurdity in which they are too often placed, and whence they are only brought out for amusement and comic relief. They need to be treated with respect, for otherwise understanding will forever elude us.

Plates

Plate 1. The tomb of St Osmund. Now in the south nave arcade of Salisbury cathedral, the tomb was originally in the Lady Chapel.

Plate 2. Becket's tomb. One of the stained glass windows in the Trinity Chapel aisles, Canterbury. A pilgrim gives thanks at the tomb of St Thomas Becket, clearly showing the two oval foramina.

Plate 3. The tomb of St Edward the Confessor. An illustration from 'La Estoire de Seint Aedward le Rei', CUL, MS Ee.3.59, f. 30. Pilgrims crawl in and out of the foramina. By permission of the Syndics of Cambridge University Library.

Plate 4. The Trinity Chapel, Canterbury. The site of the shrine of St Thomas Becket still retains much of the beautiful mosaic floor. A lone candle signifies the fact that St Thomas's cult is not quite extinct. This view plainly shows the wear in the stones which surround the area once covered by the dais of the shrine.

Plate 5. The feretory chapel of St Richard, Chichester. The modern
embellishments of the chapel, such as the altar and lectern, are very different from
what the original appearance must have been. However, the platform survives
though reduced in size, and the height of the modern reredos, concealed by the
flamboyant tapestry, gives an impression of the medieval barrier cutting this area
off from the high altar. The cult of St Richard still flourishes in a small way,
represented by candles and the sale of cards bearing a prayer composed by the saint.

Plate 6. The shrine of St Hugh's Head. This is the surviving base, in the north east corner of the Angel Choir, Lincoln cathedral, which once supported Hugh's head reliquary. A twentieth-century sculpture has been added to it, which is partly shown in this photograph.

Plate 7. The western Angel Choir, Lincoln cathedral. This is the original site of the shrine of St Hugh, now crowded with monuments. The dark stone table to the far right marks the spot where Bishop Sanderson saw the irons which were presumed to be the site of the shrine. The reredos is modern, but in the same position as its medieval counterpart.

Plate 8. The tomb of King John. In the middle of Worcester cathedral's choir, St Wulfstan's shrine was probably to the north (left) and St Oswald's to the south (right).

Plate 9. The Winchester retrochoir, looking west. A modern catafalque stands over the site of St Swithun's shrine from 1476 to 1539. Note the two huge chantry chapels of Bishops Beaufort and Waynflete, the Holy Hole, the small screen blocking off the area of the feretory chapel, and the back of the great reredos looming in the distance.

Plate 10. The Lady Chapel, Lichfield cathedral, looking east. A probable site for the shrine of St Chad is marked by modern ironwork.

Plate 11. The Great Screen at Winchester. The mighty reredos, erected at the end of the fifteenth century, almost obscures the east window beyond.

Plate 12. A view through the choir screen, Canterbury. This view is taken from very near the steps up to the choir, about where the medieval rood screen would have been. It illustrates how the height of the stairs can impede the sighting of objects in the distance. One of the tourists in the photo, of whose body only the head and shoulders can be seen, is actually in the nearer part of the choir. Those further back are invisible. It also shows the impressive height of the screen. Note that the near altar is off-centre.

Plate 13. The Arundel Screen, Chichester. A much more open choir screen, although originally the arches were probably filled with altars and may have been blocked.

Plate 14. The Martyrdom, Canterbury cathedral. The site of Becket's death and later a 'subshrine' to St Thomas. Although the altar is very modern, it is in the same position as the medieval altar where pilgrims offered to the sword's point. This view also shows the stairs by which pilgrims ascended to the choir aisles or descended to the crypt.

Plate 15. The Holy Hole, Winchester. The doorway set into the east face of the feretory platform.

Plate 16. Reliquary chests on the screen around the choir, Winchester.

Tables

Table 1. The Saints

Church/Saint	Death	Canonised	Translations
Canterbury (Christ Church)			
Dunstan	988	Traditional	1180, 1508
Thomas	1170	1173	1220
Alphege	1012	Traditional	1023, 1180
Anselm	1109	1494	(1124)
Wilfrid	709	Traditional	948, late 11thc., late 12thc.
Chichester			
Richard	1253	1262	1276
Ely			
Etheldreda	679	Traditional	695, 1106, 1252
Sexburga, (etc.)	c.700	Traditional	1102, 1252
Durham			
Cuthbert	687	Traditional	698, 999, 1104, 1380
Hereford			
Thomas	1282	1320	(1287), 1320 (?), 1349
Lichfield			
Chad	672	Traditional	1148, 1296
Lincoln			
Hugh	1200	1220	1220(?), 1280
Little Hugh	1255	Unofficial	
London			
Erkenwald	693/4	Traditional	1140, 1148, 1326
Norwich			
William	1137	Unofficial	1151, 1278
Rochester			
Paulinus	644	Traditional	late 11thc.
William	1201	1256	
Salisbury			
Osmund	1099	1457	1456
Winchester			
Swithun	863	Traditional	971, 1093, 1150, 1476
Aethelwald	984		1111, 1148
Worcester			
Oswald	992?		1002, c.1086
Wulfstan	1095	1203	1196–8, 1218
York			
William	1154	1227	1224(?), 1283, 1470(?)

Some saints in abbeys and collegiate churches

Church/Saint	Death	Canonised	Translations
Beverley			
John	721	Traditional	1197
Bury St Edmunds			
Edmund	869	Traditional	1095/1198, 1292
Canterbury (St Augustines)			
Augustine	c.604	Traditional	613, 1091, c.1300
St Albans			
Alban	c.300	Traditional	793, 1129
Amphibalus	c.300	Traditional	1177
Tynemouth			
Oswin	651	Traditional	1065, 1103, 1110, 1190s
Westminster			
Edward	1066	1161	1163, 1269

Offerings to Shrines. The following tables document receipts at shrines and other places of interest. If a date is uncertain, it is followed by a question mark. If an account covers a period less than eleven months or more than thirteen then that year is followed by an asterisk (e.g. 1410*) and is not included in the graphing data. If the period of the account cannot be known then it is assumed to be a full year, but the year in question is followed by a swung dash (e.g. 1410~).

Table 2. St Thomas Becket: oblations to the four stations connected with the cult of St Thomas at Canterbury

Treasurers' accounts

Year	Shrine			Corona			Martyrdom			Tomb		
	£	s.	d.	£	s.	d.	£	s.	d.	£	s.	d.
1198/9				40			33	6	8	455		
1199/1200				35			25			315	3	
1200/1				62			44			431		
1201/2				50			35			355	10	
1202/3				33	11		20			237	8	
1203/4				27			14			180		
1205/6				30			15			230		
1206/7				16	10		27	5	6	320		
1213*							5	10		60	17	
1213/14							31	5		300		
1214/15							20	16		72	16	6
1215/16							10	11		65	13	9

Year	Shrine			Corona			Martyrdom			Tomb		
	£	s.	d.	£	s.	d.	£	s.	d.	£	s.	d.
1216/17							12	5	2	97	13	
1217/18							21	9		212	12	
1218/19							12	8	7	186	11	
1219/20	702	11					93		2	275	9	
1220/1	429	8		71	10					31	3	3
1221/2	478	10		80	10		40	5	6	34	18	6
1222/3	505	1					40	4		32	16	
1223/4	420						29	1		25	7	6
1224/5	236	8					15			11		
1225/6	330						21	8		13	16	9
1226/7	256						13	12	3	7	6	2
1227/8	287	10		19	17		16			7	2	
1228/9	271	5		29	12		15			6	11	6
1229/30	200			50	11		10			4	3	2
1230/1	207	13		37	6	8	12			5	1	
1231/2	253			50			18			11	17	12
1232/3	212			35			14	10		11	15	
1233/4	127			24	5		8			6		2
1234/5	149	5		34			15	1s		10	12	
1235/6	228	10		40	7		16			11	4	
1236/7	182			36	3	6	14			11	1	
1237/8	127	3	4	26	2		10	10		9	10	
1238/9	132	6		27			10	11		9		
1239/40	114			25			9			8		
1240/1	130			28			3	14		8		
1241/2	122	10		25	14		8	1	6d	6	17	3
1242/3	125			26	5		7	10		6	13	4
1243/4	137	17		31	5		11	17		10		
1244/5	146	14		32			14			8	10	
1245/6	147	10		32	10		13	5		11		
1246/7	88			25			13			6	5	
1247/8	131	7		26	10		10	2		5		
1248/9	100	13		20	2		5	9		5	3	
1249/50	75			21			6	3		4		
1250/1	90	14		30			6	4	6	6		
1251/2	70			37			9	4		9	10	
1252/3	57	15		21	3		9	10		5	7	6
1253/4	92	2		27	1		102			7	10	
1254/5	100			34			10	6		6	1	
1255/6	80	1	8	24	10		9	10		3	10	
1257/8	46			18	10		5	10		1	8	3
1258/9	65			19			7			2	10	

Year	Shrine			Corona			Martyrdom			Tomb		
	£	s.	d.	£	s.	d.	£	s.	d.	£	s.	d.
1259/60	55			16	4		6	17		3	1	
1261/2	60	12		20	10		9	5		5		
1262/3	48	5		20			10			5		
1263/4	76			19			11	15		4	15	
1265/6	60			21	10		7	12		4		6
1266/7	71	5		26			7	5		3	15	
1267/8	93			40			11	10		9		
1268/9	92	12		30			12	14		6	10	
1269/70	100	12		32			11			7	14	
1270/1	70			30			9	13		4	10	
1271/2	71			34			5			2	5	6
1272/3	106	13		37	3		10			4		
1273/4	120			47	5		10			9	3	
1274/5	130			21	17		9			7		
1275/6	111	1s		38	3		7	8		6	17	
1276/7	100	10s		40			7	15	3	5		
1277/8	104			40			9	14		6	6	
1278/9	150			45			13			11	13	
1279/80	160			28			11			6		
1280/1	123	16		30			7			2	11	
1281/2	101	12		26			6			1	10	
1282/3	101			30			8			4	14	
1284/5	165			47			13	10		6	15	
1285/6	180			50	2	6	14			6		
1286/7	174			50	5		13			5	12	
1287/8	210			60			12			6	10	
1288/9	232			51			10	19		8		
1289/90	233	6	8	55			9	14		8		
1290/1	190			48	2		9	10		8		
1291/2	200			44			10			8		
1292/3	200			45			12			8		
1293/4	140			31			7	13	6	7	10	
1294/5	154			32			6	6		5		
1295/6	170			17			10			4		
1296/7	233	7s		35			12			5		
1297/8	250			40			14			5		
1298/9	260			50			14			9		
1299/1300	£260			28			10			8		
1300/1	231			28			7			8		
1301/2	210			32			8	5s	6d	8		
1302/3	210			33			10			8		
1303/4	216			29			8			7	10	

Year	Shrine			Corona			Martyrdom			Tomb		
	£	s.	d.	£	s.	d.	£	s.	d.	£	s.	d.
1304/5	220			30	5		9			7	10	
1305/6	230			40			11			8		
1306/7	220			40			15			8		
1307/8	220			37			15			7	10	
1308/9	260			45			14			9		
1309/10	300			40			12			12		
1310/11	300			50			12	12		12		
1311/12	320			50			12			9		
1312/13	360			50			12			10		
1313/14	360			35			10			9		
1314/15	380			45			10			9		
1315/16	200			15			1			3		
1316/17	250			16			4			3		
1317/18	460			37			5			7		
1318/19	470			47			7			7		
1319/20	500			50			9			12		
1320/1	430			32			8			6		
1321/2	220			10								
1322/3	370			23			5			40		
1323/4	460			37			8			9		
1324/5	310			36			5			7		
1325/6	350			28	4		7			7		
1326/7	390			20			3			9		
1327/8	350			20			5			7		
1328/9	320			20			3			6		
1329/30	300			20			4	10		5		
1330/1	320			24	2	1	4	6	8	10		
1331/2	330			20	2		4			9		
1332/3	323			23	8		9			8	10	
1333/4	330			32	15		11			5		
1334/5	300			30						4	11	2
1335/6	400			30			10			7		
1336/7	330			26			9			5	10	
1350/1	667			60			10			14		
1351/2	526			25			6	10		5	17	8
1370/1	466			73			27			20		
1371/2	501			62			10			6	13	4
1372/3	500			55			14			5	10	2
1373/4	340			60			13			3		
1374/5	381			62			15	5		6	14	
1375/6	440			70			12			7	7	6
1376/7	550			70			13	17	7	7		

Year	Shrine			Corona			Martyrdom			Tomb		
	£	s.	d.	£	s.	d.	£	s.	d.	£	s.	d.
1377/8	478			56			14			1	13	4
1378/9	403			65			9	10		4	10	
1379/80	352			54			14					
1380/1	350			56			9			2	11	4
1381/2	295			34			3	10				
1382/3	307			40			11					
1383/4	347			61			7	13	4			
1384/5	332			30			7	4				

Priors' accounts

Year	Shrine			Corona			Martyrdom			Tomb		
1396/7~	386	17	?	75	7		13			6		
1410/1	221	15		33	6	8		10		2		
1411*	120			4				6	8	2	13	4
1419/20	360			150			37			23		
1436/7	30	15		20						2		
1437?	Heavily damaged											
1444?	10			12								
1445/6	19	8	5	17	6	8						
1446/7	15			22								
1447/8	30			28								
1448/9	6	13		19	10							
1449/50	13	6	8	19	18	4						
1453/4	3			20								
1455?	(20s.)			10								
1455/6	1	6	8	18								
1467/8~				1	3							
1472/3	1	6	8	6	13	4						
1473/4				7								

The feretrarian account

Year	Shrine		
1397/8	249	19	7

Table 3. The Ely Sacrists' Rolls: offerings at Ely

Roll	Date	Etheldreda £	s.	d.	Great Cross £	s.	d.	Font Cross £	s.	d.	St Mary's £	s.	d.	Fetters £	s.	d.
1	1291/2				11	16	1	6	7		10	15	4			
2	1302/3	11			21	4	8	9	5	4	7	1	4			
3	1322/3	21			6			5			6	12	2	1	10	1
4	1323/4	34			13	12		5	15	10	7	7	3	2		
6	1334/5	31	4	5	16	5		3			9	16		2	11	
7	1336/7	26			15	6		2	14		12		12	3	18	4
8	1339/40	27	2		15	10		2	13	9	10	10		3	18	
9	1341/2	32	1		19	1	8	1	17		15	2	10		?	
10	1345/6	35	13	4	20	17	8	1	10	7	10	14		3		2
11	1351/2	39	14	8	7	13		2	3		7	5		4	1	
12	1352/3	41			5	19		2	12		4			3	3	
13	1354/5	41	2	6	4	12	11	2	11		5	2	5	3	2	
14	1357/8	40	2		5	2	10	2	2		5	15	4	3	14	4
15	1359/60	37	18	8	6	4	5	2			5		11	3	6	
16	1368/9	46	6		20	5	1	1	8	2	7	4		3	1	
18	1371/2	41	4		6	11	10	1	5	10	3			3	6	11
19	1374/5	50	6		16	10		1	6		6	1	8	2	16	
20	1386/7	86	19	3												
21	?	56	7	8												
25	1407/8				10	16	3	1		4	3	16	2			
26	1408/9	94	9	10	9	6	4	1	3		6	10	7			
30	1419/20	87	15	8		?		1	10		4		12			
32	1438/9	64	15		8			1			4	9	5			
34	1458/9	43	15	10	3	2		1			2	13	10			
35	1477/8	39	9	4	12	19	8					?				
36	1478/9	43	5			6	8									
37	1483/4?	31	15			10					6	6	8			
38	1485/6	36	9	8												
40	1487/8	34	9	8		7										
41	1494/5	36	4			6	8									
43	1509/10	39	2	8		2	5	5	18	1						
44	1516/17	36	17	8		1	4	4	7	3						
33	1535/6	4	13	8	7	18	7									

Note: The left hand column refers to the number of the Sacrist Roll. Sums are rounded to the nearest penny for the sake of space. The fetters are combined with the Cross at the Font in rolls 25 and 26.

Table 4. The Ely Feretrars' Rolls: oblations to the relics and receipts from sales of wax, indulgences and silk.

No.	Year	Feretrarius	Oblations			Wax sales			From the indulg.			Silk		
			£	s.	d.	£	s.	d.	£	s.	d.	£	s.	d.
1r	1420/1	John Yaxham	2	12	0½			7	10					
1v	1421/2	John Yaxham	13	5	3	1	1	4	7	6	8			
2	1422/3	John Yaxham	14	10	7½	2	14	8	6	1	5			
3	1423/4	John Yaxham	15		9	2	18		8	8	10			
4r	1424/5	John Yaxham	16	18	3	2	2	4	7	17	6			
4v	1425/6	John Yaxham	16	18	8½	2	8	8	6	17	6			
5r	1426/7	John Yaxham	14	14	5	2	7	4	7	1				
5v	1427/8	John Yaxham	14	19	3	2		8	6	5	4			
	1428/9	John Yaxham	11		6½	1	3	1	7	12	9			
7i	1464/5	William Tylney	8	8	6									
7ii	1465/6	William Tylney	7	18	10									
7iii	1466/7	William Tylney	8	11	4									
7iv	1467/8	William Tylney	8		6									
7vi	1469/70	William Tylney	7	11	2									
7vii	1470/1	William Tylney	8	10	2									
7viii	1471/2	William Tylney	8	3										
7ix	1472/3	William Tylney	9	13	5									
7x	1474/5	William Tylney	8	2										
7xi	1475/6	William Tylney	5	18	3		7	6				3	19	
7xii	1476/7	William Tylney	10	1	4				1	12	11			
8	1490/1	Thomas Denuca	7	6	1	1	10		1	10	6	12	17	
10r	1497/8	William Cotnam	4	3	1½				3	4	5¾	12	20	
10v	1498/9	William Cotnam	5		9½				2	3	0½	10		4

Note: Oblations includes wax sold and the profit from silk in those years when they are not listed seperately. 'Indulg.' is that money, from oblations, wax and silk, from all shrines in the period of the indulgence.

Table 4a. Oblations by Time of Year: the Ely feretrars' rolls 1464–77

Year	Mich. to Fair		to Christmas			to Easter		to Nat. St John			toTemp. indulg.		
	s.	d.	£	s.	d.	s.	d.	£	s.	d.	£	s.	d.
1464/5	5		6			3	6	1	2			18	
1465/6	4	6	5	10		3	4	1	5			16	
1466/7	4	10	5	16	10	3	8	1	6		1		
1467/8	3	10	5	13	4	3	8	1		10		18	10
1468/9	4	5½	6			3	6	1	6	10		18	10
1469/7	3	2	5			4		1	5			18	10
1470/1	4	10	6			3	10	1	2			19	6
1471/2	4	8	5	10		3	10	1	5	6		19	
1472/3	4	8	7			3	10	1	6			18	11
1474/5	4	11	5			5	6	1	9			18	10
1476/7	5	10	7			5	6	1	10	1	1		?

Note: The five terms are for Michaelmas to the time of the Fair, from the Fair to Christmas, from Christmas to Easter, from Easter to the Nativity of St John the Baptist, and from the feast of St John to the time of the indulgence.

Table 5. The Norwich Sacrists' Rolls: oblations to St William,
the High Altar and elsewhere

Year	High altar			St William			Trunk of Walter			Relics			Cross	
	£	s.	d.	£	s.	d.	£	s.	d.	£	s.	d.	s.	d.
1272/3	13		8½											
1273/4	16	4												
1275/6	21	3	4[1]											
1278/9	26	10												
1283/4	35	12	9				2	4					36	6
1288/9	40	4					4	16	7½	3	4		46	1½
1290/1	37	5	6[2]											
1292/3	32	10					3	10		6			60	
1296/7	35	2	7½				4	18	6¾	6	9	8½	62	0½
1299/														
1300	47	4	5¾d				2	18	3	9	14	6	110	6¾
1300/1	43	16	7				2	16	5	8	16	7	137	2¾
1304/5	45	10	7½			9	3	3	3	10	10	6	188	5½
1306/7	42	3	2				2	10	10	10		3	153	6½
1313/14	41	10	4	21		5½	1	13	1½	14	13	4	252	2
1319/20	41	19		12	1		2	1	5	24	3		251	5
1321/2	29	3	7							5		3	166	3

[1] The high altar here includes the offerings to St William, as do the offerings to 1301.
[2] Includes income from churches in Norfolk and Suffolk.

Year	High altar			St William			Trunk of Walter			Relics			Cross	
	£	s.	d.	£	s.	d.	£	s.	d.	£	s.	d.	s.	d.
1322/3	23	4	10		1	12¼[3]	1	2	9½	16	11	11	185	4
1324/5	46	3	1		18	5[4]		19	3	16	9	10	139	9½
1328/9	35	17	7		16	5½		10	10¼	12	4	7	103	2
1330/1	25	4	11		15	2¾[5]		11	1½	13	6	5	122	6
1332/3	26	1	1		13	8¼		8	6	14	14	9	168	3
1333/4	31	9	10		14	0½		6	4¾	16	15	9	187	5
1334/5	24	18			15	11½		6	6½	11	4	9	124	6
1335/6	24	18	3		17	8¼		7	1¼	11	19	9	156	0½
1339/40	21	17	10		25	7¼[6]		5	10¾	9	8	8	139	
1340/1	21		5			5¾[7]		4	5	8	19	10	377	5
1342/3	21	18	2¼			4		4	5	9		2¾	292	2½
1363/4	54	7	1¾			2			9¾	7	8	2¾	439	7
1366/7	49	17	8						3	5	4	0¼	458	0¼
1368/9	49	13	8		4	0¾			3	7	8	7¼	340	4½
1385/6	31	1	6		393	6½				2	3	6	121	6¾
1389/90	41	17	4¼		236	6¼			6¾	4		3	127	5¼
1390/1	51	9	9		275	6½			4½	3		11	76	3½
1393/4	62	6	10		182	3¾				2	13	6	58	3
1395/6	62	7			154	8				2		4	45	0½
1399/														
1400	40	12			98	3½					19	4	70	10½
1400/1	57	17	7		19	8				1	8	1		
1401/2	62	7	3		110	9d				1	15	7	45	11
1403/4	77	17	8¼		97	6d			1½	2	7	2	52	3
1404/5	73	19	6½		87	3¼			1	1	19	6½	42	9
1405/6	78	10	2		92				1½	1	19		50	2
1406/7	98	3	7		66				4	2	2	1½	42	1½
1411/12	88	1	3¾		29	1			2½	1	4	4½	43	2½
1414/15	71	15	6		22	10							56	8
1417/18	60	15	3½		15	10				2	9	6½	49	6½
1419/20	81	4	2½		29						16	3	58	9½[8]
1420/1	58	19	11		14	4½				1	7	6	37	10
1422/3	78				16	11				3	11		42	3
1424/5	88	4	11		9	3½				1	8	6	14	8
1425/6	86	5	8		6					1	9		9	
1426/7	74	16	5		7	6½				1	2	11	16	8

3   Income is combined with that to the new cross.
4   Income also combined with that to St Stephan and St Ypolito.
5   Income also combined with that of St Anne.
6   Now just called pixidibus.
7   Money to St William only, from here onwards.
8   With other chests.

Year	High altar			St William			Trunk of Walter			Relics			Cross	
	£	s.	d.	£	s.	d.	£	s.	d.	£	s.	d.	s.	d.
1427/8	65	12	4		6	9				1	3	2	13	3
1428/9	67	15	1		7	2				1	5		14	4
1429/30	62	6	1½		9	0½				1	18	2½	5	8½
1430/1	66		7		5	1½				1	14	8	4	2
1431/2	60	1	1		4	9½					15	9½	13	9½
1432/3	68	9	9		6	10¼				1	14	4	9	2
1433/4	68	18	9		4	6				1	2	5	10	7
1434/5	58	6	0½		4	4								
1438/9	51	15	5		4	5½					15	8	6	4
1439/40	61	3	3		7	6				1		11¼	7	10¾
1440/1	54	6	5½		2	7				1		6½	2	10½
1441/2	54	6	8		1	9¼					11	9	2	5½
1451/2	33	14	3								11	2½	32[9]	
1452/3	36	2	4							2	16	7½	38	5
1454/5	49	7								4	3		49	7
1456/7	35	3	4							2	17	6	46	3
1457/8	35	3	4							2	2	8½	34	1
1459/60	29	10								2	5	8	27	10
1461/2	26	7	8		5	7½					16	2½	30	
1464/5	21	7	2¼			9					13		8	11
1465/6	23	16	7			9					9	9	12	6
1468/9	21	1	3								17	0¾	10	2
1469/70	16	11	6¼								16	6	8	6¾
1471/2	24	15	5½								11	6¼		
1473/4	19	7								1	11			
1474/5	21	5	7¼								13	1		
1477/8	17	17	4								6	9¼		
1481/2	20	9	5½								9	3		
1483/4	20	8	4½								13	10		
1484/5	19	16	8¼								13	0½		
1485/6	16	10	5½							1	5	4		
1486/7	18	16	9½							1	13	5		
1487/8	15	13	1½							1	12	8½		
1491/2	8	15	8								15	6		
1492/3	12	1	6½								11	10		
1493/4	15		6½								15	10		
1494/5	16	16	8								17	2		
1504/5	13	14	9	1	8						14	3d	7	
1505/6	15	10	2	1	0½					1		8d	5½	
1510/11	13	16	6½	2							18	6		

[9] With other chests.

Year	High altar £	s.	d.	St William £	s.	d.	Trunk of Walter £	s.	d.	Relics £	s.	d.	Cross s.	d.
1511/12	14	12	2								14	2½		4½
1513/14	17	4	6½							1		2½		17½
1515/16	17	8	1							1	3	5		22½
1517/8	16	8	9½							1	3	5½		13½
1518/9	14	4	8								17	11		
1521/2	16	19	0½								19	8½		12
1522/3	6	2	10[10]					17	1					
1525/6	8	16	0½					15	2½					
1528/9	12	15	9											
1529/30	12	12	8½				1	2	8					
1530/1	11	6	3				1		4					
1531/2	10	17	6					6	8½					
1534/5	5	8	5½					8	3½					
1535/6	4	15	3					1	8½					

10 This and the next entry do not include money already diverted to the subsacrist.

Table 6. The Hereford Clavigers' Accounts: income at St Thomas Cantilupe's shrine and other places

Year	Shrine £	s.	d.	Head £	s.	d.	Relics £	s.	d.	Wax £	s.	d.	Silver £	s.	d.	King Henry £	s.	d.
1478/9	21	14	2		19	8			5			2						
								(6	5)									
1490/1	13	16	4				(1		1½)	1	4	8		6	4	1	7	3
1505/6	11	16	10+			2		1	1		1	3					1	3
							(1	15	10+)									
1506/7	9	8	3					(14	8)				1	1	4		1	2
1507/8	9	18	8				(1	7	4)	1	5	1		4	8			5½
1508/9	13	10		1	5	3		15	7	1				2	6			7½
								(2	3)									
1512/13	11				10	8		5	4		19	6						
								(5	4)									
1522/3	5	16	10				(1	2	2)					18	7½		7	

Headings: Offerings to the shrine of St Thomas, to the Head (ad capud St Thome), to the relics, wax sold, broken silver sold and offerings to the pyx of King Henry.

Note: The entries followed by a plus sign (+) indicate that the figure is the minimum legible, the 1505/6 account having been damaged somewhat in the receipts section. The figures in brackets are the total of the terms when the offerings to the head of St Thomas and to the relics were combined in a single entry.

Table 7. *'Aperturæ' at Lincoln, offerings to the shrine of St Hugh*

Year	Pentecost			Trans. St Hugh			Year total		
	£	s.	d.	£	s.	d.	£	s.	d.
1334/5	15	18	11	12	12	6	28	11	5
1338/9				11	13	10			
1339/40	26	12	1						
1343/4	20			15	7	5	35	7	5
1345/6	18	12	8	11	2	6	29	15	2
1346/7	18	8		16	2	11	34	10	11
1347/8	16	7		12	5	8	28	12	8
1348/9	22			18	13	2	40	13	2
1349/50	33	3		12	6		45	9	
1350/1	32			13	8	0½	45	8	0½
1351/2	22			18	2	7	40	2	7
1352/3	25	6	3	15	4	8	40	10	11
1353/4	27			17	7	1	44	7	1
1354/5	27	11		16	11		44	2	
1355/6	30	1	8	16	3		46	4	8
1356/7	27	16		15	10		43	6	
1357/8	27	18	6	15	10	7	43	9	1
1358/9	27	6	8	14	16	8	42	3	4
1359/60	25			15			40		
1360/1				28	3				
1361/2	38		3	13	9	1½	51	9	4½
1362/3	21	4		13	9		34	13	
1363/4	40	13	4	26	10	2	67	3	6
1364/5	37	14	8						
1365/6	34	15	11	14	3	7	48	19	6
1366/7	37	10	8	20	11	7	58	2	3
1367/8	32	2	9	22	10		54	12	9
1368/9	22	4	4	27	8	4	49	12	8
1369/70	25	4	3	20	2	4	45	6	7
1370/1	30	10	4	23	13		54	3	4
1371/2	22	3	4	21			43	3	4
1372/3	33			18	13		51	13	
1373/4	31			22			53		
1374/5	30	6	8	22	10		52	16	8
1375/6	25	10		22	8		47	18	
1376/7	31	10		15			46	10	
1377/8	21	8		15	10	2	36	18	2
1378/9	19	16		14			33	16	
1379/80	18	10		15	13	4	34	3	4
1380/1	19	6	8	14	9	4	33	16	

Year	Pentecost			Trans. St Hugh			Year total		
	£	s.	d.	£	s.	d.	£	s.	d.
1381/2	19	5		13	7	8	32	12	8
1382/3	15	5		16	5		31	10	
1383/4	15	5		10	10	10	25	15	10
1384/5	14	1	11						
1385/6	14	5		11	10	3	25	15	3
1386/7	14						14		
1388/9				11	19				
1389/90	14	6	8	13	17		28	3	8
1390/1	13	15	8	12	18	2	26	13	10
1391/2	17	18	7	14	4	7	32	3	2
1392/3	13	12	8	14	6	7	27	19	3
1393/4	14	2	2	12	19	8	27	1	10
1394/5	12	4	4	13		9	25	5	1
1395/6	12	16	9	12	5	4	25	2	1
1396/7	13	15	1	11	16	9	25	11	10
1397/8	12	16	9	12	3	2	24	19	11
1398/9	9	8	7	10	2	10	19	11	5
1399/									
1400	13	17	4	8	3	9	22	1	1
1400/1	9	3	4½	6	13	7½	15	17	
1401/2	9	3		8	17	4	17		4
1402/3	10		11½	8	11	4	18	12	3½
1406/7	10	2		10	2	7	20	4	7
1407/8	10	13	9	9			19	13	9
1408/9	12	2	10	10	6	6	22	9	4
1409/10	9	14	8	10	2	10½	19	17	6½
1410/11	11	12		9			20	12	
1411/12	8	13	4	7	13	6	16	6	10
1412/13	8	13	4	8			16	13	4
1413/14	7	6	8	8	4	6	15	11	2
1414/15	7	9		9	9	1	16	18	1
1415/16	7	4	1½	6	12	4	13	16	5½
1416/17	7	15	1	9	2	2	16	17	3
1417/18	6	9	9½	11	2	8½	17	12	6
1418/19	7		7	9	1	9	16	2	4
1419/20	6	14	0½	11	4	11½	17	19	
1420/1	6		6½	11	7	8½	17	8	3
1421/2	6	5	4	11	10	3	17	15	7
1422/3	6	6		11		1½	17	6	1½
1423/4	6	13	4	11	4	2	17	17	6
1424/5	6	3	6	6	3	6	12	7	
1425/6	6	2	5	10		5½	16	2	11

Year	Pentecost			Trans. St Hugh			Year total		
	£	s.	d.	£	s.	d.	£	s.	d.
1426/7	6	15	5	11	6	4	18	1	9
1427/8	6	1		8	8	4	14	9	4
1428/9	6		1	9	14	10	15	14	11
1429/30	4	8	10	7	16	11	12	5	9
1430/1	9	18	5	8	2	4	17		9
1431/2	5	14	1	6	8	9	12	2	10
1432/3	5	7	4	6	18	4	12	5	8
1433/4	4		7	7	3	1½	11	3	8½
1434/5	4	2	2	6	12		10	14	2
1435/6	4			6	5	5	10	5	5
1436/7	4	2	1	7	6	8	11	8	9
1437/8	5	6	5	7	1	2	12	7	7
1438/9	3	2	8	3	14	11	6	17	7
1439/40	5	6	8	5	19	10	11	6	6
1440/1	7	6	8	6	9	8	13	16	4
1441/2	6	7	5	2	12	9	8		2
1442/3	10	1	6	4	8	6	14	10	
1443/4	7	4	10	5	9	11d	12	14	9
1444/5	7	18	4	18	14		26	12	4
1445/6	11	5	4	14	3	4d	25	8	8
1446/7	8	3	5½	11	8	8d	19	12	1½
1447/8	10	13	4						
1448/9	10	12	1						
1449/50	6	3	7	10	12		16	15	7
1450/1	10	13	5	7	17	7	18	11	
1451/2	8	12	9	8	9	6	17	2	3
1452/3	7	6	2	8	7	7	15	13	9
1453/4	6	18	11½	5		6½	11	19	6
1454/5	7	2	2	6	2	9½	13	4	11½
1455/6	4	19	4	7	3	2	12	2	6
1456/7	6	11	10	7		11	13	12	9
1457/8	5	11	2¼	5	11	2	11	2	4¼
1458/9	5	17	2½	8	6		14	3	2½
1459/60	5	16	4	5	14	2	11	10	6
1460/1	7	16	9	6	6	10	14	3	7
1461/2	8	4	6	5	7	4	13	11	10
1462/3	6		1	5	6	8	11	6	9
1464/5	5	3	5	6	19	2½	12	2	7½
1465/6	5	16	10	6	17	7	12	14	5
1463/4	6	11	10	7	18	4	14	10	2
1466/7	5	18	2	5	12	6	11	10	8
1467/8	7	6	5	7	1	4	14	7	9

Year	Pentecost			Trans. St Hugh			Year total		
	£	s.	d.	£	s.	d.	£	s.	d.
1468/9	4	19	1	4	19	1	9	18	2
1469/70				6	1	10½			
1470/1	6	13	6	5	8		12	1	6
1471/2	7		2¼	9	9	5½	16	9	7¾
1472/3	6	1		6	1	1	12	2	1
1473/4	6	1	3	3	10	2	9	11	5
1474/5	5		1½	6	11	6	11	11	7½
1475/6	4	13	9	7	17	3	12	11	
1476/7	9	19	3	14		3	23	19	6
1477/8	4	1	11	5	11		9	12	11
1478/9	5	10	3	4	4	10	9	15	1
1479/80	5	7	11	5	16	8	11	4	7
1480/1	3	11	2	4	8	0½	7	19	2½
1481/2	5	13	3	7	7	11	13	1	2
1482/3	3	19	3	6	2	4	10	1	7
1483/4	8	7		5	12	3	13	19	3
1484/5	3	19	2	5	7	7½	9	6	9½
1485/6	5	12		5	16		11	8	
1486/7	4	2	8	4	16	9	8	19	5
1487/8	3	17	10	6		4	9	18	2
1488/9	4	7	5	4	13	11	9	1	4
1489/90	4	1	8	4	19	7	9	1	3
1490/1	4	13	0½	3		3	7	13	3½
1491/2	3	6	1	4	3	6	7	9	7
1492/3	3	8	4	3	7	7	6	15	11
1493/4	3	19	3	4	16	2	8	15	5
1509/10		19	7½	11			11	19	7½
1510/11	4	8	8	4	13	5	9	2	1
1511/12	3	11	3	6	1	10½	9	13	1½
1512/13	4	9	7	4	1	4	8	10	11
1513/14	4	17	10	4	15		9	12	10
1514/15	2	12	5½	4	8	6	6		1
1515/16	2	12	2	6	8	7	8		9
1519/20	3	1	8	5	18	2	8	19	10
1520/1	2	2			18	7	2		7
1521/2	2	6	1	3	11	11	5	18	
1522/3	1	14	5	2	19	5	4	13	10
1523/4	1	11	1	2	1	8	3	12	9
1524/5	1	1	10	2	9	2	3	11	
1525/6	1	3	9	3	6	7½	4	10	4½
1526/7	2		8	1	15		3	15	8
1527/8	2		8	3	4	11	5	5	7

Year	Pentecost			Trans. St Hugh			Year total		
	£	s.	d.	£	s.	d.	£	s.	d.
1528/9	1	3		4	18	3	6	1	3
1529/30	2	12	9						
1530/1	1	8	8		3	4	1	12	
1531/2	2	3	5	4	2	1	6	5	6

Table 8. The Durham Feretrars' Accounts: the shrine of St Cuthbert

Year	Months	Pyx Income		
		£	s.	d.
1376	4	7	6	11
1376/7	12	34	6	10½
1377/8	13	36	7	3½
1378/9	12	38	4	4
1379/80	12	32	8	
1380/1	12	44	17	5½
1381/2	12	29		11
1382/3	12	28	5	1
1383/4	12	46		3½
1384/5	11	29	14	4
1385/6	12	63	17	8
1386/7	12	28		8½
1387	5	18	10	4½
7 months missing				
1388/9	12	37	4	6
1389/90	12	32	2	3
1391	3	16	2	11
69 months missing				
1397/8	12	27	8	7½
1398/9	12	28	12	5½
1399/1400	12	31	2	11
1400/1	12	56	5	7½
1401	5	13	10	0½
6 months missing				
1402/3	13	31		10
1403/4	12	28	11	2½
1404/5	18		Missing	
1405/6	12	31	13	11½
1406/7	12	30	16	7½
1407/8	12	25	2	10
1408/9	4	4	7	10½

Year	Months	Pyx Income		
		£	s.	d.
31 months missing				
1411/12	12	28	12	8½
1412/13	12	27	15	4½
1413/14	12	28	1	1
1414/15	12	26	7	9½
1415/16	12	24	6	6
1416/17	12	25	19	10½
1417/18	8	11	6	8½
1418/19	12	30		9½
1419/20	12	27	19	11
1420/1	12	23	7	4
1421/2	12	21	12	4
1422/3	12	20	5	6½
1423/4	12	33	4	7
1424/5	12	24	2	7
1425/6	12	21	2	6
1426/7	12	21	9	7
1427/8	12	22	12	11
1428/9	12	22	3	5
1429/30	12	25	17	11
1430/1	12	25	12	2
1431/2	12	22	13	4
1432/3	12	21	5	8
1433/4	12	16	13	5
1434/5	12	24	15	9
1435/6	12	25	13	3
1436/7	12	36	3	11
1437/8	12	19	12	7
1438/9	12	14	18	7½
1439/40	12	15	10	9
1440/1	12	22	15	5½
1441/2	12	20	16	2
1444/5	12	17	10	11½
1445/6	12	17	1	1
1446/7	12	21	5	9
1447/8	12	19	6	1
1448/9	12	23	1	1
1449/50	12	25	17	8
1450/1	12	20	3	10
1451/2	12	16	11	11
1452/3	12	12	4	6
1453/4	12	15	3	5

Year	Months	Pyx Income					
		£	s.	d.			
1454/5	12	14	12	4½			
1455/6	12	18	6	8	*Wharton's tomb*		
1456	3+3 wks	9	18	7	£	s.	d.
1456/7	12	18	15	9½	5	14	9½
1457/8	12	11	18	5	4	4	6
1458/9	12	13	3	2	5	2	
1459/60	12	15	5	5	4	9	3
1460/1	12	24	14	11½			
1480/1	12	24	12	3			
1488/9	12	4	19	9		16	6
1501/2	12	8	2	11½		13	4
					Nil, 'Because it did not have keys'		
1513/4	12	left blank				15	
1525/6	12	11	8	2		8	
1536/7	12	7	10	3		10	
1537/8	12	4	7	5½		12	

Table 9. *A Sample Receipt Indenture for the Shrine of St Cuthbert, 1375/6*

Date	Days	Receipt				Pence/day
		£	s.	d.		
Apr. 28	—		18	4		
Jun. 9	42		49	6		14.1
Jun. 18	9		120	10½		162.3
Jun. 28	10		57	3½		68.8
Jul. 18	20		25	4		15.2
Aug. 24	37		28	10		9.4
Sept. 4	11		200	½		218.2
Sept. 15	11		48	8½		53.1
Sept. 29	14		43	10		37.6
Oct. 27	28		44	7½		19.1
Dec. 6	40		23	5¼		7.0
Dec. 22	16		8	3¾		6.2
Jan. 20	29		26	2¼		10.8
Feb. 6	17		9	6		6.7
Mar. 16	39		18	7		5.7
Mar. 20	4		96	9		290.2
Apr. 11	22		15	1		8.2
Apr. 25	14		25	0		21.4
May 21	26		16	¼		7.4
Totals	389	43	17	1		27.1

Table 10. *Selected Sources of Offerings from the Sacrists' Rolls of Westminster Abbey*

The years 1318 and 1347 contain two offering sources: the Shrine of St Edward and the Relics, the latter including the Offerings to the High Altar. After 1355, the shrine is combined with the relics, and other sources come and go, including the Chapel of Mary at the North door, the Old Cross, The Chapel of St Mary 'le Pewe', and the 'New Pyx'.

Year	Shrine £	s.	d.	Relics + H.Altar £	s.	d.	£	s.	d.	£	s.	d.
1317/8	26	3	1	10		6						
1346/7	16	14		1	16	3						
	Shrine + Relics			*Mary, N door*								
1354/5	30	9	8	15	16							
1358/9	74	3		24	6							
1361/2	89	12								*Old cross*		
1364/5	73	1		10						5		
1370/1					32							
1372/3	103			12	16	7						
1373/4	94	10		12								
1374/5	91			12	3	6						
1377/8	77			7	3		*Mary le Pewe*					
1379/80	78			7	13		93					
1382/3	62			5			43	6				
1385/6	47			3		5	37	8		3	3	
1386/7	41			2	14	6	26	8		2		
1387/8	32			2	12	4	20	6				22
1388/9	37			2	4	11	22	5½				2½
1389/90	50			2	1	9	19	6½		3	1	
1390/1	47				37	0½	12	3		2		0¾
1391/2	46				26	1¼	14	1¼				21
1392/3	34				19	5½	10					16¼
1393/4	47				19	8¾	11	8½				20½
1394/5	30				9	5	9	9¾				9½
1395/6	40				3	2½	2	0½				5¼
1396/7	40				4		2	10½				13
1397/8	23				3	11½	3	3¾				12½
1399/ 1400	15											
1407/8	21											
1422/3	25	3	4	2	4		5					7
1423/4	18	3	4		15		5					6
1424/5	19				16		5					6
1425/6	18			2	6		5					6
1426/7	25	15		2	8		5					6
1427/8	23		4		16		5					6

Year	Shrine			Mary, N door			Mary le Pewe			Old cross		
	£	s.	d.	£	s.	d.	£	s.	d.	£	s.	d.
1428/9	17	13				15		5				6
1430/1	16	2				8		5				3
1431/2	9	11	5			8		5				4
1432/3	10	9				8		5				3
1433/4	6	19	10			6½		2				2½
1434/5	5	14	7½			4		2				1¼
1436/7	7					7½						2
1437/8						8¾						2¾
1438/9	4					9½		16				3
1440/1	7	6	8					5				
1444/5	7	9	8					5				3½
1445/6	11	11	8			8		5				5
1448/9	10	6	8			4		5				4
1449/50	5	4	18					5				
1450/1	11	13	4					5				
1451/2	10							5				
1452/3	10							5				
1453/4	12							5				
1455/6	10							5				
1456/7	9							5				
1457/8	9	6	8					5				
1458/9	8	4						5				
1459/60	5							5				
1462/3	7	5	10½					5				
1463/4	6	6	8					5				
1464/5	6	6	2					5				
1465/6	6	1	5					5				
1466/7	6	13	4					5				
1470/1	20							15				
1471/2	21							8	7			
1473/4	21	7						10				
1474/5	15	6	8					10	5			
1475/6	15	3						11	15			
1476/7	11	7	0½					39	0½			
1477/8	14	18						33	9½			
1478/9	6	17	6					33	15			
1481/2	9	13	4¼					76	11¾			
1483/4	11	3	4					45	7			
1484/5	8	3	4					20				
1485/6	16	6	8	*High altar*				21	4			
1486/7	6	13	10¾		20			11	10			
1487/8						8		13	9			

Year	Shrine			High altar			Mary le Pewe		
	£	s.	d.	£	s.	d.	£	s.	d.
1488/9	7	14	9					13	8
1489/90	7	16	5					18	0½
1490/1	4	17	9			12½		9	6
1492/3	6	13	5					9	11
1493/4	8	5	9					5	9
1495/6	9	3	4		15			19	
1496/7	9	5	2¾					9	2
1497/8	9	7	4½					6	3
1498/9	6		22½					4	4
1499/ 1500	4	12	7					4	6
1500/1	4	15	11					2	3
1501/2	7	13	2					2	1½
1503/4	10	6	9	New Pyx				5	2
1504/5	5	6	8			23		4	9
1505/6	5				23	7		17	10
1506/7	4	9	4		28	8		5	6
1507/8	6	13	5		20			5	6
1508/9	9	7	3					4	
1509/10	5	13	11					4	9½
1510/1								5	2½
1511/2					9	9		4	9
1512/3		46	4		11	7½		5	8
1513/4	4	12	5½		9	4½		4	7½
1514/5	4	12	5½		9	4½		4	7½
1515/6		21	4		8	10½		2	3½
1516/7		7	4		20				5
1517/8					19				
1518/9		26	6		14	7½			7¼
1519/20	4	8	8		22	9¾			5
1520/1		20	3½		20	10¾			8
1521/2					19	6			6
1522/3					20	6			14½
1523/4					18				5½
1524/5						14			1
1525/6						18		2	2
				Mary, N door					
1526/7					11	6			4
1527/8					13				5½
1528/9					10	2			5
1529/30					8	5			8
1531/2					9	3¾			14½

Graphs

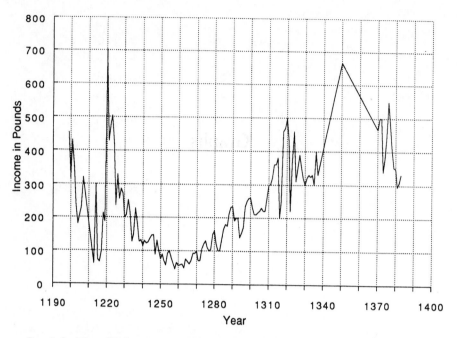

Graph 1. The offerings to the tomb of St Thomas at Canterbury to 1220, and to the shrine from 1220, from table 2.

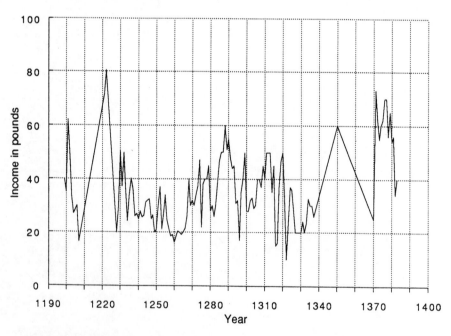

Graph 2. Income to the Corona, Canterbury, from table 2.

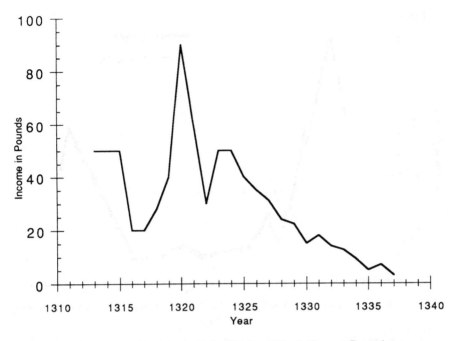

Graph 3. Offerings to the tomb of Archbishop Winchelsey at Canterbury cathedral.

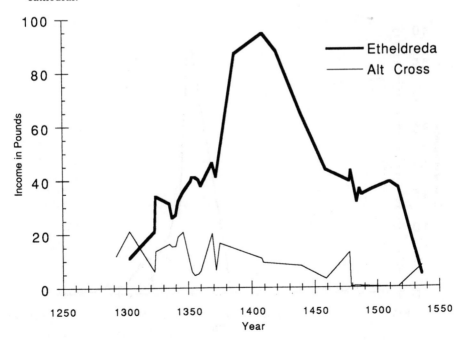

Graph 4. The receipts at the shrine of St Etheldreda and at the Great ('alta') Cross in Ely cathedral, from table 3.

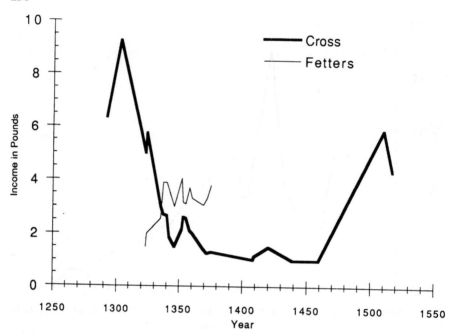

Graph 5. Receipts at the Cross at the Fountain and the Fetters (*boiis*), two devotional stations in Ely cathedral, from table 3.

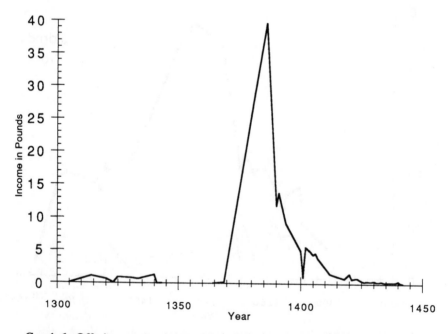

Graph 6. Offerings to the shrine of St William, Norwich cathedral, based on table 5.

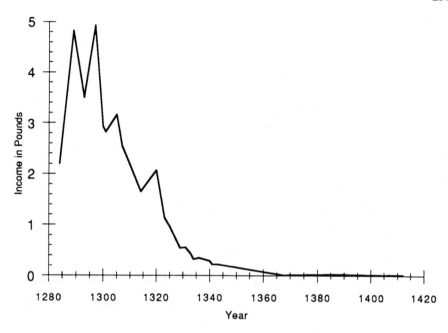

Graph 7. Offerings to the chest at the tomb of Bishop Walter (*trunco Walteri*), Norwich cathedral, from table 5.

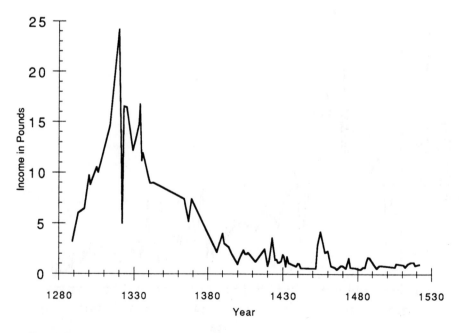

Graph 8. Graph of offerings to the relics at Norwich cathedral, from the sacrists' rolls.

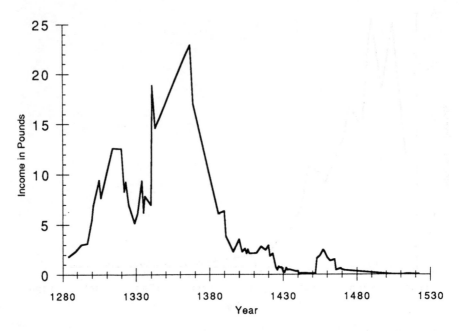

Graph 9. Offerings to the Cross at Norwich cathedral, from the sacrists' rolls.

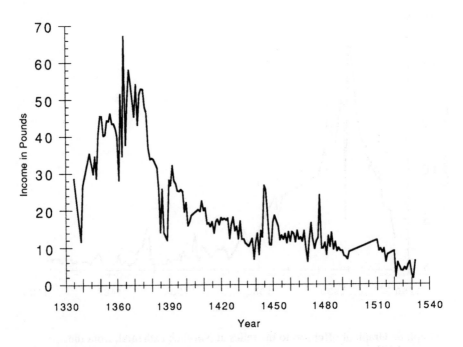

Graph 10. Offerings at the shrine of St Hugh, Lincoln, based on table 7.

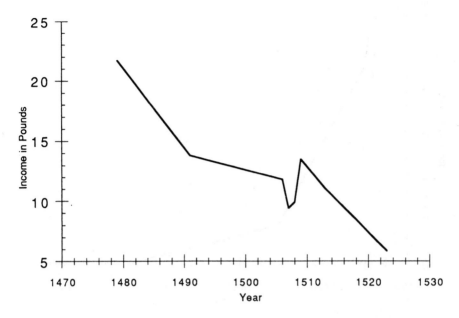

Graph 11. Offerings to the shrine of St Thomas at Hereford, based on table 6.

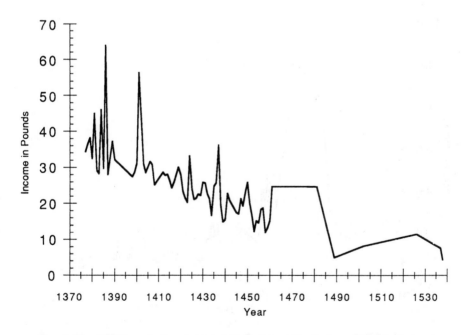

Graph 12. Offerings to the shrine of St Cuthbert, Durham cathedral, from table 8. Accounts for eleven- and thirteen-month periods have been included.

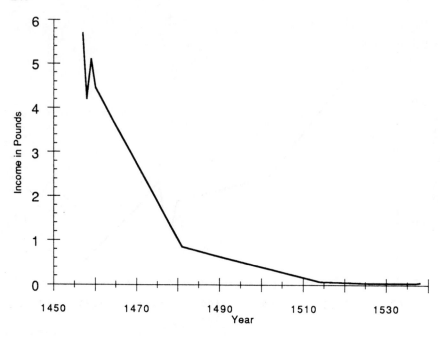

Graph 13. Offerings to the shrine of John Wharton, from table 8.

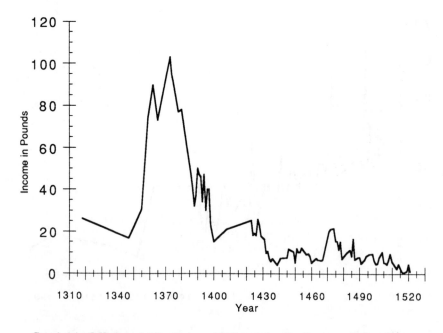

Graph 14. Offerings to the shrine of Edward the Confessor and the relics, Westminster Abbey, from table 10.

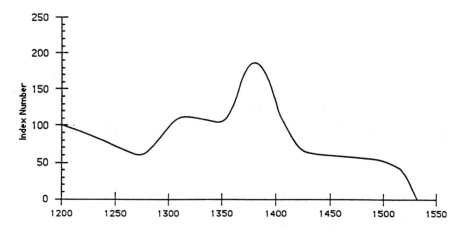

Graph 15. Model graph of income from offerings to English shrines, 1200–1540.

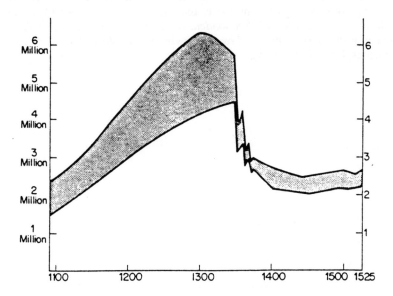

Graph 16. Graph of population estimates; from John Hatcher, *Plague, Population and the British Economy, 1348–1530* (London: Macmillan Press Ltd, 1977), p. 71.

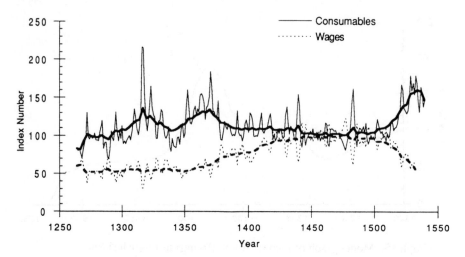

Graph 17. The price of a unit of consumables and wage rates over time, both indexed at 1450 = 100. Based on Brown and Hopkins's index: E.H.P. Brown and S.V. Hopkins, 'Seven Centuries of the Prices of Consumables, Compared with Builder's Wage Rates', *Economica*, vol. 23 (1956), pp. 311–13. The trend of each factor is indicated by the heavier line, produced by computer-defined smoothing.

Bibliography

Manuscript Sources

London, British Library (BL):
    Harl. MS 3721 (Chronicon Ecclesiae Eliensis)
    Add. MS 59616 (Customary of the Shrine of St Thomas)
    MS Harl. 2278 (Lydgate's Life of St Edmund)
    Add. MS 7965 (Wardrobe Accounts 25 Edward I)
Cambridge University Library (CUL):
    MS EDC 5/10, 1–44 (Ely Sacrists' Rolls)
    MS EDC 5/12, 1–10 (Ely Feretrars' Rolls)
    MS Ii.2.3 (Henry of Huntingdon, 'Historia Anglorum')
    MS Ee.3.59 (La Estoire de Seint Aedward le Rei)
    MS G/1/2 (The Register of Bishop Thomas Arundell)
Canterbury Cathedral Archive (CCA):
    DCc/Feretrarian 1 (Feretrarian Roll)
    DCc/Prior 1–15; DCc/MA 4 (Priors' Accounts)
    DCc/Sacrists 7–73; DCc/MA 7, 9, 10, 11, 30; DCc/Reg. R (Sacrists' Accounts)
    Lit MS D4; DCc/MA 1, 2; DCc/Treasurer 26, 27 (Treasurers' Accounts)
    DCc/Reg. K (List of Works of Henry of Eastry)
    DCc/DE 163; DCc/Lit. MS C11; DCc/Regs A, E, H (Miscellaneous Accounts
        and Registers)
Durham, Dean and Chapter Archive (DDCA):
    Feretrar's Account Rolls, 1375–1538
Hereford Cathedral Archive (HCA):
    MSS R.369, R.584–6 (Clavigers' Accounts)
    MSS 2368, 2370, 2371, R.621 (Fabric Rolls)
    MSS 1436, 1437, 1440 (Various Receipts)
Lichfield Cathedral Library:
    MSS XXVI–XXVIII (Cantaria Sancti Blasii)
Lichfield Joint Record Office (LJRO):
    B/A/1/3 (The Register of Bishop Norburgh)
    Chapter Act Books I–IV
Lincoln County Archive (LCA):
    D&C Bj/5/16/1, 2 (*Aperturæ* Accounts)
Norwich County Archive (NCA):
    DCN 1/4/1–125; MC 136/1 (Sacrists' Rolls)
Salisbury Cathedral Archive (SCA):
    MS 132 (Fabric Accounts)
    Machon Register
    Account of the Warden of the Shrine of St Osmund, 1493/4
Westminster Abbey Muniment Room (WAM):
    MSS 19618–19807 (Sacrists' Rolls)
Worcester Cathedral Archive (WCA):
    MSS AXII, A22 (Misc. Volumes)
    MSS C.425–30 (Sacrists' Rolls)

MSS B936, B1039, B1089, B1135, B1214, B1299, B1549 (Grants of lights to the shrines)
Prior William More's Journal
York Minster Library Archive (YMLA):
E/3/1–45 (Fabric Rolls)

Printed Sources

An Account of the Altars, Monuments, and Tombs Existing A.D. 1428 in Saint Alban's Abbey, trans. R. Lloyd (Saint Albans, 1873).
Accounts of the Priory of Worcester for the Year 13–14 H. VIII, AD 1521–2, eds J.H. Bloom and S.G. Hamilton (London, 1907).
Acta Sanctorum, October, vol. 1, ed. J. Ghesquiero (Antwerp, 1765).
Adae Murimuth Continuatio Chronicorum, ed. E.M. Thompson (RS, vol. 93, 1889).
Adam of Eynsham. *Magna Vita Sancti Hugonis: The Life of Saint Hugh of Lincoln*, eds D.L. Douie and D.H. Farmer (Oxford, 1985).
Ailred of Rievaulx. *De Sanctis Ecclesiæ*, in *Priory of Hexham; Its Chroniclers, Endowments, and Annals, The*, ed. J. Raine (SS, vol. 44, 1864).
Amundesham, John. *Annales Monasterii S. Albani*, ed. H.T. Riley (2 vols, RS, vol. 28, 1870–1).
Anglia Sacra, ed. J. Wharton (2 pts, London, 1691).
The Anglo-Saxon Chronicle, a Revised Translation, ed. D. Whitelock (Westport, 1961).
Annales Cestriensis, ed. R.C. Christie (Lancashire and Cheshire Record Soc., vol. 14, 1886).
Annales de Burton, in *Annales Monastici*, vol. 1, ed. H.R. Luard (RS, vol. 36, 1864).
Annales de Theokesberia, in *Annales Monastici*, vol. 1, ed. H.R. Luard (RS, vol. 36, 1864).
Annales Monasterii de Waverleia, in *Annales Monastici*, vol. 2, ed. H.R. Luard (RS, vol. 36, 1865).
Annales Monasterii de Wigornia, in *Annales Monastici*, vol. 4, ed. H.R. Luard (RS, vol. 36, 1869).
Annales Monasterii de Wintonia, in *Annales Monastici*, vol. 2, ed. H.R. Luard (RS, vol. 36, 1865).
Annales Monastici, ed. H.R. Luard, 4 vols (RS, vol. 36, 1864–9).
Annales Prioratus de Dunstaplia, in *Annales Monastici*, vol. 4, ed. H.R. Luard (RS, vol. 36, 1866).
Bartholomew de Cotton. *Historia Anglicana*, ed. H.R. Luard (RS, vol. 16, 1859).
Bede. *Bede's Ecclesiastical History of the English Nation*, trans. J. Stevens (London, 1910).
The Book of Prests, of the King's Wardrobe for 1294–5, ed. E.B. Fryde (Oxford, 1962).
Building Accounts of King Henry III, ed. H.M. Colvin (Oxford, 1971).
Burton, Thomas. *Chronica Monasterii de Melsa*, ed. E.A. Bond (3 vols, RS, vol. 43, 1868).
Calendar of Close Rolls, Edward III, A.D. 1330–33, ed. H.C.M. Lyte (London, 1898).
Calendar of Close Rolls of the Reign of Henry III, A.D. 1234–1237, ed. H.C.M. Lyte (London, 1908).
Calendar of Entries in the Papal Registers Relating to Great Britain and Ireland, Papal Letters, vol. 2, ed. W.H. Bliss (London, 1895).
Calendar of Entries in the Papal Registers Relating to Great Britain and Ireland, Petitions, vol. 1, ed. W.H. Bliss (London, 1896).
Calendar of Patent Rolls, ed. H.C.M. Lyte (London, 1891–1903).
Calendar of the Liberate Rolls (London, 1916–64).
Candidus, Hugh. *The Peterborough Chronicle of Hugh Candidus*, eds C. Mellows and W.T. Mellows (Peterborough, 1941).
'The Canonization of St. Hugh of Lincoln: The text of Cotton Roll xiii, 27', ed. H. Farmer.

Lincolnshire Architectural and Archaeological Soc. Reports and Papers, vol. 6, pt 2 (1986), 86–117.

The Canonization of Saint Osmund, ed. A.R. Malden (Salisbury, 1901).

Capgrave, John. *The Chronicle of England by John Capgrave*, ed. F.C. Hingeston (RS, vol. 1, 1858).

Ceremonies and Processions of the Cathedral Church of Salisbury, ed. C. Wordsworth (Cambridge, 1901).

Chapter Acts of the Cathedral Church of St. Mary of Lincoln, A.D. 1520–1536 ed. R.E.G. Cole (Lincoln Record Soc., vols 12 & 13, 1915–17).

Chapter Acts of the Dean and Chapter of the Cathedral Church of Chichester, 1472–1544 (The White Act Book), ed. W.D. Peckham (Sussex Record Soc., vol. 52, 1951–2).

Charters and Records of Hereford Cathedral, ed. W.W. Capes (Hereford, 1908).

The Chartulary of the High Church of Chichester, ed. W.D. Peckham (Sussex Record Soc., vol. 46, 1942 and 1943).

Chronicles and Memorials of the Reign of Richard I, ed. W. Stubbs (2 vols, RS, vol. 38, 1864–5).

Chronicles of the Mayors and Sheriffs of London and The French Chronicle of London, ed. H.T. Riley (London, 1863).

Chronicles of the Reigns of Edward I and Edward II, ed. W. Stubbs (2 vols, RS, vol. 76, 1882–3).

Chronicles of the Reigns of Stephen, Henry II, and Richard I, ed. R. Howlett (4 vols, RS, vol. 82, 1884–90).

Chronicon Abbatiæ de Evesham, ad Annum 1418, ed. W.D. Macray (RS, vol. 29, 1863).

Chronicon Abbatie de Parco Lude, ed. E. Venables (Horncastle, 1891).

Chronicon Petroburgense, ed. T. Stapleton (Camden Soc., no. 47, 1849).

Chronicon Vulgo Dictum Chronicon Thomæ Wykes, in *Annales Monastici*, vol. 4, ed. H.R. Luard (RS, vol. 36, 1869).

Code of Canon Law, Latin-English Edition, ed. Canon Law Soc. of America (Washington, 1983).

Collection of All the Wills, Now Known to be Extant, of the Kings and Queens of England, A, ed. J. Nichols (London, 1780).

Compotus Rolls of the Obedientiaries of St. Swithun's Priory, Winchester, ed. G.W. Kitchin (London, 1892).

Compotus Rolls of the Priory of Worcester of the XIVth and XVth Centuries, trans. S.G. Hamilton (Oxford, 1910).

Concilia Magnae Britanniae et Hiberniae, ed. D. Wilkins (4 vols, London, 1737).

The Correspondence, Inventories, Account Rolls, and Law Proceedings of the Priory of Coldingham, ed. J. Raine (SS, vol. 12, 1841).

Councils and Synods, with Other Documents Relating to the English Church. Vol. I, AD 871–1204, eds D. Whitelock, M. Brett and C.N.L. Brooke (Oxford, 1981).

Customary of the Benedictine Monasteries of Saint Augustine, Canterbury, and Saint Peter, Westminster, ed. E.M. Thompson (2 vols, Henry Bradshaw Soc., vol. 33, 1902, 1904).

Daniel, Walter. *The Life of Ailred of Rievaulx*, trans. F.M. Powicke (London, 1950).

Decreta Lanfranci: Lanfranc's Monastic Constitutions, ed. D. Knowles (London, 1951).

Documents Illustrating the Activities of the General and Provincial Chapters of the English Black Monks, 1215–1540, ed. W.A. Pantin (Camden Soc., 3rd ser., vols 45, 47, 54, 1931–7).

Documents Illustrating the History of S. Paul's Cathedral, ed. W.S. Simpson (Camden Soc., ns. vol. 26, 1880).

Documents Relating to the Foundation of the Chapter of Winchester, A.D. 1541–1547, eds G.W. Kitchin and F.T. Madge (London, 1889).

Eadmer of Canterbury. *Historia Novorum in Anglia*, ed. M. Rule (RS, vol. 81, 1884).

———— 'Edmeri Cantvariensis Nova Opvscvla de Sanctorum Veneratione et Obsecratione', ed. A. Wilmart, *Revue de Sciences Religieuses*, vol. 15 (1935), 362–70.

———— *Eadmer's History of Recent Events in England*, trans. G. Bosanquet (London, 1964).

—— 'Eadmer's Life of Bregwine, Archbishop of Canterbury, 761–764', ed. B.W. Scholtz, *Traditio*, vol. 22 (1966), pp. 127–48.

—— *The Life of Anselm, Archbishop of Canterbury*, ed. R.W. Southern (Oxford, 1972).

—— *Vita Sancti Oswaldi*, in *Historians of the Church of York*, vol. 2, ed. J. Raine (RS, vol. 71, 1886).

Early Charters of the Cathedral Church of St. Paul, London, ed. M. Gibbs (Camden Soc., 3rd ser., vol. 58, 1939).

Early Communar and Pittancer Rolls of Norwich Cathedral Priory, with an Account of the Building of the Cloister, eds E.C. Fernie and A.B. Whittingham (Norfolk Record Soc., vol. 41, 1972).

'Early Statutes of the Cathedral Church of the Holy Trinity, Chichester, with Observations on its Constitution and History, The', ed. M.E.C. Walcott, *Archaeologia*, vol. 45 (1877), 143–234.

Edward VI. *Iniunccions geuen by the moste exellente Prince, Edwarde the .vi.* (London, 1547).

Ely Chapter Ordinances and Visitation Records, 1241–1515, ed. Seriol J.A. Evans, in *Camden Miscellany*, vol. 17 (Camden Soc., 3rd scr., vol. 64, 1940).

English Historical Documents, 1042–1189, eds D.C. Douglas and G.W. Greenaway (London, 1953).

The Episcopal Register of Robert Rede, Ordinis Predicatorum, Lord Bishop of Chichester, 1397–1415, ed. C. Deedes (Sussex Record Soc., vols 8 and 11, 1908 and 1910).

Erasmus, Desiderius. *Pilgrimages to Saint Mary of Walsingham and Saint Thomas of Canterbury*, trans. J.G. Nichols (2nd edn, London, 1875).

Extracts from the Account Rolls of the Abbey of Durham, from the Original MSS., ed. J.T. Fowler (SS, vols 99, 100, 103, 1898–1901).

Extracts from the Cathedral Registers, A.D. 1275–1535, trans. E.N. Dew (Hereford, 1932).

The Fabric Rolls of York Minster, ed. J. Raine (SS, vol. 35, 1859).

Fifty Pictures of Gothic Altars, ed. P. Dearmer (London, 1910).

The First Register of Norwich Cathedral Priory, ed. H.W. Saunders (Norfolk Record Soc., vol. 11, 1939).

Flete, John. *The History of Westminster Abbey by John Flete*, ed. J.A. Robinson (Cambridge, 1909).

Florence of Worcester. *Florentii Wigorniensis Monachi Chronicon ex Chronicis*, ed. B. Thorpe (2 vols, London, 1849).

Flores Historiarum, ed. H.R. Luard (3 vols, RS, vol. 95, 1890).

Gervase of Canterbury. *The Chronicle of the Reigns of Stephen, Henry II, and Richard I, by Gervase, the Monk of Canterbury*, in *The Historical Works of Gervase of Canterbury*, vol. 1, ed. W. Stubbs (RS, vol. 73, 1879).

—— *The Gesta Regum, with its Continuation the Actus Pontificum, and the Mappa Mundi*, in *The Historical Works of Gervase of Canterbury*, vol 2, ed. W. Stubbs (RS, vol. 73, 1880).

—— *Of the Burning and Repair of the Church of Canterbury in the Year 1174*, trans. C. Cotton (2nd edn, Cambridge, 1932).

Giraldus Cambrensis. *Vita S. Remigii et Vita S. Hugonis*, in *Opera*, vol. 7, ed. J.F. Dimock (RS, vol. 21, 1877).

—— *The Life of St. Hugh of Avalon, Bishop of Lincoln 1186–1200*, ed. R.M. Loomis (New York, 1985).

Goscelin. 'Historia Translationis S. Augustini Episcopi', ed. J.P. Migne (PL, vol. 155, 1854), cols 13–46.

Great Register of Lichfield Cathedral known as the Magnum Registrum Album, The, ed. H.E. Savage (London, 1926).

Guthlac Roll, The, ed. G. Warner (Oxford, 1928).

Harpsfield, Nicholas. *Historia Anglicana Ecclesiastica*, ed. E. Campion (London, 1622).

Henry of Avranches. *The Shorter Latin Poems of Master Henry of Avranches Relating to England*, eds J.C. Russell and J.P. Hieronymous (Cambridge, Mass., 1935).

Henry of Huntingdon. *Historia Anglorum*, ed. T. Arnold (RS, vol. 74, 1879).

Heremannus the Archdeacon. *Miraculis S Edmundi*, in *Memorials of St. Edmund's Abbey*, vol. 1, ed. T. Arnold (RS, vol. 96, 1890).

Higden, Ralph. *Polychronicon Ranulphi Higden Monachi Cestrensis*, ed. J.R. Lumby (9 vols, RS, vol. 41, 1865–89).

Historiæ Dunelmensis Scriptores Tres, ed. J. Raine (SS, vol. 9, 1839).

Historians of the Church of York, ed. J. Raine (3 vols, RS, vol. 71, 1879–94).

The History and Constitution of a Cathedral of the Old Foundation, ed. C.A. Swainson (London, 1880).

The Holy Lyfe and History of Saynt Werburge, Very Frutefull for all Christen People to Rede, ed. E. Hawkins (Chetham Soc., vol. 15, 1845).

Inventories of Christchurch Canterbury, eds J.W. Legg and W.H. St John Hope (Westminster, 1902).

'Inventories of Plate, Vestments, etc., belonging to the Cathedral Church of the Blessed Mary of Lincoln', ed. C. Wordsworth, *Archaeologia*, vol. 53, pt 1 (1892).

'Inventories of Westminster Abbey at the Dissolution', ed. M.E.C. Walcott, *Trans. of the London and Middlesex Archaeological Soc.*, vol. 4 (1875), 313–64.

Jehan de Waurin. *Recueil des Croniques et Anchiennes Istoiries de la Grant Bretaigne, a Presente Nomme Engleterre*, ed. W. Hardy (5 vols, RS, vol. 39, 1864–91).

Jocelin of Brakelond. *The Chronicle of Jocelin of Brakelond*, ed. H.E. Butler (London, 1949).

Johannes de Oxenedes. *Chronica Johannis de Oxenedes*, ed. H. Ellis (RS, vol. 13, 1859).

John de Shalby. *The Book of John de Shalby, Canon of Lincoln (1299–1333) Concerning the Bishops of Lincoln and their Acts*, trans. with notes by J.H. Srawley, Lincoln Minster Pamphlets, no. 2 (Lincoln, 1949).

John of Worcester. *The Chronicle of John of Worcester, 1118–1140*, ed. J.R.H. Weaver (Oxford, 1908).

Knighton, Henry. *Chronicon Henrici Knighton*, ed. J.R. Lumby (2 vols, RS, vol. 92, 1889, 1895).

Langton, Stephen. 'Tractatus de Translatione Beati Thomae', ed. J.-P. Migne (*PL*, vol. 190, 1854), cols 407–424.

Leland, John. *The Itinerary of John Leland in or About the Years 1535–1543*, ed. L. Toulmin-Smith (London, 1907).

Letters and Papers, Foreign and Domestic, of the Reign of Henry VIII, ed. J. Gairdner (33 vols, London, 1862–1910).

The Liber Albus of the Priory of Worcester, ed. J.M. Wilson (London, 1919).

Liber Ecclesiae Wigorniensis: A Letter Book of the Priors of Worcester, ed. J.H. Bloom (London, 1912).

Liber Eliensis, ed. E.O. Blake (Camden Soc., 3rd Ser., vol. 92, 1962).

Liber Niger, Statutes of Lincoln Cathedral, vol. 1, eds H. Bradshaw and C. Wordsworth (Cambridge, 1892).

Liber Regie Capelle, ed. W. Ullmann (Henry Bradshaw Soc., vol. 92, 1961).

Lincoln Wills Registered in the District Probate Registry at Lincoln, vols. 1–3, ed. C.W. Foster (Lincoln Record Soc., 1914, 1918, 1930).

Literæ Cantuarienses, ed. J.B. Sheppard (3 vols, RS, vol. 85, 1887–9).

Lives of Edward the Confessor, ed. H.R. Luard (RS, vol. 3, 1858).

Materials for the History of Thomas Becket, eds J.C. Robertson and J.B. Sheppard (7 vols, RS, vol. 67, 1875–85).

Memorials of St. Edmund's Abbey, ed. T. Arnold (3 vols, RS, vol. 96, 1890–96).

Memorials of Saint Guthlac of Crowland, ed. W. de G. Birch (Wisbech, 1881).

'Miracles of St Osmund', ed. D. Stroud, *The Hatcher Rev.*, vol. 3 (1987), 107–15.

'The Miracles of the Hand of St James', trans. B. Kemp, *The Berks. Archaeological J.*, vol. 65 (1970), 1–19.

Miracula Sancti Johannis, Eboracensis Episcopi, in *The Historians of the Church of York and Its Archbishops*, ed. J. Raine, vol. 1 (RS, vol. 71, 1879), 261–510.

'A Monastic Chronicle Lately Discovered at Christ Church, Canterbury: with Introduction and Notes', ed. C.E. Woodruff, *Arch. Cant.*, vol. 29 (1911), 47–84.

The Monastic Constitutions of Lanfranc, ed. D. Knowles (London, 1951).

Monasticon Anglicanum, ed. W. Dugdale (London, 1655), new edn, eds J. Caley, H. Ellis and B. Bandinel (6 vols, London, 1830).

'Notes on an Inventory of Westminster Abbey, A.D. 1388, Now in the Library of Canterbury', ed. M. Walcott (London-Middlesex Record Soc., vol. 5, 1881), 425–32, 39–40.

Orderic Vitalis. *The Ecclesiastical History of Orderic Vitalis*, ed. M. Chibnall (Oxford, 1969).

Odo of Ostia. 'An Early Twelfth-Century Account of the Translation of St. Milburga of Much Wenlock', trans. A.J.M. Edwards, *Trans. of the Shropshire Archaeological Soc.*, vol. 57 (1961–4), 143–51.

Ordinal and Customary of the Abbey of Saint Mary, York, eds the abbess of Stanbrook and J.B.L. Tolhurst (Henry Bradshaw Soc., vol. 73, 1936).

Paris, Matthew. *Matthaei Parisiensis, Monachi Sancti Albani, Chronica Majora*, ed. H.R. Luard (5 vols, RS, vol. 57, 1872–80).

———— *Chronicles of Matthew Paris*, ed. R. Vaughan (Gloucester, 1984).

———— *Historia Anglorum*, ed. F. Madden (3 vols, RS, vol. 44, 1866–9).

Paston Letters and Papers of the Fifteenth Century, ed. N. Davis (2 pts, Oxford, 1971, 1976).

The Priory of Hexham; Its Chroniclers, Endowments, and Annals, ed. J. Raine (SS, vol. 44, 1864).

Privy Purse Expenses of Elizabeth of York, ed. N.H. Nicolas (London, 1830).

Reading Abbey Cartularies, ed. B.R. Kemp (Camden Soc., 4th ser. vol. 31, 1986).

Records of Antony Bek, Bishop and Patriarch, 1283–1311, ed. C.M. Fraser (SS, vol. 162, 1953).

Records of the Wardrobe and Household, 1285–1286, ed. B.F. Byerly and C.R. Byerly (London, 1977).

Records of the Wardrobe and Household, 1286–1289, ed. B.F. Byerly and C.R. Byerly (London, 1986).

Reginald of Durham. *Reginaldi Monachi Dunelmensis Libellus de Admirandis Beati Cuthberti Virtutibus quae Novellis Patratae sunt Temporibus*, ed. J. Raine (SS, vol. 1, 1835).

The Register of Bishop Robert de Stretton, A.D. 1360–1385, ed. R.A. Wilson (2 vols, Collections for a History of Staffordshire, n.s. vol. 8, 1905, 1907).

The Register of John Morton, Archbishop of Canterbury 1486–1500, ed. C. Harper-Bill (2 vols, Canterbury and York Soc., vols 75, 78, 1987, 1991).

The Register of Thomas Langley, Bishop of Durham, 1406–1437, ed. R.L. Storey (SS, vols 164, 166, 169, 170, 177, 182, 1956–67).

Registrum Ade de Orleton, Episcopi Herefordensis, A.D. mcccxvii–mcccxxvii, ed. A.T. Bannister (Canterbury and York Soc., vol. 5, 1908).

Registrum Antiquissimum of the Cathedral Church of Lincoln, ed. C.W. Foster (Lincoln Record Soc., various vols. 27–67, 1931–73).

Registrum Johannis de Trillek, Episcopi Herefordensis, A.D. mcccxliv–mccclxi, ed. J.H. Parry (Canterbury and York Soc., vol. 8, 1912).

Registrum Johannis Gilbert, Episcopi Herefordensis, A.D. mccclxxv–mccclxxxix, ed. J.H. Parry (Canterbury and York Soc., vol. 18, 1915).

Registrum Ricardi de Swinfield, Episcopi Herefordensis, ed. W.W. Capes (Canterbury and York Soc., vol. 6, 1909).

Registrum Statutorum et Consuetudinum Ecclesiae Cathedralis Sancti Pauli Londinensis, ed. W.S. Simpson (London, 1873).

A Relation, or Rather a True Account, of the Island of England, ed. C.A. Sneyd (Camden Soc., vol. 37, 1847).

Report of the Royal Commission on Historical Manuscripts (London, 1874).

Richard of Cirencester. *Speculum Historiale de Gestis Regum Angliæ*, ed. J.E.B. Mayor (2 vols, RS, vol. 30, 1863, 1869).

Rishanger, William. *Willelmi Rishanger, Quondam Monachi S. Albani, et Quorundam Anony-*

morum, Chronica et Annales, Regnantibus Henrico Tertio et Edwardo Primo, in *Chronica Monasterii S. Albani*, ed. H.T. Riley (RS, vol. 28, 1865).

Rites of Durham, Being a Description or Brief Declaration of All the Ancient Monuments, Rites and Customs Belonging or Being within the Monastical Church of Durham before the Suppression, ed. J.T. Fowler (SS, vol. 107, 1903).

Robert de Tautona. 'The Relics of St Petroc', trans. C.G.H. Doble, *Antiquity*, vol. 13 (1939), 403–15.

Roger of Hovedon. *Chronica Magestri Rogeri de Houedene*, ed. W. Stubbs (4 vols, RS, vol. 51, 1868–71).

The Rule of St. Benedict, ed. J. McCann (London, 1952).

The Sacrist Rolls of Ely, ed. F.R. Chapman (2 vols, Cambridge, 1907).

'Sacrist's Roll of Lichfield Cathedral Church, A.D. 1345', ed. J.C. Cox (Collections for a History of Staffordshire, vol. 6, part. 2, appendix I, 1886), 199–221.

'St Austin's Abbey, Canterbury. Treasurers' Accounts 1468–9, and Others', ed. C. Cotton, *Arch. Cant.*, vol. 51 (1940), 66–107.

The Saint of London: The Life and Miracles of St. Erkenwald, ed. E.G. Whatley (Birmingham, N.Y., 1989).

Sampson. *Samsonis Abbatis Opus de Miraculis Sancti Ædmundi*, in *Memorials of St. Edmund's Abbey*, ed. T. Arnold (RS, vol. 96, 1890).

Sanctuarium Dunelmense et Sanctuarium Beverlacense, ed. J. Raine (SS, vol. 5, 1837).

Sede Vacante Wills: A Calendar of Wills proved before the Commissary of the Prior and Chapter of Christ Church Canterbury, During Vacancies in the Primacy, ed. C.E. Woodruff (Kent Archaeological Soc., Records Branch, vol. 3, 1914).

Simon Semeonis. *Itinarium Symonis Semeonis Ab Hybernia Ad Terram Sanctam*, ed. M. Esposito (Dublin, 1960).

'Some Early Kentish Wills', ed. C.E. Woodruff, *Arch. Cant.*, vol. 46 (1934), 27–35.

Some Oxfordshire Wills, eds J.R.H. Weaver and A. Beardwood (Oxford Record Soc., vol. 39, 1958).

Spicilegium Liberianum, ed. F. Liverani (Florence, 1863).

Statutes and Constitutions of the Cathedral Church of Chichester, eds F.G. Bennett, R.H. Codrington and C. Deedes (Chichester, 1904).

Statutes of Lincoln Cathedral, eds H. Bradshaw and C. Wordsworth (3 vols, Cambridge, 1897).

Stephanus, Eddius. *The Life of Bishop Wilfrid by Eddius Stephanus*, ed. B. Colgrave (Cambridge, 1927).

Stone, John. *The Chronicle of John Stone*, ed. W.G. Searle (Cambridge Antiquarian Soc., vol. 34, 1902).

Stow, John. *The Annales of England* (London, 1592).

Stubbs, T. *Chronica Pontificium Ecclesiæ Eboraci*, in *Historiæ Anglicanæ Scriptores X*, no ed. given (London, 1652).

Sussex Chantry Records, ed. J.E. Ray (Sussex Record Soc., vol. 36, 1931).

Symeon of Durham. *Historia Ecclesiæ Dunhelmensis*, in *Symeonis Monachi Opera Omnia*, vol. 1, ed. T. Arnold (RS, vol. 75, 1882).

The Tale of Beryn, eds F.J. Furnivall and W.G. Stone (London, 1887).

Taxatio Ecclesiastica Angliæ et Walliæ Auctoritate P. Nicholai VI, Record Commission (London, 1802).

Testamenta Vetusta: Being Illustrations from Wills, ed. N.H. Nicolas (London, 1826).

Thomas of Elmham. *Historia Monasterii S. Augustini Cantuariensis*, ed. C. Hardwick (RS, vol. 8, 1858).

Thomas of Monmouth. *The Life and Miracles of St. William of Norwich*, eds A. Jessopp and M.R. James (Cambridge, 1896).

Thómas Saga Erkibyskups, ed. E. Magnússon (RS, vol. 65, 1875–83).

Thorpe, John. *Registrum Roffense* (London, 1769).

Three Chapters of Letters Relating to the Suppression of Monasteries, ed. T. Wright (Camden Soc., vol. 26, 1843).

Transcripts of Sussex Wills, vol. 1, ed. R.G. Rice (Sussex Rec. Soc., vol. 41, 1935).

'Translatio Corporis Sancti Hugonis Lincolniensis Episcopi', *Catalogus Codicum Hagiographicorum Bibliothecae Regiae Bruxellensis, pars I, Codices Latini Membranei, vol. I*, eds Hagiographi Bollandiani (Brussels, 1886), 191–93.

'Translation de S. Hugues de Lincoln, La', ed. A. Poncelet, *An. Boll.*, vol. 31 (1912), 463–5.

The Travels of Leo of Rozmital, ed. M. Letts (Hakluyt Soc., ns. vol. 108, 1957).

Trivet, Nicholas. *Annales*, ed. T. Hog (London, 1845).

Trokelowe, Johannis de, et al. *Johannis de Trokelowe, et Henrici de Blaneforde, Monachorum S. Albani, Necnon Quorundam Anonymorum, Chronica et Annales, Regnantibus Henrico Tertio, Edwardo Primo, Edwardo Secundo, Ricardo Secundo et Henrico Quarto*, ed. H.T. Riley (RS, vol. 28, 1866).

'Two Inventories of the Cathedral Church of St Paul, London, dated Respectively 1245 and 1402', ed. W.S. Simpson, *Archaeologia*, vol. 50 (1887), 439–524.

Un Procès de Canonisation à l'Aube du XIIIe Siècle (1201–1202: Le Livre de saint Gilbert de Sempringham, ed. R. Foreville (Paris, 1943).

Valor Ecclesiasticus, Tempore Henrici VIII, ed. J. Caley (6 vols, London, 1810–34).

'Vie de S. Édouard le Confesseur par Osbert de Clare, La', ed. M. Bloch, *Anal. Boll.*, vol. 41 (1923), 5–131.

Vita Ædwardi Regis qui apud Westmonasterium Requiescit, trans. F. Barlow (London, 1962).

Vita Oswini, in *Miscellanea Biographica*, ed. J. Raine (SS, vol. 8, 1838).

Walsingham, Thomas. *Gesta Abbatum Monasterii Sancti Albani a Thome Walsingham*, ed. H.T. Riley (3 vols, RS, vol. 28, 1867–9).

—— *Historia Anglicana*, ed. H.T. Riley (2 vols, RS, vol. 28, 1863–4).

Walter of Coventry. *The Historical Collections of Walter of Coventry*, ed. W. Stubbs, 2 vols (RS, vol. 58, 1872–3).

The Westminster Chronicle, 1381–1394, eds L.C. Hector and B.F. Harvey (Oxford, 1982).

William Glastynbury. 'The Chronicle of William of Glastynbury, Monk of the Priory of Christ Church, Canterbury, 1419–1448', ed. C.E. Woodruff, *Arch. Cant.*, vol. 37 (1925), 121–51.

William of Malmesbury. *The Chronicle of Glastonbury Abbey*, ed. J.P. Carley (Woodbridge, 1985).

—— *De Gestis Pontificium Anglorum*, ed. N.E.S.A. Hamilton (RS, vol. 52, 1870).

—— *De Gestis Regum Anglorum*, ed. W. Stubbs (2 vols, RS, vol. 90, 1887–9).

—— *The Vita Wulfstani of William of Malmesbury*, ed. R.R. Darlington (Camden Soc., 3rd ser., vol. 40, 1928).

Williams, Sir John. *Account of the Monastic Treasures Confiscated at the Dissolution of the Various Houses in England*, ed. W.B.D.D. Turnbull (Edinburgh, 1836).

Wills and Inventories Illustrative of the History, Manners, Language, Statistics, etc. of the Northern Counties of England from the Eleventh Century Downwards, ed. J. Raine, part 1 (SS, vol. 2, 1835).

Worcester, William. *Itineraries*, ed. John H. Harvey (Oxford, 1969).

Wriothesley, Charles. *A Chronicle of England During the Reigns of the Tudors*, ed. W.D. Hamilton (Camden Soc., ns. vol. 11, 1875).

Wulfstan of Winchester. *The Life of St Æthelwold*, eds M. Lapidge and M. Winterbottom (Oxford, 1991).

Secondary Sources

Altham, H.S. 'St. Swithun's Shrine', *Winchester Cathedral Record*, no. 17 (1948), 13–15.

Anderson, C.H.J. *The Lincoln Pocket Guide, being a short Account of the Churches and Antiquities of the County, and of the Cathedral of the Blessed Virgin Mary of Lincoln, commonly called the Minster* (London, 1880).

Anderson, M.D. *A Saint at Stake* (London, 1964).

────── *History and Imagery in British Churches* (London, 1971).

Andrew, M.R.G. 'Chichester Cathedral, The Original East End: A Reappraisal', *Sussex Archaeological Collections*, vol. 118 (1980), 299–308.

Ariès, P. *Western Attitudes toward Death*, trans. P.M. Ranum (London, 1974).

Aston, M. *Lollards and Reformers: Images and Literacy in Late Medieval Religion* (London, 1984).

Atkinson, T.D. *An Architectural History of the Benedictine Monastery of Saint Etheldreda at Ely* (2 vols, Cambridge, 1933).

Baddeley, St.C. 'The Holy Blood of Hayles', *Transactions of the Bristol and Gloucestershire Archaeological Soc.*, vol. 23 (1900), 276–84.

Bailey, R.N. 'St Cuthbert's Relics: Some Neglected Evidence', in *St Cuthbert, His Cult and his Community to AD 1200*, eds G. Bonner, D. Rollason and C. Stancliffe (Woodbridge, 1989), 231–46.

Bailey, T. *The Processions of Sarum and the Western Church* (Toronto, 1971).

Bannister, A.T. *The Cathedral Church of Hereford, its History and Constitution* (London, 1924).

Barber, P. *Vampires, Burial and Death* (New Haven, 1988).

Barlow, F. *Edward the Confessor* (London, 1970).

────── *Thomas Becket* (London, 1986).

Barrett, I. 'The Relics of St Thomas Cantilupe', in *St. Thomas Cantilupe, Bishop of Hereford: Essays in his Honour*, ed. M. Jancey (Hereford, 1982), 181–8.

Barrett, P. 'A Saint in the Calendar: the Effect of the Canonization of St. Thomas Cantilupe on the Liturgy', in *St. Thomas Cantilupe, Bishop of Hereford, Essays in his Honour*, ed. M. Jancey (Hereford, 1982), 153–8.

Baskerville, G. *English Monks and the Suppression* (London, 1937).

Batsford, H. and C. Fry. *The Greater English Church of the Middle Ages* (2nd edn, London, 1943–4).

Bazeley, W. 'The Abbey of St. Mary, Hayles', *Trans. of the Bristol and Gloucestershire Archaeological Soc.*, vol. 22 (1899), 257–71.

Bean, J.M.W. 'The Black Death: The Crisis and Its Social and Economic Consequences', in *The Black Death: The Impact of the Fourteenth-Century Plague*, ed. D. Williman, Medieval and Renaissance Texts and Studies (Binghamton, 1982), 23–38.

Bennett, F. *Chester Cathedral* (Chester, 1925).

Benson, E.G. 'The Lost Brass of the Cantilupe Shrine', *Trans. Woolhope Field Club*, vol. 33 (1949–51), 68–76.

Bentham, J. *The History and Antiquities of the Conventual and Cathedral Church of Ely* (Norwich, 1812).

Bethell, D. 'The Making of a Twelfth-Century Relic Collection', in *Studies in Church History*, vol. 8, eds G.J. Cuming and D. Baker (1972), 61–72.

Beveridge, W. 'The Yield and Price of Corn in the Middle Ages', *Economic History*, vol. 1 (1926–9), 155–67.

Biddle, M. 'Excavations at Winchester 1967: Sixth Interim Report', *Ant. J.*, vol. 48–50 (1968–70), 250–85.

────── 'Alban and the Anglo-Saxon Church', in *Cathedral and City: St Albans Ancient and Modern*, ed. R. Runcie (London, 1977), 23–42.

────── 'Archaeology, Architecture, and the Cult of Saints in Anglo-Saxon England', in *The Anglo-Saxon Church*, eds L.A.S. Butler and R.K. Morris (London, 1986), 1–31.

Biddle, M. and D.J. Keene. 'Winchester in the Eleventh and Twelfth Centuries', in *Winchester in the Early Middle Ages*, ed. M. Biddle (Oxford, 1976).

Binnall, P.B.G. 'Notes on the Medieval Altars and Chapels in Lincoln Cathedral', *Ant. J.*, vol. 42 (1962), 68–80.

Binski, P. 'The Cosmati at Westminster and the English Court Style', *Art Bull.*, vol. 72 (1990), 6–34.

Bishop, E. 'On the History of the Christian Altar', *Downside Rev.*, vol. 5 (1905), 154–82.

Blore, G.H. *Notes on the Monuments of Winchester Cathedral* (Winchester, 1935).

Boase, T.S.R. *Death in the Middle Ages* (London, 1972).

Bolton, J.L. *The Medieval English Economy, 1150–1500* (London, 1980).

Bond, F.B. *Gothic Architecture in England* (London, 1905).

—— 'Medieval Screens and Rood-Lofts', *Trans. of the St. Paul's Ecclesiological Soc.*, vol. 5 (1905), 197–220.

—— *Screens and Galleries in English Churches* (London, 1908).

—— *Westminster Abbey* (London, 1909).

—— *An Introduction to English Church Architecture from the Eleventh to the Sixteenth Century* (2 vols, London, 1913).

—— *Dedications and Patron Saints of English Churches: Ecclesiastical Symbolism, Saints and their Emblems* (London, 1914).

—— *Ely Cathedral* (Ely, 1919).

Bond, F. and W. Watkins. 'Notes on the Architectural History of Lincoln Minster from 1192 to 1255', *J. of the Royal Institute of British Architects*, 3rd ser., vol. 18 (1911), 84–97.

Bonner, G. 'St Cuthbert at Chester-le-Street', in *St Cuthbert, His Cult and His Community to AD 1200*, eds G. Bonner, D. Rollason and C. Stancliffe (Woodbridge, 1989), 387–96.

Bonser, W. 'The Cult of Relics in the Middle Ages', *Folklore*, vol. 73 (1962), 234–56.

Boulter, B.C. *Pilgrim Shrines of England* (London, 1928).

Boutell, C. 'The Tombs and Monumental Sculpture in Hereford Cathedral', *JBAA*, vol. 27 (1871), 191–202.

Branner, R. 'Westminster Abbey and the French Court Style', *J. of the Soc. of Architectural Historians*, vol. 23 (1964), 3–18.

Braun, H. *English Abbeys* (London, 1971).

—— *Cathedral Architecture* (London, 1972).

Bray, J.R. 'Concepts of Sainthood in Fourteenth-Century England', *Bull of the John Rylands University Library of Manchester*, vol. 66, no. 2 (1984), 40–77.

Britton, J. *The Architectural Antiquities of Great Britain* (London, 1809).

—— *The History and Antiquities of the Cathedral Church of Salisbury* (London, 1814).

—— *The History and Antiquities of the See & Cathedral Church of Norwich* (London, 1816).

—— *The History and Antiquities of the See and Cathedral Church of Winchester* (London, 1817).

—— *The History and Antiquities of the Cathedral Church of Wells* (London, 1824).

—— *The History and Antiquities of the Cathedral Church of Hereford* (London, 1831).

Bromley, F.E. 'A Note on the Corona of St. Thomas of Canterbury', *Arch. Cant.*, vol. 46 (1934), 102–9.

Brooke, C.N.L. 'The Earliest Times to 1485', in *A History of St Paul's Cathedral*, ed. W.R. Matthews and W.M. Atkins (London, 1957).

—— 'The Cathedral in Medieval Society', introduction to W. Swaan, *The Gothic Cathedral* (London, 1969).

—— 'Religious Sentiment and Church Design in the Later Middle Ages', in *Medieval Church and Society* (London, 1971), 162–82.

—— 'St Albans: The Great Abbey', in *Cathedral and City: St Albans Ancient and Modern*, ed. R. Runcie (London, 1977), 43–70.

Brooke, R. and C. Brooke. *Popular Religion in the Middle Ages* (London, 1984).

Brown, A. 'The Financial System of Rochester Priory: A Reconsideration', *Bull. of the Institute of Historical Research*, vol. 50 (1970), 115–20.

Brown, E.H.P. and S.V. Hopkins. 'Seven Centuries of the Prices of Consumables, Compared with Builder's Wage Rates', *Economica*, vol. 23 (1956), 296–314.

—— 'Wage Rates and Prices, Evidence for Population Pressure in the Sixteenth Century', *Economica*, ns. vol. 24 (1957), 289–306.

Brown, E.A.R. 'Death and the Human Body in the Later Middle Ages: The Legislation of

Boniface VIII on the Division of the Corpse', in *The Monarchy of Capetian France and Royal Ceremonial* (Aldershot, 1991), 221–70.

Browne, A.L. 'The Cathedral Treasurer in the Middle Ages', *Church Quarterly Review*, vol. 133 (1941–2), 197–207.

Browne, G.F. *An Account of the Three Ancient Cross Shafts, the Font and St Bertram's Shrine at Ilam* (London, 1888).

——— *St. Aldhelm: His Life and Times* (London, 1903).

Browne, J. *The History of the Metropolitanical Church of St. Peter, York* (2 vols, London, 1847).

Browne, P. *An Account and Description of the Cathedral Church of the Holy Trinity, Norwich, and its Precincts* (2nd edn, London, 1807).

Brown, P. *The Cult of the Saints: Its Rise and Function in Latin Christianity* (London, 1981).

Bruce-Mitford, R. 'The Chapter-House Vestibule Graves at Lincoln and the Body of St. Hugh of Avalon', in *Tribute to An Antiquary; Essays Presented to Marc Fitch by Some of his Friends* (London, 1976), 127–40.

Bund, J.W.W. 'A Fourteenth-Century Pilgrimage', *Ass. Architectural Societies Reports and Papers*, vol. 34, pt. 1 (1917), 103–26.

Burne, R.V.H. *Chester Cathedral, From its Founding by Henry VIII to the Accession of Queen Victoria* (London, 1958).

——— *The Monks of Chester: The History of St. Werburgh's Abbey* (London, 1962).

Bussby, F. *Winchester Cathedral: 1079–1979* (Southhampton, 1979).

Calkins, R.G. *Monuments of Medieval Art* (New York, 1979).

Calthrop, M.M.C. 'Priory of St Mary of Worcester', *VCH Worcester*, vol. 2, eds J.S.W. Bund and W. Page (1906), 94–112.

Carley, J.P. *Glastonbury Abbey: The Holy House at the Head of the Moors Adventurous* (Woodbridge, 1988).

Caröe, W.D. 'Canterbury Cathedral Choir during the Commonwealth and After, with Special Reference to Two Oil Paintings', *Archaeologia*, vol. 62, pt. 2 (1911), 353–66.

Carolus-Barré, L. 'Saint Louis et la Translation des Corps Saints', in *Études D'Histoire du Droit Canonique*, vol. 2 (Paris, 1965), 1087–1112.

Carpenter, D.A. 'The Gold Treasure of Henry III', in *Thirteenth Century England I*, eds P.R. Coss and S.D. Lloyd (Woodbridge, 1986), 61–83.

Carpenter, E. *House of Kings* (London, 1966).

Carter, E.H. *Studies in Norwich Cathedral History* (Norwich, 1935).

Cave, C.J.P. *The Roof Bosses of the Cathedral Church of Christ, Canterbury*, Canterbury Papers no. 4 (Canterbury, 1934).

Caviness, M.H. *The Early Stained Glass of Canterbury* (Princeton, 1977).

Cheney, C.R. 'Church Building in the Middle Ages', *Bulletin of the John Rylands Library*, vol. 34 (1951–2), 20–36.

Church, C.M. *Chapters in the Early History of the Church of Wells* (London, 1894).

Clapham, A.W. *English Romanesque Architecture Before the Conquest* (Oxford, 1930).

——— *English Romanesque Architecture After the Conquest* (Oxford, 1934).

——— *Romanesque Architecture in Western Europe* (Oxford, 1936).

Clapham, A. 'Salisbury Cathedral: Churches and Religious Building, Monuments and Sculpture', *Arch. J.*, vol. 104 (1947), 144–5.

Clarke, W.K.L. *Chichester Cathedral in the Nineteenth Century*, Chichester Papers no. 14 (Chichester, 1959).

Cohen, K. *Metamorphosis of a Death Symbol: The Transi Tomb in the Late Middle Ages and the Renaissance* (Berkeley, 1973).

Coldstream, N. 'English Decorated Shrine Bases', *JBAA*, vol. 129 (1976), 15–34.

Cole, R.E.G. 'Proceedings Relative to the Canonization of Robert Grosseteste, Bishop of Lincoln', *Ass. Architectural Soc.s Reports and Papers*, vol. 33 (1915), 1–34.

——— 'Proceedings Relative to the Canonization of John de Dalderby, Bishop of Lincoln', *Associated Architectural Soc. Reports and Papers*, vol. 33 (1915), 243–76.

Cole, R.E.G. and J.O. Johnston. 'The Body of Saint Hugh', *Associated Architectural Soc. Reports and Papers*, vol. 36, pt 1 (1921–22), 47–72.

Colgrave, H. *St Cuthbert of Durham* (Durham, 1947).

Colvin, H.M. *The History of the King's Works*, vols 1–3 (London, 1963, 1975).

Conant, K.J. *Carolingian and Romanesque Architecture 800 to 1200* (3rd edn, Harmondworth, 1973).

Constable, G. 'Opposition to Pilgrimage in the Middle Ages', *Studia Gratia*, vol. 19 (1976), 123–46.

Conway, W.M. 'Portable Reliquaries of the Early Medieval Period', *Proc. of the Soc. of Antiquaries of London*, vol. 31 (1919), 218–40.

Cook, G.H. *Old St Paul's Cathedral: a Lost Glory of Medieval London* (London, 1955).

——— *English Monasteries in the Middle Ages* (London, 1961).

——— *Medieval Chantries and Chantry Chapels* (London, 1963).

——— *Letters to Cromwell on the Suppression of the Monasteries* (London, 1965).

Cotton, C. *The Saxon Cathedral at Canterbury and the Saxon Saints buried therin* (Manchester, 1929).

Couteur, J.L. and D.H.M. Carter. 'Notes on the Shrine of St. Swithun formerly in Winchester Cathedral', *Ant.J.*, vol. 4 (1924), 360–70.

Cowdrey, H.E.J. 'An Early Record of the Export of Becket's Relics', *Bulletin of the Institute of Historical Research*, vol. 54 (1981), 251–3.

Cox, J.C. *The Sanctuaries and Sanctuary Seekers of Medieval England* (London, 1911).

Cox, J.C. and A. Harvey. *English Church Furniture* (London, 1907).

Craster, H.H.E. *Tynemouth Priory* (Newcastle, 1907).

Crook, J. *A History of the Pilgrim's School and Earlier Winchester Choir Schools* (Chichester, 1981).

——— 'The Romanesque East Arm and Crypt of Winchester Cathedral', *JBAA*, vol. 142 (1989), 1–36.

——— 'King Edgar's Reliquary of St Swithun', *Anglo-Saxon England*, vol. 21 (1992), 177–202.

——— 'St Swithun of Winchester', in *Winchester Cathedral; Nine Hundred Years, 1093–1993* (Chichester, 1993), 57–68.

Crossley, F.H. *English Church Monuments A.D. 1150–1550* (London, 1921).

——— *English Church Design, 1040–1540 A.D.* (London, 1945).

Daly, P.H. 'The Process of Canonization in the Thirteenth and Early Fourteenth Centuries', in *St Thomas Cantilupe, Bishop of Hereford: Essays in his Honour*, ed. M. Jancey (Hereford, 1982), 125–36.

Dart, J. *The History and Antiquities of the Cathedral Church of Canterbury* (London, 1726).

Davis, J.F. 'Lollards, Reformers and St. Thomas of Canterbury', *Univ. of Birmingham Historical J.*, vol. 9, no. 1 (1963), 1–16.

Dearmer, P. *Fifty Pictures of Gothic Altars* (London, 1910).

Delehaye, H. 'Loca Sanctorum', *Analecta Bollandiana*, vol. 48 (1930), 5–64.

Dendy, D.R. *The Use of Lights in Christian Worship* (London, 1959).

Dickens, A.G. *Lollards and Protestants in the Diocese of York, 1509–1558* (London, 1982).

Dickinson, J.C. *The Shrine of Our Lady of Walsingham* (Cambridge, 1956).

Ditmas, E.M.R. 'The Cult of Arthurian Relics', *Folklore*, vol. 75 (1964), 19–33.

Dix, G. *A Detection of Aumbries* (Westminster, 1942).

Dixon, W.H. *Fasti Eboracensis* (London, 1863).

Doble, G.H. 'The Leominster Relic List', *Transactions of the Woolhope Naturalists' Field Club*, vol. 31 (1942), 58–65.

Dobson, R.B. *Durham Priory 1400–1450* (Cambridge, 1973).

——— 'Cathedral Chapters and Cathedral Cities: York, Durham and Carlisle in the Fifteenth Century', *Northern History*, vol. 19 (1983), 15–44.

Douie, D.L. 'The Canonization of St. Thomas of Hereford', *Dublin Rev.*, vol. 229, no. 469 (1955), 275–87.

Draper, P. 'The Retrochoir of Winchester Cathedral', *Architectural History*, vol 21 (1978), 1–17.

——— 'Bishop Northwold and the Cult of Saint Etheldreda', in *Medieval Art and Architecture at Ely Cathedral* (BAACT, vol. 2, 1979), 8–27.

——— 'The Sequence and Dating of the Decorated Work at Wells', *Medieval Art and Architecture at Wells and Glastonbury* (BAACT, vol. 4, 1981), 18–29.

——— 'William of Sens and the Original Design of the Choir Termination of Canterbury Cathedral 1175–1179', *J. of the Soc. of Architectural Historians*, vol. 42 (1983), 238–48.

——— 'King John and St Wulfstan', *J. of Medieval History*, vol. 10, no. 1 (1984), 41–50.

——— 'The Retrochoir of Winchester Cathedral: Evidence and Interpretation', *JBAA*, vol. 139 (1986), 68–74.

Duchesne, L. *Christian Worship: Its Origin and Evolution*, trans. M.L. McClure (5th edn, London, 1919).

Duffy, E. *The Stripping of the Altars: Traditional Religion in England, c. 1400–c. 1580* (London, 1992).

Dufty, A.R. 'Lichfield Cathedral', *Arch. J.*, vol. 120 (1963), 293–95.

Dugdale, W. *Monasticon Anglicanum* (London, 1655).

——— *The History of St Paul's Cathedral in London from its Foundation* (2nd edn, London, 1716).

——— *Monasticon Anglicanum: A history of the Abbies and other Monasteries, Hospitals, Frieries, and Cathedral and Collegieate Churches, with their dependancies, in England and Wales*, 2nd edn, eds John Caley, Henry Ellis and Bulkeley Bandinel (London, 1830).

Duggan, A.J. 'The Cult of St Thomas Becket in the Thirteenth Century', in *St Thomas Cantilupe, Bishop of Hereford: Essays in his Honour*, ed. M. Jancey (Hereford, 1982), 21–44.

Duncan-Jones, C.M. *S. Richard of Chichester* (London, no date).

Dyer, C. *Lords and Peasants in a Changing Society: The Estates of the Bishopric of Worcester, 680–1540* (Cambridge, 1980).

——— *Standards of Living in the Later Middle Ages; Social Change in England c. 1200–1520* (Cambridge, 1989).

Eames, E. 'Notes on the Decorated Stone Roundels in the Corona and Trinity Chapel in Canterbury Cathedral', in *Medieval Art and Architecture at Canterbury before 1220* (BAACT, vol. 5, 1982), 67–70.

Ellis, D.M.B. and L.F. Salzman. 'Religious Houses: The Abbey and Cathedral Priory of Ely', *VCH Cambridge and the Isle of Ely*, vol. 2, ed. L.F. Salzman (1948), 199–209.

Emmerson, R. 'St Thomas Cantilupe's Tomb and Brass of 1287', *Bull. of the International Soc. for the Study of Church Monuments*, vol. 2 (1980), 41–5.

Erskine, A.M. *The Accounts of the Fabric of Exeter Cathedral, 1279–1353* (Devon and Cornwall Record Soc., ns. vols. 24, 26, 1981, 1983).

Essex, J. 'Some Observations on Lincoln Cathedral', *Archaeologia*, vol. 4 (1777), 149–59.

Everett, A.W. 'The Rebuilding of Exeter Cathedral c. 1270–1360', *The Devonshire Association for the Advancement of Science, Literature and Art, Report and Transactions*, vol. 100 (1968), 179–90.

Eward, S. 'St Osmund: The Building of the Shrine', *Salisbury Cathedral News*, no. 148 (April, 1952), 5–7.

Farmer, D.H. *Saint Hugh of Lincoln* (London, 1985).

——— 'The Cult and Canonization of St Hugh', in *St Hugh of Lincoln: Lectures Delivered at Oxford and Lincoln to Celebrate the Eighth Centenary of St Hugh's Consecration as Bishop of Lincoln*, ed. H. Mayr-Harting (Oxford, 1987), 75–87.

Farmer, D. 'Prices and Wages, 1350–1500', in *The Agrarian History of England and Wales*, ed. J. Thirsk, vol. 3 (Cambridge, 1991), 431–525.

Fernie, E. 'St. Anselm's Crypt', in *Medieval Art and Architecture at Canterbury before 1220* (BAACT, vol. 5, 1982), 27–38.

—— 'Archaeology and Iconography: Recent Developments in the Study of English Medieval Architecture', *Architectural History*, vol. 32 (1989), 18–29.

Finucane, R.C. 'The Use and Abuse of Medieval Miracles', *History*, vol. 1, no. 198 (1975), 1–10.

—— *Miracles and Pilgrims: Popular Beliefs in Medieval England* (London, 1977).

—— 'Sacred Corpse, Profane Carrion: Social Ideals and Death Rituals in the Later Middle Ages', in *Mirrors of Mortality: Studies in the Social History of Death*, ed. J. Whaley (London, 1981), 40–60.

—— 'Cantilupe as Thaumaturge: Pilgrims and their Miracles', in *St. Thomas Cantilupe, Bishop of Hereford: Essays in his Honour*, ed. M. Jancey (Hereford, 1982), 137–44.

Flower, C.T. 'Obedientiar's Accounts of Glastonbury and Other Religious Houses', *Trans. of the St Paul's Ecclesiological Soc.*, vol. 7 (1911–15), 50–62.

Foreville, R. *Un Procés de Canonisation à l'Aube du XIIIe siècle, 1201–2: Le Livre de Saint Gilbert de Sempringham* (Paris, 1943).

—— *Le Jubilé de Saint Thomas Becket* (Paris, 1958).

Fowler, J.T. 'On a Window Representing the Life and Miracles of S. William of York, at the North End of the Eastern Transept, York Minster', *Yorkshire Archaeological and Topographical J.*, vol. 3 (1875), 198–348.

—— 'On an Examination of the Grave of St. Cuthbert in Durham Cathedral in March 1899', *Archaeologia*, 2nd ser. vol. 57 (1900), 1–28.

Frankl, P. *The Gothic: Literary Sources and Interpretations through Eight Centuries* (Princeton, 1960).

Fraser, C.M. *A History of Antony Bek* (Oxford, 1957).

Frere, W.H. *Pontifical Services Illustrated from Miniatures*, Alcuin Club Collections, vol. 4 (London, 1901).

Galbraith, V.H. *The Abbey of St Albans* (Oxford, 1911).

Gasquet, F.A. *English Monastic Life* (London, 1904).

Gauthier, M.-M. *Highways of the Faith: Relics and Reliquaries from Jerusalem to Compostella* (London, 1983).

Gee, E. 'The Topography of Altars, Chantries and Shrines in York Minster', *Ant. J.*, vol. 64 (1984), 337–350.

Gem, R.D.H. 'The Anglo-Saxon Cathedral at Canterbury: A Further Contribution', *Arch. J.*, vol. 127 (1971), 196–201.

—— 'Bishop Wulfstan II and the Romanesque Cathedral Church of Worcester', in *Medieval Art and Architecture at Worcester Cathedral* (BAACT, vol. 1, 1978), 15–37.

—— 'Chichester Cathedral: When was the Romanesque Church Begun?', in *Anglo-Norman Studies*, ed. R.A. Brown, vol. 3 (Woodbridge, 1981), 61–4.

—— 'The Significance of the 11th-century Rebuilding of Christ Church and St. Augustine's, Canterbury, in the Development of Romanesque Architecture', in *Medieval Art and Architecture at Canterbury before 1220* (BAACT, vol. 5, 1982), 1–19.

—— 'The Romanesque Architecture of Old St Paul's Cathedral and its Late Eleventh-Century Context', in *Medieval Art, Architecture and Archaeology in London* (BAACT, vol. 10, 1990), 47–63.

Gerould, G.H. ' "Tables" in Medieval Churches.' *Speculum*, vol. 1 (1926), 434–40.

Glenn, V. 'The Sculpture of the Angel Choir at Lincoln', in *Medieval Art and Architecture at Lincoln Cathedral* (BAACT, vol. 8, 1986), 102–8.

Goldberg, P.J.P. 'Mortality and Economic Change in the Diocese of York, 1390–1514', *Northern History*, vol. 24 (1988), 38–55.

Goodich, M. 'A Profile of Thirteenth Century Sainthood', *Comparative Studies in Society and History*, vol. 18 (1976), 429–37.

Gottfried, R.S. *Epidemic Disease in Fifteenth-Century England* (no place, 1978).

—— *The Black Death* (New York, 1983).

Gough, R. *Sepulchral Monuments in Great Britain* (London, 1786).

Goulburn, E.M. 'The Confessio, or Relic Chapel; An Ancient Chamber in Norwich Cathedral, on the North Side of the Presbytery', *Norfolk Archaeology*, vol. 9 (1884), 275–81.

Green, A.R. 'The Romsey Painted Wooden Reredos: With a Short Account of Saint Armel', *Arch. J.*, vol. 90 (1934), 306–14.

Haigh, C. and D. Loades. 'The Fortunes of the Shrine of St Mary of Caversham', *Oxoniensia*, vol. 45 (1980), 62–72.

Hall, D.J. *English Medieval Pilgrimage* (Bath, 1965).

Hallam, E.M. 'Royal Burial and the Cult of Kingship in France and England, 1060–1330', *J. of Medieval History*, vol. 8, no. 4 (1982), 359–80.

Hampson, E.M. and T.D. Atkinson. 'The City of Ely', in *VCH: Cambridge and the Isle of Ely*, vol. 4, ed. R.B. Pugh (1953), 28–89.

Hardin, J.A. *Modern Catholic Dictionary* (London, 1981).

Harvey, B.F. 'The Population Trend in England between 1300 and 1348', *Trans. Royal Historical Soc.*, 5th ser., vol. 16 (1966), 23–42.

Harvey, J.H. 'The Building of Wells Cathedral', in *Wells Cathedral; A History*, ed. L.S. Cochester (Over Wallop, 1982).

Harvey, P.D.A. 'The English Inflation of 1180 to 1220', *Past and Present*, no. 61 (1973), pp. 3–31.

Hatcher, J. *Plague, Population and the English Economy, 1348–1530* (London, 1977).

Head, T. *Hagiography and the Cult of Saints: The Diocese of Orléans, 800–1200* (Cambridge, 1990).

Hearn, M.F. 'The Rectangular Ambulatory in English Mediaeval Architecture', *J. of the Soc. of Architectural Historians*, vol. 30, no. 3 (1971), 187–208.

Heath, S. *The Romance of Symbolism* (London, 1909).

———— *In the Steps of the Pilgrims* (2nd edn, London, no date).

Heffernan, T.J. *Sacred Biography: Saints and Their Biographers in the Middle Ages* (Oxford, 1988).

Herrmann-Mascard, N. *Les Reliques des Saints: Formation Coutumière d'un Droit* (Paris, 1975).

Hewitt, J. 'The "Keeper of Saint Chad's Head" in Lichfield Cathedral, and other matters Concerning that Minster in the Fifteenth Century', *Arch. J.*, vol. 33 (1876), 72–82.

Hill, J.W.F. *Medieval Lincoln* (Cambridge, 1948).

Hills, G.M. 'The Architectural History of Hereford Cathedral', *JBAA*, vol. 27 (1871), 46–84.

Hoade, E. *Western Pilgrims* (Jerusalem, 1970).

Hole, C. *English Shrines and Sanctuaries* (London, 1954).

———— 'Some Instances of Image-Magic in Great Britain', in *The Witch Figure*, ed. V. Newall (London, 1973), 80–94.

Hope, W.H. St John, *English Altars* (London, 1899).

———— *Architectural History of the Cathedral Church and Monastery of Rochester* (London, 1900).

———— 'On the Great Almery for Relics of Late in the Abbey Church of Selby, with Notes on Some Other Receptacles for Relics', *Archaeologia*, vol. 60, pt 2 (1907), 411–22.

———— 'Notes on the Holy Blood of Hayles', *Arch. J.*, vol. 68 (1911), 166–72.

———— 'Twelfth-Century Pulpitum or Rood Loft Formerly in the Cathedral Church of Ely, with Notes on Similar Screens in English Cathedral and Monastic Churches'. *Proc. of the Cambridgeshire Antiquarian Soc.*, vol. 21 (1919), 19–73.

———— 'The Sarum Consuetudinary and its Relation to the Cathedral Church of Old Sarum', *Archaeologia*, vol. 68 (1917), 111–26.

———— 'Quire Screens in English Churches, with Special Reference to the Twelfth-Century Quire Screen Formerly in the Cathedral Church of Ely', *Archaeologia*, vol. 68 (1917), 43–110.

Hope, W.H. St John and W.T. Bensly. 'Recent Discoveries in the Cathedral Church of Norwich', *Norfolk Archaeology*, vol. 14 (1901), 105–27.

Hope, W.H. St John and J.W. Legg. *Inventories of Christchurch Canterbury* (Westminster, 1902).

Horlbeck, F.R. 'The Vault Paintings of Salisbury Cathedral', *Arch. J.*, vol. 117 (1962), 116–30.

Horne, E. 'The Head of St. Thomas of Hereford', *The Clergy Rev.*, ns. vol. 28 (1947), 99–104.

Hoving, T.P. 'A Newly Discovered Reliquary of St Thomas Becket', *Gesta*, vol. 4 (1965), 28–9.

Jackson, T.G. 'Winchester Cathedral: An Account of the Building and of the Repairs Now in Progress', *Trans. of the St. Paul's Ecclesiological Soc.*, vol. 6 (1906–10), 217–36.

Jacob, E.F. 'St. Richard of Chichester', *J. of Ecclesiastical History*, vol. 7 (1956), 174–88.

James, M.R. *On the Abbey of S. Edmund at Bury* (Cambridge Antiquarian Soc., vol. 28, 1895).

Jancey, E.M. *St. Thomas of Hereford* (Newport, 1978).

―――― 'A Servant Speaks of his Master: Hugh le Barber's Evidence in 1307', in *St. Thomas Cantilupe, Bishop of Hereford: Essays in his Honour*, ed. M. Jancey (Hereford, 1982), 191–201.

Johnson, C. 'The System of Account in the Wardrobe of Edward I', *Trans. of the Royal Historical Soc.*, 4th ser., vol. 6 (1923), 50–72.

Jones, D.J. 'The Cult of St. Richard of Chichester in the Middle Ages', *Sussex Archaeological Collections*, vol. 121 (1983), 79–86.

Jones, D. *The Church in Chester 1300–1540* (Chetham Soc., 3rd ser., vol. 7, 1957).

Jones, W.H. 'On the Original Position of the High Altar at Salisbury Cathedral', *The Wiltshire Archaeological and Natural History Magazine*, vol. 17 (1878), 136–46.

Jones, W.R. 'Lollards and Images: The Defense of Religious Art in Later Medieval England', *J. of the History of Ideas*, vol. 34 (1973), 27–50.

Kaufman, P.I. 'Henry VII and Sanctuary', *Church History*, vol. 53 (1984), 465–76.

Kemp, B. *English Church Monuments* (London, 1980).

Kemp, E.W. *Canonization and Authority in the Western Church* (Oxford, 1948).

Kettle, A.J. and D.A. Johnson. 'The Cathedral of Lichfield', in *VCH: Stafford*, vol. 3, ed. M.W. Greenslade (London, 1970), 403–15.

Kidson, P. 'St. Hugh's Choir', in *Medieval Art and Architecture at Lincoln Cathedral* (BAACT, vol. 8, 1986), 29–42.

Kitchin, G.W. *The Great Screen of Winchester Cathedral* (3rd edn, London, 1899).

Klukas, A.W. 'The Architectural Implications of the *Decreta Lanfranci*', in *Anglo-Norman Studies*, ed. R.A. Brown, vol. 6 (Woodbridge, 1984), 136–71.

Knowles, D. *The Religious Houses of Medieval England* (London, 1940).

―――― *The Monastic Order in England* (2nd edn, Cambridge, 1963).

L'Estrange, J. 'Description of a Chamber Formerly Adjoining the Jesus Chapel of the Cathedral', *Norfolk Archaeology*, vol. 6 (1864), 177–184.

Ladds, S.I. *The Monastery of Ely* (Ely, 1930).

Lang-Sims, L. 'Sarsnet and Old Bones', *Cant. Cathedral Chron.*, no. 75 (1981), 34–8.

Langmuir, G.I. 'Thomas of Monmouth: Detector of Ritual Murder', *Speculum*, vol. 59 (1984), 820–46.

Lasko, P. *Ars Sacra, 800–1200* (Harmondsworth, 1972).

Lawrence, C.H. 'St. Richard of Chichester', in *Studies in Sussex Church History*, ed. M.J. Kitch (London, 1981), 36–55.

Lea, H.C. *Superstition and Force* (Philadelphia, 1870).

Lethaby, W.R. *Westminster Abbey and the King's Craftsmen* (London, 1906).

―――― 'The Confessor's Shrine at Westminster Abbey', *Arch. J.*, vol. 68 (1911), 361–4.

―――― *Westminster Abbey Re-Examined* (London, 1925).

―――― 'Old St Paul's', *The Builder*, vol. 138 (1930), 671–3, 862–4, 1091–3, vol. 139 (1930), 24–6, 193–4, 791–3, 1005–7.

Lethieullier, S. 'A letter from Mr. Smart Lethieullier to Mr. Gale, relating to the Shrine of St. Hugh, the crucifyed Child at Lincoln', *Archaeologia*, vol. 1 (1770), 26–29.

Levison, W. 'St Alban and St Albans', *Antiquity*, vol. 15 (1941), 337–359.

Leyser, K. 'Frederick Barbarossa, Henry II and the Hand of St James', *EHR*, no. 356, vol. 90 (1975), 481–506.

Lipman, V.D. *The Jews of Medieval Norwich* (London, 1967).

Loomis, L.H. 'The Holy Relics of Charlemagne and King Athelstan: The Lances of Longinus and St Mauricius', *Speculum*, vol. 25 (1950), 437–56.

Lunt, W.E. *Financial Relations of the Papacy with England, 1327–1534* (Cambridge, Mass., 1962).

McCann, A. *A Short History of the City of Chichester and its Cathedral* (Chichester, 1985).

McKenna, J.W. 'Piety and Propaganda: The Cult of King Henry VI', in *Chaucer and Middle English Studies in Honour of Russell Hope Robbins*, ed. B. Rowland (London, 1974).

McRoberts, D. 'The Glorious House of St. Andrew', in *The Medieval Church of St Andrews*, ed. D. McRoberts (Glasgow, 1976), 63–120.

Major, K. 'The Finances of the Dean and Chapter of Lincoln from the Twelfth to the Fourteenth Century', *J. of Ecclesiastical History*, vol. 5 (1954), 149–67.

Marshall, G. 'The Shrine of St. Thomas de Cantilupe in Hereford Cathedral', *Trans. of the Woolhope Naturalists' Field Club*, vol. 27 (1930–2), 34–50.

—— 'Craswell Priory and the Bones of One of St Ursula's 11,000 Virgins of Cologne', *Trans. of the Woolhope Naturalists' Field Club*, vol. 31 (1942), 18–21.

—— *Hereford Cathedral; Its Evolution and Growth* (Worcester, 1951).

Mason, A.J. *What Became of the Bones of St Thomas?* (Cambridge, 1920).

Mason, E. 'St Wulfstan's Staff: A Legend and its Uses', *Medium Aevum*, vol. 53, no. 2 (1984), 157–79.

—— *St Wulfstan of Worcester, c. 1008–1095* (Oxford, 1990).

Mate, M. 'The Indebtedness of Canterbury Cathedral Priory, 1215–95', *The Economic History Review*, vol. 26, no. 2 (1973), 183–97.

Mayr-Harting, H. 'Functions of a Twelfth-Century Shrine: The Miracles of St Frideswide', in *Studies in Medieval History Presented to R.H.C. Davis*, eds H. Mayr-Harting and R.I. Moore (London, 1985).

Milman, H.H. *Annals of S. Paul's Cathedral* (London, 1869).

Milner, J. *An Historical and Critical Account of Winchester Cathedral* (2nd edn, Winchester, 1801).

Mitchell, W.T. 'The Shrines of English Saints in Wartime before the Reformation', *Pax*, vol. 30 (1940).

Morgan, P. 'The Effect of the Pilgrim Cult of St Thomas Cantilupe on Hereford Cathedral', in *St Thomas Cantilupe, Bishop of Hereford: Essays in his Honour*, ed. M. Jancey (Hereford, 1982), 145–52.

Morris, J. 'English Relics: I – St. Thomas of Hereford', *The Month*, vol. 44 (Jan–Apr., 1882), 112–26.

Morris, P. 'Exeter Cathedral: A Conjectural Restoration of the Fourteenth-Century Altar Screen', *Ant. J.*, vol. 23 (1943), 122–47.

Morris, R.J. *Cholera 1832: The Social Response to an Epidemic* (London, 1976).

Morris, R.K. 'The Remodelling of the Hereford Aisles', *JBAA*, 3rd ser., vol. 37 (1974), 21–39.

—— 'The New Work at Old St Paul's Cathedral and its Place in English Thirteenth-Century Architecture', in *Medieval Art, Architecture and Archaeology in London* (*BAACT*, vol. 10, 1990), 74–100.

Muncey, R.W. *A History of the Consecration of Churches and Churchyards* (Cambridge, 1930).

Nelson, J. 'Royal Saints and Early Medieval Kingship', in *Studies in Church History*, vol. 10, ed. D. Baker (Oxford, 1973), 31–44.

Newman, C. 'Anglo-Norman Architecture and the Conquest', *Mediaevalia*, vol. 7 (1981), 263–79.

Nieuwbarn, M.C. *Church Symbolism*, trans. J. Waterreus (London, 1910).

Noake, J. *The Monastery and Cathedral of Worcester* (London, 1866).

Norton, E.E. and M.C. Horton. 'A Parisian Workshop at Canterbury. A Late Thirteenth-Century Tile Pavement in the Corona Chapel, and the Origins of Tyler Hill', *JBAA*, vol. 134 (1981), 58–80.

O'Connell, J. *Church Building and Furnishing: the Church's Way* (London, 1955).

Oakley, A.M. 'The Cathedral Church of St Andrew, Rochester', *Arch. Cant.*, vol. 91 (1975), 47–60.

Oman, C. 'Security in English Churches, A.D. 1000–1548', *Arch. J.*, vol. 136 (1979), 90–8.

O'Neilly, J.G. 'The Shrine of Edward the Confessor', *Archaeologia*, vol. 100 (1966), 129–54.

Orme, N. 'Two Saint-Bishops of Exeter: James Berkeley and Edmund Lacy', *Analecta Bollandiana*, vol. 104 (1986), 403–18.

Owen, D.M. *History of Lincolnshire, vol. v: Church and Society in Medieval Lincolnshire* (Lincoln, 1971).

——— [as D.M. Williamson] *Lincoln Muniments*, Lincoln Minster Pamphlets no. 8 (Lincoln, 1956).

Oxford English Dictionary 2 on CD ROM (version 1.00, Oxford, 1992).

Peck, F. *Desiderata Curiosa* (London, 1779).

Peckham, W.D. 'Some Notes on Chichester Cathedral', *Sussex Archaeological Collections*, vol. 3 (1973), 20–6.

Peers, C.R. 'Rievaulx Abbey: The Shrine in the Chapter House', *Arch. J.*, vol. 86 (1929), 20–8.

Peers, C.R. and H. Brakspear. 'Architectural Description of Winchester Cathedral', in *VCH: Hampshire and the Isle of Wight*, vol. 5, ed. W. Page (Folkstone, 1912), 50–59.

Perkins, J. *Westminster Abbey; Its Worship and Its Ornaments* (3 vols, London, 1938).

Phillips, C.S. 'The Archbishop's Three Seats in Canterbury Cathedral', *Ant. J.*, vol. 29 (1949), 26–36.

——— *Canterbury Cathedral in the Middle Ages* (London, 1949).

Piper, A.J. 'The First Generations of Durham Monks and the Cult of St Cuthbert', in *St Cuthbert, His Cult and His Community to AD 1200*, eds G. Bonner, D. Rollason and C. Stancliffe (Woodbridge, 1989), 437–46.

——— 'Typescript List of Feretrar's and Their Colleagues', DCCA, Durham.

Platt, C. *The Abbeys and Priories of Medieval England* (London, 1984).

Poole, G.A. 'The Tomb of Remigius', *Associated Architectural Societies Reports and Papers*, vol. 14, pt 1 (1877), 21–6.

Postan, M.M. *The Medieval Economy and Society: An Economic History of Britain in the Middle Ages* (London, 1972).

Potts, R.U. 'The Latest Excavations at St. Augustine's Abbey', *Arch. Cant.*, vol. 35 (1921), 117–26.

Prestwich, M. 'The Piety of Edward I', in *England in the Thirteenth Century*, ed. W.M. Ormrod (Woodbridge, 1985), 120–8.

Prideaux, E.K. 'Illustrated Notes on the Church of St. Candida and Holy Cross at Whit-church Canonicorum, Dorset', *Arch. J.*, vol. 64 (1907), 119–50.

Quirk, R.N. 'Winchester Cathedral in the Tenth Century', *Arch. J.*, vol. 114 (1957), 28–68.

Raby, F.J.E. 'The Tomb of St Osmund at Salisbury', *Arch. J.*, vol. 104 (1947), 146–7.

Radford, C.A.R. 'The Excavations at Glastonbury Abbey, 1951–5', *Somerset and Dorset Notes and Queries*, vol. 27 (1955–6), 72.

——— 'Two Scottish Shrines: Jedburgh and St. Andrews', *Arch. J.*, vol. 112 (1956), 43–60.

——— 'The Bishop's Throne in Norwich Cathedral', *Arch. J.*, vol. 116 (1961), 115–132.

Radford, U.M. 'Wax Images Found in Exeter Cathedral', *Ant. J.*, vol. 29 (1929), 164–8.

Raine, J. *St. Cuthbert: With an Account of the State in Which his Remains were Found Upon the Opening of his Tomb in Durham Cathedral, in the Year MDCCCXXVII* (Durham, 1828).

Ramsay, N. and M. Sparks. 'The Cult of St Dunstan at Christ Church, Canterbury', in *St Dunstan: His Life, Times and Cult*, eds N. Ramsay, M. Sparks and T. Tatton-Brown (Woodbridge, 1992), 311–24.

Rawlinson, R. *The History and Antiquities of the City and Cathedral-Church of Hereford* (London, 1717).

Redmond, R.X. 'Altar: 3. In the Liturgy', in *New Catholic Encyclopedia*, vol. 1 (New York, 1967), 347–51.

Richardson, J.S. 'Saint William of Perth, and his Memorials in England', *Transactions of the Scottish Ecclesiological Soc.*, vol. 2, pt 1 (1906–7), 122–6.

Richmond, C. 'Religion and the Fifteenth-Century English Gentleman', in *Church, Politics and Patronage in the Fifteenth Century*, ed. B. Dobson (Gloucester, 1984), 193–208.

Ridyard, S.J. '*Condigna Veneratio:* Post-Conquest Attitudes to the Saints of the Anglo-Saxons', in *Anglo-Norman Studies*, ed. R.A. Brown, vol. 9 (Woodbridge, 1987), 179–208.

—— *The Royal Saints of Anglo-Saxon England: A Study of West Saxon and East Anglian Cults* (Cambridge, 1988).

Robertson, W.A.S. 'The Crypt of Canterbury Cathedral', *Arch. Cant.*, vol. 13 (1880), 17–80, 500–51.

Rodwell, W. 'Archaeology and the Standing Fabric: Recent Studies at Lichfield', *Antiquity*, vol. 63 (1989), 281–94.

Rollason, D.W. *Cuthbert: Saint and Patron* (Durham, 1987).

—— *Saints and Relics in Anglo-Saxon England* (Oxford, 1989).

Rothkrug, L. 'Popular Religion and Holy Shrines: Their Influence on the Origins of the German Reformation and Their Role in German Cultural Development', in *Religion and the People, 800–1700*, ed. J. Obelkevich (Chapel Hill, 1979), pp. 20–86.

Routledge, S. Robertson and Sheppard. 'Report (1888), on Discoveries in the Crypt of Canterbury Cathedral', *Arch. Cant.*, vol. 18 (1989), 253–6.

Royal Commission on Historical Monuments (Eng.). *An Inventory of the Historical Monuments in London, vol. i, Westminster Abbey* (London, 1924).

Rubin, M. *Corpus Christi: The Eucharist in Late Medieval Culture* (Cambridge, 1991).

Russell, J.C. *Population in Europe, 500–1500* (London, 1969).

Sanderson, R. *Lincoln Cathedral: an Exact Copy of All the Ancient Monumental Inscriptions there, as they stood in 1641* (London, 1851).

Sandquist, T.A. 'The Holy Oil of St. Thomas of Canterbury', in *Essays in Medieval History Presented to Bertie Wilkinson*, ed. T.A. Sandquist and M.R. Powicke (Toronto, 1969), 330–44.

Saunders, H.W. *An Introduction to the Obedientiary and Manor Rolls of Norwich Cathedral Priory* (Norwich, 1930).

Scarfe, N. 'The Body of St. Edmund; An Essay in Necrobiology', *Suffolk Institute of Archæology*, vol. 31 (1970), 303–17.

Scholz, B.W. 'The Canonization of Edward the Confessor', *Speculum*, vol. 36 (1961), 38–60.

Scott, G.G. 'Hereford Cathedral', *Arch. J.*, vol. 34 (1877), 323–48.

Sekules, V. 'The Tomb of Christ at Lincoln and the Development of the Sacrament Shrine: Easter Sepulchres Reconsidered', in *Medieval Art and Architecture at Lincoln* (*BAACT*, vol. 8, 1986), 118–31.

Shinners, J.R. 'The Veneration of Saints at Norwich Cathedral in the Fourteenth Century', *Norfolk Archaeology*, vol. 40 (1988), 133–44.

Simpson, W.S. *Chapters in the History of Old St Paul's* (London, 1881).

—— *S. Paul's Cathedral and Old City Life* (London, 1894).

Singleton, B. 'The Remodelling of the East End of Worcester Cathedral in the Earlier Part of the Thirteenth Century', in *Medieval Art and Architecture at Worcester Cathedral* (*BAACT*, vol. 1, 1978), 105–15.

Smith, R.A.L. 'The Central Financial System of Christ Church, 1186–1512', *EHR*, vol. 55 (1940), 353–70.

—— 'The Financial System of Rochester Cathedral Priory', *EHR*, vol. 56 (1941), 586–95.

—— *Canterbury Cathedral Priory* (2nd edn, Cambridge, 1969).

Society of Antiquaries. 'Proceedings for Thursday, Jan. 27th, 1876', *Proc. of the Soc. of Antiquaries of London*, 2nd ser., vol. 6 (1873–6), 476–9.

Solloway, J. *Archbishop Scrope* (London, 1927).

Somner, W. *The Antiquities of Canterbury* (London, 1640).

Southern, R.W. *Saint Anselm and his Biographer: A Study of Monastic Life and Thought* (Cambridge, 1963).

Sox, D. *Relics and Shrines* (London, 1985).

Spencer, B. 'Medieval Pilgrim Badges', *Rotterdam Papers*, vol. 1 (1968), 137–54.

────── 'Two Leaden Ampullae from Leicestershire', *Trans. Leicestershire Archaeological and Historical Soc.*, vol. 55 (1979–80), 88–9.

────── 'Pilgrim Souvenirs', in *Medieval Waterfront Development at Trig Lane, London*, eds G. and C. Milne, London and Middlesex Archaeological Soc. Special Paper no. 5 (London, 1982), 106–7.

────── 'Pilgrim Souvenirs from the Medieval Waterfront Excavations at Trig Lane, London 1974–76', *Trans. of the London and Middlesex Archaeological Soc.*, vol. 33 (1982), 304–23.

────── 'A Thirteenth-Century Pilgrim's Ampulla from Worcester', *Trans. of the Worcester Archaeological Soc.*, 3rd ser., vol. 9 (1984), 7–12.

Spufford, P. *Money and its Use in Medieval Europe* (Cambridge, 1988).

Srawley, J.H. *Robert Grosseteste, Bishop of Lincoln 1235–1253* (Lincoln Minster Pamphlets no. 7, Lincoln, 1953).

Stanley, A.P. 'The Shrine of St. Thomas of Canterbury', in *Historical Memorials of Canterbury* (12th edn, London, 1891), 179–294.

────── *Historical Memorials of Westminster Abbey* (7th edn, London, 1890).

Stewart, D.J. *On the Architectural History of Ely Cathedral* (London, 1868).

Stewart, D.J. and R. Willis. 'Notes on Norwich Cathedral', *Arch. J.* vol. 32 (1875), 16–47.

Stocker, D. 'The Tomb and Shrine of Bishop Grosseteste in Lincoln Cathedral', in *England in the Thirteenth Century: Proceedings of the Harlaxton Symposium*, ed. W.M. Ormrod (Woodbridge, 1985), 143–8.

────── 'The Shrine of Little St Hugh', in *Medieval Art and Architecture at Lincoln Cathedral* (BAACT, vol. 8, 1986), 109–117.

────── 'The Mystery of the Shrines of St Hugh', *St. Hugh of Lincoln: Lectures delivered at Oxford and Lincoln to celebrate the eighth centenary of St Hugh's Consecration as Bishop of Lincoln*, ed. H. Mayr-Harting (Oxford, 1987), 89–124.

Stranks, C.J. *This Sumptuous Church* (London, 1973).

────── *St Etheldreda, Queen and Abbess* (Ely, 1975).

Strik, H.J.A. 'Remains of the Lanfranc Building in the Great Central Tower and the North-West Choir/Transept area', in *Medieval Art and Architecture at Canterbury before 1200* (BAACT, vol. 5, 1982), 20–6.

Stroud, D. 'St. Osmund: Some Contemporary Evidence', *Hatcher Rev.*, vol. 2, no. 16 (1983), 243–50.

────── 'The Cult and Tombs of St. Osmund at Salisbury', *The Wiltshire Archaeological and Natural History Magazine*, vol. 78 (1984), 50–4.

Stubbs, C.W. *Historical Memorials of Ely Cathedral* (London, 1897).

────── 'The Hereford Miracles', *Trans. of the Woolhope Naturalists' Field Club*, vol. 18 (1902–4), 377–83.

Stukeley, W. *Itinerarium Curiosum, or, an Account of the Antiquitys and Remarkable Curiositys in Nature or Art, observ'd in Travels thro' Great Brittan* (London, 1724).

Sumption, J. *Pilgrimage: An Image of Medieval Religion* (London, 1975).

Sutherland, C.H.V. *English Coinage 600–1900* (London, 1973).

Tanner, N.P. *Heresy Trials in the Diocese of Norwich, 1428–31* (Camden 4th ser., vol. 20, 1977).

────── *The Church in Late Medieval Norwich 1370–1532*, Studies and Texts 66 (Toronto, 1984).

Tatton-Brown, T. 'The Trinity Chapel and Corona Floors', *Canterbury Cathedral Chronicle*, no. 75 (1981), 50–6.

────── 'The Buildings and Topography of St Augustine's Abbey, Canterbury', *JBAA*, vol. 144 (1991), 61–91.

Taylor, A.J. 'Royal Alms and Oblations in the Later 13th Century', in *Tribute to an Antiquary; Essays presented to Marc Fitch by Some of his Friends*, eds F. Emmison and R. Stephens (London, 1976), 93–125.

────── 'Edward I and the Shrine of St Thomas of Canterbury', *JBAA*, vol. 132 (1979), 22–8.

Taylor, H.M. 'Corridor Crypts on the Continent and in England', *North Staffordshire J. of Field Studies*, vol. 9 (1969), 17–52.

——— 'The Anglo-Saxon Church at Canterbury', *Arch. J.*, vol. 126 (1969), 101–30.

Thacker, A. 'Lindisfarne and the Origins of the Cult of St Cuthbert', in *St Cuthbert, His Cult and Community to AD 1200*, eds G. Bonner, D. Rollason and C. Stancliffe (Woodbridge, 1989), 103–24.

——— 'Cults at Canterbury: Relics and Reform under Dunstan and his Successors', in *St Dunstan: His Life, Times and Cult*, eds N. Ramsay, M. Sparks and T. Tatton-Brown (Woodbridge, 1992), 221–45.

Theilmann, J.M. 'Communitas among Fifteenth-Century Pilgrims', *Historical Reflections*, vol. 11 (1984), 253–70.

Thomas, C. *The Early Christian Archaeology of North Britain* (London, 1971).

——— *Bede, Archaeology, and the Cult of Relics* (Jarrow, 1973).

Thomas, W. *A Survey of the Cathedral-Church of Worcester* (London, 1736).

Thompson, A.H. *The Building of York Minster* (London, 1927).

——— *The Medieval Chapter*, York Minster Historical Tracts, vol. 13 (London, 1927).

Thompson, J.A. 'Piety and Charity in Late Medieval London', *J. of Ecclesiastical History*, vol. 16 (1965), 178–95.

Thurstan, H. *The Life of St. Hugh of Lincoln* (London, 1898).

——— *The Physical Phenomena of Mysticism* (London, 1952).

Torrance, W.J. *The Story of Saint Osmund, Bishop of Salisbury* (Salisbury, 1978).

Toynbee, M.R. *S. Louis of Toulouse and the Process of Canonisation in the Fourteenth Century* (Manchester, 1929).

Trollope, E. 'Little St. Hugh of Lincoln', *Associated Architectural Societies Reports and Papers*, vol. 15 (1879), 126–31.

Tudor, V. 'The Misogyny of St. Cuthbert', *Archaeologia Aeliana*, 5th ser., vol. 12 (1984), 158–64.

——— 'The Cult of St Cuthbert in the Twelfth Century: The Evidence of Reginald of Durham', in *St Cuthbert, His Cult and Community to AD 1200*, eds G. Bonner, D. Rollason and C. Stancliffe (Woodbridge, 1989), 447–68.

Tudor-Craig, P. 'Archbishop Hubert Walter's Tomb and its Furnishings: The Tomb', in *Medieval Art and Architecture at Canterbury before 1220* (BAACT, vol. 5, 1982), 71–93.

Tudor-Craig, P. and L. Keen. 'A Recently Discovered Purbeck Marble Sculptured Screen of the Thirteenth Century and the Shrine of St Swithun', in *Medieval Art and Architecture at Winchester Cathedral* (BAACT, vol. 6, 1983), 63–72.

Tummers, H.A. *Early Secular Effigies in England: The Thirteenth Century* (Leiden, 1980).

Turner, D.H. 'The Customary of the Shrine of St. Thomas Becket', *The Canterbury Cathedral Chronicle*, no. 70 (April 1976), 16–22.

Twigg, G. *The Black Death: A Biological Reappraisal* (London, 1984).

Urry, W. *Canterbury under the Angevin Kings* (London, 1967).

——— 'Some Notes on the Two Resting Places of St Thomas Becket at Canterbury', in *Thomas Becket, Actes du Colloque International de Sédières*, ed. R. Foreville (Paris, 1975), 195–210.

Vallance, A. *Greater English Church Screens* (London, 1947).

Vaughan, R. *Matthew Paris* (Cambridge, 1958).

Venables. 'Some Account of the Recent Discovery of the Foundations of the Eastern Termination of Lincoln Minster, as Erected By St. Hugh', *Arch. J.*, vol. 44 (1887), 194–202.

——— 'The Shrine and Head of St. Hugh of Lincoln', *Arch. J.*, vol. 50 (1893), 37–61.

Walcott, M.E.C. *Memorials of Chichester* (Chichester, 1865).

——— *Traditions and Customs of Cathedrals* (London, 1872).

——— 'The Bishops of Chichester from Stigand to Sherbourne', *Sussex Archaeological Collections*, vol. 28 (1878), 11–58; 29 (1879), 1–38.

——— 'The Inventories of Westminster Abbey at the Dissolution', *Trans. of the London and Middlesex Archaeological Soc.*, vol. 4 (1875), 313–64.

Walker, J.W. 'The English Mediaeval Altar', *The Modern Churchman*, vol. 27, no. 10 (1938), 564–7.

Wall, J.C. *Shrines of British Saints* (London, 1905).

Ward, B. *Miracles and the Medieval Mind: Theory, Record and Event 1000–1215* (2nd edn, Aldershot, 1987).

Webb, G. *The Liturgical Altar* (2nd edn, London, 1939).

Westlake, H.F. 'The Church of Edward the Confessor at Westminster', *Archaeologia*, vol. 62 (1910), 81–97.

——— *The Parish Gilds of Medieval England* (London, 1919).

——— *Westminster Abbey* (2 vols, London, 1923).

Willis, B. *A Survey of the Cathedrals of York, Durham, Carlisle, Chester, Man, Lichfield, Hereford, Worcester, Gloucester and Bristol* (London, 1727).

——— *A Survey of the Cathedrals of Lincoln, Ely, Oxford and Peterborough* (London, 1730).

Willis, R. *The Architectural History of Canterbury* (London, 1845).

——— 'The Architectural History of Winchester Cathedral', *Proceedings at the Annual Meeting of the Archaeological Institute*, vol. 1 (1845), 1–80.

——— 'On the Foundations of Early Buildings Discovered in Lichfield Cathedral', *Arch. J.*, vol. 18 (1861), 1–24.

Willson, T.J. 'The Tomb of St. Hugh at Lincoln', *Arch. J.*, vol. 51 (1894), 104–8.

Wilmart, A. 'Les Reliques de Saint Ouen à Cantobéry', *Analecta Bollondiana*, vol. 51 (1933), 285–92.

Wilson. 'John de Wyke, Prior of Worcester, 1301–17. Some Glimpses of the Early Years of his Priorate from the "Liber Albus" ', *Associated Architectural Societies Reports and Papers*, vol. 34, pt 1 (1917), 131–52.

Wilson, C. *The Shrines of St William of York* (York, 1977).

——— 'The Neville Screen', in *Medieval Art and Architecture at Durham Cathedral* (*BAACT*, vol. 3, 1980), 90–104.

——— *The Gothic Cathedral* (London, 1990).

——— 'The Early Thirteenth-Century Architecture of Beverley Minster: Cathedral Splendours and Cistercian Austerities', in *Thirteenth Century England*, vol. 3, eds P.R. Coss and S.D. Lloyd (Woodbridge, 1991), 181–95.

Wolffe, B. *Henry VI* (London, 1981).

Wood, A. *'Survey of the Antiquities of the City of Oxford' Composed in 1661–6 by Anthony Wood*, ed. Andrew Clark (3 vols, Oxford, 1890).

Woodman, F. *The Architectural History of Canterbury Cathedral* (London, 1981).

——— 'The Retrochoir of Winchester Cathedral: a New Interpretation', *JBAA*, vol. 136 (1983), 86–97.

Woodruff, C.E. 'The Chapel of Our Lady in the Crypt of Canterbury Cathedral', *Arch. Cant.*, vol. 38 (1926), 153–71.

——— 'The Financial Aspect of the Cult of St. Thomas of Canterbury', *Arch. Cant.*, vol. 44 (1932), 13–32.

——— 'Some Early Kentish Wills', *Arch. Cant.*, vol. 46 (1934), 27–35.

——— 'Notes on the Inner Life and Domestic Economy of the Priory of Christ Church, Canterbury, in the Fifteenth Century', *Arch. Cant.*, vol. 53 (1940), 1–16.

——— 'The Sacrist's Rolls of Christ Church Canterbury', *Arch. Cant.*, vol. 48 (1936), 38–80.

Woodruff, C.E. and W. Danks. *Memorials of the Cathedral and Priory of Christ in Canterbury* (London, 1912).

Woodward, G.W.O. *The Dissolution of the Monasteries* (London, 1966).

Wooley, R.M. *St. Hugh of Lincoln* (London, 1927).

Wordsworth, C. *Notes on Mediaeval Services in England, with an Index of Lincoln Ceremonies* (London, 1898).

Wormald, F. 'The Rood of Bromholm', *J. of the Warburg Institute*, vol. 1 (1937–8), 31–45.

Wright, T. 'On the Municipal Archives of the City of Canterbury', *Archaeologia*, vol. 31 (1846), 198–211.

Yates, W.N. 'The Fabric Rolls of Hereford Cathedral 1290/1 and 1386/7', *The National Library of Wales J.*, vol. 18 (1973–4), 79–86.

Index

UNIVERSITY LIBRARY
NOTTINGHAM